THE

EMPTY CRADLE

OF DEMOCRACY

✥

SEX, ABORTION,

AND NATIONALISM

IN MODERN GREECE

✥

Alexandra Halkias

DUKE UNIVERSITY PRESS

DURHAM AND LONDON

2004

© 2004 DUKE UNIVERSITY PRESS

All rights reserved

Printed in the United States of America on acid-free paper ∞

Designed by Amy Ruth Buchanan

Typeset in Scala by Keystone Typesetting, Inc.

Library of Congress Cataloging-in-Publication Data appear

on the last printed page of this book.

✣

For Christos C. Halkias

with love

✣

CONTENTS

Acknowledgments xi

Introduction 1

PART 1 *The Agoras of Agon*

1. Setting the Stage: Athens, Greece, Fantasy, and History 19
2. Stage Left: Greek Women 35
3. Center Stage: What Is Greece? 53
4. Stage Right: The Demografiko 77

PART 2 *In Context, in Contests*

5. In the Operating Room: On Cows, Greece, and the Smoking Fetus 89
6. Give Birth for Greece! Abortion and Nation in the Greek Press 113

PART 3 *Sexing the Nation*

7. Navigating the Night 135
8. The Impossible Dream: The Couple as Mother 207
9. Abortion, Pain, and Agency 235

PART 4 *Instigating Dialogues*

10. Reprosexuality and the Modern Citizen Face the Specter of Turkey 291

11. A Critical Cartography of the Demografiko's Greece 319

Epilogue: Theory and Policy 345

Notes 349

References 381

⊹

> This is just a hypothesis, but I would say it's all against all. There aren't immediately given subjects of a struggle, one the proletariat, the other the bourgeoisie. Who fights against whom? We all fight against each other. And there is always within each of us something that fights something else.
> —MICHEL FOUCAULT, *The History of Sexuality, Vol. 1*

> The role for theory today seems to me to be just this: not to formulate the global systematic theory which holds everything in place, but to analyze the specificity of mechanisms of power, to locate the connections and extensions, to build little by little a strategic knowledge (*savoir*).
> —MICHEL FOUCAULT, *Power/Knowledge*

ACKNOWLEDGMENTS

⁘

This book addresses the research done for my dissertation in Athens, Greece, in 1994. Yet the project of the book is different from that of the dissertation defended in 1997. This book develops a line of analysis and argumentation that became visible once the dissertation was complete. The focus shifted from abortion and national identity to sexuality and nationalism, and to re-theorizing the gendered subject of late modernity by exploring new relations between elements of the historically situated discourses that produce it in a formally democratic context. The social relationship between agency, violence, and discourse became central.

Through every stage of developing this book, from the formation of the original idea all the way through the dissertation and then the additional years of radical reworking, I have benefited from the scholarly advice, intellectual friendship and support of many. Some generously offered me their thoughts and comments during the first formative phase of this project. Of these, I am most grateful to the chair of my doctoral committee, rigorous and yet creative sociologist, and relentless editor, Chandra Mukerji, as well as to Dan Hallin and Michael Schudson, both of whom not only inspired the media analysis but also helped to hone the larger argument concerning liberal democracy. Lisa Lowe also made important insightful comments throughout, especially with regard to feminist theory, and lightly offered vital practical and intellectual assistance at a determining moment in the book's development. Without Page DuBois and her incisive comments at critical junctions from the very beginning of the project as a research proposal in 1991, this book might not have been born(e). Last but not at all least, Michael Herzfeld carefully read and meticulously commented on the full doctoral dissertation, in addition to supporting this work since then in multiple crucial ways, and also became a very good friend. The standards of excellence set by each of these scholars were inspirational and established the domain within which the doctoral dissertation went on, with five more years of hard work, to become this book.

In many cases, the right scholar with the right advice, commentary on some portion of the manuscript, or other related form of assistance showed up at just the right time. I am grateful for important forms of help received from the following scholars. In the United States, Bennett Berger, Judith Butler, Craig Calhoun, Vangelis Calotychos, Jane Cowan, Eugenia Georges, Faye Ginsburg, Joseph Gusfield, Val Hartouni, Jean Jackson, Anastasia Karakasidou, Irving Markovitz, Adamandia Pollis, Maggie Sale, Stefan Senders, Yasemin Nuhoglu Soysal, and Karen Van Dyck. Academics in Greece who have assisted with this project are the faculty of the Department of Sociology, Panteio University, by showing faith in this project when some others did not. I especially thank Neoklis Sarris for his steadfast support despite some intellectual differences. I also thank Maria Andonopoulou and Nota Kyriazi for their warm support and their comments on the manuscript. I am grateful for the administrative support given by Irene Chiotaki, Maria Gofa, and Petros Koulouras. At the Department of Political Science at the University of Athens, I would like to acknowledge Kyrkos Doxiadis, the first in Athens to read, comment on, and endorse an earlier version of the entire manuscript, also recommending me for my first post in Athens as a visiting scholar at the department from 1999 to 2000, where I found the gift of a thriving intellectual community of faculty and students. Of the former, I would like to note my gratitude to Nikos Tatsis, with whom I cotaught my first Greek Introduction to Sociology course to an amphitheater of three hundred students; Constantinos Tsoukalas, with whom I enjoyed a warm intellectual friendship and twice cotaught a course on the State and Society that proved helpful for certain aspects of this book; and Maro Pandelidou-Malouta, who read the dissertation and offered helpful comments. I also thank graduate student Tasos Pehlivanidis, who offered crucial research assistance with the historical portion of the book, in addition to a refreshing spirit in the final stages of the book. All the students of the seminar I taught on Time and Society in the spring of 2000 offered intellectual sustenance as well as stimulating conversation in our postclass bar meetings, and I thank them.

For further assistance with the historical sections of the book I thank faculty members Panos Tsakaloyiannis of the Athens University of Economics and Business, and I am especially grateful for the eagle-eye reading of Katerina Gardika of the University of Athens, Department of History and Archaeology. A Panteion University student, Chrisanthi Niyianni, offered appreciated help with the process of verifying the historical sources. Dina

Sassani efficiently checked the comparative demography discussion. I was fortunate to have the research assistance of Penelope Topali, a graduate student at the University of the Aegean, Mytilini, for whose meticulous research skills and calm efficiency I am most grateful. Last, and importantly, Eleni Papadopoulou gracefully assisted with confirming sources and data.

Without the help of all the women who agreed to give of their time and their thoughts in the interviews and other conversations, this book would not exist. In many ways, their work with me in the field is the foundation of this book. I interviewed a total of ninety women who used the services of the Family Planning Center of Alexandra's Hospital in Athens during 1994 and I observed the interactions and gynecological examination of a total of four hundred women visiting the same site. An additional thirty women were interviewed based on a snowball sample started from doctors, friends, and acquaintances. I preserve the anonymity of all these women, as promised. Of those who assisted me with the practicalities of my fieldwork I especially thank Julia Balaska, Yiota Bouziou, Gerasimoula Haralambous, Marina Meidani-Papayianaki, Eleni Pambouki, Eleni Papagaroufali, and Katia Roumelioti, all originally strangers to me who very generously offered their time, their knowledge, and their contacts to assist this research.

I also thank the midwives and nursing personnel of the Family Planning Center at the Alexandra University hospital during 1994 for having accepted my presence there and facilitated the research process in important ways. I do not name them to preserve their anonymity. In addition, I acknowledge the numerous ob/gyn doctors who spoke with me. Of special significance were Dr. G. Dasopoulos, Dr. G. Kalipolitis, Dr. E. Leontidou, and Dr. L. Mavridaki, all of whom generously shared their knowledge of their practice; Dr. Dasopoulos and Dr. Leontidou also provided vital in-depth accounts of other aspects of Greek women's physical well-being, such as specific medical developments, in Dr. Dasopoulos's case, and the autonomous feminist movement's mobilization around such issues, in Dr. Leontidou's case. I am also very grateful for the invaluable help offered by my aunt, an anesthesiologist, Dr. Vivi Chrysovergi.

The institutions that constituted sites for the fieldwork are the Family Planning Center, the Sterility Department and the Ultrasound Department of the state-run University Hospital Alexandras, where Dr. Aravandinos, the director of the hospital in 1994, generously granted me permission to conduct my research; a private ob/gyn clinic; the prenatal unit at the private clinic Mitera, where I conducted secondary research on women coming for ultrasounds of their pregnancy, thanks to Dr. Nikolaidis's permission; and the private fertility clinic run by Dr. E. Kapetanaki, where, thanks to the mediation of a good friend and biologist at the clinic, Nelly Michas, I was granted permission to interview thirty women who had just undergone embryo implants. The data from these last two sites have not been directly included in this book, though they have offered valuable context and inform the analysis presented here.

The institutions that provided financial and other material support during this project are the Department of Communication, University of California, San Diego, with a series of scholarships from 1991 to 1996; the Michael Schudson research award in 1994, which helped pay the wonderful team at Textco, Pangrati who did the transcribing of many interviews; and, in Greece, the Institute for Language and Speech Processing directed by George Karagiannis, which granted me a much appreciated scholarship to help complete the writing in 1999–2000. To Arhio ton Yinaikon and the archive of the Syndesmo gia ta Dikaiomata tis Yinaikas provided valuable access to important archives on feminism and women in Greece.

Intellectual institutional support was offered by a graduate seminar held during the spring of 1994 by Pandeio University's Department of Anthropology and, in particular, Professor Demetra Madianou, who expressed a strong interest in my project at that time; the Onassis Center for Greek Studies of New York University, where I worked as a visiting researcher during the spring of 1997; and the Department of Anthropology at Harvard University, with which I was affiliated as a research assistant in the later stages of the project. I would also like to acknowledge Bryn Mawr College for the lessons of intellectual fortitude and courage that I gained there, and especially Professor Robert Washington, the first who taught me how to "think sociologically."

Aspects of this work have been presented in numerous conferences over the years. I especially appreciate the comments I received from fellow panelists and audience members of the annual conferences of the American Anthropological Association, the American Sociological Association, the International Communication Association, and the Pacific Sociological Association; also the UC Davis Frontline Feminists Conference in 1995, the graduate student workshop on Politics and Identity Formation in Contemporary Europe at Harvard in April 1997, and the 1998 Modern Greek Studies Association Conference.

Others, scholars or not, who each uniquely helped with the process of creating this book by offering valuable comments and advice, disparate forms of support, as well as insight, encouragement, and often 100 percent on-target humor at important moments in its development include Alexandra Alexandri, Michael and Cathy Dertouzos, Cindy DuPray, Rod Ferguson, Marga Gomez-Reino, Nea Herzfeld, Anna Kent, Stuart Price, Alexander Tristan Riley, Levente Soysal, Robert Walker, and Leslie and Wren Yoder. For the same reason, I also thank Costis Akritidis, Nikos I. Athanasakis, Angie Athanasiadi, Antonis Balassopoulos, Patricia Barbeito, Elena Evaggelatou, Anna Frangoudaki, Adrianne Kalfopoulou, Dimitris Karmakolias, Christina Katsoulou, Nikos Kotaridis, Nota Kyriazi, Yiorgos Lakopoulos, Arsenoe Laniotis, Pandelis Lekkas, Andreas Lytras, Lyda Masoura, Haris Mylonas, Filippos Nikolopoulos, Roula Pandazi, Eleni Papadopoulou, Akis Papatxiarchis, Ron Rein, Telemache Serassis, Dr. L. Tapp, Maria Topali, Kostas Vlahos, Peter Wilkins, Nikos Xyrotiris, and George Yiannoulopoulos.

I also need to acknowledge the three anonymous reviewers at Duke University Press, all of whom were especially meticulous and rigorous. I especially thank editorial assistant Christine Dahlin for her reliability and method throughout the process and for her work in the final stretch. I am very grateful to my editor, Ken Wissoker, for his patience and his intelligence.

Crucial for the completion of this book was the friendship of Diamanda Galas, Jackie Gately, Jonathan Markovitz, Yorgos Rammos, and Sassy Tzavara. Diamanda offered inspirational strength, in addition to a generous series of interviews, which are being saved for another project. Sassy has been a true friend and a source of encouragement for the past twenty years. Yorgos's courage and razor-sharp mind was a beacon of light during darker parts of the later years of the journey. Both Jackie and Jonathan offered gifts of great kindness. Jonathan has been an active source of strength in my life for over a decade in addition to relentlessly reading, editing, and incisively commenting on numerous drafts of this book.

Finally, I am grateful for the assorted forms of vital nourishment, along with steadfast optimism, offered by my family, Chris C. Halkias, Demetra S. Halkias, Helen J. Halkias, and Myrella. My father, Christos C. Halkias, worked to understand my project and supported it with invaluable Internet and other research assistance. I am grateful both for his genuine interest and support, and for the spark with which he ignites life! The book is devoted to him. I also want to acknowledge my two grandmothers, Alexandra Halkia and Ioanna Saras, for their efforts to understand my pursuit of "all those letters" *tosa grammata paidaki mou, ti tha ta kanis,* and for their disparate lessons in grace.

To all of the above, I extend gratitude. Bringing this book to life has been a very difficult and solitary process. Yet, it could not have been done without them. Of course, as per the mandates of dominant discourses at the present historical moment, I alone am responsible for this book.

INTRODUCTION

✥

This book traces the social and cultural construction of the nation, the body, gender, and sexuality in Greece, a nation that is in many ways located at the crossroads of East and West, a charged site of conflict and conjunction between modernity and tradition. This process of construction is a deeply political project. My ostensible focus is on abortion, of which there have been anywhere from 150,000 to 400,000 annually throughout the 1990s, and on the perceived national problem of a low birth rate, approximately 110,000 births annually for a population of close to 11 million, that is popularly called *to demografiko*.[1] Even *The Economist* noted in a special 2002 issue on Greece, "Greece has an exceptionally high incidence of abortion."

What can we learn about the construction of the subject and the nation in late modernity from this high rate of abortion in Greece? Rather than asking why there are so many abortions in Greece at the present, I ask *how* is it that there comes to be a high incidence of abortion in a country where the low birth rate is a national issue. In pursuing this paradox, the book attempts to chart the discursive production of the gendered and nationed subject in present-day Greece. My objective is to trace the vexed operation of power in the recesses of the national imaginary, as it is expressed, for instance, in press coverage of the demografiko and in the capillaries of daily social life, such as sexuality and erotic relationships. In effect, this involves an exploration of the meanings of love, life, the divine, and agency and their very intimate affiliations with stories about what it means to be Greek.

Unraveling this tangled set of discourses, I find that the same stories of Greekness that produce the specific construction of the demografiko as a major national problem also yield forms of sexuality, personhood, and "the couple" that result in the high rate of abortion, which the demografiko discourses penalize even though the medical act itself has been legal since 1986 and easily and safely available even before then. In arguing thus, I offer a case study of the ways nationalism permeates and shapes the body and of how understandings of gender and sexuality animate nation-building projects of late modernity. The primary material considered consists of in-depth interviews, and often a series of follow-up conversations, with 120 women living in Athens who reported having had two or more abortions and all mainstream newspaper articles on abortion or the demografiko that were published during the calendar year 1994, a year that Greece presided over the European Council. Also, my observation of over four hundred ob/gyn exams performed in a state clinic and of the surrounding interactions between medical personnel and the women visiting the clinic constitute an important part of the material used in developing my analysis.

Thus, this book is not *about* abortion. Rather, it examines the vexed constitution of subjects, political subjects, and the larger national community to which they imagine they belong. Their sense of who they are and what has meaning to them is what affects their actions, and their sense of who they are is grounded in particular understandings of what it means to be *Greek*. This book traces some of the discourses of gender and of nation at one particular geopolitical site. Using abortion and the demografiko as a point of entry, I map some of the narratives and the discursive practices through which the body politic and the physical body are together founded in Greece. The book follows the junctions, the collusions, and the sometimes violent collisions that occur between disparate stories about what it means to be properly Greek and stories about what it means to be a good Greek *woman,* as these are inscribed on the different, but similarly intimate—and, as I suggest here, intrinsically linked—domains of sex and the national imaginary.

This book is also not just about Greece. Although in "the margins of Europe" in many ways, Greece is not only at the "crossroads of East and West" but also at the heart of the so-called West (Herzfeld 1987). At the level of the international imaginary, if we can speak of such, Greece seems to occupy a privileged position as a symbol of passion, of freedom and, in the consumerist contexts of globalization, of fun and pleasure, if one judges from the promotional materials the tourist industry produces every summer concerning the Greek islands. In addition, Greece is seen as "the cradle of democracy," the phrase used by many Western news media to refer to the country. In mapping the meanings of nation, sex, and the body in Greece, I attempt to expose the shaky foundations at the heart of contemporary liberal democracy and to chart the troubled waters of agency in late modernity as it is shaped in typically very densely woven cultural and historical political contexts.

At the present historical moment, the cornerstone of liberal democracy in Europe, the United States, and elsewhere and the driving force behind most projects of modernization globally are the presupposed "autonomous" and "rational" individual and the purportedly secular modern nation-state. This book sheds light on the shadows, that is, on the *lived* aspect of these two constructs and suggests that these are laboriously crafted, often contradictory, and certainly only tenuously achieved fictions that rely on a sterilized and clinical view of complex social realities that are in fact laced with contest.

Analysis of the decision-making process in modern Greek sexual contexts thus extends beyond the sexual act, its pleasures, its multiple dangers, and its ramifications to demonstrate that the postulated political subject of late modernity, the independent and rational individual, cannot be taken as a given. At the same time, its home, the nation, is not merely "out there" in the state, in formal political discourse, or in citizen's transactions with the state, but also very deeply within, as it colors and shades human beings' most intimate moments, including their own sense of their body. Thus, policy efforts that are based on different definitions of the subject and the nation are themselves smuggling in forces conducive to deepening social injustices rather than remedying them. The currently popular discourses of state-building modernization projects across the globe, that presuppose populations as a collection of individuals, often not even aware of this assumption as a problematic and supremely political move, obfuscate and silence the fraught and often dangerous arena of agon within which everyday life takes place in late modernity.

Incidents such as the July 2001 Genova uprising and the September 2001 attacks on core symbols of U.S. financial and political domination are but small signs of the cost of continuing to use discourses in public policy that, whether economic or social, gloss the often harsh specificities of the lived experience of the self in disparate geopolitical contexts of globalizing high modernity. Violence that is less visible, but perhaps more profound, than that witnessed at the Twin Towers has been occurring in particular cultural habitats all along. At issue is not the elimination of violence, for the very constitution of the subject involves certain forms of violence, as Butler (1993) persuasively argues,[2] but a higher awareness of its strategic deployments and of the depth of the "collateral damage" that is caused, even by ostensibly peaceful and well-meaning state-building projects, whether they are directly aimed at individual citizens, categories of them, or nations as a whole. At stake in this analysis of what goes on in people's bedrooms and within their imagination in contemporary Greece is an interrogation of the premises of liberal democracy. This book seeks to contribute to the project of understanding that what we have come to think of as being properly democratic might not be quite so democratic after all.

The Plot: Greece, Modernity, and the Body

The extent of the coverage of Greece's currently low birth rate in all sectors of the Greek press, as well as its status as the object of study of one of Greece's few interparty parliamentary committees (1993–94), among other developments, indicate the significance of the demografiko as a contemporary Greek cultural phenomenon. It is the premise of this book that the sheer numbers are not relevant. First, there is the technical problem of an absence of formal national statistics on abortion, which makes all numbers suspect. Second, abortion aside, when a population of 11 million (including anywhere from 500,000 to 1 million foreign immigrants) has a yearly number of births of 100,000–120,000, this is not in itself, and certainly not self-evidently, a major national problem. We live in an era when national prowess is established and gauged by technological sophistication, in the military or in industry, and by capital consolidation; at the same time, scientific developments in DNA research and reproductive technologies are increasingly challenging the centrality of "natural" human births as a prerequisite for the survival of a population. Third, even if the numbers did indicate a very sharp decrease in the size of the population and not just "a difficulty with reproducing the population," as the Greek demografiko is usually defined, of deeper interest is how this particular aspect of social reality is being interpreted, deployed, and invested in by different parts of society or "constituencies." How are larger narratives at play? Most important, what types of political orders and subjects do the discourses relating to the demografiko attempt to install and secure?

Part of the argument put forward is that the preoccupation with Greece's biological "robustness" can be seen as a product of friction between the discursive "plates" of modernity and tradition.[3] The media's articulation of the demografiko reveals evidence of a diffuse and always incomplete conjunction between various culturally specific discourses and their associated practices. On the one hand are the European Union's various mandates to rationalize business and state operations and the cultural concomitants of a long-standing Greek desire to become fully "European." On the other hand are both the much bemoaned yet tenacious clientelistic party relations, inherited by social structures put in place during the Ottoman Empire and shaping not only contemporary Greek politics but many facets of life in Greece, and the communitarian ethics associated with Greek Christian Orthodoxy.

The heightened concern over productivity in the economy does not eliminate the fear of invasion by Turkey but, rather, *displaces* it so that it is often transmuted into the more modernly palatable, if Orientalizing, notion that Greece will be overrun by (unmodernly, as this narrative goes) proliferating Muslims and other "foreigners" who are more and more immigrating to Greece. The only protection "we" have from such a prospect, according to this story, is if Greek women do their part to protect the nation in these dire straits by ceasing to abort, themselves quite unmodern and thus bizarrely Muslim-like in this instance, and fulfilling what emerges as their civic duty to be a mother. This complex and always open-ended struggle to *be* modern, as well as the occasional truces in the struggle, create a friction between the cultural "tectonic plates" of the social formations and discursive practices associated with modernity and tradition.

The pressures exerted by the confrontations and unexpected alliances between aspects of these larger social and discursive formations, otherwise called the condition of modernity, are an important factor shaping contemporary Greek political culture in general. In addition, the current location of the demografiko in a historical moment of fairly pronounced nationalism and in the shadow of a public discursive space formally ruled by the strong, if ambivalent, desire to modernize the Greek nation renders it a space within which the national imaginary lets its hair down, so to speak. In effect, the demografiko as a discursive domain serves as a repository, as well as a catalyst, for the fears, anxieties, and yearnings that are increasingly disallowed as inappropriate in the actively modernizing discourses articulated elsewhere. Similarly, the 120 women living in Athens who have had two or more abortions whom I interviewed constitute a very particular boundary group wherein one is likely to find a condensed version of the discourses, and the paradoxes, animating the body politic at large.

A key characteristic of contemporary Greek domestic and foreign politics is the tension resulting from a vexed desire: on the one hand, to surrender to the seduction of the modern and, on the other, to remain loyal to and continue to benefit from social formations (institutions, social relations, and identities) that are not consistent with a society that is highly rationalized in the Weberian sense. My argument is that the demografiko and the high rate of abortion in Greece are in fact firmly connected, though not, as the Greek press suggests, in the linear sense that abortions are a causal factor contributing to the national crisis of an aging population. The relationship, rather, is an underground one. Both the demografiko and the high rate of abortion are *symptoms*, each manifested on a different plane of social life, of the fraught encounter between what is commonly envisioned in Greece today as modernity and tradition.

Certainly, the high national rate of abortion presents an appearance, if not more, of opposition to the cultural mandate for more births that the demografiko authorizes. In this context, abortion in the formal public sphere frequently takes on the significance of an antipatriotic act. Yet, closer examination reveals that abortion at the site of the gendered subject actually figures primarily as a reactionary or even a conservative expression of the very same larger sociopolitical tensions producing the racializing and sexualizing nation-building technology that the demografiko operates as. That is, the demografiko works both to *engender* the Greek nation and to give it a racialized identity and, as a by-product of this very process, women have embodied subjectivities and couples have sex of the type that produce many abortions. As I argue in this book, the demografiko is animated by a powerful reactionary reassertion of the I of the nation—that is, of what is seen as *the core* of its identity—as what looks much like a religious state. Yet, the practice of repeat abortion, which ostensibly appears to be at odds with this construction of Greece, stands as evidence of an endorsement of the affiliated reactionary definition of "woman" as the subject whose body is seen as *essentially* reproductive and of Greek female bodies as "inherently" adverse to "invasions" such as those most methods are seen as being. In this context, abortion actually shifts meaning from that of an antipatriotic or even treasonous act, as it is represented in public sphere demografiko discourses, and emerges at the site of Greek women's subjectivity as an act that is to varying degrees natural.

At this level, the intertwining of gendered and nationalist discourses yields a politicized syntax of sexuality that is filled with contradictions. Modern birth control methods are figured as "invasive" and constituting "foreign bodies," whereas both heterosexuality itself and abortion are together *naturalized*. The demografiko is thus constituted as a national drama in which gender has a central role. Patrolling the borders of the modern nation-state is a project linked to the fortification of a particular configuration of gender, and the demografiko operates as a powerful technology that helps to manage both of these. In this sense, a critical reading of abortion can nonetheless also find in it a significant element of counterhegemonic praxis.[4]

That is, the popularity of abortion in Greece today can be seen as strong and suggestive evidence of the bankruptcy of some of the founding fictions of the modern Greek nation. The very same stories of struggle, valor, passion, and resistance to control, violation, invasion, and hostile foreign bodies, which work to make dominant an idea of the nation as vitally needing more *Greek* babies, are, I argue, those that, installed at the site of the subject's sexuality and body, make abortion itself seem natural, and birth control very often a threatening or alien force. If seen in the light of its co-implication with the stories that in the public sphere represent it as a national problem, abortion in Greece may emerge as a fruitful opportunity for a radical reassessment and reworking of popular national narratives. It is political praxis in more and unexpected ways, and it needs to be read as such.

In brief, the media's portrayal of a national demographic problem operates as a reproductive technology in the following senses: (1) it promotes a national agenda that prioritizes the biological reproduction of Greeks and redeploys a cultural discourse of compulsory motherhood that is already in wide circulation, hence operating as a reproductive technology in a literal sense; (2) it concretely engenders the nation itself by emphasizing a need for male babies, as one of the main mandates behind the demografiko is for more *male* soldiers; and (3) it uses religion to advance a particular racialized notion of Greece and "Greekness" while obscuring, at best, other configurations of these. Moreover, all this is done in a way that firmly heterosexualizes the nation and, at the same time, renders motherhood the normative requirement for Greek female citizenship. Thus, the demografiko works as a complex reproductive technology by reproducing and naturalizing particular institutions, including political forms of reproduction (heterosexual nuclear families and a particular matrix of the modern nation-state) and certain political configurations of subjects (Greek Orthodox *mother* citizens and Greek Orthodox male citizens).

Beyond Greece

As noted, the project of this book extends beyond Greece. The subtext running throughout, and which I flag at appropriate junctions, involves the main currency of liberal humanism and the democratic state-building projects it fuels in high modernity. In probing the demografiko press coverage, for example, we are confronted by some of Greece's cultural preoccupations, even obsessions, as they emerge at this historical moment.[5] This analysis of Greek configurations of nationhood and personhood in the mainstream press, however, in conjunction with the interviews and the follow-up conversations that typically ensued, also illuminates the assumptions and cultural contradictions limiting liberal democratic projects in other geopolitical contexts.

Moreover, the findings of this research challenge those rigid disciplinary understandings of social and political institutions that do not properly take account of the foundational role played in the latter not only by culture, but specifically by discourse and communication. I argue that a more useful unit of analysis, for scholarly research, policy formation, and national debate alike, in Greece as well as elsewhere, is in fact the *textuality* of both subject and nation. In particular, specific constellations of discursive practices that implicate gender in the formation of national identity, and vice versa, require attention if public policy aimed at any level of a society is to be effective. Thus, my research raises serious questions about the transportability of conceptions of the liberal subject of modernity, "the individual," and of the modern nation-state to settings outside those of abstract theory. Certainly, these constructs project and presuppose a social and political environment that is much more *peaceful* than most.

THE THEORY: DISCOURSES, SUBJECTS, AND THE NATION

In the beginning, there was the Word.

As Foucault convincingly argued, discourses effectively produce the body. To secure the anchor of my project it is useful to briefly consider Foucault's own words on this score.[6] Describing his own project, Foucault states, "What I want to show is how power relations can materially penetrate the body in depth, without depending even on the mediation of the subject's own representations" (1980c, 186). This understanding of power clearly posits the body firmly within the field of power rather than as something that is, at least initially, external to power's efforts to dominate. Foucault elaborates: "If power takes hold on the body, this isn't through its having first to be interiorized in people's consciousnesses. There is a network or circuit of bio-power, or somato-power, which acts as a formative matrix of sexuality itself as the historical and cultural phenomenon within which we seem at once to recognize and lose ourselves" (186). In effect, this is an understanding of power as radically constitutive, where its repressive qualities are almost secondary to its fundamental productive operation. In this view, the body itself, and sexuality as the site of truth of the subject, are more the products of power than its victims.

Thus, Foucault offers a different positioning for those interested in a critique of power. Instead of "the problem of sovereignty (What is the sovereign? How is he constituted as sovereign? What bond of obedience ties individuals to the sovereign?)," Foucault suggests that political analysis have a different subject:

the analysis of a whole range of areas; I realize that these can seem over-empirical and secondary, but after all, they concern our bodies, our lives, our day-to-day existences. As against this privileging of sovereign power, I wanted to show the value of an analysis which followed a different course. Between every point of a social body, between a man and a woman, between the members of a family, between a master and his pupil, between every one who knows and every one who does not, there exist relations of power which are not purely and simply a projection of the sovereign's great power over the individual; they are rather the concrete, changing soil in which the sovereign's power is grounded, the conditions which make it possible for it to function. . . . For the State to function in the way that it does, there must be, between male and female or adult and child, quite specific relations of domination which have their own configuration and relative autonomy. (187–88)

Pivotal to this type of analysis of power is the understanding that much of what is taken for granted in contemporary social science and observed as a neutral datum or unit of analysis is itself a historically and culturally specific product of power, just as much as are the particular practices of scientific observation and knowledge production. This includes our notion of the individual (firmly bounded and characterized by "rational" thought and "free" choice), the family, and sexuality, indeed reproduction itself. To clarify this aspect of Foucault's argument, consider what he says, having first noted the contrast with feudal societies: "In the seventeenth and eighteenth centuries a form of power comes into being that begins to exercise itself through social production and social service. It becomes a matter of obtaining productive service from individuals in their concrete lives. And in consequence, a real and effective 'incorporation' of power was necessary, in the sense that power had to be able to gain access to the bodies of individuals, to their acts, attitudes and modes of everyday behavior" (125).

This development had an important corollary. The theoretical significance of the project of this book hinges on the two together. Foucault continues, "But at the same time, these new techniques of power needed to grapple with the phenomena of population, in short to undertake the administration, control and direction of the accumulation of men (the economic system that promotes the accumulation of capital and the system of power that ordains the accumulation of men are, from the seventeenth century on, correlated and inseparable phenomena): Hence there arise the problems of demography, public health, hygiene, housing conditions, longevity and fertility. And I believe that the political significance of the problem of sex is due to the fact that sex is located at the point of intersection of the discipline of the body and the control of the population" (125).

In sum, many domains of social life, including the very topos of the body and the individual, that have become naturalized through discourses, are, with a Foucauldian perspective, denaturalized and reposited as themselves products and instruments of power that require analysis. Many Foucault scholars have subsequently argued that discourses produce the body in *gendered* and *racialized* ways (see especially de Lauretis 1987). There is a significant body of literature focused specifically on theorizing the political significance of the gendered production of the body.[7]

The case of abortion and the demografiko in Greece provides an opportunity to contribute to this theorization of the subject while also providing vivid empirical evidence of how this process works and of how profound its effects may be. Examining the phenomenon of Greece's high rate of abortion by tacking among Greek medical, media, and personal sites, I show how the discourses of nation specifically and their deployments of gender, race, and religion effectively *create* the Greek body, its sexuality, and, quite literally, the very possibility of life itself. Thus, I offer an analysis of how the controversial and, at some level, absurd-sounding theoretical claim *Discourses produce worlds* is borne out at one site. In so doing, following the epigraphs opening this book, my aim is to map discursive contestation in order to contribute to contemporary social and political theory.

I investigate the historically specific contemporary Greek manifestations of (1) Benedict Anderson's (1983) nation as "imagined community"; (2) Foucault's (1977) modern subject as a dynamic product of power operating from within, at the level of desire, as well as from without; and, very importantly, (3) the interanimation of these two. Toward these ends, I approach the narratives women shared with me about their lives and the mainstream coverage of the perceived national problem with a low birth rate (called, for short, the demografiko) as expressions of collective memory in which national identity is being negotiated.[8] The crux of my argument is that the stories told at these sites in effect create *Greece* and a particular range of Greekness, at the same time that they also actually produce, and reproduce, Greek human bodies.[9]

Many of the 120 women living in Athens who were interviewed expressed disagreement with the terms of the discussion about Greece's birth rate as they are presented in the public sphere. Some put forward their own incisive social critiques of the country's current state of affairs. All their narratives also indicate that the configuration of personhood that underlies these discussions, as well as the liberal democratic projects with which reactionary manifestations such as the demografiko are intimately linked, are not always pertinent to the ways these women experience themselves and their lives. For the Greek women living in Athens who participated in this research, although abortion may be about the nation in some sense, it is not at all about the nation in the terms of the Greek press. And although women are often only too aware of the expectation that they must either breed or properly contracept in order to be "good Greek women," the ways they spoke to me of heterosexuality, conception and contraception, love and betrayal, and dreams and loss suggest that most of the time abortion, even repeat abortion, actually makes a lot more sense to them than do any of the other options. With what follows, I hope to instigate a dialogue, a coming together, and a mutual interrogation of the sets of discourses shaping the understandings of the Greek press or a more formalized public sphere, on the one hand, and those of the women I spoke with, on the other. In so doing, I propose, we can come to see in a new light, and retheorize, important aspects of the larger liberal democratic discourses with which these Greek phenomena are affiliated.

One part of the project of this book, then, is to map the meanings of abortion and plot their contestation in Athens today. But, more important, because abortion is as prevalent as it is in the experience of modern Greek women (second-highest frequency after Rumania, despite easier access to contraception), I have taken abortion in Greece as a useful point of entry for studying Greek configurations of gender and personhood. Because of the country's preoccupation with the demografiko and the frequent public deployments of a connection between the frequency of abortion and the demografiko problem, I have also looked at both women's narratives and the media's discourse on abortion as important grounds for an analysis of representations of Greek national identity. Given the historical specificities of Greek conceptions of the nexus of nationhood and personhood, the demografiko and the narrated experiences of sexuality by Greek women are important, and telling, shards of modern Greek culture. Finally, because of Greece's unique cultural and geopolitical position "in the margins" of Europe, the stories articulated at these sites help to put together a "representative anecdote" (Ortner 1989) that at the present historical moment offers a privileged vantage point from which to view the larger social, cultural, and political terrain of not only Greece and the unifying European Community, but "the West" wherever it occurs.[10]

Thus, this book outlines some of the ways in which the historically specific concept of struggle, agon, or *agona,* and concern with various forms of intervention, interference, or invasion (*epemvasi*), especially that of a foreign body (*to xeno soma*), animate or inanimate, barbarous or civilized, help to constitute a particularly Greek syntax for more and less local narratives of nation and person—or "allegories of identity."[11] These narratives viscerally shape Greek women's understandings of their body, of sexuality, contraception, and abortion. I attempt to place the public sphere discussion of the demografiko, as well as the larger concern with Greek national identity, into conversation with the stories told by women about abortion, identity, and politics in Greece.

Both the narratives of the women I spoke with and the press coverage of the demografiko, when positioned against the backdrop of the other sources I draw from (ranging from the detailed kaleidoscopic views of the history and culture of this territory that I put forward in part 1, to the currently popular songs and local scholarly work on nationalism analyzed at the opening of part 3), constitute uniquely rich sites for furthering the theorization of the subject-nation nexus, as well as for examining the specifically Greek conceptions of nationhood and personhood.[12] In all, this work seeks to contribute to the project of illuminating the politics of late modernity by studying what is particular in how nation and gender are *cofounded* at the present historical moment in Greece, which is arguably at the center of the pervasive margins of European modernity. Thus, this is a study of how nationalisms, genders, and sexualities come together and how, in late modernity, they sometimes fall apart.[13] At the same time, this book also puts forward another story, one that suggests that prevailing notions of liberal democracy rely on truncated understandings, at best, of the profoundly political construction of the subject.

A Map of This Book

Thus, the explicit project of this book is to plot the coordinates of Greece as an imagined community at the present historical moment. Under examination are the political categories of nation, citizenship, gender, sexuality, and race as they are shaping and animating the contemporary Greek national imaginary.

In part 1, I initiate this project by putting forward significant aspects of the politics of Greek identity and the present state of Greece, including its historical contexts. Beginning with a description of Athens in the present, I move to the historical development of Athens in chapter 1, keeping Greece in the background for a moment, and, then in chapter 2, to the social and cultural context of contemporary Greek women's life. After that, in chapter 3 I survey the historical development of Greece itself and discuss salient aspects of the broader context that make up the stage on which the drama analyzed in this book is performed. I also advance the argument for the charged role race and religion have historically played in the politics of identity at this site while gesturing toward the gendered field of power in which this process currently takes place. In chapter 4, I turn back to the present, to how the demografiko itself is defined in contemporary Greece and position it in comparative context.

The focus in part 2 is on two vital aspects of the contestation involved in abortion and the demografiko in Greece. In chapter 5, I offer a straightforward ethnographic narrative describing one day at a clinic where abortions are performed, while also positioning myself as researcher in the field. In chapter 6, I focus on the letters to the editor of mainstream newspapers expounding on the demografiko and abortion to probe the underlying common matrix of nationhood in the public sphere. Analysis of the press coverage puts in bold relief how the historically specific manifestation of anxiety about foreign bodies, invasion, and struggle come together in this sector of the Greek public sphere to produce a variety of competing explicit understandings of national identity and a nonetheless common implicit underlying matrix of nationhood in which Greece figures as a genre of religious state.

In part 3, consideration of the ways abortion is talked about by the women I interviewed reveals how the matrix of nationhood driving the Greek public imaginary in effect *creates* Greek sexuality, contraceptive behavior, and even life itself. Underlying the analysis of these interviews is my observation of more than four hundred gynecological exams performed by medical interns at one of the prototype State Family Planning Clinics of Athens and of innumerable instances of contraceptive advice given by midwives, interns, and doctors at the Family Planning Center run by the same Clinic, as well as other interactions between and among these groups. As a result, it becomes possible to show how the various nationalist and religious discourses that permeate the press and other sectors of the public sphere, and that work to tentatively establish the boundaries of "Greece" as it is popularly imagined, also work *viscerally* to produce culturally specific configurations of the boundaries of Greek bodies and to shape perceptions and experiences of sexuality, of love, and of relationship. Thus, in chapters 7, 8, and 9, I argue that the same stories that contribute to the social construction of the demografiko as a major national problem also help naturalize precisely what many demografiko discourses configure as the main enemy: abortion.

More specifically, in chapter 7 I examine the dynamics through which abortion emerges as a more natural method of birth control while others are configured as varyingly invasive, alien, or violating of core understandings of both Greekness and trust. In chapter 8, we see how, in addition, abortion operates as politics by other means and has positive uses within the fraught field of power constituted by the heterosexual couple. In chapter 9, I explore the ways abortion in Greece is nonetheless also experienced as painful in different ways. Thus, this part of the book explores sites of sexuality, the body, and *erota* or love/passion and reveals a different configuration of subjectivity than that typically presupposed when speaking of the modern liberal, rational, and autonomous individual. The implications for theorization of agency are elaborated here.

In part 4, I attempt to bring to the fore and to instigate a dialogue in multiple directions. That is, in chapter 10 I return to the demografiko discourses in the mainstream press with a focus now on the politics of representation of Greek women, rather than of the nation. I deepen the argument about how the nexus of meanings of contemporary Greece is articulated at the site of sexuality and reproduction by exploring the refractions projected in the public sphere. I argue that this occurs in such a way as to yield the contradictory public representations of Greek women both as signs of the *nation-state's* modernity via appropriate contraceptive behavior, and as protectors of the more traditional *homeland* or *patrida* by being good breeders. This is in direct counterpoint to part 3, where analysis of women's narratives tells a very different story about how it is Greece comes to have a high rate of abortion.

In the last chapter of the book, chapter 11, I return to the conversations I had with the women, though this time to examine their own opinions and critiques of the demografiko. This body of material constitutes a fairly direct response to the media discourses on the demografiko from a site that has not yet been heard. At the same time, this chapter also critically reads the women's responses and charts the circulation of nationalism within their own narratives. I trace the formation of alternative configurations of nationhood and conclude by providing a further illustration of how subject and nation alike are often discursively produced in contradictory ways, yet always refracting both entrenched patterns of power and resistance in the process. In effect, even as almost all the women I spoke with were strongly opposed to the demografiko, and often incisive in their analysis of why, I argue that overall, the resistances they express, much like the relationships and sexuality they describe, nonetheless exhibit the endorsement of pronouncedly nationalist understandings of Greekness. This has serious implications for current theory on agency, democracy, and the subject. In the final section on theory and policy, I explicitly draw a link between the theoretical argument explored throughout and social and public, domestic or foreign, policy.

Embedded within the text at critical junctions are short Greek phrases written in English characters for readability. In most cases, these phrases are the Greek for whatever has just been said in English. This use of Greek is meant to underscore and guard against the danger of developing a sense of a "complete understanding" of the charged and continuously contested multivocality and polysemy of the field of national politics and gender in Greece. The book is an exploration of this field, of the often paradoxical stories of what is true and what is real and what is good at this geopolitical site. As an exploration, it cannot but be open-ended, partial, and, potentially, disruptive of taken-for-granted ideas about social reality. An exploration of rugged terrain, no matter how thorough or penetrating it might be, does not make that terrain one's own. The occasional Greek phrases, written in English characters, usually mirroring the Greek spelling, serve as a reminder of ever-present alterity, of the limits of our field of vision.

I take seriously Donna Haraway's argument that "one cannot relocate in any possible vantage point without being accountable for that movement. Vision is *always* a question of the power to see—and perhaps of the violence implicit in our visualizing practices. With whose blood were my eyes crafted?" (1991, 193). Throughout the book, I attempt in different ways to render visible some of the violence inherent in the observations and analysis that I support and, where appropriate, to gesture toward the "blood" of which my own "personal" eyes are indeed crafted. As Haraway argues, "The 'eyes' made available in modern technological sciences shatter any idea of passive vision; these prosthetic devices show us that all eyes, including our own organic ones, are active perceptual systems, building in translations and specific ways of seeing, that is, ways of life. There is no unmediated photograph or passive *camera obscura* in scientific accounts of bodies and machines; there are only highly specific visual possibilities, each with a wonderfully detailed, active, partial way of organizing worlds" (190). The path that remains, once this is fully acknowledged, is to participate in the effort to build "situated and embodied knowledges" without engaging in "the god-trick of seeing everything from nowhere" (189) and also without falling prey either to relativism or to "a serious danger of romanticizing and/or appropriating the vision of the less powerful while claiming to see from their positions" (191). This is the path I try to follow in this book.

❖

PART ONE

The Agoras of Agon

In the beginning was the wrath of the earth.

Later Apollo came and killed the chthonic serpent, Python.
It was left to rot. It is said that this is where the first name
of Delphi, Pytho, came from. In such a fertilizer, the power
of the god of harmony, of light and of divination took root
and grew. The myth may mean that the dark forces are the
yeast of light; that the more intense they are, the deeper the
light becomes when it dominates them. One would think that,
if the landscape of Delphi vibrates with such an inner radiance,
it is because there is no corner of our land that has been so
much kneaded by chthonic power and absolute light.

—George Seferis, *Delphi*

Part 1 situates and thus initiates a cartography of discourses of national identity and of gender that are in circulation in Athens at the topos of abortion. Part 1 offers a kaleidoscopic view of Greek society, culture, and politics, historically and in the present. The focus is on mapping some of the forces characterizing the geopolitical field of Athens at the present, including the historical dimension of the politics of Greek identity, so as to firmly situate the critical analysis of discourses this book puts forward.

In many ways, Athens is an agora of agon—an agora or marketplace, where different sites peddle different wares, different kinds of struggle, engaging subjects and thus *creating* them. The scent of one field of power, we might imagine, intermingles with those of others. Streams of discourse flow from one place to another, congealing into different categories of subjects, with unpredictable order, noise, shoving, and arguments. From time to time, something falls and breaks. The sound of shattering is absorbed and transmuted into a sound like that of a wind chime, punctuating the pervasive background sound of tinkling coins changing hands. Thieves move through the crowd easily, taking one form of agon from one stand, grabbing another, a prized new possession paid for dearly, from the crowd. Posing as detached observers, other thieves stuff their pockets. In the distance, somebody blows a whistle. Someone is arrested. The streams of humans continue to flow, the forms of struggle coagulate and mutate.

Pushing this metaphor just a little more, Athens is also an agora in the more traditional sense of "a marketplace of ideas." As I show, it is not the clear or abstract well-argued ideas of ancient philosophers, nor is it ideologies in a Marxist sense, that are at a premium here, but rather the far more nebulous and less easily identified discourses and discursive practices of national identity and gender. It is these that give shape to the mob. In what follows, we join the crowd. And yet, we must not forget, we also remain radically separate.

Chapter 1

SETTING THE STAGE:

ATHENS, GREECE, FANTASY,

AND HISTORY

Certainly, "the Greek light" that so many have written of, as has the Nobel prize-winning poet Seferis in the excerpt opening this part of the book, is a prominent part of the Greek landscape. Whether there are perceivable physical differences to the light in this part of the Mediterranean is hard to tell. What matters is that Greeks and foreigners alike tend to share a belief in its uniqueness. The metaphoric sense of light is operative because the link is often explicitly made between the quality of the light here, an almost relentless brightness, and the clarity of thought of especially Ancient Greek thinkers. Moreover, as Seferi suggests, a narrative about good and evil also seems to be intertwined with those relating to the Greek light.

Glossy images of whitewashed little houses perched on a barren slope of one or another island with the sparkling sea below and the clear blue sky above tend to be connected to a romanticized idea of a starkly simple and wholesome mode of life. The image may appear as seductive as it does because it is superimposed on an imaginary snapshot of "the Ancient Greek world." This double exposure, gilded by fragments of more recent historical narratives about Greece and Greeks, may be what is read as evidence of a distinctly Greek *spirit*. Incisive thinking, uncompromising conviction in high ideals, including a superior aesthetic such as that exhibited in the ancient ruins scattered across the country, relentless freedom and independence, and an inferred readiness to take absolute and passionate action in heroic ways are vital parts of the contemporary Greek myth. This, I think, is what "the Greek light" is made of. This representation of Greece, even if muted locally by the hectic rhythm of life, the high stakes of bipartisan micropolitics, petty clientelism, and other stressful aspects of Greek late modernity, no doubt constitutes an important part of the context of contemporary Athens, the site of my research (see figure 1).

Figure 1. The Greek National Tourist Organization reinscribes a popular image of Greece in its ad campaigns. The viewer of this ad is humbly invited to draw a parallel between Great Western Art and the painted walls of "the *homes* of Greece," while the caption strategically calls on the English-speaking visitor's quest for his or her own creativity. At stake in this representation is the contemporary economic survival of the modern nation via the tourism industry.

There are other, less noble but equally important features.[1] Athens today is a city whose busy central Constitution Square sports a thriving McDonald's, only the first of several now operating in the larger Athens area, that is surely host to almost as many as those who come to visit the Parthenon, a mere mile away from Syntagma, also the home to the Greek Parliament, i Vouli ton Ellinon. The adjacent old town areas of Monastiraki and Plaka are filled with tourist shops selling Greek memorabilia. This area gives way to the increasingly posh areas of Thisseio, Psirri, and Gazi, where the natural gas factory used to operate and workers' dwellings have been renovated to become some of the more fashionable restaurants and bars frequented by the Athenian elite. Little bars and tavernas can be found in abundance in most neighborhoods of Athens, assuming one is willing to negotiate with the unbelievable traffic found at almost all times of day and night! This city, representing less than 5 percent of Greece's territory, is where 34 percent of the approximately 11 million Greeks live.[2]

In the upper-class neighborhood of Kolonaki, as well as the nearby northern suburbs of Psyhico and Filothei, Filipino cleaning women, considered the elite of the caste of Russian, Ukrainian, Bulgarian, and Albanian cleaning women now employed regularly even by middle-class households, keep house for the aging and diminishing class of Athenian aristocracy as well as for the newly rich. These are also areas where one rarely sees in public any of the thousands of Albanians who entered the country legally or illegally during the 1990s. Further downtown, as well as along parts of the avenue along the coast, Greek prostitutes are joined by a growing number of male and female Russian, Ukrainian, Albanian, and other prostitutes, some of whom also double as "California Girls" dancing at some of the fancier strip joints.

Athens, specifically Exarhia, the area neighboring Kolonaki, is the base for what has been called Europe's most enduring anarchist movement. Even today, police vans often line its central street or park outside the headquarters of the party in office, the Panhellenic Socialist Party (PASOK), in an attempt to ward off "trouble." *Fasaria. Klouves.* Athens has also been the main site of action for a twenty-year-old revolutionary organization called the 17th of November (commemorating the day in 1973 when students took over the Athens Polytechnic in protest of the U.S.- supported Papadopoulos dictatorship) that the United States ranked as one of the most dangerous terrorist groups in the world. In a larger global context of entities such as the IRA and ETA, and of course now Al Qaeda, this is a puzzling title, because the 17th of November has engaged in highly focused strategic actions resulting in some damage to property and the death of twenty-three people, almost exclusively members of the Greek and foreign elite, since its operation began in 1975. Nonetheless, it has increasingly been the subject of heated discussion in the public sphere, and in June 2001 highly contentious legislation was passed to help "fight the terrorist threat." U.S. and British pressure played an important part in this new wave of effort to find and arrest members of this group, which culminated, in the summer of 2002, in the arrest of several alleged members.[3]

Another especially prominent aspect of the contemporary Athenian public sphere are the 2004 Olympic Games that the city fought for and won under the mostly inspired leadership of Iana Aggelopoulou, the wife of a very wealthy industrialist, though of working-class background herself. Putting aside the scandals associated with the allocation of the related funds that have sent shock waves through Greek society on more than one occasion, preparations for the Games—necessary to create an infrastructure capable of supporting the expected massive influx of people to an already very congested Athens—are affecting many facets of life in Athens today. The new Eleutherios Venizelos airport, built in the remote area of Spata, opened in March 2001 and the new roads constructed to facilitate traffic to and from it are two of the proud achievements of the currently governing PASOK; both have received extensive media coverage.

Other significant features of the Athenian social landscape include the largest professional association of lawyers in all of Europe, the highest per capita concentration of doctors, at least twenty well-equipped high-tech Centers for Assisted Reproduction, innumerable art galleries and gyms, many theaters, *barakia* (little bars with music), a few of which cater to a gay clientele, and tavernas and *kentra* (places to drink and eat that also usually have music) as well as *kafeteries* and *fast-foodadika*. For several years now, Greece reportedly has had the highest per capita consumption of scotch and of cigarettes in Europe. Cafés are ever-present and crowded at most hours of the day; there people sit talking with one another, sipping a *portokalada,* an orange drink, or *frappe,* a foamy iced coffee drink that, along with the iced cappuccino, *freddo,* have almost replaced the traditional *tourkiko* or *elliniko,* the small cup of thick espresso-like coffee called Turkish or Greek depending on the degree of one's nationalism.[4]

The fairly loud voices, honking cars, and overall ruckus heard in Athens are punctuated by the sound of phones ringing. The center of Athens today is a site inhabited by humans whose most prominent feature, male and female alike, might well be the contraptions they hold firmly in their hands and into which they talk very loudly and often. In a very short period of time, the mobile phone, *to kinito,* has become a vital appendage for many Greeks whose dense social networks now have another outlet for further *zimosi* ("kneading"), as social interaction with a purpose is called, or simply casual gossip (*koutsobolio*). The Greek market for mobiles is at 59 percent saturation; the average in other countries of Europe is 65 percent.[5] In Athens, as well as elsewhere, the kinito has become in a very few years an important accessory with which, as many claim openly, there is a powerful relationship of dependence.

Fervently trying to connect some of the disparate points of the Athenian landscape is an erratic public transportation system and thousands of taxis. The massive construction undertaken to build a tunnel for a new underground train (*to metro*), which kept encountering ancient ruins, finally yielded results. It is another of the proud and well-publicized accomplishments of PASOK and is making its mark on Athenian traffic, often as much by creating yet more congestion at the stations where commuters' cars park erratically as by somewhat diminishing the flow on some of the main arteries of the city. Indeed, the traffic is often the reason cited for the need of the omnipresent mobile phones. Surrounding all this, and enveloping it, is the pervasive smog (*to nefos*), which is routinely at levels comparable to that of Los Angeles.

Historical Background of the City

Athens was not always like this. In this section I track significant events in the city's historical development, leaving the details of the various histories of Greece itself in the background for the moment. Greece was formally declared an independent state, having successfully won a fierce and bloody struggle for independence from the Ottoman Empire, with the Protocol of London on 3 February 1830. In 1822, one year into the revolution, Athens was a city of eight thousand (Leondidou 1989, 48). When, in 1834, Athens was declared the capital of the Greek Kingdom, it was basically a city in ruins with twelve thousand inhabitants.[6] Barely three thousand houses remained intact (Markezinis 1966, 126). The adjacent port of Piraeus, famous in antiquity and now again thriving, was a wild coast with a few moorings. Although interesting versions of Athens existed in ancient times, the Roman or Middle Ages, and the immediately preceding period of the Ottoman Empire, in many ways, the history of contemporary Athens as a city begins in 1830. After its declaration as the capital of Greece, a highly centralized state apparatus developed and replaced the decentralized modes of administration that existed during Ottoman rule. The government, the king, and social classes that serve the state were installed. Athens became a city with power and control over the nation, without itself having any directly productive economic activity.

Figure 2. *I Sholi ton Athinon No. 2* (The School of Athens No. 2), 1974, Yiorgos Vakirtzis. Courtesy of National Gallery of Art of Greece.

This began to change in 1870 to marked effect by 1880. The Greeks living in their own communities outside of Greece, mostly in Western and Eastern Europe and in northern Africa, who had kept their businesses outside of Greece, began to settle in Greece and to invest. As they settled in Athens, the city began to operate as a mercantile center and the new bourgeoisie became a dominant economic force. A capitalist mode of production developed during the 1880s and Athens proper began to grow. Thus, whereas there were 87,117 inhabitants of the Athens-Piraeus area in 1879, by 1889 there were 144,589. From that time on the population exploded.[7]

The next significant change came after the military uprising against the king in the Athens area of Goudi, in 1909.[8] The process of industrialization, which intensified during World War I, gradually transformed the Athens-

Piraeus area from a small-scale base for bourgeois and petit bourgeois classes to the productive center of Greece (Leondidou 1989, 96). This transformation intensified after 1922, when the refugees from the Asia Minor disaster arrived in Greece. As per the agreement made by Greece and Turkey (more on this in the section on the history of Greece), there was an "exchange of populations" wherein a total of 1.3 million refugees arrived in Greece in "exchange" for 500,000 Turks who left Greece for Turkey (151). Of this number of returning Greek refugees, it is estimated that in 1928 about 250,000 had settled in the larger Athens area (table 16, 159). Thus, between 1920 and 1928 the population doubled, from 453,000 to 802,000 (156; table 15, 158). During the nineteenth century, Athens never had more than 4 to 6 percent of the country's population, but after the arrival of the refugees this figure climbed to 13 percent.[9]

After the refugees' arrival, a wave of internal immigration to Athens, along with continuing industrialization and urbanization, all played a role in transforming postwar Athens into "the crossroads of Greece." A survey of Athens in 1960 counted 690,000 "local" Athenians and 867,000 who had been born in other parts of the country or elsewhere.[10] By 1981, despite a slowdown in internal immigration during the 1970s, 31 percent of the country's population resided in the larger area of Athens. Today, that larger area (including Piraeus and suburbs) is home to 3,761,810 Greeks.[11]

SOCIAL STRATIFICATION AND THE ECONOMY

The social structure of Athens has gone through several changes. During the nineteenth century, the Greek bourgeoisie was located outside of Greece, in Europe and northern Africa, where Greeks had settled to take advantage of economic opportunity, and in Asia Minor, where they continued a long history of Greek presence. At this time, there were two phases to the socioeconomic development of Athens. In the first, lasting roughly until the early 1870s, the population consisted primarily of urban-dwelling bourgeois, public servants, and petit bourgeois. Primary economic activity was minimal (i.e., by 1876, there are reports of a mere eleven factories in Athens and twenty-seven in Piraeus).

The second phase of development occurred in the 1870s: the Greeks abroad begin to return, establishing Athens as the base for their financial enterprises. In the Balkans of this time, there were significant investments in large-scale transportation projects. Indeed, in Greece the 1880s have been called "the decade of the railways." The wealthier Greeks who returned from abroad also began to invest in banks, mining, shipping, and commerce. Industrialization gradually changed the economic profile, specifically of Piraeus from a services-centered city to a more directly productive one. At the end of the nineteenth century there were roughly six thousand workers in the larger Athens-Piraeus area.[12]

Greece recovered in the first decade of the twentieth century. After the Goudi uprising in 1909, many productive units were created. In 1910 there were reports of 243 factories in the Athens-Piraeus area, of which 12 were large. The area was radically transformed by industrialization, which intensified during World War I. The diaspora bourgeoisie, made up of wealthier Greeks who had come to settle, was joined by a newly developing "domestic" bourgeoisie, and the mercantile class continued to thrive. At the same time, a workers' movement developed, as workers multiplied and lived in poverty and socialist ideas began to circulate. The second Panhellenic Workers Conference in Athens in 1918, partly an effect of the October Revolution, resulted in the foundation of the General Federation of Workers of Greece (Leondidou 1989, 113). The same year saw the founding of the Socialist Workers' Party of Greece, later to become the Communist Party of Greece (KKE). The influx of the Asia Minor refugees in 1922 further enhanced Athens's economic development, as many of them became a source of cheap labor. More women also joined the active workforce, mostly in the area of tapestry and rug making (Leondidou, 198). The area of Nea Ionia became a weaving center; the areas of Kaisariani and Virona developed several small industries; the Piraeus areas of Kokkinia and Drapetsona became large workers' towns (174, 178).

However, the Athens economy did not fully absorb the new populations. Rather, as the population grew between the two World Wars, so did the problems associated with rapid urbanization. Unemployment was endemic and especially pronounced during the Metaxas dictatorship (1936–40). The working class lived in poverty, poor living conditions became even worse during the 1940s, unemployment increased.

The class divisions in Athens were mapped spatially. The ruling class and bourgeoisie lived in "their own" neighborhoods, around Constitution Square, in Kolonaki, and in the new "garden towns" that later became the northern suburbs of Psyhico, Filothei, and Ekali. These areas were far removed from the more congested workers' neighborhoods that developed in areas of Piraeus such as Kokkinia and Korydallo, or eastern and northern suburbs of Athens such as Vironas, Kaisariani, Nea Ionia, and Nea Filadelfia. In these working-class neighborhoods a distinct culture emerged where tightly knit bonds within and between families served as a bulwark against the dangers of the exploitative financial environment of Athens. Political differences created lines of division between the internal immigrants to Athens from other parts of Greece, who tended to be opposed to Venizelos, and the refugees from Asia Minor, whose beliefs ranged from supporting Venizelos to communism. Other aspects of a common culture were strong, though. For example, a genre of music stemming mostly from the subproletariat, the songs of *rebetika*, were enjoyed by most.[13]

In postwar Greece, after the civil war and with U.S. aid from the Marshall Plan, Athens went through a boom. Architecturally, construction increased from 1957 to 1963. New buildings were built and prominent landmarks in the Athens landscape were created. The imposing Hilton Hotel in the center of Athens was built in 1958–63 according to the design of architects E. Bourekas, P. Vasiliadis, and S. Staikos (Wharton 2001). Its novel size, along with the implications of its being a highly visible symbol of U.S. capitalism, generated both local and international criticism.[14] However, the construction of the Hilton, along with the creation of Mont Parnes, which was the first luxury hotel to begin operations in Athens in 1961, and other large hotels whose construction was decided in the late 1950s, seemed to some to herald a new era. Slowly, Greece entered what was to become a crucial sector of the economy: the international tourist industry. In addition, a surge in investments in housing resulted in Athens undergoing a phase of massive reconstruction.

At the same time, there was rapid economic growth. A marked improvement in the conditions of life for the entire population took place. The poverty of the period between the two World Wars became a thing of the past and the population of the subproletariat sharply diminished. The working class grew so that by 1971 about 42 to 45 percent of those living in Athens were workers, whereas in 1928 it accounted for 38.1 percent of the working population (Leondidou 1989, 188). All public and most private sector activities had made Athens their base. In postwar Greece, Athens played the main role in the financial development of the country.[15]

POLITICS

This does not mean that social conflict disappeared. Class stratification was complex in a polarized economy such as Athens. On the one hand, there were increasing units of mass production, and on the other, the thriving merchants and petite bourgeoisie. Between the two was a growing working class with some upward mobility. The fluidity of occupations during the postwar period, and the tendency toward multiple occupations, led to a fair measure of mobility from the working class to the petite bourgeoisie. This created peculiar social relationships. During the nineteenth century the pivotal factor leading to alliances and strong group ties was the particular area of Greece that inhabitants of Athens came from. Moreover, *Athenian* Athenians distinguished their position from that of Athenians coming from other areas. As this friction subsided and socialist ideas supported by the large working class began to be more visible, another, stronger conflict emerged between Greek Athenian members of the working class and Athenians from Asia Minor. Politically, this was expressed as anti-Venizelism opposed to a pro-Venizelist position.

However, due to the fluidity of the economic base of lower strata of Athenian society, political movements were usually associated with a broader base rather than an exclusively working-class base. This became clear in the 1940s, when EAM, the left-wing organization of resistance to the Nazis, helped unify Greek Athenians and refugees in a larger popular front. A somewhat similar range of mobilization can be seen in the radicalization of the 1960s as well.

It is important to keep in mind here that the manner in which modern Athens became populated, along with the specificities of its financial development, were associated with fracture lines in the body politic that often ran deep and, at the same time, occasionally shifted abruptly. In addition, Greeks actively *remember;* that is, the personal histories of their families' experiences (throughout the World Wars, civil war, and population relocations) are relayed from generation to generation and constitute an important part of the socialization of new members of the family. Also, the radio, which a select few had as early as 1938, and television, which entered Greek homes in its black-and-white version in 1965, both relied heavily on the dramatic representation of historical events that took place in Athens and Greece in general.[16] The occasionally dormant but easily accessed sites of conflict in contemporary Athens, a dense and vibrant agora of agon, layered as they are in assorted representations of this history of Athens, in addition to aspects of the history of Greece that are discussed further below, are multiple and strongly charged. Trauma is at the center of this.

LORD BYRON AND "THE MAID OF ATHENS"

To conclude this historical review of contemporary Athens, I offer a quick look at how narratives of gender intertwine with those of the city's character in a lighter incident that actually took place in Athens before Greece had become an independent nation-state. More than two centuries ago, at the end of the eighteenth century, Athens was a city of approximately ten thousand people. At that time, history gives us an intriguing incident that brings to the fore the historical context of the nexus of discourses of national identity with those of gender in modern-day Athens. It was in November 1797 that Teresa Makris was born in Athens, in the area of Psirri. Psirri itself does not have many ancient ruins, though it is adjacent to the areas of Plaka and Monastiraki, which are riddled with ruins. At that time, Psirri had 997 small houses, thus rendering it one of the more vital areas of Athens.[17] Teresa's father, Prokopis Makris, was the consul of England to Athens. When Teresa was two years old, her father died. Her mother, Tarsi Makri, marshaled her resources to make a living for herself and her three daughters and started renting out rooms in their home.

Mrs. Makri rented rooms to foreign travelers, usually English. One of these, Lord Byron, arrived Christmas afternoon in 1809 and stayed through March 1810. He spent the days walking and exploring the ancient ruins of the surrounding area with his traveling companion, J. Hobhouse. In the afternoon he visited with Mrs. Makri and her three daughters. One such afternoon the twenty-one-year-old poet played "the stiletto game," a courtship practice common at that time. Kneeling before Teresa and acting as though he would commit suicide for her, he brought his knife to his chest expertly, the story goes, yielding but one drop of blood. A brief but intense infatuation ensued between Byron and the thirteen-year-old Teresa.

This in itself might not be significant were it not for the fact that in 1810 Lord Byron wrote the poem "Maid of Athens ere we part" that was to become famous when published in 1812. Byron was a strong supporter of the Greek struggle for liberation from the Ottoman Empire. The poem is seen as having been written as part of his effort to support the independence of Greece.[18] Since then, most of the travel books of the time would mention Teresa and Byron, and it is said that many readers of his "International" visited the neighborhood of Psirri hoping to catch a glimpse of the young Athenian woman who had captured his attention.[19]

The poem he wrote for Teresa is worth looking at more closely.

Maid of Athens, ere we part,
Give, oh, give back my heart!
Or, since that has left my breast,
Keep it now, and take the rest!
Hear my vow before I go,
Zoi mou sas agapo.

By those tresses unconfined,
Wooed by each Aegean wind;
By those lids whose jetty fringe
Kiss thy soft cheeks' blooming tinge;
By those wild eyes like the roe,
Zoi mou sas agapo.

By that lip I long to taste;
By that *zone*-encircled waist;
By all the token-flowers that tell
What words can never speak so well;
By love's alternate joy and woe,
Zoi mou sas agapo.

Maid of Athens! I am gone:
Think of me, sweet! when alone.
Though I fly to Istanbul,
Athens holds my heart and soul:
Can I cease to love thee? No!
Zoi mou sas agapo.

Zoi mou sas agapo means "My life, I love you," though with an interesting use of the plural "you" that likely references Byron's having learned the formal form. Beyond an indication of Byron's feelings for Teresa, we see in this poem the conflation of an idealized and romanticized Teresa with the city of Athens itself and, judging from the intimacy with which he pictures the Aegean winds in her hair, with a notion of Greece as a whole. The use of the term of endearment "zoi mou," more often used by mothers to their children, is interesting, as there are an array of other such terms that might have been used (*matia mou, kali mou, psixi mou, kardia mou,* meaning, respectively, my eyes, my good one, my soul, my heart). "Zoi mou" epitomizes a particular sense of Greece, a feminized Greece clearly, and a Greece that is somehow in the role of child to the Western "other," yet that also gives life in some important way to the civilized world as Lord Byron knew it.

Back to Contemporary Athens

Returning to present-day Athens, the fumes from the cars and the *nefos* make the Aegean winds Byron refers to seem even further away than they are. The many bars and tavernas sprouting up among the abandoned and now de-

Figure 3. *Eis tou 1797 Hmera Tetradi,* painting of Teresa Makri, collection of Dimitri Tsitoura, reprinted in Lisa Miheli, 1987, *I Athina se Tonous Elassones* (Athens: Dromena).

crepit old homes in Psirri, and the always present gypsy children passing from table to table asking for a few coins, would no doubt have shocked Teresa and Byron alike were they to stroll down its narrow streets today. In addition, as is revealed by the juxtaposition of Athens's billboards today and one of the several paintings of Teresa (figure 3), the representations of femininity have changed from the romantic and ambivalently innocent-looking Teresa of Lord Byron's poem to the aggressive, often predatory-looking, "lean and mean" models of the present that are very similar to those of contemporary U.S. and British advertisements.

Certainly an emphasis on beauty characterizes contemporary Athens as well. Athenians are noted, at least in the national imaginary, for a special pride in discerning what they see as being *kalaisthito* or, more frequently, *kompso,* meaning aesthetically pleasing or tasteful, a judgment not always shared by Greeks elsewhere. This domain seems to occupy a boundary position between things that are classical, distinguished from those that are *traditional* though they also have their place, and the cutting-edge modern. As a guiding principle, the quest for this version of beauty seems to affect choices in the whole range of everyday life in Athens, including architecture, cuisine, clothing, and cars.

This sensibility is perhaps most evident, and more broadly based, in the realm of personal appearance. In the past, the stores of Athens (*ta emborika*), especially along Ermou street near Syntagma, were considered *the* venue for sophisticated modern shopping. As more Greeks travel abroad this has diminished, but only slightly. The Internet also has entered the scene. According to a study using a sample of seven hundred inhabitants of Athens, Salonica, and other large cities, 800,000 Greeks are connected to the Internet and approximately 100,000, of which men seem to be the heavier spenders, are estimated as active online consumers.[20] In fact, men, especially the growing group of businessmen, are increasingly conscious of their appearance and partial to well-tailored suits, as a casual glance at the pedestrians in the center of Athens reveals. Recently advertisements have appeared that seem to capitalize on a sense of men's hair as a vital part of their appearance, something that, in the not too distant past, would have been considered an effeminate interest. Meanwhile, the social construction of the *Athinaia,* the Athenian woman, as Teresa Makris also was called almost two centuries ago, today above all connotes a "superior," more modern way of dress, in addition to a slightly aloof or snobbish mode of conduct.

Women in general like to be seen as being *peripoiimenes*. The word literally means that one merely *takes care* of one's appearance, though it has come to mean wearing stylish, clean, and well-pressed clothes, even if they are not particularly expensive, having one's hair done professionally, and regularly wearing carefully applied makeup. In effect, being peripoiimeni is an understatement for a complex monthly, weekly, and daily regimen of maintaining approximation to a fairly polished ideal of femininity that is not that different from that of other cosmopolitan European cities.

Younger women and single women tend to accentuate their body, wearing tight clothing and high heels. Many are very thin, but there are also curvier bodies in abundance. During the scorching hot Athenian summer, one sees, and *feels*—for, among other things, physical boundaries are much more diffuse here—a lot of flesh. This past summer, two otherwise happily involved male friends of mine, on two separate occasions, expressed pleasure and frustration when commenting that all the sexy bodies surrounding them were a very difficult temptation to deal with. Meanwhile, the huge advertising

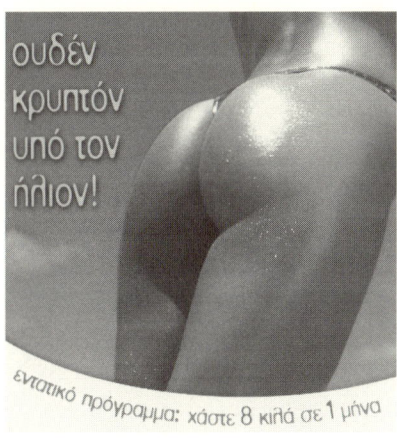

Figure 4. The pervasiveness of flesh in the visual landscape of modern Athens is markedly gendered. Almost all diet "institutes" and companies marketing the delivery of packaged diet food target their predominantly female clientele with images that foreground and forcefully reinscribe the valorization of the image of women's bodies as the determining factor in their sense of well-being.

billboards that crowd the Athens horizon, especially those promoting one of the many dieting centers or "centers of beauty" where various dieting methods are offered along with high-tech skin treatments and hair-removal technologies, often exhibit seminaked female bodies (figure 4). Many current jokes are either about Pontious, the minority of Greeks who came with the exchange of populations from the northeastern Pontos of Asia Minor and spoke a dialect that sounded strange to many other Greeks (a U.S. equivalent are the jokes about Polish people), or about "the blond woman" (*anekdota gia xanthies*), or about sex. All in all, Athens is distinctly a sexy city.

Chapter 2

STAGE LEFT:

GREEK WOMEN

✥

Other important aspects of the polyphony of Athens today have already been described in detail by Faubion (1993). This chapter explores characteristic social and cultural dynamics of daily life in Athens as it presents itself to women more specifically.

Work

According to figures publicized in 2001, women constitute 60 percent of the total of unemployed Greeks.[1] Moreover, women make up 74 percent of the total of *long-term* unemployed Greeks and 90 percent of those working in flexible and informal (*evelikti kai atypi apasxolisi*) occupations. Overall, many women lack benefits such as medical coverage and pension, unless they are covered through their husband's policy. In addition, a woman's salary for the same work done by a man is about 70 percent of his salary. Meanwhile, Greek women, including Athenian women, continue to be almost exclusively responsible for housework and child-raising.

According to George Romania, an economist and consultant for the Institute of Occupation (GSEE-ADEDY), whereas European social policy has made provisions for the principle of equal pay for equal work and appropriate absorption of women into the workforce, Greece has not yet been able to realize this goal:

> [This is so] because, unfortunately, there is a prevalent mentality that sees a woman as having special physiological conditions which diminish her productivity. This mentality places her in lower positions in the public sector and it also exists amongst employers in the private sector. The horizons for a woman, professionally speaking, are clearly limited and this has numerous conse-

quences.... Women in the private sector suffer the harshest consequences due to the specificities of their coverage and the work environment. For example, working overtime is considered a prerequisite for many jobs women hold and, since there are so many unemployed women, working women are put under a lot of pressure to work past the eight-hour day.[2]

It should be noted that along with the sense that women's primary duty is to be in charge of the home, there is also a lingering expectation, at a cultural level, that women bring a dowry to their marriage. Typically, this consists of household goods such as sheets, towels, special plate sets, and silverware. In many instances, it also includes the apartment for the new couple. The logic of the dowry is rooted in the time when women were seen as belonging to men and women's work was not part of the market economy and thus would not visibly contribute to the family's income. The dowry residence was seen as payment to the husband for his assumption of the responsibility for the woman, her *apokatastasi* both socially and financially. The transformed Family Law passed by PASOK in 1981 made the bold move of abolishing the legal requirement of a dowry. Yet, my ethnographic data suggest that at an informal level, there continues to be a strong expectation that the new couple's home be a "gift" from the wife's family.

Currently receiving significant public attention is PASOK's attempt to make the Greek pension system "equal for all." In the context of a large-scale revamping of the pension system to compensate for the diminishing contributions of the aging Greek population, an important aspect of the concern with the demografiko, and also to meet the economic requirements for economic alignment with the European Union, PASOK, using British consultants, announced a new program for the population's retirement. In this context, it announced the intention to eliminate the option for early retirement that had previously been offered to Greek women. Different retirement funds have established their own guidelines, but generally, working Greek mothers have had the option to retire with a full pension almost ten years before their male counterparts. In an intriguing deployment of feminist discourse, the new move proposed in the spring of 2001 was explained in the public sphere as a just redress of an unjust system.[3] However, as the government's Secretary for Equality E. Bekou commented, Greek society is characterized by a fundamental injustice in the structure of the family. The woman continues to be almost exclusively responsible for running the home and raising the children; in the meantime, the Greek state has not been able to cover the population's needs for day care centers. This, Bekou noted, con-

Figure 5. Cartoon by K. Mitropoulos that appeared in *Ta Nea* the day after Minister of Labor Giannitsi made the unexpected statement that women "have nothing to worry about." A woman, flat on the ground with a huge boulder on her back, bears the title "Women's Burdens" and the minister of labor stands before her. He looks down at her and says, "And don't worry! The limits of Equality remain as is!" The woman mumbles, "Thank God, Mr. Giannitsi."

tinues today, when it is both financially and psychologically important for women to also work outside the home.[4]

With regard to the demografiko, Bekou made reference to a European study showing that whether working outside the home or not, women actively choose to have fewer children. This, she said, emphasizes that it is a *family* decision to have children and that *families* are deciding to have fewer children. Thus, she argued, the claim that Greece is suffering from a low birth rate (which is putting more pressure on the pension system) because Greek women *prefer* to work outside the home does not hold.

The issue of the pension system has shaken the party in office, and it will continue to do so, if the spring 2001 massive workers' strikes were any indication. Indeed, at midnight on 25 April the minister of labor announced, per order of Prime Minister Simitis, that the new measures would be put on hold.[5] Nonetheless, this did not stop the large strike of 26 April, accompanied by statements of support from prominent members of the New Democracy Party. During the summer of 2001, public debate on the retirement system, as well as negotiations with the GSEE, continued. It shall be interesting to see how the issue of women's pensions will be resolved and whether it incites more gender-specific types of worker mobilization.[6]

Politics

After years of struggle, Greek women received the right to vote in the municipal elections of 1930 under the condition that they knew how to read and write and were over thirty years old.[7] Neither of these two limitations existed for male citizens. Nonetheless, a portion of the National Council of Greek Women in the 1920s had been sufficiently swayed by the discourse representing women as intellectually immature, both by nature and due to a lack of education, to embrace this position. In one of its publications, the Council reiterated this position and called for women to "educate women and fight against *the uneducated vote.*"[8] Mosxou-Sakorafou (1990, 224) comments, "These women, pioneers in social change and feminists, some of whom were the most active members of the National Council of Greek Women, seemed to forget that if men waited for even the last worker and villager to mature and learn how to read and write, neither would they have yet achieved the right to vote." Those women who met these requirements, about 10,500 in all, voted for the first time in the municipal elections of 1934. The reasons for the low turnout seem to have been: (1) not all women had registered, as the obligatory registration of women had only begun in 1925; (2) public opinion strongly felt that the vote was men's affair; and (3) about 55 percent of women were completely uneducated (231).

During the subsequent Nazi Occupation, in the areas dominated by the left-wing EAM, women could vote in the local council elections and in the general elections (in Free and Occupied Greece) for the National Council. In postwar Greece, the law of 29 April 1949, which gave the right to vote to all women over age twenty-one in local council elections, was ratified by Parliament in 1951. Women over age twenty-five were also given the right to be elected to municipal offices, except for the office of mayor. In the municipal elections of April 1951, 734,750 women voted and 71 were elected to municipal offices out of 40,000 offices available (Mosxou-Sakorafou 1990, 232).

The Constitution that was adopted on 1 January 1952 established the right to vote for all citizens over twenty-one years of age. Also, women twenty-five or older can be elected members of Parliament. Elections for an office in Parliament were declared for November 1952, but women's right to vote was rescinded with the argument that the voters' registration lists of women had not been updated. Thus, women voted in the by-election of Thessaloniki in 1953 and finally, for the first time in general national elections, in 1956.[9] From this time onward, all Greek women are registered in a separate list of voters and they vote in centers separate from male voters. Those who choose to run as candidates for an office themselves remain very few.

This situation continues to the present. In 2000 the discussion of establishing quotas for the election of women in municipal elections became more pronounced, largely because of the European Union's guidelines concerning equality. At the present, the Greek Parliament of three hundred has thirty women members. Although official quotas have not yet been instituted as this book goes to print, the issue of quotas is being seriously discussed and meets with significant resistance from many sectors of Greek society, including women across the political spectrum.

Nevertheless, Greek women's participation in political offices at various levels is fairly visible. The actress Melina Merkouri's political career with the Panhellenic Socialist Party is perhaps the best example of a highly visible female politician. Dora Bakoyianni, the daughter of Konstadinos Mitsotakis, former leader of the right-wing New Democracy Party and the wife of a member of Parliament who was killed by the 17th November organization, is now a prominent politician in her own right, elected mayor of Athens in 2002. Another woman politician who has been visible and important in the sphere of Greek politics for the past twenty years is Vaso Papandreou, the current minister of the interior, rumored to be a former girlfriend of the late Prime Minister Andreas Papandreou. A younger politician, Fofi Gennimata, the daughter of a prominent and well-respected representative of PASOK, was elected mayor of Piraeus in the same elections. Another female addition to the PASOK government, Milena Apostolaki, also a younger woman, was the assistant minister of work and then, in 2002, moved to the Central Committee of PASOK. Due to her young age and attractive image, as well as her blend of discreet yet firm assertiveness, she stands out in the Greek public sphere.[10] Women politicians from the left with high visibility are members of parliament Maria Damanaki, former president of the Coalition of the Left and Progress (and the anchor voice on the radio station the Polytechnic students created when they took over the Polytechnic buildings in November 1973 to protest the Papadopoulos regime), and Aleka Papariga, the current Secretary General of the Communist Party of Greece.

Women's ostensibly low degree of participation in formal politics is considered systematically in a study by Pandelidou-Malouta (1992), who argues that the reasons for much-discussed underrepresentation are disparate and specific to subcategories of women (e.g., older and mostly uneducated Greek women have little interest in participating in the political system). Pandelidou-

Malouta suggests that the real difference between Greek men and women as "individuals with political agency" may rest with the respective degree of legitimacy that each subject category attributes to the political system. If this is correct, as my fieldwork suggests it indeed is, it raises deeper questions about the rates of women's formal participation in politics in contemporary Greece. That is, the relative absence of formal participation may reflect the lower levels of legitimacy that Greek women grant the political system.

Play

Another important aspect of the social conditions for women has to do with their sexuality and reproductive and contraceptive choices. Quantitative data concerning these matters are problematic at best in a culture where subjects have had very good historical reasons to veil motives and conceal some actions from the controlling and judging gaze of assorted monitors. In Greece, the shadow economy reigns supreme and as noted, formal discourse is often at a fair distance from actual practice. In this context, questionnaires cannot generate fully reliable information about a sensitive topic such as sexuality. Nonetheless, some statistical information in this regard may provide conditional insight into the contraceptive behavior of Greeks.

The facts and figures reported below come from the most recent large-scale scientific research project conducted by Dr. Haris Symeonidou and published in the 2002 *Country Report of Fertility and Family Surveys* of the United Nations.[11] The data provided here include results from surveys conducted in 1969 by another researcher, Valaoras, and in 1983, 1997, and 1999 by Symeonidou. These data may help situate some of the topics I examine in more depth. However, the interview materials discussed in part 3 shed light on the cultural dynamics that operate as serious constraints on the efficacy of large-scale quantitative research on the topic of sexuality and birth control. In presenting some of the data from the UN report here, I gesture toward a few of these issues, as well as noting some methodological considerations of the surveys. In another brief statistical section appearing in part 3, I specifically discuss the cultural practices conditioning reports of the use of birth control methods in Greece.

The 2002 UN report states that the average age at first intercourse in Greece is nineteen years for women and seventeen years for men. This is not much different, the report notes, from the respective ages reported forty years ago in the first national fertility survey conducted in the 1960s (Valaoras

1969, cited in UN-Greece 2002 Report, 136). The age at first use of contraception, however, has declined from 22.4 years for women born in 1950–54 to 19.3 years for women born in 1975–79. For men also there has been a respective decline, from 18.4 to 17.6 years. In addition, the percentages of women and men reporting use of contraception at first intercourse are much higher now than in the past. For example, of the younger cohort of the most recent survey, 87 percent of women and 92 percent of men reported using contraception at their first sexual experience, whereas the figures for the oldest cohort of this survey were 48 percent and 64 percent, respectively (UN-Greece 2002 Report, 136).

Despite the high reported use of contraception at first intercourse, the 2002 UN report cites the reliance on so-called traditional contraceptive methods, including coitus interruptus, as the reason for the continued high number of unplanned pregnancies and hence "the wide practice of abortion as a main birth control method in Greece" (UN-Greece 2002 Report, 137). Exploring the "how" of this process is one part of the project of this book. My answer differs from that of the report above. That is, I argue that there are deeper cultural and political reasons for "the extremely high rate of artificially disrupted pregnancies in Greece [which] might even be termed an abortion syndrome," as anthropologists Loizos and Papataxiarchis (1991, 224) have noted. But I concur with the report that the frequency of abortion is high enough to suggest that it is being used by some as a preferred method of birth control.

Abortion has always been widely practiced in Greek clinics and hospitals.[12] However, the revised Family Law of 1981 and other efforts to modernize Greek legislation, prodded from the activism of local feminist groups, especially the autonomous women's movement, resulted in Law 1609 of 1986, which fully legalizes the termination of a pregnancy before the twelfth week under the conditions that (1) the termination is conducted by a medical practitioner with specialization in gynecology or obstetrics and with the assistance of an anesthetic; (2) the pregnant woman is informed of the consequences of terminating the pregnancy, including the fact that the state can provide some protection for the mother and child, as well as other family planning issues, before the operation (*epemvasi*); (3) the mother's health is examined; and (4) the hospital or private clinic where the abortion is conducted meets particular specifications. Beyond the twelfth week, abortion can still be legally performed if serious defects are diagnosed in the embryo and the woman has been pregnant for less than twenty-four weeks, or if there is an unavoidable risk to the woman's physical or mental health. Abortion is also permitted if the pregnancy is the result of rape, seduction of a minor, incest, or the abuse of an incapacitated woman, this time provided the pregnancy has not advanced beyond nineteen weeks.

Yet, despite the legality of abortion in Greece, it remains a medical act that is significantly underreported. Almost ten years after the 1986 formal legalization of abortion, in 1995 the officially reported number of induced abortions (legal and illegal) was 6,242 and the total number of abortions in general (including miscarriages) was 9,876, according to the National Statistics on Social Security and Health (1995). The fertility surveys of the UN report show much higher frequencies, although here too, as it notes, there is underreporting. For example, in the 1983 national fertility survey, 51 percent of the women had had at least one abortion whereas in the sixties it was 34 percent (UN-Greece 2002 Report, 137, 135). Perhaps partly in response to the great disparities in the reports of abortion frequency, the UN-Greece report underscores the need for further research, noting that "attitudes towards abortion have also to be examined carefully."[13]

The cumulative percentages of women in the 1999 sample having a first induced abortion by age group are quite high, and, as the 2002 UN report yet again emphasizes, these percentages "most probably underestimate the incidence of abortions" (UN-Greece Report 2002, 138). In particular, based on respondents' reports, up to the age of twenty-four years, 7.8 percent of women born in 1970–74 reported having experienced at least one induced abortion; the percentage increases considerably in older cohorts (i.e., 17.5 percent for the 1960–64 cohort; 138). Meanwhile, however, the figure typically cited at medical conferences and by various experts in the press for the actual annual rate of abortion during the past twenty years ranges from 150,000 to 400,000, with 250,000 reported as the more recent rate.[14]

A closer look at the data concerning the use of contraception further problematizes the reported rates of abortion for women in Greece. The 2002 UN report shows that the earlier 1983 national fertility survey conducted on a sample of 6,534 married women age fifteen to forty-four found that a remarkable 80 percent of the women reported using contraception at the time of the survey (for this same sample, recall, the report refers to an abortion rate of 51 percent). Moreover, when the UN report compares the 1983 data to the 1969 Valaoras sample of 13,838 married women, the surprising comment is made that "fertility regulation does not present important changes in Greece *during the last four decades*" (UN-Greece 2002 Report, 135; my emphasis). The 1969 total percentage of reported contraceptive use is almost identical, indeed a little higher, being 84 percent, whereas the rate of induced abortions is cited as 34 per 100 live births. Meanwhile, in the 1997 follow-up survey Symeonidou conducted on a subsample of 507 of the 6,534 married women from the 1983 sample, the reported total contraceptive use was higher than both that of 1969 and that of 1983, at an astonishing 91.3 percent (135). Thus the UN report presents both a very high rate of use of contraception and a surprisingly steady one despite the deep cultural change in Greece during the past forty years.

Of additional interest, though harboring similar sampling problems, are the 2002 UN report findings from the most recent 1999 survey of 3,048 women and 1,026 men age eighteen to forty-nine (UN-Greece 2002 Report, ix). This is the only survey used in the 2002 UN report that included men, though the report actually processed only the data pertaining to those members of the sample who were women and married (135). These findings, described again as "quite similar to the findings of the previous surveys," actually show that of the nonpregnant and sexually active women living in couples, 24.8 percent were not using any contraceptive method! In addition (and, I note, this figure is not in fact similar to those of the earlier surveys), "The percentage of all non-pregnant sexually active women living with a partner and using contraception among the sample of women living in couples equals 55.5 percent" (135). The remainder were either pregnant or sexually inactive. Moreover, for a sense of the breakdown of this figure by method, consider that of those women "living in a union" who do use contraception, the most recent 1999 results indicate that 39.6 percent use the condom, 45 percent use withdrawal, 4 percent use the Pill, and 6.5 percent use the IUD. Finally, the UN report states that 4.3 percent of the more recent sample of women in the Greater Athens area use the method of "periodic abstinence." The contraceptive diaphragm continues to appear to be unknown, as it was in the earlier 1983 survey (135).

The figures of reported birth control use for 1969, 1983, 1997, and 1999 are surprising. Very significant changes have occurred in Greek society during the past forty years, as the earlier chapter on the historical development of Athens and the next one on Greece show in some detail. Yet, we see a consistently very high reported overall use of birth control methods, as though the realm of sexual behavior has remained unaffected. On the other hand, as the UN report itself states, there are also internal reasons having to do with the sample of each of these surveys that render these comparisons problematic. I go into this in more detail when the frequencies for the specific methods are analyzed in part 3.

The above data are best treated as indications or a type of snapshot of one aspect of the conditions within which a crucial domain of Greek women's life, sexuality, and reproduction takes place. However, this snapshot is constrained by a range of factors. Some constraining factors, which I mentioned at the beginning of this section, have to do with external issues, such as how Greeks are likely to publicly make statements concerning sexual practices. Others, which the report itself underlines, pertain to the inner logic of the sampling procedure of each of the surveys under consideration, as well as to the limitations of formal abortion statistics.

There are additional, quite serious constraints. For example, it is significant that, as I noted above, "in the present report [on the most recent 1999 survey with the most diverse sample, we presume] information on contraceptive use patterns was gathered only for sexually active *women* who *live in a union*, while the contraceptive behavior of those *not* living in a union was not collected" (UN-Greece 2002 Report, 135; my emphasis). It is also significant that a few paragraphs later the report nonetheless goes on to mention that "the contraceptive patterns *for men* are alike to those for women regarding the use and the type of contraception." Finally, it is especially significant that the only elaboration given to this particular statement, which indicates that in fact another aspect of the sample may indeed have been analyzed, occurs in the next sentence, where we are told that "men tend to report—as expected—the use of condom more often than women do" (135).

This last statement raises yet other important issues. First, although the more recent 1999 sample consisted of 1,026 men and 3,048 women aged 18–49 years, the original Valaoras 1969 sample consisted of 3,838 married women in its 1962–63 phase and 6,500 in 1965–67; the subsequent 1983 survey of 6,534 married women aged 15–44 years; and the 1997 follow-up survey of a subsample of 507 of the 1983 women (who were by then fifteen years older); and the 1999 sample of 1,026 men and 3,048 women 18–49 year old. All these results are compared to one another within the same report. Second, the statement speculating on how men may differently represent usage of the condom is important because it explicitly opens up the issue of the politics of the representation of different methods in respondents' reports, specifically addressing their gendered dimension and thus implicitly suggesting that *women's* reporting of the use of condoms or other methods may also be a particular *representation* of actual usage. It is important to consider that, if reports of abortion frequency are as severely *underreported* in Greece as it is claimed that they are, and as the UN report repeatedly notes that they are, it is equally possible that some of the factors resulting in this also contribute to a similar, and related, drastic *overreporting* of usage of other forms of birth control.

In sum, the preceding data are best treated as signifiers, in Barthes's sense, not as signifieds. That is, they gesture toward a landscape, but they are not the actual terrain, as is the case, after all, to greater or smaller degrees with all attempts to scientifically know social reality. The difference here is that the emphasis on numbers and percentages implies an accuracy and precision that other social scientific methods do not claim. Also, the UN report may deepen the reader's understanding of the complexity of Greek culture, especially if reread later in light of the findings of my qualitative research on a very specific group: Greek women living in Athens who have had two or more abortions. Finally, as the most recent and ostensibly most "scientific" data, indeed the formal report of the United Nations Economic Commission for Europe, they are useful as additional fragments in the mosaic of the physical-sexual politics of nationalism in Greece that this part of the book seeks to create.

To render visible another aspect of this context that is indisputably a powerful factor influencing Greek women's lives, including both their actual and reported reproductive choices, it is important to review the role of religion in daily life.

Religion

According to formal census figures, anywhere from 97.7 to 99 percent of the population is Greek Orthodox. To a large extent, Greek Orthodoxy concerns the practices of people rather than formal Church doctrine, and it is not uncommon for Jewish or Catholic Greeks to participate in some aspects of lived Greek Orthodoxy. In this sense, ritual activities, many of which take place outside both the physical and ideological space of the Greek Church, are often those that in reality compose and constitute what counts as religion for Greeks.[15]

In Greece saints are often incorporated into the daily lives of people, who may develop a strong personal relationship of mutual obligation with them. The saints of the Orthodox Church are spiritual beings that in many ways have the status of subjects of the polity. They act as intermediaries between God and humans. Many Greeks, men and women alike, turn to saints when they find themselves in difficult situations. Emotions are ascribed to the saints, personalities with strengths and weaknesses, and they are often associated with specific domains of life and rendered patrons of that domain. Indeed, the celebration of saints can extend beyond the limits of a particular geographic area or a given professional association to include the boundaries of the state (e.g., saints who are considered protectors of the various wings of the Armed Forces of Greece). Furthermore, saints are called on by nickname or abbreviated versions of their formal name, thus indicating an intimacy and a proximity that facilitates requests for help.[16] *O Ai Yiorgis.*

Worship of saints occurs in the home, via icons, especially by women, and in or near churches that carry the saint's name. The public space for worshiping a saint, a church in his or her name, is usually founded on the basis of a vision or dream or on the discovery of a buried icon or other holy instrument. Women who develop yet further intimacy with the particular saint usually undertake the care of the church. Especially in rural Greece, which is where many older Athenian women grew up, women clean the church, bring flowers to decorate it, and light the candles and lanterns on the eve of significant celebrations. Men, even in Athens, with the exception of clergy and of the one- to four-member male chorus some churches have, tend to limit themselves to the financial support of the church. Both men and women give some money to light a candle when visiting a church. In special cases, men may make a donation of a larger sum of money and buy a large votive candle to make a prayer concerning a particular business matter, and women may give smaller amounts usually for issues of health, childbirth, or marriage. This does not mean that men's faith or "bartering" efforts with the saints, the Virgin Mary, or Christ is necessarily less than women's. (For an interesting parody of this dynamic, see figure 6.) Nor does it mean that women do not also make significant gifts to a church, indeed sometimes stipulating in their will that property belonging to them be given to a particular church. *Afto to horafi einai tou profiti Ilia.* Rather, the issue here is the gendered division of religious labor.

In Greece the nation itself is intimately bound up with stories of the divine (figure 7). In practice, this means that the nation-state, or parts of it, participates actively in the worship of certain saints or the Virgin Mary and Christ. In addition, new companies, factories, institutions such as hospitals and schools, and other sites of work commence their formal operations only after a priest has blessed the premises in a formal ceremony. Each September, when the school year begins, students are similarly blessed, along with their school, in a special ceremony. The classrooms in many older schools and universities, as well as many offices in government buildings, have an icon of Christ hanging on one of their walls.[17]

Homes are routinely blessed. Usually the neighborhood priest, at the re-

Figure 6. Cartoon by K. Mitropoulos in his series "Wild Babes" in *Ta Nea*, 13 August 2001. It shows one older man, carrying a votive candle, who says to a younger man, "You think I was going to sit and pray for a miracle! I bought Viagra, Joe." In the background are two boys. One boy says to the other, "So, what did he want the votive for then!" The other responds, "I guess he can't find a woman, you idiot!"

Figure 7. Cartoon by K. Mitropoulos in *Ta Nea*, 13 August 2001. It shows a woman wearing a green dress (the color of PASOK) and carrying a handbag that reads "the government" (female in Greek) talking to one of the women selling large votive candles for special prayers in church. She says, "OK, so we have: 'Economy, Health, Education, Retirement issue and (the party's autumn) Conference. Five votives please.'"

quest of the woman of the house, visits to say a special prayer and burn incense (of course, he receives a tip for these services). Many homes, even in Athens, maintain a small icon station with the icon of the Virgin Mary and/or Christ and a special saint, along with a candle. Again, the woman of the house may light the candle routinely and also offer *tamata* (symbolic offerings) to accompany a prayer for some special request (e.g., a child doing well on exams or the successful resolution of a health difficulty).

Greek Orthodoxy has several fasting periods, most of which are well-known and honored by many Greek women, including Athenians, who may also try to keep their families on a similar dietary regimen at that time. In this way, the *noikokyra* of the house tries to assure a form of religious purity for her family, even in social classes where a rural past is almost forgotten. In addition, all major life events, christening, marriage, and death are marked by special blessings within the framework of the Greek Orthodox Church. It is women who are usually the main protagonists here, after the male clergy.

Of special interest to the lived aspect of Greek Orthodoxy is the use of tamata, or offerings, as well as the use of objects considered to have protective powers, called *fylahta*. Tamata are usually plaques made of tin, silver, or gold; it has the image of a specific part of the body if it is a *tama* asking for the return of health, or of an object if it is being offered to ask for some other success for the family. These are positioned on or near the icon of the relevant saint or the Virgin Mary, either in a church or, less frequently, at the icon station of the home. Another form of tama is in the nature of a promise: the subject promises to do something, often to visit a particular church of the saint being appealed to, in exchange for being granted the fulfillment of a prayer. The tama may be accompanied by a financial gift to the church, depending on the resources of the person concerned. In some cases, the performative tama is offered as a promise and fulfilled either in advance or retroactively, after the prayer has been answered. *Ehi dosi orko*. For example, when a relative of mine finally was able to have a child, she fulfilled her tama to the Virgin Mary by going to the Church of the Virgin Mary on the island of Tinos, considered a particularly miraculous church. In the vast majority of cases, tamata are conducted by women when significant crises occur in their daily life.[18]

Each year on 15 August the Virgin Mary is celebrated. This day is a national holiday. All churches of the Panagia have a special sermon. It is also a time of heightened offerings. The Church of the Virgin Mary, on the island of Tinos, has the limelight at this time. *I Panayia tis Tinou*. According to the Panhellenic Holy Foundation of the Evaggelistria of Tinos, the total revenue of this church during 2000 was 3,228,173 Euros; this represents an increase from 1999, when the total revenues were 2,846,661 Euros.[19] Not all of this is from the resale of the tamata, but they account for a significant part of the revenues.

Also testifying to the broad-based interest, if not belief, in the powers of the Virgin Mary, every 15 August the news media report on how many faithful went to visit the church. Much time and space is devoted to interviews with people outside the church asking them what miracle they are asking for. Many of those visiting the Panagia tis Tinou climb up the stairs on their knees as part of their tama. In all cases there is some special request that either has been fulfilled or that the visitor is coming to deposit with the Virgin Mary. Most of these people are women, with men watching from a slight distance, though there are men who crawl on their knees as well. In 2001, the head of the main opposition party New Democracy, Constantine Karamanlis, visited the church on the holy day with his wife, Natassa. Another example of how the faith in the miraculous powers of the Virgin Mary intersect with the nation and the public sphere can be seen in the fact that even the now deceased former prime minister and head of the socialist party PASOK, Andreas Papandreou, visited the church with his new wife, Dimitra Liani, to fulfill a tama Dimitra had reportedly done asking that her husband recover from his heart surgery, as he did.[20]

Fylahta are small objects that may be purchased from specific churches or monasteries and often contain amber or dried flowers that had been offered to the Church by other faithful Greeks. One of the most powerful fylahta is a small object containing a piece of wood that is said to come from the Holy Cross. Fylahta are considered significant agents of protection for those who carry or wear them. Of similar usage are the crosses and blue "eyes" that are placed on infant's clothes, in cars and houses, and often hung by a dainty chain around the neck, again especially by women. Even in Athens, it is common to see women wearing these little blue beads on a bracelet or necklace, and many cars sport a cross or a blue eye hanging from the front mirror. These charms are thought to protect the bearers from "the evil eye," the power of other people to practice evil through the envious gaze of their eyes.[21] A similar means of protection is to say "ftou, ftou, ftou" when something is said that could lead to the incitement of the evil eye. Here, the faithful person calls on the name of the Father, the Son, and the Holy Spirit to spit on evil and thus banish it. This expression is commonly used by Athenians today, again mostly though not exclusively women. In some intellectual and leftist circles, it may raise eyebrows.

All in all, Greek Orthodoxy is a vital part of Greek life and in markedly gendered ways. Although all clergy are male, as is the leadership, and girls and women are never permitted to enter the sacred part of the church or to partake of communion when they have their period, the vast majority of those who attend church regularly, as well as those who perform many of the other tasks outlined above, are women. Perhaps most important, Greek women have an investment in protecting and preserving particular religious ties for themselves and their families. As Jill Dubisch says, "[Religion in Greece] is less an object or means of contemplation than a set of acts one performs, not only inevitably, but almost *naturally* (part of what Bourdieu has termed habitus)" (1995, 58; my emphasis).

When Kostas Kenderis won the gold medal in his race in the eighth World Championship at Edmonton in 2001, Greek television news reports repeatedly showed him at the beginning of the race closing his eyes and firmly setting right the clasp of the gold chain on which he wore a small gold cross. This was not by chance. The message conveyed then and in much of the subsequent coverage was: He was running, with the help of God, for (H)is nation. Thus, it made perfect sense for the news anchor of Antenna channel to emphasize Kenderis's time in the race, 20:04 minutes, and comment, smiling, that this is "a symbolic number, we must note, with the upcoming Olympic Games to be held in Greece in 2004." *A sign from God.* It is perhaps one of the marked incongruities of an otherwise very cosmopolitan modern Athens that such practices, and a pervasive "magical way of thinking," continue to be widely upheld.

Culture

I turn here to a different facet of the cultural context of Athenian women's lives. I ask that you follow me to one particular part of the Athenian landscape, an art exhibit that took place during the spring and early summer of 1995 at the National Art Museum on Kifisias and Vasilisis Sophias, across from the Hilton Hotel. The title of the exhibit of ancient art is "From Medea to Sappho: Insubordinate Women in Ancient Greece" ("Anypotahtes Gynaikes stin Arhaia Ellada"). The collection included many Greek vases and other artifacts of antiquity that depict representations of female characters, ranging, as the exhibit's title states, from Medea to Sappho. Shown first in Portugal, the official Cultural Center of Europe for 1995, the exhibit was a tribute to Melina Merkouri, the former culture minister and a popular actress. Of particular interest for my purposes here is the pamphlet published by the National Archeological Museum that accompanied the exhibit. It states: "Through murder, suicide, infanticide—for the woman/mother a double suicide—the women of myth re-discover their voice. Again. Their voice has reached us through the mouths of the poets, the men who sang their praises, censored them, hated them and loved them. They allowed them to speak as long as they were images, confused allegories and imaginary figures, while at the same time muzzling the real women that lived alongside them. There are few exceptions to this rule and only a single voice, that of Sappho, breaks through the barrier of time, struggling against oblivion and anonymity."

I have lived with strength and feeling,
With passionate emotions. (Zoi Karelli, *The Last Song of Sappho*)

Things are more complicated, in Athens certainly, than the exhibit's literature suggests. The hold of Greek antiquity on all facets of contemporary life, from politics to popular culture, is indeed very strong, but Greece today is a site, a topos, consisting of many "real women," who in fact live "with strength and feeling, with passionate emotions." Some of today's women are artists, poets, and writers. Others are teachers, some are lawyers and doctors, some businesswomen, a very few are politicians, and some are a combination of these and other roles. Many others work at family businesses, such as shops or tavernas. Almost all also work hard in the home, where the tenacious ideal of the good homemaker, *i noikokyra*, and the lived practice of persistently firm traditional gender roles result in an especially heavy workload.

Certainly, very few of these women perceive themselves as "muzzled." To the contrary, many Greek women are outspoken and articulate. What is true is that there are rules about what can be said and to whom. Emotional pain, for instance, is rarely a legitimate topic for conversation in Greece. And silence can be strategically deployed in certain contexts to convey this pain. Within the limits of what can be verbalized, women try in different ways to communicate their strength and what vision a relentless dailiness will permit. However, not many of these voices are actually being heard in those parts of the public domain defined as formally political. Nor are they being granted the capacity to significantly affect domestic and foreign policy.

There are exceptions, as I have noted. One of these, the woman in whose name the exhibit was organized, Melina Merkouri, was until her death a strong woman. For a variety of reasons—her family's history in politics, her initial entry into the public sphere as a beautiful and spirited actress, her strong antijunta stand during the Papadopoulos regime—she was able to see ways through various national impasses, speak her mind publicly, and, in many instances, not only be heard but be taken seriously. Her impact on Greek political culture was significant and her accomplishments extend far beyond the much publicized rejuvenation of dialogue with England about the return of the Elgin marbles to Greece. There are a few other women like her.

Overall, however, the narratives of the female subject in Greece—both those concerning the production of herself as subject and those involved with the identity of her familial and/or national community—are shaped by what Herzfeld (1991b) has alluded to as "a poetics of womanhood." Among other things, this poetics does in fact lead to words that are, in different ways, hard to hear. That is, I would argue, they may be pitched in low tones, they may serve as veiled weapons against others, or they may bespeak the pain of the self in a scrambled code, in addition to simply being difficult to understand by "outsiders," of whom, in what remains very much a xenophobic society, there are many. As a result of this, and of other social forces as well, the voices of women are not much heard in public debate.

Chapter 3

CENTER STAGE:

WHAT IS GREECE?

✣

Meanwhile, in the public sphere, a heated debate again takes place on how best to (re)define Greece as a modern nation-state so as to bolster its vulnerable position in the European Union, in the Balkans, vis-à-vis Turkey, and within late modernity more generally. The fervor of the debates on modernity that took place among Greeks locally and in the diaspora during the nineteenth century reverberates in the current debate fueled by efforts to fully align the country with the European Union. Challenges of modernization, which range from eliminating party clientelism to privatizing and streamlining segments of the monumental public sector, are being treated as a matter of the highest priority. This constitutes a formidable project for contemporary Greece as it strives to recraft its identity.

Evidence of this can be seen in the debate that occurred after the spring 2000 government announcement of an impending decision to change the format of Greek ID cards. These are something like the U.S. social security cards, issued by local police stations and mandatory for all Greek citizens.[1] Until the year 2000, it was obligatory to list religion on the card, although previous governments had also raised this issue for discussion. Now, however, the Committee for the Protection of Personal Information had made a decision. And Prime Minister Simitis, under pressure from European Union mandates, eventually announced the firm decision to eliminate this entry. Also eliminated was the line requiring a statement of marital status. Although this second change received almost no attention in the public sphere, the elimination of the statement of religious affiliation provoked intense debate.

Reactions occurred in many segments of Greek society. As a consequence of the debate taking place both in the public sphere and among citizens, Archbishop Chrystodoulos, the head of the Greek Orthodox Church, started

GREECE

A country on the edge

THE Greeks, as they cheerfully explain, are a special people. They are not quite like anybody else, anywhere, and they are especially different from the Slavs and Turks and Arabs who occupy so much of the neighbouring part of the world. When the introspective mood is upon them, as it is today, the Greeks will add that being special is not all fun. When you are a small country as well as a special one, and when you live on the edge of things, it can be dangerous.

These 10m people live at the south-eastern edge of the culture-area called the West. Their Parthenon-building ancestors began that culture, and their Byzantine ancestors kept it alive when the rest of Europe had fallen into the dark ages. If the West eventually gave the world the Enlightenment, it was Greeks who had provided much of the light.

The Greeks of 1993 are still recognisably their ancestors' descendants. The original blood has been blended with the blood of Turks and Slavs and others, but the face in a modern Athens street or a rural corner of the Peloponnese is not a face from Istanbul or Belgrade. The language has changed hugely since classical times, but the Greeks are the only people in the world, apart from the Chinese, who can look at a 2,500-year-old inscription and recognise in it their own tongue. To argue with a Greek today is to experience the same mixture of exhilaration (because he is so full of ideas, so quick with logic) and exasperation (when he slides around awkward facts) that many a growlingly impressed Roman experienced two millennia ago.

The trouble is that, since those days, the West has moved steadily westward, and has left Greece isolated at the bottom right-hand corner of Europe. This does not matter when Greece can present itself as a lonely outpost of western ideas, defying the barbarians; then the West rallies round. Sometimes Greece's place on the map can even help, in the periods of history when Europe is on easy terms with its neighbours to the east. Then geography, and the entrepreneurial cleverness that Greeks seem to carry in their bones, make their country a natural trading post between Europe and the countries of south-west Asia and northern Africa.

Unfortunately, such periods are rare. For much of the time, perched on the end of its European promontory, Greece feels lonely and insecure. It does not know quite where it belongs, or what it stands for. It is currently going through a bad patch of such uncertainty.

Since they won their independence from the Ottoman empire 170 years ago, there have been only three times when Greeks could justifiably feel the world was smiling on them. There was the brief glory of the 1820s, when Greece was the first part of south-eastern Europe to break free from the Turks, and high-minded liberals all over Europe thought

History and geography have conspired to bring Greece to a moment of decision. The decision it takes will be a rare test of national character. Brian Beedham explains

THE ECONOMIST MAY 22ND 1993

Figure 8. This *Economist* 1993 story on Greece describes the country as a site of uncertainty. The smog-covered Athens next to the Acropolis statues of the ancient women caryatids in the photo may also be read as a reflection of the hazy understanding of *contemporary* Greece that informs the international imaginary of late modernity.

collecting signatures from those desiring a plebiscite on the matter. As this book goes to print, he claims to have collected 3 million signatures. Priests appeared outside courts, parish members in tow, protesting the new decision. This was not just the Church responding to an attack on its symbolic status, of which there have been many in Greece's modern history as the modern nation-state has sought to become increasingly secularized. Elimination of this line was seen by many as a denial of the crux of what it means to be Greek. The swift response of Minister of the Exterior George Papandreou, who stated that he did not see personal beliefs as appropriate content for a public document, did not fully succeed in containing the swell of opposition to the new measure. However, Prime Minister Simitis has remained steady with his decision, and it seems this display of strength and firmness has quieted opposition.

Another telling example of current concern with Greek identity occurred on 28 October 2000, the day on which the sixtieth anniversary of "No Day," 28 October 1940, was celebrated. On that day, the dictator Prime Minister Metaxas responded to the ultimatum issued by the head of the Italian Fascist Party, Mussolini, that no, Greece would not surrender. As a result, Italy launched an invasion, using troops based in Albania primarily, to take over Greece. Greece resisted ferociously. After six months of fierce fighting, Greece occupied the larger part of southern Albania, a country that had been under Italian rule since early the previous year. Some local analysts speculate that it is this historical event that anchors the image of Greeks in the modern global imaginary as free spirits who resist oppression.

The day is celebrated throughout Greece every year as a holiday. Businesses are closed and all schools participate in local parades, in addition to the large parade in Athens and Thessaloniki, where representatives from all the Armed Forces march. Tradition has it that the school parades are headed by one student, selected on the basis of his or her grades, carrying the flag (*simaioforos*). During the academic year 2000–2001, the top student of one of the schools in northern Greece was an Albanian boy, a resident of Greece for most of his life. This created a nationwide uproar. The Greek flag could not be carried by an Albanian, argued many of the parents of students attending this school, and many Greeks agreed. The story was covered in all news media. Ultimately, the boy himself turned down the honor, choosing simply to march in the parade along with his classmates, and the flag was carried by the female student who had the next highest grades, and Greek citizenship.

This incident helps illuminate how charged a matter Greek national identity is at the present. Some of the television news coverage displayed both local inhabitants of the particular village and Athenians, outraged by the very idea that an Albanian student might carry the Greek flag. In interviews the boy himself seemed modest enough, clearly treating it as an honor that he might carry the Greek flag and not registering any anger, though he seemed a little sad, that he might be denied what he clearly saw as an honor. His Greek was fluent, a fact that did not go unnoticed by the media.[2] Interestingly, at the same time, in a school in central Greece, the simaioforos of the parade was an Albanian girl. In this case, there was almost no opposition expressed. The news item was given minimal coverage; where it was mentioned, it was as an aside. Indeed, the very fact was not reported until the day of the parade itself. Nowhere were the two situations analyzed in relationship with one another.

The incident of the Albanian boy illustrates the defensiveness experienced in Greece concerning the issue of national identity. The two situations together reveal yet more. Certainly, the geographic location of the two schools is an important factor. The Albanian boy attended school in a region very close to the border; the Albanian girl attended school further inland. This may account for some of the differences in local reaction.

At a national level, it is important to note the larger context. According to the figures of the Ministry of Education for the academic year 2001–2002, Greek elementary, secondary, and high schools will have a total of 100,000 foreign (alien) students.[3] More specifically, as a newspaper article reporting on this states, "from 1995–1996 to the present, total student population in elementary schools has dropped by 5% whereas foreign enrollments in elementary school has risen by 400%."[4] The article later reports that foreign students account for a more modest 12.5 percent of the entire primary and secondary school student population. In this larger context, the sex of each of the two children described in the incidents above may be especially significant. The idea of the flag being carried by a male "alien," even if underage, in an area very close to the border may be fundamentally more threatening than the idea of almost any female "alien" being a simaioforos. Certainly, qua male, the Albanian boy is, by sexist definition, more threatening than the Albanian girl. Add to that the different relationship to the borders of the two school regions and the Albanian boy emerges as distinctly more threatening. In addition, however, Albania is more feminized than Greece in the national imaginary. Thus, altogether the idea of one of "Albania's sons" carrying the Greek flag close to the border may symbolically emasculate Greece in a way that the Albanian girl in a more remote region cannot. In this sense, the specifically gendered ways in which the Greek nation and the Albanian are locally imagined may also be significant.

Greek History in Brief: So Close, and Yet So Far

The geographic area of the modern Greek nation-state has been animated historically by a variety of different civilizations. Aspects of some of these live on, very vividly, in the present national imaginary. Some are also fairly common knowledge to those who live outside of Greece; others are not. In what follows we traverse a span of many centuries, briefly visiting some key sites of Greece.

The Greek city-states of antiquity, and their colonies on the shores of Asia Minor, created a civilization based on an apparent linguistic homogeneity (Hall, 2002, 48). This civilization was at its peak in classical Athens (fifth–fourth century B.C.), when the Athenian democracy we think of today was at its prime. There was a council of five hundred men, Vouli ton Pendakosion, that prepared the topics to be discussed and decided on by an assembly of the "total" population, the Ekklisia tou Demou. Thus, the heretofore explicitly religious and racial basis for organizing the population was transformed. Power is transferred to the *demos,* a version of civil society, hence "democracy." Importantly, foreigners and slaves, as well as all women, as noncitizens, were excluded from this category.

This civilization ends when the city-states lose their independence and freedom in 338 B.C. to the Macedonian Dynasty of Philip, and later his son Alexander. As Alexander's conquests grew, the intellectual aspects of the city-state civilization ignite the East, leading to the division of the empire into Hellenistic kingdoms after the death of Alexander in 323 B.C. The Greek and the Hellenistic worlds during the second and first century B.C. became attached to the Roman Empire. Yet, at the same time, Rome was culturally Hellenized (in philosophy, art, and philology). Usage of the Greek language became more widespread. Elite Roman society was diglossic and circles of Hellenic intellectuals were formed. The same occurred in Asia Minor. Nonetheless, the inhabitants of this area called themselves Romans, or Romaioi, and all were granted the status of Roman citizens.

However, in A.D. 330 Constantinople became the second capital of the empire. After the Gothic peoples of the North and eastern Europe took over Rome in A.D. 476, only the eastern part of the empire, with the capital of Constantinople, was left. Latin remained the language of administration up to the end of the sixth century, at which time Greek gained supremacy. Greek also became the language of the Christian Church of this eastern part of the empire. The Gospels were written in Greek. Beginning in the seventh century, Greek became the language of the state and the state became formally

Christian. It is at this time that the history of the Byzantine Empire begins, with its foundation in Christianity.

In the middle of the eleventh century the Catholic and Orthodox Churches split. A great conflict occurred between the Pope and the Patriarch of Constantinople, culminating in the occupation of Constantinople by the Crusaders in 1204 and the division of the lands of the Empire by the Latins. This division continues to the present, in the split between the two churches and, importantly, in its contribution to the development of one of the two major political cultures of modern Greece, which is characterized by a distrust of the West (Diamandouros 2000, 41–49).

Constantinople was regained by the Byzantines in 1261. The Empire's commerce by sea was now in the hands of the *Frangoi* (French and northern Italian cities). In 1453, however, "the City," was conquered by the Ottoman Turks, as were the remaining areas shortly thereafter. The subjected peoples of the Ottoman Empire were organized into millets, a unit based on religion rather than ethnic origin. The Orthodox patriarch of Constantinople had tremendous power over the Christian peoples of the Ottoman Empire, indeed more power than during the Byzantine Empire, for now he had civil as well as religious power (Clogg 1992, 10–13. See also Kitromilidis 1996, 25–27).

The long-standing hostility of the Orthodox Church toward Catholics met with the distrust of Ottomans toward the European forces that were trying to impede the further expansions of the Empire. This coincidence of interests led to an unlikely alliance: an anti-Western bloc that offered the Church strong resistance against the new trends in European thought. Greek remained a dominant language, both in its archaic form for the Church and intellectuals and in its spoken form for other sectors of the population. As the Empire's commerce passed into the hands of Greeks during the eighteenth century, Greek also became the language of commerce in the Empire. These Greeks, or Hellenes, thanks to their Greek education and simultaneous contact with the European Enlightenment, became an avant-garde in the construction of the modern conception of Greek ethnic/national identity (Kitromilidis 1996, 23–25; Svoronos 1999, 154–61).

COMPETING DREAMS OF GREECE

Commerce, the Greek communities abroad, and the many Greeks who left to study at universities in Italy or France near the end of the eighteenth century made inroads for the ideas of the Enlightenment to "reach" the Balkans. Educational centers were created for a modern education, to coexist with the traditional education controlled by the Church. The Church was wholly opposed to these new ideas and attempted to build a sense of national identity based on the history of ancient Greece. Through the end of the revolution in 1830, Greeks, including most of the nineteenth-century nationalists, seemed to have had a vague but firm sense of continuity from ancient to modern Greece, though this was not articulated in racial terms but on the basis of a common language, history, and consciousness. In effect, at this time, whoever called themselves a Greek was a Greek. It is because of this that many Greek-speaking Albanians, Slavs, Rumanians, and Vlachs were easily assimilated and indeed became important players in Greek patriotism at that time (Dakin 1972, 8).

Until the beginning of the nineteenth century, the average inhabitant of Greece called himself or herself a Roman (Romios), and the (Greek) language Romeika. There was a sense of an ancient Greek heritage, though; as Dakin (1972, 2) notes: "To some extent—the consciousness of the modern Greek of his classical ancestry is a product of Western scholarship." As a result of the introduction of Enlightenment ideas, primarily via the works of Adamandios Korais (1748–1833), a significant portion of the Greek population acquired a distinct consciousness of national identity by the beginning of the nineteenth century. They believed in a liberatory vision that saw them as free from the Ottoman Empire and were opposed to those groups (kotzabasides, Church hierarchy, and Fanariots) that enjoyed positions of power in the Ottoman Empire.

In 1797 Rigas Ferraios (1757–1798), a highly educated Vlach, circulated several revolutionary pamphlets, including his map of Greece, in which he called for the Balkan peoples to rebel against the Ottoman oppression (Kitromilidis 1996, 289–335). In 1814, the secret society Filiki Eteria was founded in Odessa with the goal of "liberating the homeland" via armed resistance. The Greek revolution occurred in 1821. In 1827, the navies of England, France, and Russia sank the Ottoman navy during the battle of Navarin. This offered some form of independence to Greece. In 1828, after intense discussions and constitutional processes between 1821 and 1827, Ioannis Kapodistrias (1776–1831) became governor. This may be viewed as a sign of the entry of the trope of "modernization" in Greek public sphere discourse. Kapodistrias attempted to build the infrastructure of a modern state (bureaucracy, educational system, military, transportation) while also nonetheless concentrating power in his own hands. His efforts met with resistance both from those who were inspired by the liberalism of the Enlightenment (constitutionalists) and by the traditional elites. He was murdered in a confrontation with a family of the traditional elite in 1831.[5]

"INDEPENDENCE"

The Allied Forces, namely Britain, France, and Russia, installed Otto as king of Greece in 1832 and the country was declared a monarchic independent state. The borders were drawn in such a way that the larger number of Greeks were left outside the state (750,000 Greeks within, 2 million in the Ottoman state or in the Ionian islands under English rule) (Dakin 1972, 64). Thus, the issue of irredentism arose, defined as the need to liberate the remaining Greeks from Ottoman rule.

In 1843 a rebellion led to the Constitution of 1844, wherein Greece was defined as a constitutional monarchy. That same year, Ioannis Kolettis, the leader of the "French" party, announced the "Great Idea" of a Greece that extended to Constantinople, "the holy city of Greeks," as Dakin (1972) says, and formed a regime of parliamentary dictatorship. Greeks in the northern regions of Thessaly and Ipiros rebelled in 1854, and the English and French occupied Piraeus; Otto remained neutral and did not declare war on Ottoman Turkey. In 1862 there was a revolution, Otto departed, and a National Assembly took place. A new constitution in 1864 changed the government to monarchical democracy and established the union of the Ionian islands. In 1866 the revolution of Crete erupted, and in 1869 it fell apart. With the consent of the Great Powers, in 1881, Thessaly and Arta were ceded to Greece. In 1882, the first government headed by Harilaos Trikoupis was formed and launched a concerted nation-building program of, this time, explicit "modernization." At the time, this translated into such works as the railroad connecting Athens and Piraeus to the Peloponnese and the railway network of Greece.

In 1895 there was another rebellion in Crete and Greece joined the war against the Ottoman Empire in Thessaly in 1897, both with an unsuccessful outcome. The Great Powers intervened and the terms of peace were generous, though they included the condition that there be a Committee of International Economic Monitoring with representatives from England, Russia, France, Germany, Austro-Hungary, and Italy to ensure that the interest was paid on the large foreign debt Greece had accrued. Crete was granted relative autonomy under Ottoman domination.

In the beginning of the twentieth century a series of revolutionary movements occurred in Macedonia with the objective of winning "Macedonia for the Macedonians." These movements were splintered by inner conflicts and clans. They were mobilized primarily from Bulgaria and were both anti-Turkish and anti-Greek. Greek organizations mobilized to protect Greek priests and teachers, among others. In this instance, there was a strategic alliance between Greeks and Turks to fight the Internal Macedonian Revolutionary Organization (EMEO) that was controlled by Bulgaria and Slavomacedonians. From 1904 to 1908, when the conflict ended, Greece fortified its position in Macedonia and sent more forces to fight the Bulgarians (primarily) and the Serbs.

In 1909, there was a movement against King George I in the Athens area of Goudi by a group of lower-ranking officers. The movement led to the arrival of Eleftherios Venizelos (1864–1936), a prominent politician of Crete, and the formation of his first government in 1910. He was considered a modernizer. He represented the emerging bourgeoisie and supported the capital of Greeks abroad. In many ways, the modern state apparatus was his creation. From 1912 to 1913 there were two wars of the Balkans, from which Greece emerged with a 70 percent increase in territory, incorporating eastern Macedonia with Thessaloniki, southern Eipiros, and a large part of the Aegean islands. In 1913 the formal union of Crete with Greece was proclaimed.

The end of World War I found Greece on the side of the Entente at Venizelos's decision, with deep internal conflict between those who supported Venizelos, culminating in the movement of "the National Defense," and those who, opposed to him, supported the king. Greece staked a claim on areas with Greek populations in Asia Minor, especially Smyrna, an old dream of the Great Idea. The same region was claimed by Italy. When Smyrna was targeted in an unexpected Italian military move, France, England, and the United States agreed to the landing of Greek troops. On 15 May 1919, Greece, protected by allied warships, occupied the city. The stated goal was to protect the Greek population from Turkish reprisals. In the process, 350 Turks were killed or wounded (Clogg 1992, 94). Soon after, violent conflicts occurred between Greek and Turkish forces. Italy and France arrived at agreements with Mustafa Kemal (Ataturk) and relinquished their claims.

With the Treaty of Sèvres in 1920 Greece was a significant winner of World War I. However, the victory of the royalists in 1920, in the middle of the war, provided a rationale for allied forces to withdraw support from Greece. By 1921, all the allies had declared neutrality. Greeks launched another major offensive in March 1921 that left them in a vulnerable position. A year later, they announced agreement with a British proposal for compromised peace. The Turks refused, and on 26 August Mustafa Kemal launched a massive offensive. The Turkish occupation of Smyrna led to the massacre of approximately thirty thousand Greek and Armenian Christians (Clogg 1992, 97). There was a great fire after which only the Turkish and Jewish quarters of Smyrna survived. Five hundred thousand ran to the port hoping to get away from the fire, but the allies' ships moored there held a position of neutrality.

These events have since remained in Greek memory as the "catastrophe of Asia Minor" in 1922, and they signaled the end of the Greek presence in Smyrna and the end of the "Great Idea."

In 1923, the king resigned and the liberals acquired power. The same year, an agreement was signed with the Treaty of Lausanne that set the borders of Greece and Turkey and established terms for the exchange of populations targeting Turkish citizens of Orthodox religion living in Turkish territory and Greek citizens of Muslim religion living in Greek territory, with the exception of the Greeks of Constantinople, the inhabitants of Imvros and Tenedos and the Muslims of Western Thrace. In a violent uprooting, 380,000 Muslims were transferred to Turkey, and Greece received approximately 1.1 million Orthodox refugees, of which a disproportionate number were women (many widowed) and orphans (Clogg 1992, 101). In 1924, Parliament proclaimed the first Greek Republic.

The period that followed was characterized by economic and political instability, which resulted in the return of the king; in August 1936, with the king's backing, the dictatorship of Metaxas began. Metaxas was an admirer of the internal policy of Nazi Germany and Fascist Italy. He also believed there could be a synthesis of the pagan values of Ancient Greece with the Christian values of the Byzantine Empire to create a "Third Hellenic Civilization." In 1940, Italian forces torpedoed a Greek warship. On 28 October Metaxas rejected Mussolini's ultimatum. Greek troops fought valiantly against Mussolini's. The Greek army crossed the Albanian border and captured three towns, Koritsa, Agioi Saranda, and Argirokastro, that had many Greek inhabitants. This victory occupies a prominent position in the collective memory deployed by Greek nationalism.

During the Nazi occupation of Greece in World War II, there was poverty, fear, and a devastating famine. There was also a strong resistance movement. One of the leading forces was the National Liberationists Front (EAM), primarily controlled by communists. Britain continued to intervene in Greek politics and strove for the return of the king after Greece was freed. Once Greece was freed, a government of national unity was formed, with British support, led by George Papandreou. As an old Venizelist, he could not be accused of being pro-monarchy. In December 1944, communists accused Papandreou of moving away from commitments he had made and the left-wing ministers of his government resigned. A large protest was organized by EAM that ended with a violent encounter with the police, during which many protesters were killed. Churchill told his General Skoby to treat Athens as an occupied city. In 1945, Papandreou was replaced by the republican officer Plastiras in the hope of diffusing the tension. The military branch of EAM, ELAS, handed over its arms after an agreement made in the coastal area of Varkiza. Plastiras, however, did not have control of the right, sectors of which began active persecution of leftists, while those Greeks who had cooperated with the Nazis were treated with leniency. From 1946 to 1949 there was a civil war in Greece. Churchill and Stalin had agreed on postwar spheres of influence and Greece was to go to the Americans and British. Greek communists, as Mazower (2000b, 117) states, "refused to believe there had been a carve-up, and were only defeated after a long civil war, which when it ended in 1949 left more people dead, imprisoned and uprooted than the German occupation had done."

During the 1950s, after the Truman Doctrine of 1947, the United States began to intervene in Greek politics more visibly. In the context of the cold war, the United States supported the king as a point of stability within the unstable Greek political climate. The United States intervened in the law governing elections and used the economic aid they offered Greece (under the Marshall Plan) as leverage to support those Greek governments that actively prosecuted leftists or suspected leftists. Exiles continued. This culminated in the constitution of 1952 that, while granting certain liberties (such as women's right to vote), preserved a law on the basis of which files were kept on leftists. Greeks were obliged to petition for "certificates of social beliefs" (*pistopoiitiko koinonikon fronimaton*), a document issued by the police and a prerequisite for being hired in the public sector, for a driver's license and a passport, for entrance to the university, and so on. In the context of this monitoring of political identity, in 1952 N. Belogiannis, a member of KKE, the Communist Party of Greece, was executed by a military court under the charge of espionage.

CYPRUS

During the 1950s, the problem in Cyprus intensified. The island of Cyprus had been under English rule since 1878 and its population in the 1950s was 600,000 inhabitants, of which 80 percent were Greek and 18 percent were Turkish (Clogg 1992, 150, 154). Greek Cypriots persistently asked for a union with Greece throughout the 1950s. The British used the Turkish minority as leverage against the Greek Cypriot demands and encouraged the government of Turkey to assess its own interests in the island. For its part, the Greek government supported guerrilla resistance against the English forces. Archbishop Makarios of Cyprus also supported unification. He contacted the rightist Colonel Griva, Cypriot-born Greek head of the National Organization of Cypriot Combatants (EOKA), in this regard. In 1959, the prime ministers of

Greece, Karamanlis, and Turkey, Menderes, signed an agreement in Zurich under pressure from England to grant Cyprus independence within the framework of the British Commonwealth, also ceding England bases in Cypriot territory. As a result of the policy of the Papadopoulos junta in Greece (1967–73), a coup occurred against Archibishop Makarios in 1974 under the guidance of the Greek Ioannidis, who replaced Papadopoulos as the head of the regime. The coup led to the invasion of the island by Turkey and the Turkish occupation of 38 percent of the island's territory.

The British had attempted to convert the struggle of the Cypriots into a conflict between Greece and Turkey. On 28 August 1955, they invited the prime ministers of each side to find a solution. As the tripartite conference took place, the Turkish government organized a pogrom against the Greeks of Istanbul and Smyrna (Sarris 1982, 117–85). In 1963, there was another bloody conflict between Greeks and Turks on the island; this resulted in the first dichotomization of the population.

The story of Cyprus occupies a prominent part in the contemporary Greek national imaginary, at least partly because it concentrates aspects of the Greek-Turkish conflict, of the always imminently betraying Allied "friends," of Greeks' aversion to dictatorships, and, of course, of the by now eclipsed dream of territorial expansion.

APPROACHING THE PRESENT

In 1955, Karamanlis formed ERE, the National Radical Union, a party following from the Greek Rally (Ellinikos Synagermos), the right-wing party that had been in office from 1952 under the leadership of Papagos. ERE was given the order to govern from the king. EDA, the United Democratic Left—basically a front for the illegal KKE, the Communist Party of Greece—also participated in the elections. In 1961, G. Papandreou created the Center Union Party, unifying the fractioned parties of the center. These three parties expressed the two cleavages in the political history of Greece in the twentieth century. These consisted of the tension between pro-Venizelos liberals and those royalists and others opposed to Venizelos, and communists and anticommunists who, after the civil war, become non-*ethnikofrones* (leftists but not exclusively) and *ethnikofrones* (whose motto was "Homeland, Religion, Family": *Patris, Thriskia, Oikoyenia*). In the tumultuous and often violent elections of 1961, Karamanlis won. Papandreou began a struggle for new elections against both Karamanlis and the king. In 1963, the M.P. of EDA, G. Lambrakis, was killed by ethnikofrones. Karamanlis entered into a conflict with the palace, basically over the privileges of the monarchy, and he resigned and left for Paris. He eventually returned when the Papadopoulos regime fell in 1974.

Papandreou won the elections of 1964 with 53 percent of the votes and continued to be in conflict with the palace (Clogg, 159). He positioned K. Mitsotakis, as well as his own son, Andreas Papandreou, as ministers, and began to free leftists who had been imprisoned or exiled for crimes of the civil war. In 1965, the king forced Papandreou to resign. The king tried to break up the Union of the Center party and forty-five members of parliament, including Mitsotakis, abandoned the party. This group formed a new government. Rumors concerning the role of the king and the U.S. Embassy abound at the time. Another year of instability followed and in 1967 the military dictatorship of G. Papadopoulos began.

The king tried to organize his own coup but failed and left Greece. The United States supported the junta.[6] The involvement of the United States throughout this period, both supporting the palace (1950–60) and the junta of the colonels after that, in addition to the U.S. position of not intervening in the Turkish invasion in Cyprus (in contrast to the firm stance held by President Johnson in 1964, when a Turkish invasion was prevented at that time), all led to the development of quite strong anti-U.S. feelings in many sectors of the population.[7]

After 1974, Greek politics became more stable. A plebiscite ended the reign of monarchy in Greece, a new constitution was voted declaring Greece a presidential democracy, and the party of Karamanlis, New Democracy, stayed in power until 1981, at which time Andreas Papandreou won the elections with the Panhellenic Socialist Party. PASOK has remained in office since then, with the exception of the period 1989–93. From 1991 to 1993, New Democracy was the party in office, with Mitsotakis as prime minister.

Today, the leader of the opposition party New Democracy is K. Karamanlis, the namesake and nephew of the founder of the party. The daughter of Mitsotakis, Dora Bakogianni, is considered one of the main future contenders for the leadership of the party. Meanwhile, in the ruling party PASOK, the leader who took over shortly before the death of Andreas Papandreou is Kostas Simitis. He continues to be the prime minister after the very close elections of 2000. The next elections are planned for the spring before the Olympic Games are held in Greece in 2004. A potential future contender for the leadership of PASOK is the son of Andreas Papandreou, grandson of George Papandreou, and presently minister of the exterior, George Papandreou, although there are several others and increasingly polarized cleavages within the party. All in all, politics in Greece, as elsewhere, remains very much a family affair.

Negotiating National Identity

The above narrative puts forward a very partial and anecdotal overview of the historical development of Greece. The guiding principle is a desire to put forward moments in history that are vividly remembered in contemporary collective memory. The most evident characteristics are courageous resistance toward those perceived as foreigners, a distrust of allies that is amply justified by past events, and a passion for freedom that does not hesitate to use violence if needed. At this junction, it is useful to focus more closely on the historical context of the politics of national identity specifically and their often vexed interface with disparate discourses of ethnicity, race, and religion. One example that powerfully illustrates this complex dynamic and the intricate and charged ways with which a homogeneous national identity is crafted in modern Greece is the case of Greek Macedonia.[8] In this section, I present a few significant instances where national and ethnic identity were negotiated, often in violent ways. First, there is a brief consideration of the politics of Hellas and its conjunctions with Greece in earlier times. A series of three short reviews of contemporary Greek minorities follow, whose situations illuminate the dynamics underlying the politics of national identity at the present.

ROMIOI, GRAIKOI, AND HELLENES

Until the revolution of Greece against the Ottoman Empire, the matrix of nationhood was one of a fully religious collectivity, the Romioi, who were the Christian subjects of the Roman Empire. The Graikoi, a particular subset of Roman citizenry, were those who paid special attention to Ancient Greek culture. As noted, modern efforts to found a Greek nation proper begin around the revolution. The help of Philhellenes was significant and also involved strategic redeployments of Ancient Greece. As Herzfeld notes (1982, 3), "Their goal was far more ambitious than freedom alone, for they proclaimed the resurrection of an ancient vision in which liberty was but a single component. That vision was Hellas—the achievement of the ancient Greeks in knowledge, morality, and art, summed up in one evocative word. What was more, the new Greek revolutionaries went one step further than their forebears had ever managed to do: they proposed to embody their entire vision in a unified, independent polity. This unique nation-state would represent the

Figure 9. In Greece today there are a few suggestive examples of a redeployment of traditional notions of Greekness and its ancient history. In the case of this international advertisement for a top high-tech company, the specifically Ancient Greek, Hellenistic strain of nationalism is used to market technological products and to assert a sophisticated modern Greek future.

GREECE.
EVERYTHING COMES FROM ITS HISTORY.
NOW ITS FUTURE COMES TO YOU.

ultimate achievement of the Hellenic ideal and, as such, would lead all Europe to the highest levels of culture yet known."

The realities of the Greece struggling to free itself from the Ottoman Empire were contradictory to the vision of Greece as Hellas advanced at that time. The paradoxes that unfolded from this were multiple. For example, there was the issue concerning Hellene as meaning pagan in the early years of Christianity.[9] Since then, the term had been deployed at certain times in different ways, but the fact remained that it was now being used to reference a people who felt Greek Christian Orthodoxy to be one of its constitutive elements. Also, as Herzfeld (1982) emphasizes, there was the issue of language. The daily language of Greek men and women at the time, Romeic, was conceptually opposed to ancient Hellenic Greek language.

Finally, what of all the customs, mores, and habits that had resulted from the many years of living as subjects of the Ottoman Empire and coexisting with quite ethnically diverse populations? According to Herzfeld, "Greeks

What Is Greece? 67

who were quite willing to condemn the Turks on religious grounds nevertheless would not purge all the secular traces of a Turkish-dominated past." What might these be? Herzfeld continues in his analysis of the tension between the Hellenic ideal and the Greek social and historical experience: "The flaws that the Turks supposedly brought to the Hellenic perfection included shiftiness, double-dealing, illiteracy, influence-peddling and rule-bending, disrespect for norms and admiration for cunning individuals who could twist them to their own advantage" (1987, 29).

The Austrian scholar Jakob Philip Fallmerayer (1835) produced an extensive work Orientalizing his contemporary Greeks, emphasizing such attributes, though presenting them as *Greek*. This was a blow that the Greek historian Paparigopoulos responded to in his own work. Paparigopoulos (1853) presented a history of Greece that essentially argued against the discontinuity that Fallmerayer claimed existed between Ancient Greeks and their modern corollaries by presenting evidence favoring a cultural continuity running through Byzantium and beyond. All in all, a basic tension that remains a powerful undercurrent in contemporary political culture is that between *Romiosini* and *Ellinismos,* or Hellenism. In important ways, this is the backdrop against which the current politics of national identity get played out in Greece.

ASIA MINOR REFUGEES

Region is an important factor in internal conflict in Greece. Regional conflicts were further complicated in the 1920s when the refugees from the Asia Minor disaster arrived, creating a demographic explosion. Approximately 1.5 million came, making up 20 percent of the total population of the country and almost 50 percent of the active population in the urban centers of Greece (Polyzos 1984). With the influx of refugees, the ranks of the working class swelled. However, half of them were of bourgeois or petit bourgeois background. At the same time, the arrival of the refugees in northern Greece and especially Macedonia was considered a remedy for the demographics of that area as well as a boost to its Greek culture.

Wherever they settled, many of the refugees had to face the consequences of sudden poverty and the loss of property. For some, linguistic difference further increased the difficulties of assimilation.

The inhabitants of "Old Greece" feared this strange category of new Greeks. On the one hand, they were impoverished and forcibly rendered members of the proletariat; on the other, they were often more advanced professionally and culturally. This dissonance led to negative reactions on the part of the old Greeks. Those who were part of the population exchange were called "Turkish seeds" or "christened in yogurt" (*tourkosporoi, yiourtovaftismeni*). The word "Smyrnia," which used to mean a woman from Asia Minor, became synonymous with the word for prostitution. The exemplary cleanliness of many homemakers from Asia Minor, called *pastra,* is linguistically transformed to *pastrikia,* which is also used as a synonym for prostitute. Even the word "refugee" is transmuted to acquire heavily negative connotations. Many refugees change their last name, "cleaning" them of the telling prefix Kara- or the ending -oglou (Rigos 1992, 227–28).

This form of racism built momentum. Toward the end of the 1920s, far rightists begin to use it toward their own ends. In 1933 the newspaper *Typos* asked that it be mandatory for refugees to wear yellow bracelets so they could be easily identified and avoided by "Greeks." Anti-Venizelist Greeks were also negatively predisposed toward them and proposed that they should be persecuted. In an intriguing redeployment of a racializing antirefugee rhetoric, the publisher of the daily *Kathimerini,* G. Vlahos, wrote several articles before the elections of 1928. He was vehemently opposed to his party's efforts to gather refugee votes and to propose two refugee members of parliament in Athens. In one article he referred to refugees as "the refugee herd." In another, he wrote, "But they are Greeks of the same blood and brothers. Let them be brothers and cousins. When they acquire a political consciousness and the will of free citizens—something which will never happen—then they will have the right to be considered one of us, not just as voters but also as candidates" (quoted in Mavrogordatos 1982, 94–95).

Bringing religion in, the member of Parliament for the island of Spetses, Periklis Bouboulis, on 24 January 1934, made a statement in Parliament that the Jews of Thessaloniki, themselves the object of persecution in other contexts, were more Greek than the refugees (Mavrogordatos 1982, 49). This racism also took the form of physical violence by anti-Venizelists both before they were in office and after 1934, when they took the state in their hands. The expression "Let us burn the refugee settlements" was common.[10] One of the reasons mentioned for this was the fear that if the refugees were not properly "managed" they might turn to communism.

After the movement of support for Venizelos was quelled in 1935, when he lost the elections, Laikos Synaspismos (Popular Coalition), a collection of rightist parties, took office. The new state waged an open war against refugees in Macedonia. According to Deputy District Attorney of Thessaloniki, A. Vazouras, this involved the following: "The state military . . . which consisted of special forces of old Greeks was permitted by their pathetic leaders to indulge in violent crowd behavior against the population. Homes were

Figure 10. This contemporary painting refers to the refugees' cultural background, referencing the significance of music in their struggle to adjust, while underlining how they and their dream for just remuneration of lost property were left hanging. The label at the top, "To Live, or Not to Live," underscores the great depth of feeling with which histories of Greece have been experienced. The painting reverberates with the larger "dance-as-you-cry" Zorba theme. "Trompe-L'oeil-Realité," Costas Haralambìdìs, 2000, Argo Gallery, Athens, Greece. Used by permission of the artist.

robbed, people were beaten, women were raped, all in all this move had the form of the invasion of a barbarous military into an enemy country.... Out of the blue, without any provocation or cause, as though there was an organized plan for revenge or terror of the portion of the population seen as 'enemy' by the government. Arrests occurred everywhere. The police holding cells were jammed full. Most of the records that came through the district attorney's office documented violent beatings [and] injuries."[11]

The above anecdotal evidence paints a vivid picture of the racism that refugees from Asia Minor suffered and of the battleground that national identity can be in Greece.

The refugee support for Venizelos had an edge to it. Based on the Treaty of Lausanne, Greece and Turkey were each to pay the population departing from the respective territory for the property being left behind. As per a bilateral agreement reached with Turkey on 29 October 1930, Venizelos agreed to "forget" the money Turkey owed the Orthodox Turks who had returned to Greece in the population exchange. Although this resolved some tension at an interstate level, it meant, in effect, that the refugees had lost the value of their properties. Before this, the social consciousness and ideology of the refugees, many of whom had been of bourgeois or petit bourgeois standing in Asia Minor, did not meld with that of the working class. During the 1930s, perhaps partly because of the racism they experienced and partly because of what they saw as the "gift" Venizelos gave Turkey at their expense, the refugees began to work as a catalyst and the feared communist threat became more of a reality as many refugees turned toward the left of the political spectrum.

MUSLIM GREEKS IN THRACE

The Muslim minority in Thrace is the only minority whose existence as Muslim citizens of the Greek state is acknowledged by an international treaty, the Treaty of Lausanne, signed after the disaster of Asia Minor, between Turkey and the victors of World War I, including Greece, in 1923. The Greek claim was for the recognition of the Muslim minority here and the Christian Orthodox one there, as *ethnic* minorities. The Turkish side, perhaps concerned about the implications of such a claim, given the millions of Kurds on Turkish territory, agreed to sign the treaty only if the minorities were named as *religious* minorities.[12]

The Muslims in Greece retained their habitus of inhabiting and cultivating land from the leading religious and political groups that governed during the Ottoman khalifat. Thus, whereas the new Turkish state run by Mustafa Kemal began a process of modernizing and westernizing its population, the Muslims in Greece continued to live under a theocratic power of traditional structures. For example, the role of the muftis took on an ethnarchic in addition to its previous religious quality. Thus, whereas in Turkey the religious community was separated from the state, in Greece the muftis became public servants with juridical powers over the community on issues of family and inheritance law. The Greek state maintained a hostile stance toward the minority, and this in turn brought the minority closer to Turkish nationalism. At the beginning of the 1990s, they were granted further rights and the previous policy of ghettoizing them within the districts in which they live, Rodopi and Xanthi, began to change. At the present, there are two Muslim members of Parliament, one in each of the two main parties. The Pomaks are another Muslim minority, said to descend from a people of ancient Thrace. They also have a traditional societal structure. They live at the border of Greece and Bulgaria in the district of Xanthi. While the language they speak is considered closer to Bulgarian than to Turkish, they maintain a hostile stance toward both Bulgaria and Turkey. However, between the two World Wars, Greece registered Pomaks in the voters' lists for Turks of Western Thrace and has since treated them as though they are a part of the same minority.

Who, Then, Is Greek?

Clearly, the borders of who is Greek and who is not have been vehemently, indeed explosively, both contested and patrolled at particular moments and sites of Greece. As the preceding illustrates, the constitution of the category of subjects deemed properly Greek is neither unproblematic nor seamless.[13]

Graphically illustrating this highly complex field of power in which ethnic and national identities are crafted, and also highlighting the ways narratives about gender underlie and animate this field, is a joke made by Professor Neoklis Sarris, a contemporary scholar in Turkish studies and a professor of sociology at Panteio University, and himself a descendent of Greek refugees from Istanbul. Speaking often on television on a range of current issues, including Greek-Turkish relations, Sarris has many critics and has alternately been called both a Turkophile, intended as very much of an insult by those delivering it, and, most often, a Turkofagos (a person who wants to destroy/devour the Turks). Recently he was invited to attend a conference held in Bulgaria. As he told me, during a break in the proceedings one of the Bulgarian officials present turned to him and commented, somewhat playfully, that because of his blue eyes and fair coloring, perhaps he is a Slav! Sarris

Figure 11. As this Greek National Tourist Organization ad suggests, ancient Greek monuments tenaciously dominate the vastly larger contemporary Athenian urban landscape, much as public discourse concerning the demografiko and Macedonia obfuscate the specificities of the nation's historical present.

responded, "Listen, it is simple. If you look closely at the map of the Balkans, you see that they are shaped like a cunt. The various peoples would masturbate, and then ejaculate in here. Therefore, we are all the product of the same masturbation!"[14]

I relay this as he told it to me, exploding into laughter with his own punch line, for several reasons. One, I find it a vivid illustration of the profound constructedness of national identity in the region. Even as the anecdote relies on a genetic discourse, it redeploys it, showing that at its extreme it collapses. Two, this comment, made to me "on the record" by a man often locally perceived as a vehement nationalist and anti-Turk, is revealing of the distinct limits that history imposes on essentialist postulations of the Greek nation. Indeed, it is important to keep in mind that this joke is made by someone who repeatedly refers to "Greek blood" in public statements. Sarris insists that he is using the phrase metaphorically, yet it is indisputable that whatever his intentions, some of his statements are used by overtly hard-core essentializing Greek nationalists and this is something he is aware of. The sarcastic redeployment of a story concerning whose genes you have and whose genes I have, coming from this particular subject, thus carries special significance. Finally, I share the anecdote because it illuminates the inextricable political conjunction of gendered, often clearly sexist, discourses with nation-building ones.

In Sarris's joke, the Balkans are not only feminized but, in a sense, relegated to the status of prostitute. Although, in the joke, the Balkans are clearly the receptacle for "the seed" of other peoples, the use of the masturbation dynamic rather than sex as the causative mechanism suggests that the status of the Balkans is distinctly lower than that of the masturbating agent. That is, we are not speaking of two equals having sex but of one agent and one receptacle. In addition, given the contemporary connotations of masturbation, the joke also attributes a form of futility or vacuity to the history of Balkan peoples. Unstated in this joke, the implication nevertheless remains, if some of us who are "here" can claim that we *always were* here, then we may have a trace of superiority over the descendents of the adolescently masturbating others.

Back to Present Greece

Whatever may be the connections of present Greece to various aspects of the past of this geographic area, my primary interest in this book is the present and how at the present historical moment Greece struggles to fortify its position as a modern nation-state. As the preceding eclectic review of Greek history illustrates, the past is indeed crucial for situating and understanding the contestation of the present. For example, key discourses currently in circulation in the public sphere in an effort to resolve Greece's problems are firmly rooted in history. Yet, in the present, some of these are, at best, of deflated currency. These have emerged in recent years in particularly condensed form especially around two issues, which themselves are occasionally connected: one is the Skopiano, or the problem of the former Yugoslav Republic of Macedonia's (successful) claim for autonomous statehood, and the other is the demografiko, the perception that Greece's low birth rate is a serious problem. The failure of hegemonic stories of Greekness is perhaps most tangibly driven home in the outcome of the Skopiano; the stories themselves—their plot lines, their specificities—are perhaps nowhere as clear as they are in the coverage of the demografiko. Here, we are told, one of Greece's biggest national problems, as it charts its way through modernity, is that not enough babies are being born.

Chapter 4

STAGE RIGHT:

THE DEMOGRAFIKO

❖

Relations between Greece and Turkey have been tumultuous, as we have seen, since the foundation of the modern Greek nation and its individuation from the Ottoman Empire. Greek-Turkish relations constitute an important site of friction within the very volatile region of southeastern Europe today. Incidents of military planes flying into other countries' airspace have been occurring almost routinely throughout most of modern Greece's history. Nationalist sentiment regarding "the other side" has its own ebb and flow. Despite important diplomatic moves that have yielded significant results, Greek civil society remains concerned.

Also causing anxiety at the present is the large number of Albanian and other Balkan immigrants who entered Greece during the 1990s. Informal estimates claim that there are now 1 million immigrants living in Greece. Although few of them have been granted legal status, numerous Albanians are currently employed illegally as cheap manual labor. In an attempt to gain control of the immigrant situation, the Ministry of the Interior announced a "free" period for all immigrants to register for legal resident status. The result of this effort in the spring of 2001 was that 350,000 immigrants declared their residency, of which 300,000 proved that they have or can find both work and insurance. The title of a newspaper article, "A Pleasant Surprise from the Immigrants," reporting this outcome is indicative of the nonetheless entrenched negative feelings associated with immigrants, despite their contributions to the Greek economy.[1] The picture accompanying this article shows a plainclothes guard or clerk of one of the centers where immigrants were asked to appear; standing over a crowd of immigrants with his hand stretched straight out in the air, his palm facing down, in a gesture resembling a Nazi salute, the clerk or guard glares out toward the crowd (figure 12). This image argues both that immigrants need to be controlled and that state authority may be exceeding the limits of appropriate governmentality in its treatment of them. Certainly in the context of the article describing the new measure that was largely deemed generous, the photo seems to be suggesting that the measure is too generous. Reflecting yet another inconsistency between the needs of the economy and formal policy, the police routinely sweep areas where immigrants camp or live in abandoned buildings and expel them, in fairly violent fashion, from the country. Whether or not the new measure means these practices are going to stop is uncertain as the ongoing influx of immigrants continues.

In addition, the international acknowledgment of independent statehood to Macedonia, a region bordering the north of Greece, and the subsequent violent ethnic conflict taking place in this area placed more pressure on a heavily indebted Greece that is simultaneously struggling to define itself and consolidate its position in the international political scene, primarily now as an equal member of the European Union.

In the midst of this, and in the shadow of the concerted public attention being paid to the pressures of modernization and Prime Minister Simitis's efforts to improve Greece's position with the European Community, Greece has witnessed renewed concern with the chronically low birth rate of the country. The peak of this concern occurred in 1993–95, the same time the autonomy of Macedonia was at issue. Experts in demography and several politicians (mostly of the right), as well as doctors, have all contributed to the definition of what is widely seen as Greece's major national problem. Numerically this is defined as a birth rate of roughly 110,000 per year, a figure insufficient for the full replacement of the existing population of over 11 million. The simultaneous very high rate of abortion, anywhere between 100,000 and 400,000 per year throughout the 1990s, has been locally interpreted as an important part of the demografiko. While a global concern with the planet's overpopulation and a need to limit population growth largely remains a moot point in Greek discourse about the low national birth rate, the consistently booming population of approximately 80 million in neighboring Turkey is cited time and again as the main reason that Greece, and Greek women in particular, need to increase the rate of births.

In effect, a pronounced cultural fear of the proliferating and allegedly potentially invading Muslims—itself a displacement of the suppressed fear that modern Greece is not holding its own economically, politically, or in the area of foreign diplomacy—is being linked to a strong, also long-standing preoccupation with the performance of Greek wombs. The junction of these concerns is not new for Greece. The numbers themselves do not indicate a

Figure 12. This image undercuts the positive tone of the article reporting on the success of the August 2001 attempt to legalize alien immigrants in Greece. This layout, especially given the power of the image, indicates the strength of an undercurrent of xenophobic sentiment in contemporary Greece.

drastic change. Yet, the fervor with which the perceived problem is discussed has been at an exceptionally high level in some sectors of the press, especially between 1993 and 1995, and in the proceedings of the tripartisan parliamentary committee established in 1993 per the proposal of K. Mitsotakis to propose solutions to this problem. My assumption in this book is not that the numbers are not what they are, but that what is significant and interesting from the perspective of a critical analysis of power is what and how certain numbers are made to mean at a particular historical moment. Throughout the 1990s, the demografiko constituted a prominent issue in the Greek national imaginary, and the terms in which it is articulated, as I show, are quite specific.

The parliamentary committee authored a report and presented a proposal in 1993 that included a series of measures to induce the population to reproduce itself at a higher rate. The bill was initially defeated but it has been resurrected several times since then, and there are not a few who predict that it, and perhaps its restrictions on abortion, may eventually be approved. In the summer of 2000, several members of Parliament posed another question in Parliament relating to the demografiko and authored a report advocating a version of the bill aimed at "controlling" the demografiko.

In addition, during the 1990s, several institutes and research foundations were founded in Greece with the mission of researching the demografiko. Not all of these were active. But they received ample coverage from the press and numerous interviews were taken with academics affiliated with them. Connected with this phenomenon is the number of books published on both the general topic of demography and the specific Greek "demographic problem" during the 1990s.[2] In addition, the fact that the women I interviewed recognized the demografiko as a phenomenon considered "by some" a major national problem is itself a powerful indication of the penetration of demografiko discourses in Greece at the present historical moment.

Moreover, the demografiko, with its strident, at times even fundamentalist postulations of nation, race, religion, gender, and sexuality, and the high frequency of abortion that occurs under its sign, together constitute a condensation of the politics of modernity taking place elsewhere in Europe, such as England, France, and Germany, where the agon between subjects of purity and "contaminating" forces, state-building projects and their disassembling specters, different versions of "East" and "West," or "modernity" and "tradition," is neither as dense nor as acute.

Nation Building and Reproduction around the World

Abortion is certainly represented as a nationalist issue in other countries as well. The Hungarian memorial to the "holocaust" of aborted fetuses and the popularly held belief that "the unborn are also Croats" are strong examples of this. To situate the Greek demografiko in its global context, I consider briefly instances where reproduction or abortion have become strongly politicized and explicitly linked to particular nation-building projects elsewhere.[3] In this brief survey, I focus on the former socialist nations or developing nations Bulgaria, Rumania, the former Soviet Union, which all have high abortion rates, and China and India, which have the opposite situation of a very high birthrate, and return to the country along Greece's northern border, Macedonia.

BULGARIA

Although today the birth rate is not considered a problem in Bulgaria, in the past this was one of the countries that implemented an explicit demographic policy. After World War II, Bulgaria tried to encourage a steady moderate rate of population growth. In 1968 it passed a law offering subsidies that aimed at supporting families that chose to have a second and third child. These subsidies, payments to the working parent for three years after giving birth, continue to the present (Carlson and Omori 1998). With regard to birth control, from 1976 through 1995 women age twenty-five to forty-four rapidly increased their use of contraceptive pills (10 percent), condoms (19 percent), and especially IUDs (25 percent). From 1990 onward, contraceptives have been easily available, though accessibility is limited by their fairly high cost. From 1976 through the end of the 1980s, the rate of abortion remained steady. Abortions were fully legalized in 1988 in Bulgaria. From 1989, after the demise of the government at the time, through 1994 there was a notable drop in abortions (24 percent). However, this was accompanied by a drop in the number of births (50 percent) as well.[4] In 1976, the rate of births was the lowest in Europe, 7.89 births per 1,000 inhabitants. The most recent data show that in 1996, Bulgaria had 89,000 abortions, meaning 51.3 abortions per 1,000 women age fifteen to forty-four, and 55.2 abortions per 100 pregnancies.

RUMANIA

Rumania also has a fairly high rate of abortions, keeping in mind the inherent difficulties in compiling accurate abortion figures (Henshaw, Singh, and Haas 1999). In Rumania's case, this difficulty is because, as in Greece, the vast majority of abortions occur in the private sector, which is not required to report figures on abortion to the National Statistical Service. In 1990, before abortions were conducted by private doctors, the Ministry of Health reported 914,000 abortions, meaning 182 abortions per 1,000 women age fifteen to forty-four. The rate peaked in 1965 when it reached 252 abortions per 1,000 women. By 1996, Rumania was reporting 394,400 abortions, or 78 per 1,000 women and 63 abortions per 100 pregnancies. Each woman was expected to have 2.34 abortions during her lifetime. The same year, Rumania, along with Russia, had the highest rate of documented pregnancies ending in an abortion (63 percent). Two reasons cited for the high rates of abortion in Rumania are that contraceptives are exclusively imported and sold at very high prices, and there are reported incidents of Rumanian women being obliged to pay for contraceptives in foreign currency.[5]

Abortion and reproduction have been most explicitly deployed in nationalist discourse in two instances in Rumanian history (Kligman 1998). During the Ceausescu regime, the state initially allotted a central role to reproduction as the mechanism through which the workforce would multiply and thus yield "the triumph of socialism." Women who had many children were deemed "heroic mothers" as long as the children were not adopted or the result of a second marriage. Public discourse at this time also rendered abortion illegal in 1966 and offered strong financial support to the "heroic mothers." The objective, argues Kligman, was to ensure that these mothers would also continue to be productive workers. As a result, women with unwanted pregnancies resorted to illegal abortions and used contraceptive methods such as periodic abstention, or the rhythm method, and coitus interruptus. This situation changed drastically a year after the 1989 revolution, when abortions were legalized and became the main method of birth control. At this time, public discourse foregrounded the freedom to choose abortion, positioning it as a key symbol of a democratic and independent nation.

RUSSIAN FEDERATION

The rate of abortions in the Russian Federation is also very high. Indeed, it has led to the nation's being characterized as a country with "a culture of abortions," characterizing also other countries of the Eastern bloc (Schmid 2001; Da Vanzo and Adamson 1997).[6] In 1995, Russia reported 2,287,300 abortions, meaning 68.4 abortions per 1,000 women fifteen to forty-four years of age, and 62.6 abortions per 100 pregnancies. Each woman was expected to have 2.56 abortions during her lifetime. From 1991 to 1995, the number of abortions dropped by 27 percent. Yet, by 1997, abortions were back to 2.5 million, roughly double the number of births, as news reports stated.

Abortion was considered the preferred method of birth control since immediately after the Revolution. Abortion is free, assuming one goes through the complicated bureaucratic process of state facilities. As in Greece, it seems that many prefer the private route; in Russia, the cost is approximately $15. The reasons cited for the high rate of abortions are, again, the high cost of contraceptives and also difficulties in availability. In Russia, abortion is also very dangerous to the health of women. Today, abortion is increasingly being discussed as a political issue. Nationalists are opposed to it and the government struggles to institute sexual education programs in schools.

Abortion was politicized in Russia in the past (Petchesky 1990, 20–21). The legalization of abortion was an important objective of the socialist revolution. However, shortly thereafter there was a drop in births and an increase in abortion. Politicians and experts alike interpreted the two as a linked phenomenon, as do many Greek politicians and experts at the present, and

Russian women were accused of being selfish and irresponsible, again as Greek women are represented in demografiko discourses. This led to the imposition of limitations on abortion accessibility. Since then, as the figures above indicate, the situation has changed.

CHINA

A high rate of abortion, and the insertion of abortion within nation-building discourses, does not occur only in countries with a rate of birth locally perceived as being too low. The situations in China and in India, countries with birth rates perceived as being very high, are good examples. In China, the government took measures to control the annual rate of growth of the population throughout the 1990s. The objective was to keep it below 1.25 percent. Toward this end, the state propagates the idea of "one couple, one child" and encourages getting married at a more "mature" age. Urban couples are permitted to have only one child; couples in rural areas are permitted to have a second, in some regions, only if the first one is a girl. Couples who do not comply are penalized via deductions from their salary and fewer social services. This national policy for controlling births focused exclusively on the female body (Petchesky 1990, 16). It involved mandatory abortions, campaigns in favor of sterilization procedures, and an emphasis on the use of the Pill and the IUD.

There was a high level of insubordination on the part of the populace. This is usually explained as a function of the traditional cultural preference for boys and for large families.[7] In fact, statistics show that in the 1990s there were 118 boys born for every 100 girls. Until recently, this meant that there was a high rate of female infanticide in China. Moreover, one study found that 50 million females were reported "missing" in China due to institutionalized death or neglect (Yo et al. 1993).[8] More recently, ultrasound is being used to identify the sex of the embryo, which, if female, is then aborted.[9]

In 1995, China reported 7.93 million abortions, meaning 26.1 abortions per 1,000 women age fifteen to forty-four, and 27.4 abortions per 100 pregnancies. In 1998, the Ministry of Health's data indicated that there had been 7.4 million abortions; the Council of Family Planning reported 2.6 million. It is estimated that the real number of abortions is much higher because of the fairly simple process of procuring the "abortion pill" RU-486 on the black market.

In a study of the uses of the word "population" in Chinese public discourse, Anagnost (1995) finds that a notion of "the poor quality of the population" emerged in the 1980s, accompanying the policy of one child per couple.

In this discourse, used by both the government and its critics, demographics were never mentioned. Rather, the issue was the likely cultural and political crisis China would face because of "the poor quality" of the population. The way to show the world the superiority of socialism became, indirectly, the diminishment of the birth rate. One example of how this elision was accomplished was the popular phrase at the time "Fewer births, more goods." Thus, reproductive practices were powerfully linked to progress and modernization. This example from China puts in relief one of the paradoxes of the Greek case, wherein the nation-building objective of modernization is linked to a drop in abortions, which, however, is, quite unmodernly, discursively linked to an *increase* in births.

INDIA

In India, where the need to limit the number of births was a national priority as early as the 1960s, the government created the National Family Planning Program that, especially in the 1970s, focused on forced sterilization. Abortion was legalized in 1971. In the 1990s, the government reassessed its means and sought to pay more respect to the wishes of the couple, issues of women's rights, and the better quality of medical services (Visaria, Jejeebhoy, and Merrick 1999). Thus, as of 1995, there was a small increase in the use of contraceptives. Nonetheless, female sterilization continued to be the main means of birth control (71 percent of the total female population).

Another issue that has arisen in India, as in China, is the marked drop in the number of girls born (today, 917 girls are born for every 1,000 boys; Karlekar 1995). Here, too, there is a traditional preference for male children, which is based on the cultural mandate that all property be left to male children. In addition, male children carry the financial burden of taking care of the elderly parents. Upon marriage, an Indian woman becomes a member of her husband's family and it becomes her duty to take care of his parents. These mores, along with a dowry tradition and the widespread use of ultrasound to diagnose the sex of the fetus, have led to a drop in the births of female babies. Amniocentesis was used toward this end as early as 1974. Today, formal figures indicate that there are 2 million abortions of female fetuses annually; informal sources indicate that the real figure may be as high as 5 million. Legally, this type of abortion is forbidden. In practice, however, it has become a lucrative business. Meanwhile, the methods used in the past— female infanticide and the abandonment or negligence of female infants— continue to be used by some sectors of the population (Rajaretnam and Deshpande 1994). In 2001, India's Supreme Court ordered the government to enforce the prohibition against abortions of female fetuses and female infanticide. The state also offers incentives to parents who have one or two children, as long as one of the two parents has been sterilized.

In 1995–96 there were 566,500 abortions reported, meaning 2.7 per 1,000 women age fifteen to forty-four and 2.1 abortions per 100 pregnancies. However, these figures are considered far lower than the actual ones. It is estimated that private doctors perform double this amount, and nondoctors are thought to perform a multiple of this number. All in all, the Bangalore Society of Obstetrics and Gynecology estimates that there are actually 6.7 million abortions annually, many of which are performed in conditions that are dangerous to a woman's health.[10] With regard to other forms of birth control, there has been a marked increase, from 24 percent in 1982 to 43 percent in 1990.

MACEDONIA

An especially interesting example of the charged national politics of reproduction occurred just recently in the far more proximate country of Macedonia, or FYROM. Here, in this newly founded state, the ethnic conflict between Albanians, a minority, and Macedonian Slavs, a majority, in conjunction with the cultural specificity of each, has led to the sudden sharp politicization of births. To conclude this section of the global context of the politics of reproduction, I quote at some length from a *New York Times* article reporting on this situation.[11] This article puts in bold relief how births, an ostensibly straightforward biological fact, are never just births.

> Tetovo, Macedonia, Aug. 10. The girl was blessedly ordinary, if viewed as a newborn and nothing else. Healthy, peachy, maybe a little wrinkly in the face, she was fast asleep two hours after coming into the world, the third daughter of a tired 28-year-old Albanian woman, Samije Jusufi.
>
> But as a symbol, the infant is much more than a harmless, nameless baby in a maternity ward here: she is frightening and, in some ways, what the fighting in Macedonia is all about.
>
> The majority ethnic group here, the Macedonian Slavs, finally got a state to call their own in 1991 after Yugoslavia came unstrung. But simple math is undermining all that. The largest minority in the country, the Albanians, are having more babies than the Slavs are.
>
> "Sons make a family go on," said Mrs. Jusufi, explaining barely out of the delivery room why she would try again after three girls. "Daughters make someone else's family go on."

> Good numbers are hard to come by, but few dispute that if current trends continue, the Slavic majority could become a minority in this nation they consider their own, anywhere from several years to several decades from now.

The rhetoric used in the article clearly marks its positionality as a news article in the *New York Times*. The "newborn" that is "healthy, peachy," the mother who is "tired," and the Slavs who "finally got a state to call their own," as though we are talking about Virginia Woolf's room of her own (no easy task itself, but still importantly different), even if it was after Yugoslavia "came unstrung," all reveal the amalgam of Americana and exoticization with which such "problems" with reproduction in other nation-states are viewed from more westernly perspectives.

However, this rhetoric notwithstanding, the excerpt offers in condensed form the complex dynamics involved in situations where reproduction has become a charged political issue. The demonization of the infant that the article deploys is accurate, if a little Hollywood-like. The comment concerning the relative value of sons and daughters, though dramatically reiterated as a clear instance of nothing more complex than North American "sexism," nonetheless underlines the inherently gendered aspect of birth rates. Finally, this article vividly illustrates that there are also other stakes involved in such situations. These are stakes that the clinical reports of the UN, International Planned Parenthood, and other international organizations often gloss: those having to do with political, ethnic, racial, or religious differences. Clearly, part of what is at issue is the *type* of births desired. Despite the references to "simple math" and "good numbers," the implications of the article are clear. Not all births are equal. More humans are wanted, yes, but not simply so as to have more physical bodies within the given nation-state. Rather, as I go on to argue, using the demografiko in Greece as an example, more births are desired for what particular bodies are made to mean in specific nationalized, gendered, geopolitical national contexts. That is, certain births are desired because of how the body is made to mean in disparate geopolitical minefields.

PART TWO

In Context, In Contests

A game of light

like all of us after all.

—Laina, 1998

Chapter 5

IN THE OPERATING ROOM:

ON COWS, GREECE, AND

THE SMOKING FETUS

❖

It was Wednesday, 9 March 1994, 10 A.M. I had an appointment with Tasi Aspridaki, one of my aunt's friends from medical school. Tasi is an anesthesiologist who helps with abortions as well as doing the anesthesia in other operations. After I asked my aunt if she could help me with my research, she thought of Tasi. The clinic where we were to meet, Artemis, is probably the third or fourth most popular private ob/gyn clinic in the northern, more upper-class, suburban area of Athens. It is a little off the beaten path of the Greek upper class but still in the same vicinity. I got there early. I was nervous. I knew I would be going through several levels of scrutiny. At stake was my being allowed into an operating room during an abortion and, for all its legality and common usage and despite the absence of an organized anti-abortion movement and certainly any violence, abortion in Greece remains an issue and an event that, at most sites, elicits hushed tones and secrecy. In any case, as far as I could tell, this was the only connection I had that might get me into that well-barricaded part of an ob/gyn hospital.

I was wearing a white shirt buttoned up to the next to last button, with a white T-shirt showing underneath. I was also wearing khaki pants, a black and beige small-check blazer, and a pair of flat pumps instead of my fieldwork shoes. My fieldwork shoes no doubt cost me a bit in terms of making some people feel safe with me and my research, but they gave me enough sense of strength to be worth it. They looked like ordinary men's shoes. My pair was dark brown and had a thin rubber sole. I was able to walk tall and still have a very solid footing at the same time, without looking as if I was at all interested in making a pass at anyone. These shoes moved me out of the category of the "permeable," or sexually available. In fact, I think my "research uniform" had the effect of desexualizing me, in Greek straight terms at least. Anticipating all the layers of scrutiny I would encounter before being permitted entry into the high-security bowels of the clinic, which is where abortions take place in the three main private ob/gyn clinics of Athens, I decided my flat pumps were a better choice for today. Thin ankles showed under my serious pants, the better to encourage the paternalism ob/gyns seemed to feel most comfortable putting on display when faced with women who are conscious. Including, sometimes even in a more pronounced form, when they were dealing with a researcher inquiring after what constitutes the bread and butter of most Greek ob/gyn practices: abortion. For them to be even mildly cooperative with the research, I needed to put them at ease—as much as possible, that is, given the usual reaction to my research topic.

As I've noted, Greece is often reported in its own media and at Greek ob/gyn medical conferences as having the highest rate of abortion in Europe. One more symptom of the phenomenon of the Greek *para-economia,* the huge but hidden part of the Greek economy, is that very few abortions are actually formally reported. Greece's para-economy consists of a fully organized and well-functioning economic system that exists out of view of the Internal Revenue Service. Thus, for example, stores may "cut receipts" for a fraction of the merchandise they actually sell and use those for tax purposes while keeping their main business off the books. Clients who want a receipt are quoted a different price than are those who don't ask for one. In general, both the doctors performing abortions and the clinics in which they are performed do not declare abortions so that they won't be taxed for them. Also, as the doctors are always quick to note, the women want to maintain their privacy and anonymity and are not themselves at all inclined to document the abortion in any way. I was told this so often, I am sure, to give the doctors an alibi for their failure to help build my sample by allowing me to come in contact with their patients. But it is true that there is a generalized aura of secrecy surrounding abortion. Several doctors told me that most women would rather avoid a state-run clinic and prefer to pay for an abortion in a private clinic, thus avoiding having the abortion stamp put in the public health services book all insured citizens carry "for life" (*isovia,* a midwife said, the same word used for a criminal sentence). This was confirmed by many of the women I spoke with. What all this means is that there are no reliable formal statistics on abortion in Greece.

In addition to the snowball sample of thirty middle- and upper-class professional women that I built mostly thanks to friends and their friends, I also conducted interviews at a state-run clinic in Athens, considered by experts to be the prototype for all Greek state-run Family Planning Centers, where I had been granted formal permission to do research on abortion (a feat accomplished largely, I think, by virtue of my willingness to sit in the director's waiting room "just in case" he had a spare moment for each of the full five working days that his secretary told me there was no time for a proper appointment with him). Of the ninety women with a written record of two or more abortions whom I interviewed at the clinic, most of them lower and middle class, all reported having had at least one of their abortions in a private clinic and most had had all of them there. Certainly this was partly a product of the fact that abortion was illegal until 1986, when PASOK passed the law 1609/86, and hence performed only—if quite abundantly and safely—in private clinics. But even most of the younger women I interviewed said they preferred to have their abortions done in a private clinic. They might visit the state-run clinic for their routine gynecological examination and Pap test, though always under the guise of being interested in beginning to use some form of Center-sanctioned contraception. The Family Planning Center at the clinic was not authorized to offer routine gynecological services to women *unless* they were coming for advice about contraception. The midwives who staffed the center saw to it that this rule was upheld at least enough so that the women who came in had to act as though they cared about both contraception and the Center's advice on it. But a private clinic seemed to be the preferred site for abortions for women of all social classes. Of course, as I found out later, even the public clinics did not regularly report abortions, despite the fact that on the whole they did need to adhere to the state's bureaucracy to some extent to be reimbursed for services to insured people. Only abortions deemed "therapeutic" were systematically reported. Those account for approximately 1 percent of all abortions performed in Athens each year.

The figures of the National Statistical Service (1993) show that during 1992, two years before my fieldwork, there were 1,642 abortions performed in all of Greece. Yet, there was a consensus among the thirty doctors I interviewed in Athens that the more accurate figure was probably in the vicinity of 300,000 to 400,000 abortions for each year up until the mid-1990s. This, for a population of 10 million, placed Greece first or second among European Union countries with high rates of abortion throughout the late 1980s and 1990s. The effects of the European Union–funded anti-AIDS campaign—considered by many laypersons and experts alike to be a strong, if inadvertent, force against abortion—had not kicked in until later. Actually, 1993–94 was the period many doctors identified as marking a drop in Greece's rate of abortion to approximately 200,000 to 300,000 per year—still many more abortions than the number formally reported.

As I was told by Marina Meidani, a scholar at Panteio University in Athens and member of the Board of Editors of *Dini,* the only feminist scholarly journal published in Greece, this discrepancy between the formal discourse of the state and the daily practice of Greeks is typical of everyday life. However, I suggest that this discrepancy is not so easily located in the disjunctions between a firmly bounded state and the supposedly similarly separate stuff of either daily life or civil society. Rather, what I often encountered, even in my discussions with individual women, was a different tension: the tension and reversibility of "truth" as it is paraded in variously disguised forms through a minefield of erratically extended trust and distrust. Greeks, whether living in Greece or abroad, sometimes refer to their culture as "paranoic." Be that as it may, it is clear that trust is a core issue, and with good reason, as there has been a long national and personal history of often quite violent breaches of trust. I think the difference between stated facts and lived practice, or experience, has to do with fear.

The heart of what is seen locally as the problematic disjunction between formal words and informal (hence, it is implied, *real*) practice lies in the success, or lack thereof, involved in setting and defending boundaries that will be respected. Deciding just which boundaries should be set and defended is itself often a tricky and fluctuating business. The domestically prevalent stereotype of yelling Greeks notwithstanding, the confrontational approach typically used for assorted negotiations can also be misleadingly calm, when the ammo is a strategically flung "Whatever you think," for example. Either way, it tends to maximize harm to all parties even as it is fueled by a concerted attempt to avoid incurring the losses suffered in the past and, above all, to preserve face. *Opos nomizeis.* Where people's hearts are close to the skin, put on the line with a show of bravado, and then hurt, there remains little room to negotiate conflict arising at a later date without automatically upping the ante and resorting to a variety of subtle, or not so subtle, terrorist tactics. No longer as easily accessible, the heart may go underground, content to mastermind from there the infinite intricacy of the doings of the mind, with cunning, *poniria,* or its cheap substitute *koutoponiria.* The common reference to the evil eye (which can be cast, even unwittingly, when one says something very good about someone or a possession and feels some envy, or if one quite simply does not want the good of someone else) stands as good evidence of the wide range of strategies that can be used for dealing with perceived threats.

Having arrived early at the clinic, I was playing my part in a little dance with Dr. Aspridaki. Not all anesthesiologists help during abortions, as I had been told she did. Although abortion in Greece is common and routine at one level, it is nonetheless not at all a simple matter to be making part of your living from it. A Greek Orthodox version of shame attached to abortion is one reason. Another is what the mass media call the demografiko. This is, as I've noted, a statistical and cultural phenomenon perceived—mostly in the mainstream press and occasionally in Parliament as well—to be of unique proportions at the present and of great gravity: Greece's major national problem, as it is said, with a birth rate that, according to demographic conventions, is not high enough to "reproduce the generations" (which is, of course, presumed to be a positive and necessary goal for the Greek nation's welfare). In the context of public discussions on this issue in the press, TV, and radio, abortion occasionally came up as an important factor, at times the most important factor, contributing to "the demographic problem." In some contexts, abortion is actually likened to an act of treason. Surprisingly, it was the centrist press, and of course the far right's press, that stated this more than the papers of the mainstream right. All of which is to say that, while Tasi was likely flattered to be facilitating research sponsored by a U.S. university and pleased to be accruing favor with my aunt (perhaps paying off some unknown favor extended to her in the past), she also had good reason to be cautious with me.

As I had been directed to, I told the front desk of the clinic that I was there for Dr. Aspridaki. They called her and then told me to wait; she would be up to get me shortly. The lobby/waiting room of the clinic was packed. It had a slightly different feeling than that of the other private, northern suburb ob/gyn clinics. In one corner of Artemis's front lobby that morning was a fiftyish woman dressed in black holding a bag of potato chips in one hand and a soda in the other. She was nodding emphatically toward one of the two men sitting with her. One was wearing the black band on his sleeve that few Greek men in Athens still wear when they are in mourning. It continues to be a common practice in many villages, and among women, even in Athens, wearing black for one or more years is a routine part of mourning for the death of a husband. The other man sitting with them was very young. As I watched, another woman walked up to them, her hair pulled back in a big bow barrette, with more food. She had brought them some cheese pies from the canteen. A little further down on the couch-like furniture of the lobby was an older man with his head rolled forward on his chest, snoring. She woke him up and handed him a cheese pie.

I wondered whether it was a sister of one of these parties, or a brother's wife, who was giving birth. Of course, it might also be that a relative of theirs was there for an operation, a hysterectomy or the removal of a tumor. In fact, there was something about their energy; they exuded a sense of *distinction* for being present. It was in some way "big of them" to be there. Also, the joyous undertones to the anxiety that usually accompany a birth vigil were missing. Their pleasure was due to everyone facing an obstacle together, pulling together to overcome something. *Tha to perasoume mazi*. They were taking a stand in solidarity. *Na tis sibarastathoume*. But, as is the case with many such stands taken in all sorts of situations in Greece today, there was a vehemence to the gesture that seems a little too strong, driven perhaps by a guilty pleasure that the plight of the other is not one's own or, possibly, by the prejudicative comprehension that the plight of the other may in fact be a reflection on the ostensibly "innocent" other. What the vehemence was covering up in this particular case was anybody's guess. One thing was clear: were it a simple birth this group was waiting on, the pride would not have the same pitch. Their presence would have been expected, something that honored them, but not something others should be especially grateful for. Also, the joy felt in waiting for the arrival of yet another addition to the extended family was not animating this group. But perhaps it was a difficult labor. Whatever they were there as witnesses for was likely not life-threatening, but there was some *miasma* attached. It showed in the bustle.

I paced through the lobby a few times. I read the signs on the wall with the little arrows: "ultrasound," "prenatal examinations," "external laboratory." I noted the absence of an "abortion" sign and wondered what direction the abortion rooms might be in. Then I heard my name over the loudspeaker. *I Kyria Halkia na erthi stin resepsion*. My aunt's friend was at the desk. She was wearing one of the long white jackets, a *roba*, over her "citizen clothes," as the midwives at the state-run center called their street-clothes. *Ta politika*. The juxtaposition implied that being a midwife was more than being "a citizen," more like being part of an army instead. I shook hands with Tasi and we exchanged brief pleasantries. She told me to follow her and we walked down a flight of stairs, through a small hallway-cum-waiting room where she was greeted by a doctor wearing blue pants and a blue shirt. From there, we turned to a big closed door that had a little square of glass with wires running through it at face level. It looked like what I imagined a prison door would look like. She looked in quickly, punched a number on a pad to the right, the door clicked, we entered.

To the immediate left was a woman behind a desk with a computer monitor or screen of some sort placed on it. Next to this woman, to the right as we walked in, was a young man. Tasi nodded at them and indicated that I was with her and we were "just going in." As we turned into another corridor I saw doors, probably three or four on each side. We were walking fast. I glanced into one as we went by and saw several beds with women lying on them. In another room, I saw a woman wearing a bright pink uniform tucking in the sheets of one of the beds. The woman looked up at Tasi, greeted her warmly, and then looked over at me quizzically. Tasi called out "Hi there, I've got a friend with me today," and kept walking. Then a male doctor walked by us, wearing a green longish shirt over street clothes. He called "Hi" to her, and then asked, "Who is this with you?" Tasi was cool with him. First she said "Hi" back to him and then she added, "Oh, the niece of a friend." The doctor continued, "What's she doing here?" and then "Are you sure she isn't with the IRS?" *Plaka, plaka, den xereis apo pou tha sou tin feroun kamia fora.* He smiled a little, as did Tasi, nodding her head a bit. We kept walking.

Finally we got to a door on the left that was jammed open. We entered a small room that had three doors leading off it. Directly in front of us was a long basin with several water taps. One of the three doors was on the wall to the right, immediately next to the basin, another directly opposite it on the wall to the left. Opening off from the wall in front of us, a little to the left, was the third door. The change from the hall was dramatic. Here there were many people, fairly loud voices, and the smell of cigarette smoke. Tasi greeted some of the people and briskly walked by others. I heard her telling somebody that I was my aunt's niece, "You remember her from Evangelismo Hospital, she's a colleague anesthesiologist." I followed her through the door across from us into another room, almost as small as the anteroom with the three doors and sink. Here she introduced me to four people who seemed to be simply hanging out.

There were two women wearing pink uniforms, another one in pale blue, and a man in green pants and shirt. She told me the first names of the two women and said they were midwives. Then she told me the first name of the other woman and explained that she was the one who would help with the anesthesia, unless something came up. I later learned that it was fairly routine for a helper—sometimes one of the midwives, sometimes a technician not performing any of the midwives' duties—to perform the anesthesia in abortion cases. A specified anesthesiologist would be officially responsible and on call, though not present in the operating room. Meanwhile, about a third of the payment going to the anesthesiologist would be passed along to this substitute. Tasi introduced the man in green as "Mr. Filias, one of our doctors here." Somebody handed me one of the green shirts folded up neatly by the door and told me to put it on. I squeezed my big shoulder bag behind one of the chairs by the sink and hung my blazer on one of the nails by the door. I pulled on the green shirt. "Have a seat," Tasi said, and I did, increasingly aware of the butterflies in my stomach. Clanky metal medical instruments make me queasy. Blood I don't mind, but scientifically sanctioned butchering equipment gives me much more pause than any machete. The butterflies I felt in my stomach were exacerbated by my phobia. But, I realized, they are also a result of my feeling of being a complete fraud. What *am* I doing here?

Tasi turned to the doctor who had just asked me exactly that question. She told him pointedly that I was doing research on the women who come here, "for abortions" (*gia ektroseis*). She enunciated the words very carefully. Now that it is being researched, it seems, its real name can be pronounced loud and clear. Usually medical personnel of all ranks prefer to say *diakopi,* which means "interruption," or *amvlosi,* which is more formal, or simply *epemvasi,* the word for surgery that also means intervention, as well as a military operation. I myself have learned to carefully emphasize my interest in the women in particular, rather than abortion per se, when communicating with medical practitioners involved in abortions.

The doctor asked, "Research, what kind? Is she a journalist?" I quickly explained that I am a sociologist, as I have gotten into the habit of saying to avoid the questions and curious looks I am confronted with if I say my Ph.D. is in the field of communication. Because my B.A. and M.A. from Bryn Mawr were in sociology, and because most of the members of my doctoral committee at UCSD are sociologists or political scientists, I don't feel this is an out-and-out lie. Anthropology, in some ways the better "home" for the type of fieldwork I was conducting at Artemis, would have made little sense here because the lay understanding of the field in Greece remains strongly linked to archaeology. "The research is for my doctoral dissertation." I explained to the doctor. "It will be filed at the University of California," having learned that nobody listens to the whole long title of University of California at San Diego. "Oh," he said, looking away slowly toward the door. Then his head swiveled back and his eyes met mine head on. "What is it you are trying to learn?" Always that question. Again, as I have learned to do, I said that I am interested in "the women's psychological profile," especially what their emotions are with regard to the unwanted pregnancy and its termination. "However," I went on in an even voice (deflecting, deflecting), "my approach is not psychoanalytic. What I am most interested in is how they consciously perceive of, and respond to, their situation."

Meaning what, I wonder? Meaning that I am trying to convince my interlocutors that I successfully walk the straight and narrow path of not being somebody who will judge badly the doctors providing abortions—neither an overly zealous Greek Orthodox woman (*theousa*) nor some implicitly crazy feminist (*feministria*) who would think abortion is a good thing but would have a similarly negative approach toward the doctors making money from it. "My primary unit of analysis," I said as I concluded my answer to the doctor's question, "is the discourses that Greek women who have had two or more abortions articulate: *the stories they tell*, not their psyches." *As though those are so easily distinguishable.*

Highlighting my interest in the women's perspectives served to assuage the doctors' apparently quite deep concern that they, and their participation in abortion, may actually be what is under examination. In fact, the doctors have never been my central concern, though they did become a site of great interest as my research progressed. In addition, my firm disavowal of the deep unconscious, a domain that is clearly not the doctors' turf, works to accomplish two things. On the one hand, this suggests a respect on my part for the territorial boundaries of categories of knowledge in general (an issue at the core of professional life in a modernizing Greece, where regulatory boards' scant and impromptu patrolling devices operate opportunistically at best and where it is often said that "whatever you call yourself, that is what you are"). *Min benoume se xena xorafia.* On the other hand, it also serves to put the doctors at ease about volunteering their own (quite unpsychoanalytic) accounts of women's feelings as they have been exposed to them in the context of their practice. To be sure, it also grants me a little more respect, as neither psychoanalysis nor psychology enjoys the recognition and respect due them in Greece.

I remember vividly that a close friend told me several years ago that "Americans are constantly going to psychologists because they don't have friends. Imagine that you have to pay to have someone listen to you!" Since then, I have heard similar statements from other friends. I don't think that the higher concentration of psychologists now practicing in Greece has done much to change a "formal level" disbelief in the contributions of psychology. It is commonly felt that visiting a psychologist is potentially even a dangerous thing to do and that it might, in some important way, harm your soul. Yet, in the classic love-hate dynamic of xenophobia-xenomania that characterizes much of modern Greek life, Greek magazines and television talk shows almost fanatically mimic much of the popularized psychological discourses in circulation in the United States. Judging by circulation rates and show popularity, the Greek public seems to be perfectly content with this development. The doctors themselves, in fact, in the process of offering me *their* stories of the women, as they very often did, occasionally also attempted to psychoanalyze their patients. More often, though, they turned to recounting their own feelings and ideas concerning abortion and seemed to look to me for some sort of affirmation.

I had the authority to be granted their attention at all because I was, in their view, a scientist of sorts. If I were persuasive in not representing an actual threat to the doctors (either as a journalist, as someone who would report them to the Greek IRS, as an incognito *theousa*, or as a feministria[1]), it is what they saw as a sociologist's *scientific* credibility, if quite low-grade from their medical-scientific perspective, which gave them license to make pronouncements about the women (*oi gynaikes* as they called their clients/patients) that they might otherwise have censored. In most cases, I did nothing to challenge their almost automatic move to position themselves as experts *on the women themselves*, rather than on abortion as a medical act, gynecology, or even women's physical health in general.

That gynecologists so unanimously saw themselves as overall experts on the women is not just a symptom of patriarchy gone awry but a function of the specificities of the relationship between gynecologist and patient in Athens. I witnessed firsthand and had reported to me the taking of many liberties on the part of gynecologists. Yet, overall, the women supported and participated in the positioning of their doctors. In general, an exceptional degree of intimacy seems to be cultivated by both the women and their doctors. On the whole, women spoke to me of their doctors with a mixture of fondness and reverence that they did not use for anyone else, except, in some cases, when speaking of their father.

I think the experience of abortion lies at the heart of this intimacy— whether it is the disclosure of prior abortions to their current doctor, or the trust women feel they are placing on their doctor when they decide to go ahead with an abortion. Very often I was told by the women I spoke with, most middle class, as an argument against using the state-run clinics for their abortions, that they wanted "their own doctor" to do it. In those cases when I was told the woman did *not* want her own doctor to perform the abortion, and I think this may actually be the strongest evidence of the bond between gynecologists and their patients in Athens, it was because *she did not want him to know*, much as if he were actually a member of her family.

An optimistic reading of the situation I encountered when I first entered the field is that this quite powerful relationship is also at least part of the reason doctors were so reticent to help with the research. For example, in the context of an interview I had early on in the project with one of the better-known ob/gyns whose clientele is rumored to be among the most elite Athenians, I was told point-blank that I should change my research topic because no doctor would cooperate with me. When I asked why, I was told that women would not feel comfortable discussing their abortions with a stranger. I agreed and said that that was why I was hoping the doctor would recommend me as a "good" stranger to talk with, so as to facilitate the research.

I had already been told to drop the research and change topics by another ob/gyn, so I wasn't completely thrown off. Thanks, I believe, to the mutual friend who had recommended me to him for "a chat" (never an *interview* with doctors, that would be an automatic "no," no matter who intervened), one of the first doctors I spoke with confided that none of the doctors would talk, let alone help, because they were worried about the IRS. None of the abortions are declared, this doctor told me, and if I start keeping tabs on the number of research subjects I have . . . It might be dangerous. So, having had the benefit of that encounter, I knew how to respond to Dr. Polakis, who was saying he could not help me because he was worried about violating the confidentiality of his patients. I told him I could definitely see his point, though of course, I added, nodding as though he understood, "this does not mean I will not do the research," as he openly suggested I should. My topic had already been approved at the University of California, I said matter-of-factly, and the research was already underway. I was interested in talking with the women, I said, to contribute to the understanding of abortion and Greek women's perspectives on it. I was hoping this particular doctor (who was, after all, as I commented, known as one of the best in Athens), along with a few others of similar stature, might give my phone number to just a few of their patients, along with their verbal endorsement of the research I was doing, and the suggestion that they call me for a chat. At this, Dr. Polakis lost the calm he had obviously been maintaining with difficulty: "First of all, why do you want to speak with the women?! They have nothing to say. What could they say? Why did they get pregnant? They did. Why are they having an abortion? They don't want the child. They have nothing to say. Greek women are not very cultivated or very smart. *Oi Ellinides einai hamilou pneumatikou epipedou.* The way to do your research is to look at the statistics of birth control usage over time. Greece has the lowest frequency of users of the Pill. Greek women refuse to take it! That is why there are many abortions here. You can look also at the statistics for the Pill in other countries, and compare. You can do a comparative analysis."

The expression Polakis used to define the IQ of Greek women, *hamilou pneumatikou epipedou,* is a formal and somewhat elaborate phrase which I later learned was a trope fairly commonly used by experts involved in family planning in Greece. It references the liberal-humanist tone of mostly colonizing literature on family planning procedures for countries that are "underdeveloped" while also reflecting the local elite belief among many Greek gynecologists (and other scientists) that Greek women are indeed of low intelligence and uncultivated, or simply not smart. A belief apparently shared by Polakis, who had just acted as though *I* were being disrespectful of his patients by asking that he encourage them to speak with me, despite their interest in confidentiality. Overall, I think Dr. Polakis was able to say what he said to me, first of all, because he was confident we were not on tape. Since then, however, confronted with how prevalent his view is among Greek medical practitioners, it has occurred to me that he may well have said the same thing even if he did think our conversation was being recorded.

The definition of the situation that he sought to maintain between us was that of a knowledgeable expert in the field giving advice to a junior colleague in an adjacent, distinctly lesser field. The ease with which he recommended that I change both the topic and the entire methodology of my research indicates not only his own tenuous boundary management, but also the limits of the expertise he attributed to me. Yet, at the same time that his manner toward me evinced the paternalism I referred to earlier, which many Greek ob/gyns have developed as their main coping skill with patients, it also reconstructed him and me as equals (of a sort) in that neither of us were of the same caste, or *pasta,* as the subjects under discussion.

For Polakis, my UC affiliation and the fact that I was doing research on abortion in the first place—seen by many Greeks as an absurdly "hot" issue in the United States—no doubt worked to construct me as more of an American than a Greek. Also, he asked me twice whether it was a doctoral dissertation I was writing or a master's thesis. In fact, the second time he just called it a master's and then looked at me questioningly. I had the sense he felt there was a very significant, almost masculinizing difference of rank between the two. Perhaps most important, he clearly did not remember that I had visited him as a patient myself several times during my adolescence and early adulthood. The performance Polakis strove to uphold, and which I permitted, was that he and I were professionals interested in *helping* the subject population in good liberal, if not also out-and-out colonizing, reformatory fashion. Ostensibly, his expertise and experience were being used to point me in the direction of how best to go about assisting the "natives" to control the negative effects of unthinkingly following their "urges." As I was repeatedly reminded in numerous ways throughout my fieldwork, treating the population I was researching as persons, as they theoretically are according to the various oft-cited Greek and European Union legislation, was not the experienced, legitimized, professional, and *scientific* way of helping them.

This lesson was to be driven home to me the day I went to Artemis. As I said, my aunt's friend had me sitting down in the back room where two midwives and two doctors were also standing or sitting. On the right wall of this little room was a small rickety glass window with sliding panels, like the cashier window of an old Athenian movie theater. One panel was pushed all the way to the side. All I could see through it was a vague yellow, the color of the tiles on a wall. The room the window connected to, as I was soon to learn, was the operating room next door. Against the other wall of the room was a stool, where one of the midwives sat smoking.

The smoke got my attention in a bizarre way. I had quit three years earlier, after ten years as a chain-smoker, and was usually irritated by other people's smoke. That's not what was bothering me now, though. Nor was I concerned that there were oxygen tanks around, which were at times connected to anaesthetized women. Rather, the thought that would not leave my mind was that there were many wide-open cervixes that came through here each day and wouldn't having the carcinogenic particles of smoke coming in contact with them be a factor increasing their risk for developing cancer of the cervix or of the uterus. Unbeknownst to the sedated women, I thought to myself, their cervixes were being exposed to cigarette smoke.

My anxiety level was higher than I had expected. A lot of what I was seeing and hearing I could not interpret as acceptable or appropriate without serious ideological work and emotional distancing. I wondered if it was the American part of me that was seeing things this way. Was I guilty of projecting a U.S. (or Greek, I would add, much as we might hate to admit it) middle-class morality onto the scene? Americans are often mocked for their queasy stomachs and self-righteousness. The U.S. uproar about abortion itself is something that elicits amazement and has been criticized as another example of American puritanism. Sexual harassment is another of those issues. Just recently, an acquaintance had commented to me, apropos some news story, how excessive it was of Americans, all this hoopla about sexual harassment. Yes, I agreed, to the extent that it detracts attention from the fact that certain behaviors are merely an extension of the very social construction of femininity and masculinity themselves.

Might it be that what I was witnessing in Artemis's abortion department is really "normal" for Greece or Greeks proper? Perhaps, for some. Though the various signs of nervousness I witnessed from doctors, midwives, and other medical personnel suggest that even for them their daily routine is not in fact "normal." I know now that for many others it clearly is not. Yet, there is a historical pattern, especially in the Greek left, of using an otherwise very appropriate deep cultural aversion toward some American things, ideas, and people to deflect attention from women's issues. Feminism itself has been called an import from the United States—at times, in some of its variants, rightly so. But this does not do justice to the full range of Greek feminist mobilization and the salience of aspects of feminist critique to lived Greek realities.

The charge has also been redeployed in a clear attempt to contain a perceived threat and to protect the sexist structures of organizations of the Greek left, for example, from the impact of the feminist critiques many Greek women of the left launched or, more accurately, reignited in the 1960s. All critique of issues pertaining to women's rights is usually suspect as an exaggeration that might serve, if not capital's interests, as the old left used to have it, then certainly, as I believed, it might be an expression of what Nietzsche called *ressentiment,* the use of morality by the weak in a useless attempt to avenge the injustices of their station. Wendy Brown's (1991) work on modern and postmodern feminisms in the United States is an excellent analysis of the politics of this dynamic in late modernity or postmodernity, as she refers to the current era. Could it be that my response to what I was seeing was equivalent to a reactionary modern feminist ressentiment? I did not think so.

After some banter in the little room, a third woman in pink in the other room passed a little jar to the one in front of the window in the room we all were in. She got up and poured out its contents in the sink, where another doctor had just poured himself a drink of water. Some coffee cups were drying on the counter to the right. As Dr. Aspridaki and one of the ob/gyns continued to talk over my head, the midwife's eyes met mine. She smiled at me a little, and I smiled back. I gestured the question of what was in the jar, thinking it was some medicine or perhaps iodine. The conversation over my head paused and Dr. Aspridaki responded to my question by saying it contained *afta pou vgainoun apo ti mitra,* literally, "the things that come out of the uterus." The other midwife started telling me about how her daughter had been when she brought her here "just to see what happens." She told me she thought that if all adolescent girls could see an abortion, nobody would get pregnant unless they wanted to keep the child.

One of the doctors I had been introduced to before entered the room again. He was tall and very thin, compared to the short and meaty Dr. Theodorou that my aunt's colleague was having a somewhat strained conversation with.

The doctor who just entered caught a piece of the midwife's words to me and jumped in. He told me in great detail about his religious credentials: his wife's brother was a priest, his grandfather was a priest, he himself was an active member of the church of the village he was from. He said he was very concerned with the morality of abortion. On the one hand, he said, there is the church. On the other, there is the woman who is coming to her doctor for help. What are we supposed to do? Not help the woman who is asking for help? For the study to be done correctly, he told me, it needs to identify this conflict.

At this point, Dr. Theodorou also joined our conversation. He was very animated. He said one of the most important things was that, first of all, *o kathenas*, that is, anybody, and then all doctors especially, should be forbidden to appear on the media and offer their opinion about abortion. Several talk shows had focused on family planning, and one doctor in particular had been bringing up the demografiko and positioning abortion in its context as tantamount to a national evil. I smiled at Dr. Theodorou's comment and waited to hear more. Someone else interjected that Theodorou was still young and "searching himself" over abortion. At that point, Dr. Aspridaki, who had left the room momentarily, came back in and said she had been called to go upstairs. Would Dr. Theodorou take me on his rounds with him? He agreed.

The other doctor went into the room on the right and now two of the midwives were having a conversation about what they had cooked in the morning. Theodorou motioned to me and we were off for his *episkepseis*, the visits to patients of his who were in the hospital to give birth. We walked out of the cluster of rooms, down the long hall with the larger rooms of women recovering from abortions, and out the heavy metal door into the hospital proper. I was a bit confused about whether I would be able to see an abortion after all, but I decided to go with the flow.

We walked up two flights of stairs. Theodorou was talking the whole time. One comment he said stuck in my mind. He said the point was never to do anything for the money. That is, not to make the money a consideration in deciding whether or not to take on something. He said, "If you do it for the money, then it turns the other way, against you, in other words." He said he never accepted money, obviously meaning *extra* money above his fees, which were already quite high (though on a sliding scale when necessary, as he stressed). But his patients always brought him so many gifts, he said. One, whose husband owned a shoe store, brought him three pairs of shoes when his wife gave birth to a beautiful baby boy. Another, who is in the clothing business, brought him shirts. "Gifts," Theodorou said. "That's different."

We saw several women who had just given birth. One was just getting ready to leave with her new baby and had lots of questions concerning paying the clinic, paying the doctor, and how to be reimbursed by the state insurance. Theodorou appeared to be upfront in listening to her questions, but in the end his answer was that they'd talk later. Another who was also soon to leave was holding her baby son, called Kanaris, the name of a heroic fighter in Greece's struggle for independence. Theodorou made a fuss over the baby's name, proudly crooning over the baby, emphasizing that it was a heroic name. *It was almost as though he himself had created a national hero.* When he stopped to pet a new baby lying at the foot of the bed of a woman he had just chatted briefly with, he turned to me and said "See, these are what is being lost downstairs. If they saw these, nobody would do such things." *Afta einai pou hanondai kato.* The new mother in the bed looked at me with a surprisingly straight gaze. She did not say anything in agreement, or disagreement either. She was very young. I got the impression she had had an abortion herself, perhaps more than one, in the past. This was the only time Theodorou gave his patients any indication that I had any interest in, or even knowledge of, abortion per se as an activity going on in the clinic.

The way Theodorou introduced me changed as we proceeded through his rounds. Sometimes he just included me in his space, gesturing that we were together, maybe nodding in my direction to come in. Once he almost seemed to be showing me off as an affiliate of his; he said of me at that time that I was doing a study "on women and births." *Gia tis gynaikes kai tis genniseis.* Another time he said I was doing a study on "gynecological issues." When the mother of a new mother asked me if I was the clinic's social worker, I took his cue and ducked the question, answering that I was a sociologist. She said she had some questions and was hoping there might be someone to help her with them.

Theodorou and I visited another woman who had just given birth the day before. She had come to Artemis from the island of Rhodes because her doctor there had referred her to Theodorou. Her parents were in the room too. She was suffering from *sacharo,* a form of diabetes, and so apparently her pregnancy had been treated as high-risk. She hadn't yet been given pills to stop lactating and she told the doctor she was in pain. He reached down and touched one of her breasts over her nightgown very gingerly, almost tenderly. It felt strange to be watching this. I felt like an intruder, though nobody seemed to be showing any visible signs of discomfort. Except perhaps her father. He kept up an earnest monologue aimed at me about how wonderful a doctor Theodorou was and how he had helped his daughter. He labored over the details of the medication her Rhodes doctor had prescribed for her and then the treatments Theodorou had recommended at different points. He apologized to me when he could not remember the name of some of the drugs she had taken. Throughout this, Theodorou continued to handle the woman's breasts and talk from time to time.

The daughter in turn went on at great length about what an incredible man he was. She talked about his office and said she would like to send her Rhodes ob/gyn to see it so he could see what a doctor's office was supposed to look like.[2] When I think of it now, she and her mother may also have been feeling a bit strange, though perhaps more because there were witnesses to the doctor's apparent intimacy than because of the intimacy itself. Both went on at some length about how nice it was that Theodorou had his wife working as the receptionist in his office. Such a sweet woman, they both said. Had he met her in Germany when he was studying? When I eventually visited him in his office in several attempts to follow up on an offer he made that day to help me build my sample, I found out that his receptionist-wife spoke Greek with a strong foreign accent. This explained the question about where they had met.

We eventually left this room and went down to the doorway at the end of the hallway. Then he paused and said, "I have to check one more patient. Wait for me here." I waited a little bit further to the right, outside the open door of what looked to be an ultrasound examination room. A woman's belly was being scanned by a doctor who kept looking at the screen next to the woman's head. Some of the nurses walking by in the hall gave me odd looks. I was still wearing the green gynecologists' shirt but I obviously was not bustling along the way the doctors all seemed to do. Nor was I the right age, or sex. There are some female ob/gyns in Athens, but they are a very small minority. In my sample of the thirty ob/gyns I spoke with, only two were women and I searched hard to find them. Theodorou showed up a little later with wrapped packages which he said contained food. He told me patients brought him a lot of presents like that. Food, olive oil, also clothes. One man had a shoe store, he told me again, and brought him three pairs after his wife gave birth. A woman who had a clothes store gave him French shirts. As we walked down the stairs he again repeated that in his experience, he had found that if you do things for money, they turn around (or upside down). *Gyrizoun anapoda.* They go wrong, he meant. He certainly doth protest, I remember thinking at the time.

The fuller significance of his comment did not become apparent until later in the fieldwork, when I learned about the charged popularity and ongoing media debate concerning the notorious *fakellakia*. This word means "little envelopes," the not so discreet envelopes of money that have become a routine, and completely untaxable, part of remunerating doctors of all specialties for their services in both public and private sectors of the health care system in Greece. As one conservative estimation has it, approximately 30 percent of the Greek economy is believed to be "black."[3] Doctor's fakellakia, along with the pay of high school students' tutors for the entrance exams, are considered to be two large parts of Greece's black market. Reformation of the tax system involving different guestimates of an amount of income per doctor, based on his or her specialty, that comes from these envelopes was proposed in 1994. These envelopes had begun as gifts of a sort, like the tips people push into the hairdresser's pocket as they chat about how good the new cut looks. Of course, when we are talking about births, the evil eye connotations up the ante quite a bit; the thinking is that the happier the doctor is, the stronger his good wishes for the baby will be. Also, if a healthy baby was indeed delivered, it is only "right" to reward the doctor for his role. To not do so might be to risk the wrath of a God who would no doubt quickly humble the brazen. Nowadays, however, doctors are actually telling patients how much the clinic will cost, the nurse, his fees, and then, "And in an envelope, you will put X amount."

After his rounds, Theodorou wanted to go by the doctors' lounge. He pushed on a wood panel that looked exactly like the wall surrounding it. It was a door that opened into a relatively plush lounge with a big table and chairs on one end and more comfortable easy chairs scattered at the other end. Windows all around looked out on the clinic's patches of green, a few trees, and the big avenue beyond. I declined his offer of something to drink and had a seat where he pointed for me to sit.

Theodorou introduced me to two other doctors, saying I was doing research on *amvlosis*, the formal word for abortion. The first asked me the same question: What was I trying to find? *What indeed?* The connotations of this question are that there is nothing there and I am digging around for something that isn't there and, also important, that I am somehow implying there is wrongdoing going on. I said I was interested in what the reasons were for abortion from the women's point of view. In his experience, I asked, what seemed to be the reasons abortion was such a prevalent part of modern Greek reality?

He immediately noted that it was likely the case that a decline in abortion had recently begun. I asked him what he thought the causes for this decline might be. He said that part of the reason had to do with a change in women's sexuality. *Ehei allaxei I sexoualikotita ton gynaikon.* Perhaps too interested in what he meant by this, I asked him to elaborate without having first permitted him to conclude what he had clearly introduced as a list of causes for a decline. At this, he asked me if I had completed a *protokollo* (protocol). I was confused. Did he mean had I filed for permission to do this research at the clinic? Before I had a chance to respond in any way at all he turned to Theodorou and complained, as though I were not present, *"Xefevgei efkola apo to protokollo,"* meaning that I depart too easily from the protocol, which he had just asked me if I had. Theodorou glossed the implicit question, and the second doctor asked if my protocol took into account different parts of Athens. He suspected reasons for abortion might vary by neighborhood. Taking my cue from Theodorou again, I ignored the protocol part of his comment, which I simply did not understand, and said that he had a good point. Class differences might yield important differences, and in Greece, where sociologists have consistently lamented the difficulty of operationalizing class, neighborhoods might be a good index for class. He said no, it wasn't class differences he meant but neighborhood differences.

By this point, I was feeling pretty drained. Instead of asking him to elaborate on what he meant or trying to seem more interested, I turned to one of the other doctors and asked him what neighborhood his practice was located in. Then, not giving him the chance either to fully elaborate on his view of what the conclusions of the research I was in the midst of would assuredly be, I said that I hadn't yet contacted a doctor in his neighborhood and asked him if he would help me diversify the neighborhood of origin variable of my sample by putting me in touch with some of his clients.

In retrospect, this was one of those moments when I was simply too tired and no longer interested in playing the role I had decided I needed to play to facilitate the research. Instead of just letting him put in his two cents on what was "really" going on with abortion, as just about every doctor I had talked with that day had done, I was suggesting that he put his money where his mouth is and substantively help me to find out if what he was hypothesizing was true. He quickly leaned back in his chair, saying that Theodorou had many more clients than he and no doubt would help me a lot in that regard.

Eventually, Theodorou and I returned to the basement. Dr. Aspridaki also came back and, by now several hours later, I again sat on one of the stools in the little room in the back. She told me a little about her experience in medical school and how she used to be friends with my aunt. Then she said, "Let me go check what's happening, it is almost 1 P.M. now." When she returned she said we could go *mesa* (inside), where Dr. Milikakis *kani mia epemvasi*. This literally means that he is "doing one intervention," but, as I've said, in common Greek *epemvasi* has come to mean a medical operation as well. While much surgery today is called an *enhirisi*, it is also called an *epemvasi*. In this context, the correct translation of her statement is that he is performing an abortion. I got up and followed her back into the little anteroom and then through the door we had seen on our right when we first entered, into an operating room.

As we moved through the door, Tasi asked me in a hushed tone if I get dizzy, meaning, of course, do I get dizzy in such situations. Not wanting to disclose the real magnitude of my phobia, I said that yes, sometimes I did. She put her arm through the crook of my arm, as women who are friends sometimes do. But Tasi's arm was much more tightly around mine than I've ever felt this gesture before; my arm was snug against the side of her rib cage. We walked through the doorway and she steered us around to face the operating table.

The first thing I saw was a woman in bright pink at the far side of the table. She was standing up, hovering, a little to the right of the doctor, who was sitting on a stool facing both the doorway we had just come through and the butterfly-shaped outspread legs of a person who was lying down on a "boom," the gynecological table with stirrups, in front of him. I had seen those legs before. Not those particular ones, but that positioning and that weird shape. At the time of my visit to Artemis, still early in the research, I had probably witnessed around forty gynecological exams taking place in the mornings at the state-run Family Planning Center. But there the women were conscious. And the doctors were medical students in training who were always just a little nervous, no matter how well they mastered the required bravado for their performance. Here the doctor seemed completely at ease, and the woman whose legs I saw was unconscious. The doctor also wore a different uniform here, a long white bib-type apron across the whole front of his body. Complete with splatters of blood. It really was a lot like what most butchers in Athens wear, a parallel that does echo the popular reference to doctors considered to have harmed a patient with their inadequacy. The stool the doctor was sitting on had wheels and he was scooting around a bit, always within the space delineated by the legs of the woman in the stirrups. As though I had just walked into a building after having been out in the bright sun, I felt I was still adjusting and not at all clear on what was happening.

My eyes went up to the woman's arm, where I saw the rubber tie used to help the veins stick out for the anesthesia shot. Quickly I looked elsewhere. I could hear the low whir of something. The doctor was holding a long thin metal object. I heard Tasi's voice next to me saying in a loud, official-sounding voice, "This is Dr. Milikakis." She introduced me as "the niece of a colleague" who was "doing a study on abortion for her master's."

Was it so inconceivable, I wondered again, that there be a doctoral dissertation focused on abortion? Or was it that it was hard to understand that someone who looked like me—young, female—was doing a doctoral dissertation? Perhaps everything fades together after the master's from the perspective of an outsider. Actually, a Ph.D. is the only thing that is somewhere between equal to a practicing M.D. and trumping it in the Greek educational system's hierarchy, so there might have been more at stake in this innocent-seeming confusion. Either way, I was sure how I looked was also an important factor.

The woman lying on the table looked *very* young, fifteen or sixteen. And she was very big. At that moment, her flesh seemed to be everywhere. The long green robe worn by women having an abortion at Artemis was open and pushed up. Her pubic hair, reddish-brown, was exposed and I could see two large folds of skin, the lower part of her abdomen, immediately above it. Her face was turned toward the doorway, right where I stood. She looked as if she was fast asleep. Her arms were spread wide open. *Like eagle's wings.* I guessed for access. Tasi continued to speak, again with the tone of voice of one who is playing the role of teacher and working hard to maintain a natural frame over and against any other frames that might be floating around. *Like crime, I thought to myself. But not because of anything being done to the fetus.*

Now Tasi said, "Here we have one woman." *Edo ehoume mia gynaika.* The doctor smiled up at Tasi and quickly looked me over. I knew that gaze. I pretended not to, looking back in that flat, maybe-I'm-a-bit-dumb way I had learned to use to put those who felt threatened at ease, sexuality-wise and brain-wise. Then he spoke. He said, carefully underlining some words, "*If* we could ever call what you see here on the table *a woman.*" The room exploded into laughter! I was confused.

From the time I was a young child taken from New York City's Upper West Side St. Hilda's and St. Hugh's private Episcopalian *nun* school (as my sister and I would later refer to it in our own rendition of the Greek reference to such schools in Greece), where I had been placed by my mother and my father, who was then a professor of electrical engineering at Columbia, and plunged into the third grade of Paleo Psyhico's elite private Moraitis School in 1974—after the U.S.-backed dictatorship and at the beginning of a new period of pronounced anti-American sentiment in Greece—I had learned to smile, brace myself a bit, and quietly ask "Why?" to jokes that I didn't understand.

There were many. Perceived by my classmates at that time to be less of a Greek than they were (which I suppose made sense, as I was only then learning the Greek alphabet, whereas they had already started to learn how to read), and certainly some sort of proxy for the U.S. government, often the jokes made in my milieu were not at all funny. Now again, as the laughter of the doctor, the midwife, and the anesthesiologist surrounded me, I felt the wisps of an old familiar dread.

Spontaneously, I reached for the tried and true. I automatically smiled in the vague direction of the doctor, leaning into Tasi a bit, and quietly asked "Why?" Looking back at this, I can best understand that "why," especially from its quietness, as an attempt to gain time to recover from the disorientation I was experiencing. *Why else, after all?* Tasi bent toward me as the midwife across the room and the doctor kept laughing loudly. Tasi said firmly, *"Giati einai vodi."* Because she is a cow.[4]

I could not believe it. I would like to have been able not to be shocked, but I was. I had prided myself on never being shocked by anything. Nothing I saw, nothing I was told, nothing that was done to me. And that added up to a bit. Suddenly, one little word, *vodi,* seemed to have gotten me. I just could not believe it. And for some reason, my mind centered in on money as a way to keep moving forward. I kept thinking, she's paid 30,000 drachmas or more for this.[5] They took her money. Not only that, they *want* her money. Meanwhile, the lesson was continuing. Tasi was naming some of the medical instruments for me, telling me the midwife's name.[6] The doctor, whose smile had already been making me sick, now looked revolting. My field of vision suddenly was awash with shadows, and small lights started exploding behind my eyes. Sounds dropped away. I knew the signs. I gently tapped Tasi's arm and moved toward the door.

Tasi quickly removed us from the operating room and returned us to the back room with the stools. She sat down herself and told me to sit. She did not in any way show that I might have become dizzy. She didn't ask me how I was or give any sign that something might be wrong. She continued with her lesson in a voice that seemed to say that the rest was routine, there was no reason to be standing up in there. By now it was clear to me that she was afraid and had a stake in making things look like nothing was out of the ordinary. Anyway, she said twice, the whole operation takes about three minutes. *We aren't missing anything.*

In her description of the actual medical actions involved, which she proceeded with at that time, an abortion includes both *aporofisi* (suction) and *apoxynsi* (scraping). As I was told later, apoxynsi now only happens with pregnancies that are past the first trimester. It takes too much time, and effort, on the part of the doctor. It is also not supposed to be as safe. The machine used for aporofisi, called simply *to mihanima*, can much more easily and safely evacuate the uterus of its contents. Some versions of it, Tasi said, also have a blade around the mouth of the suction cup so that it is scraping at the same time that the suctioning is going on. With regard to the anesthesia, the women are injected with a mild anesthetic to put them out for a few minutes.

My mind was wandering. The whirring sound of the other room felt like it was now trapped inside my head. While we were talking, or pretending to, one of the women in pink handed something to another of the women in pink, through the little window. The same jar I had seen coming through earlier. Its contents were again poured down the sink. This time I didn't wonder what it was or where it came from. I just kept thinking how strange it was that this little jar would move back and forth through that bizarre little movie-theater-like window, passed along from the hands of one woman wearing bright pink to those of another woman wearing bright pink while one or two green-dressed men stood in the room chatting, smoking, or, as one doctor did just then, opening up the little fridge to the left of the sink looking for something to eat.

When I got home that afternoon, I called one of my best friends in the States. I didn't want to think about the cost of the call. I told him I thought the fieldwork would be done soon, hopefully in six months rather than the year I had planned for. I also told him I was feeling very nauseous. As it turned out, the nausea wouldn't go away, even after our conversation. I cancelled my afternoon appointments and lay down with a book. I couldn't read. When I finally fell asleep, it was a very deep sleep. As I drifted off, I couldn't get my mind to switch off. It kept going back to a joke I had heard a few days ago on SKY, one of the Greek radio channels.

> One morning a wife says to her husband: "Apostoli, Apostoli, the light isn't working." The husband says, "I'm not an electrician, woman, I'm a man." Then the wife says: "Apostoli, the sink is dripping." The husband responds, "I'm not a plumber, woman, I'm a man." Before he leaves for work, the woman says: "Apostoli, the furniture's leg is crooked." Apostoli retorts, "Woman, I'm not a carpenter, I'm a man." When Apostoli comes back from work that day the sink isn't dripping, the bureau does not slant anymore, and the light is working. "What happened, woman?" She tells her husband that she called the technician and he came. When he came, she says, he said he would

In the Operating Room

take care of everything if she sang for him, or if she got into bed with him. Apostoli says, "And of course you sang for him, woman." The wife responds: "Apostoli, Apostoli, I'm not a singer, I'm a woman."[7]

So who is a woman in Greece, I wondered as I drifted off to sleep. *Vodi, vodi*. That's what the research is about: plotting the coordinates of that social formation. And the fetus, being removed in the room next to the smoke-filled room, like a smoking gun, may help me trace the sociopolitical forces involved in this formation. Judging from the Apostoli anecdote, being a woman in Greece is a subject position that is centrally oriented around having sex. Gender itself clearly is an arena of contestation, given the adamant proclamations of what it means to be a man or a woman, as in the joke on the radio, and, remembering the doctor's comment, what type of gendered being does not count as a woman. Meanwhile, Theodorou's hands kept fondling a swollen breast. In a somewhat bizarre moment of that twilight zone between being asleep and being awake, and still fighting a now more low-grade feeling of nausea, I remembered the children's nursery rhyme about the cow that flew over the moon. Was the cow singing as it flew, I wondered half-asleep. And what was the moon? Was it Greece?

> I kept falling and falling, and I didn't even know who had thrown me. Around me, my girlfriends were disappearing, with skirts flying like the fins of fish around a stone that is falling. A green apple was in my hand, and as much as I went down, so it would turn red, maturing quickly within the fall. It isn't possible, I'd say inside of me. Any minute now the reverse push would come, that would send me straight up, escorted by a mass of triumphant bubbles.
>
> A cold ground accepted me, and held me. The apple in my hand, deep deep red. Nobody was coming.
> (Papageorgiou 1986; my translation)

Chapter 6

GIVE BIRTH FOR GREECE!
ABORTION AND NATION IN
THE GREEK PRESS

✥

"For every one birth, we have two abortions!"[1] This was the headline of a story published in the right-wing daily newspaper *Apogevmatini* (25 August 1993). Next to it was a drawing of a stork holding a bundle in its mouth and flying through a big cloud. On the bundle were the letters "SOS." The article told the story of a nation in crisis, of women who seemed to be having too many abortions and not enough babies, and of the existence of an important relationship between the two. In a contemporary variation of the ancient Greek saying that the biggest enemies of man are fire, woman, and water (*pyr, gini kai idor*), Greek women are portrayed here as the root of Greece's current problems.

Apogevmatini tends to be a fairly sensationalist right-wing daily, but this article emblematizes the mainstream Greek media's coverage of abortion and the demografiko. In this coverage, abortion seems to act as a lightning rod for deeply rooted cultural anxieties. Abortion in Greece is a multifaceted social phenomenon situated within fields of power shaped by particular historical relationships among the public sphere, sexuality, and the female body. As such, its coverage in the press constitutes a unique vantage point from which to view the cultural and political terrain animating current national debates, including the largest one, that of modernization.

At the present, a heated debate is taking place on how best to modernize Greece so as to bolster what is seen as its vulnerable position in the European Union, in the Balkans in general, and vis-à-vis Turkey in particular. I suggest that the specific characteristics of public consternation with abortion in Greece offer important clues revealing a largely unacknowledged common ground that is shared by the various narratives of Greek national identity circulating in the public sphere at the present.[2] This territory is marked by a belief in Greece as a religious entity, and it is shared by the press of the right, the center, and, to a lesser degree, the left alike.

As this chapter shows, the demografiko offers itself as a site for funneling the increasingly strong internal tensions that Greece faces as it crafts its own modernity. On the one hand, there is the perception of heightened danger at Greece's contested geographic borders; on the other, there is the challenge of reformulating a domestic policy that might begin to respond adequately to the conflicting demands presented by a series of long-standing problems (such as the burgeoning public service sector) and the quickly growing influence of transnationalism and the resulting waves of immigrants who entered the country during the 1990s. In this context, I argue, the demografiko operates as a powerful reproductive technology that contributes to the ongoing state-building project of policing particular configurations of race, religion, gender, and sexuality as properly "Greek," while excluding others. In addition, positioning the high rate of abortion and the low rate of births as problems threatening the country's future welfare serves as an effective coping mechanism that manages tensions resulting from the new patterns of immigration and capital consolidation while also inhibiting the interrogation of other sites about the sources of Greece's problems. Serving, in effect, as a repository or safe space for those conceptions about nationhood and personhood that are increasingly disallowed in other realms of the public sphere, demografiko coverage offers a starkly clear view of the preconceptions characterizing the Greek national imaginary at the present.

As my fieldwork revealed, the beliefs about abortion and the demografiko that are legitimized in the public sphere are different from those articulated by women in less public settings. The views analyzed in this chapter are specific to this site: published letters to the editor concerned with the demografiko and/or abortion are typically written by retired high-ranking public officials or by active middle-range public servants, almost all of whom are male. They also offer a condensed form of the themes that nevertheless reverberate in other parts of the formally recognized public sphere, as well as in narratives articulated by the women with whom I spoke. The grammar of the demografiko as a socially constructed public problem is presented in these letters. Thus, they reveal the largely unacknowledged common ground that is shared by the various narratives of Greek national identity circulating in the public sphere at present.

In this chapter, I compare the right and centrist coverage of the demografiko and in so doing plot the coordinates of that "Greece" that lies at the heart of the representatives of the two political domains that together have accounted for approximately 85 percent of the vote during the past decade. My objective is to sketch the half-buried vision of Greece that is haunting popular and policy imaginings of Greek nationhood at the present moment. Toward this end, I look to the Greek mainstream media's concern with the birth rate and with abortion throughout 1994, the year of Greece's second term presiding over the Council of the European Union.[3] I focus on the letters that were chosen for publication by the editors of the moderately right-wing *Kathimerini* and centrist *Ta Nea, To Vema,* and *Eleftherotypia*.[4]

The nationalist narratives occurring in the right and centrist sectors of the Greek press have in common a particular image of Greece as a form of a *religious state*.[5] This is somewhat surprising, given the preoccupation with modernizing Greece and consolidating its identity as an ostensibly secular liberal democratic state. Equally surprising is another finding: that the notion of abortion that is associated with this conception of the Greek ethnos does not rely on the concept of sin—not, that is, the concept of a sin against God. Rather, abortion is seen as a sin *against the nation*. I conclude this chapter by suggesting that if openly acknowledged, debated, and strategically redeployed, this already dominant image of Greece might actually help move Greece out of its current foreign and domestic impasses, including the paradox presented by strong public concern with the birth rate and abortion, on the one hand, and the persistently high rate of abortions performed on the other. I also gesture toward the critique of demografiko discourses that is put forward by the women I spoke with and discussed and analyzed in the final chapter of this book.

Narrating the Nation

Following especially from Hobsbawm and Ranger's edited collection *The Invention of Tradition* (1983) and Benedict Anderson's *Imagined Communities: Reflections on the Origin and Spread of Nationalism* (1983), I assume that the "nation" is itself a historical construct that has become naturalized in various discourses. One of the most powerful clusters of these discourses involve the nationalisms that emerge in the nation-states of modernity. As Anderson argues, the novel, and literature more generally, has served as an important instrument in the process of naturalizing both the category and the content of "the nation" in many regions.[6] Anderson's attention to the novel has led to serious consideration of literature and how it produces particular "imaginings of the nation." However, he also stresses that the press has played a key role in the process of forming and reforming the imagined community of the nation.[7] The significance of the press continues to be central for Greece, despite changes in the telecommunication industry, including the pronounced role of television in disseminating the news.

There is much being said about deployments of the past in the project of forging a contemporary national identity.[8] Greek work in this vein tends to focus on literary and historical texts. For example, a collection of work that also addresses the narratives of nation and gender that make up "Greece" (Kalogeras and Pastourmatzi 1996) focuses exclusively on literary texts. *Topographies of Hellenism* by Artemis Leontis (1995) offers insight into the nineteenth-century foreign imaginings of Greek nationhood and twentieth-century images of Greece primarily in the poetry of Seferis and Elytis. An important explication of the historical strands in the nexus of discourses making up "Greece," Stathis Gourgouris's *Dream Nation: Enlightenment, Colonization, and the Institution of Modern Greece* (1996), explores the vision of Greece that directly informed the establishment of the modern Greek nation-state.

THE PUBLIC SPHERE IN GREECE

Before proceeding, I would like to say more about my use of the term "public sphere" in the Greek context. The definition proposed by Habermas (1991, 398) helps establish a frame of reference:

> By "public sphere" we mean first of all a domain of our social life in which such a thing as public opinion can be formed. Access to the public sphere is open in principle to all citizens. . . . Citizens act as a public when they deal with matters of general interest without being subject to coercion; thus with the guarantee that they may assemble and unite freely, and express and publicize their opinions freely. When the public is large, this kind of communication requires certain means of dissemination and influence; today, newspapers and periodicals, radio and television are the media of the public sphere. We speak of a political public sphere (as distinguished from a literary one, for instance) when the public discussions concern objects connected with the practice of the state.

Certainly the situation Habermas describes is best understood along the lines of a Weberian "ideal type." As Fraser (1992) systematically shows, Habermas's concept is highly problematic as a way of describing the current state of affairs in the United States. His definition of the public sphere is also far from the specific arena of agon that the Greek press today continues to constitute.

However, for issues of the state, as Habermas puts it, the Greek press does operate as a central forum for discussion or argument as well as a key institution affecting legislation and policy decisions. My method of analysis focuses on the various discourses that are articulated by different segments of the press (rather than "voices" and the unitary individual speaker which that presupposes) and I am concerned with charting their unlikely shared alliance in forming a particular image of Greece. Habermas's vision of the public sphere as an arena in which equal and autonomous citizens all have a chance at a say is incommensurate with an understanding of the public sphere as a site where polysemic discourses are both joined and ripped apart in often unpredictable ways. His concept nevertheless captures what the Greek press in many ways claims to be, and is indeed largely seen as being.

In fact, in a recent collection of essays on Greek politics and culture, Tsoukalas, a prominent intellectual and professor of political science at the University of Athens who is also said to serve as a confidante and advisor to Prime Minister Simitis, has an essay on the law passed several years ago to prevent the press from publishing the communiqués of terrorists acting in Greece. I quote at some length from this essay as it sheds light on the specificities of the formal Greek public sphere at the present.

> In societies founded on the principles of indirect representative democracy, the citizens neither exercise nor control power. The *demos* is separated from the "state." Inevitably, the political, social, and ideological mandates slip away from the direct control and opinion of the *demos* and are named, delimited, discussed, and joined only in the framework of the appropriate political institutions and representatives. A decisive political intervention—in other words, a powerful opinion—is expressed only one day every four years with the vote. In the interval, the *demos* is left to mutter, to complain, and to wait, or is advised to forget and encouraged to be indifferent. Even if the citizen has a voice and a position, there is no way for that vote to be promoted, for it to be made a political act.
>
> Under these conditions, the press offers the only possibility for the practical promotion and publication of dissenting political discourse. The press is discourse in action and its *vema* (platform) is the poor contemporary substitute for the *vema* of the *ekklisia tou demou*. (1996, 100)

As Tsoukalas suggests, to the extent that the debates the Greek press hosts, and provokes, powerfully influence and reflect both popular and elite conceptions of nation and person as well as the state's concrete actions in Parliament or outside it, the press can be considered the heart of Greece's public sphere. In referring to it as such, I hope to highlight the ongoing significance of the press in Greece as a site for negotiating, contesting, and rationalizing state and culture alike. At the same time, my analytic focus, a demonstration of struggle and stakes, should work to challenge any sterilized postulation of a serene and firmly bounded public sphere.[9]

Mapping with nuance the cultural terrain being contested in the press, Diamandouros (1993) argues that two cultures are dominant: the Balkan-Ottoman–Greek Orthodox (or "underdog") culture, and the Enlightenment-liberal-democratic-Westernizing (or "reformist") culture. Expanding on this schema, Mouzelis (1995, 20) suggests that Diamandouros's underdog culture can be further separated into two distinct subtypes, the clientelistic and the populist, and that it is the latter, with its emphasis on *laos* (the folk, or the people) and *romiosini* (Greekness, a specific term of Greek culture foregrounding a tradition of resistance and courage), that is dominant.[10]

Similarly, Danforth (1995) argues that Greece displays two forms of nationalism: "primordial" and "modernist-constructivist."[11] Meanwhile, Herzfeld (1987) contends that all Greek nationalism at present fits into the "primordial" category. In my analysis of both the press material and the narratives of the women I interviewed, I find evidence of two distinct registers of nationalism that I refer to as "fundamentalist" and "modernizing." However, the discursive context of the specific textual evidence relating to each suggests that the modernizing nationalist rhetoric in effect consists of a particular strain of what I call fundamentalist nationalism rather that being completely separate from it. Thus the findings of my research support Herzfeld's postulation.

Meanwhile, as noted, the public sphere is once more the stage for an extensive and ongoing scholarly and media-based project examining how Greece is to go about the process of modernization.[12] Yet, given the fault lines of Greek political culture, as well as other aspects of modern Greek life, is it possible to speak of a common vision of Greece? What, in other words, might constitute the negotiable but mostly unacknowledged basis of the particular "imagined community" that is Greece at the present historical moment? Which polis haunts the diverse contemporary imaginings of the Greek nation? While the public debate on how best to modernize the Greek nation-state continues, this chapter closely examines some of the press discourse on the tandem issue of the demografiko and shows that in fact the bedrock of the contesting images of Greek national welfare is not, in the end, that of the *secular* modern nation-state.

The Respectable Right: Letters to Kathimerini

In a long letter to the editor entitled "Justifiable Anxiety," a retired member of the Supreme Court, Dimitris Tzoumas expresses his opinion on the current state of the nation.[13] In this context, he puts in relief what he sees as salient aspects of the present historical moment. I quote from this letter at length, italicizing phrases that are recurring tropes in demografiko discourse:

> The anxiety felt by the readers of *Kathimerini* for this country's present and future is apparent in the letters they write about her.[14] An exemplary case was that of Mr. Andreas Lazaris, an architect who in a letter published here on 22 December 1993 first laments the situation in which the country finds itself and the reasons that have caused this situation (geographical location, occupation, civil war, partisan state, the weaknesses of Greeks, etc.) and then adds: "The future does not bode well. I've lost my sleep. I wake up at daybreak. I read poetry . . ." This anxiety of the readers is well placed since we are indeed going through a difficult and critical period *as much for Hellenism as for Orthodoxy* because both have many difficult problems to solve and are facing serious dangers in a "society of decadence" indifferent, one would think, to the dangers that threaten her and with a strong tendency toward comfort and easy wealth, which the state itself cultivates with the various lotteries, Propo, Lotto, etc.
>
> This is a society in which we have the free operation of groups and organizations of satanists, *of heretics, of pseudomessiahs and parareligions*[15] but also various associations that are founded by and dependent upon *invisible centers abroad,*[16] under the guise of mutual aid and philanthropy. These serve foreign interests and plans unknown to their members. In addition, they undo the social foundations of our country. I would say that a serious reason for this anxiety, aside from the prevailing uncertainty and instability in the Balkans at the present, is *the zone created around Greece of non-friendly and allied states*. This zone starts from the Ionian Sea, covers almost all of the northern borders of the country and ends up in the southeast Aegean. Of course this zone does not create an immediate threat right now. However, the same won't be true in the future. And we should not delude ourselves with the idea that our country is a member of NATO and the EU. We have bitter experience with the so-called aid of our friends and allies. *Our age-old "friends" are waiting*. At the first opportunity, they will commit on the islands of the Aegean exactly what they committed on Cyprus. If we are not in a position to repel them, nobody will help us. Whoever has helped us has done so because their own interests were served too.

Another serious reason [that the future of the country does not bode well] is *the demographic problem*. This is very grave according to the experts, since births keep decreasing, creating the danger that in a few years Greece will be a country of old people. *This problem is mainly created by the low birth rate, which is due to (a) the approximately 300,000 abortions (embryocides) that happen in our country ever year,* (b) the lack of faith in God and moral decline of society, (c) economic causes, and (d) urbanization, which has changed the structure of the Greek family and *woman's exit* [sic] into the professional arena (*stivo*). A secondary factor contributing to the demografiko lies in the many deaths from (a) car accidents, (b) use of narcotics, and (c) acts of violence.

A third reason is the financial affairs of the state. They are in a worrisome condition. Suffice to say here that the public deficit (internal and external) was 253 billion drachmas in 1979, 942.8 in 1983 and 24,186.6 in 1993 (*Ikonomiki Kathimerini*, 4 January 1994). This happened, naturally, because we all try persistently to improve our finances either at the expense of the finances of the state (with strikes, lawsuits, etc.) or *by being indifferent* toward the state's finances. The state then is forced to cover its pressing needs with one loan after another and not with hard—yes, but just—taxation which is preferable to the excessive borrowing that, in the end, will hurt us and our children. In addition, tax-evasion becomes a permanent condition.

I have quoted this letter at length not because it was written by a retired member of Greece's Supreme Court and hence says something about the worldview ruling Greece, but because it stands as a miniature and yet very rich tapestry of the preoccupations, even obsessions, that characterize Greek politics at the moment. Many of these preoccupations also reverberate, and a few are challenged, in the narratives of the women I interviewed.

The excerpt highlights the currently hegemonic Greek matrix of nationhood and, in so doing, also highlights one way abortion is defined within this rubric. The 300,000 abortions, or "embryocides," as the judge calls abortions in a parenthesis, are only slightly less of a threat to Greece than are its allegedly hostile neighbors and proliferating domestic "heretics" discussed in the first few paragraphs of the letter. Indeed, if the ordering of factors implies a corresponding hierarchy of value, the abortions are more important than the nation's bleak financial status, although this rhetoric certainly suggests that the former are related to the latter by way of a self-absorption leading to an indifference to higher values. In this letter, the highest value at stake is the good of the *Greek Orthodox nation-state*. Moreover, even in the strongly religious context of this letter, abortion is a problem not because it runs counter to the divine gift of human life, for example, but because it undermines the specifically Greek Orthodox nation's welfare.

That the author calls abortion *emvrioktonia* instead of *paidoktonia* (the Greek term for both infanticide and the murder of older children) might be taken as further rhetorical evidence for a view of abortion that is only remotely about the taking of a human life, as fetal rights discourse in the United States argues, for example. The word embryocide clearly denotes a killing; indeed, it could be argued that the specification of the embryo, that is, of the maximally innocent victim, might indicate an understanding that abortion is actually worse than killing an infant or older child. However, both the immediate and the larger contexts of the letter suggest that the crime's atrocity is not based on a sense of what is being removed from the uterus as the victim of a murder but rather is based on a sense of the impact of that removal *on the nation*. What is of paramount importance, it seems, is that the woman who has an abortion is jeopardizing the well-being of the specifically Greek Orthodox nation rather than jeopardizing the embryo's spirit.[17] This is a very particular politicoreligious understanding of abortion.

Another letter, this one by a retired Air Force general, again shows a concern for the integrity of the nation, although this time concern for its spiritual integrity overshadows concern for its territorial integrity.[18] The writer responds to an earlier article, printed in *Kathimerini*, by the director of the press of the Greek Orthodox Holy Synod, I. Hatdzifotis. The latter is quoted as saying, "The church expresses concern . . . it is a disgusting way of removing life . . . that creates huge problems for the woman, not only psychologically, but also gynecologically." Karathanasis says, "To this we will add *'and spiritual problems' that concern our entire nation*." Notably, Hatdzifotis has not humanized the embryo in any way; nor, indeed, has he expressed concern for its spiritual well-being. He decries abortion not as an action "removing life" but as "a disgusting way" to do so that also creates "huge problems" *for the woman*. The general deploys a more stringent religious discourse. Where the Church's formal representative claims to see abortion's costs primarily in terms of the woman—"not only psychologically, but also gynecologically"—and not in terms of anyone's sin, Karathanasis plainly states that he will "add" to the Church's view. In so doing, he worries especially about abortion's impact on the nation by way of its assumed connection to "spiritual problems." This comment looks like a veiled reprimand to the Greek Orthodox Church for not appropriately safeguarding *the nation's* well-being and instead mistakenly, as is implied, fretting over the woman's physical and emotional health. On the other hand, Hatdzifotis's quote could easily be read as precisely a concern for

γυναίκες στην πρώτη γραμμή

Figure 13. Greece of 1919: the priest family with his wife looking on "imperiously." Used by permission of the Rizario Foundation, reprint from *Images of Greece* by Fred Boissounas, Rizario Foundation publication. Greece of 2000: Some of the few women elected to Parliament perched between the demanding norms of appropriate femininity, the maps of power, and their own strength. The shifting ground of national identity and gender is put in relief in the juxtaposition of these images. They also illustrate the friction between traditional Greek Orthodox nationhood and modern Greek femininities.

the woman's physical ability (including emotional strength) to do exactly what Karathanasis wants her to do: biologically reproduce the nation.

Could the retired officer be strategically redeploying religious discourse to reinforce his own (militaristic) image of national welfare? Probably not. On the contrary, he seems to be enlisting a secular idea of the nation in the service of a strongly religious nationalist program. The exact nature of the "spiritual problems" to which he refers becomes clearer as he continues:

> Since 1986 (law no. 1609), abortions have been legal and performed at the state's expense. The cost? It reaches up to 30 billion per year. Keep in mind that after 1833 abortion was a crime and the perpetrator was punished. What changed after 1986? Retired Archbishop Yeronimos asks: "*Because, for example, adultery (or abortion) is not punished anymore by the law, has it stopped being a sin?*" This question, which is also my own, concludes, "Do these laws of ours cease to be contrary to the Lord's commandments? Are we crazy? Are we serious or are we kidding ourselves? If we are kidding ourselves, we cannot fool God. 'Do not be deceived; God is not mocked, for whatever a man sows, that he will also reap' (Galatians 6:7). Let us see, then, what we are sowing so that we may know, too, what we shall harvest. *We are sowing death in 'defenseless beings' and creating a demographic problem.*" (emphasis added)

Here again, the demografiko is presented as a major national problem and abortion is given as its major cause. After a brief foray into some of the statistics of the demografiko, the writer of this letter returns, as he does at the end of the excerpt above, to charged tones and a specifically Christian religious discourse:

> The warning in the New Testament was clear: "And since they did not see fit to acknowledge God, God gave them up to a base mind and to improper conduct. They were filled with all manner of wickedness, evil, covetousness, malice. Full of envy, murder . . . Though they know God's decree that those who do such things deserve to die, they not only do them but approve those who practice them" (Romans 1:28–32). In other words, judgment from now to eternity!

Having reached this high pitch, the letter concludes:

> Let us do a simple calculation: The moral accessories, according to the above excerpt from the New Testament, include all those who agree with the 300,000 abortions that happen every year (although according to others they reach 500,000). They come to a total of more than two million people: the couple (legal or illegal), the obstetrician, the anesthesiologist, a nurse, and even just

one member of the circle of friends, giving a total of 7 individuals times 300,000 equals 2,100,000 people per year.

... We propose: *To return to our Orthodox roots, to become conscious Christians and to trust God so that our course can be toward eternity before it is too late ... too late for our Nation!!* (emphasis added)

Here the liberal humanist discourse of the state and its laws, along with its accompanying constructions of consent and agency as residing within the single individual, is clearly enlisted in the service of a Greek Orthodox religious state and the traces of a more collective configuration of personhood. We must strengthen our formally religious Christianity if we really wish to preserve the nation. It seems quite clear, however, that it is the Greek Orthodox part of this, rather than the secular Greek nation-state, and its variously religious citizenry, that is the primary concern.

Similar sentiments are expressed in a letter published in *Kathimerini* written by the priest of the church of St. Fotini on the island of Kalymnos.[19] Again there is an intriguing deployment of "embryos," this time by a clergyman, but this letter helps to show that the Greek Orthodox Church itself does not in fact have a monolithic position on abortion. Indeed, typically the lay clergy express less severe opinions on abortion than do members of the higher levels of the ecclesiastical hierarchy, such as the Church's spokesperson, Hatdzifotis. But here the opposite is the case. The letter that *Kathimerini* chose to publish was written by a lay clergyman very strongly opposed to abortion. A consideration of this letter permits a glimpse of the complex terrain of Greek Orthodox meanings of abortion, as well as of the ongoing interpenetration of the formal political and religious orders in Greece today. An early sentence reads:

During the premiership of Mr. A. Papandreou, law 1609/86 was passed, which tolerates and incites abortions with the expenses paid by the Greek people; thus, according to the relevant statistics, each year from 300,000 to 400,000 embryos are killed before they even see the light of life, with the result that every three years 1,200,000 infants are killed, exactly as many [of us] as the eternal enemies *of faith and of our nation,* Muslim Turks, slaughtered during the Asia Minor disaster of 1922. (emphasis added)

Here we see first how the enemy "of faith" and "of our nation" is one and the same: Muslim Turks. In equating the number of abortions per three years to the number of Greeks killed during the war with the Ottoman Empire, the paper gives a vivid picture of how abortion is also used to effect the domestication of the nation's enemy. Whoever is responsible for the abortions is bad, evidently, by dint of being responsible for violence against the nation; indeed, abortion is likened to a crime exactly equal to one of the greatest acts of war against Greece still alive in popular collective memory.

Moreover, the letter continues by referring to the demografiko, and in so doing does not consider the high rate of abortion a problem in itself. Rather, it is the demografiko that makes it a problem: "The demographic problem of Greece today is severe, since *to preserve our existence as a nation* we must have 2.4% births annually whereas today we have no more than 1.7%. It follows that we are progressing toward self-destruction and extinction [*afanismo*]" (emphasis added). Here the reference to "[our] extinction" clearly connotes a racial component to Greekness. At the same time, the letter also makes use of a common trope of Greek liberal democratic discourse—"constitutionality"— an issue raised frequently by different sectors of the Greek legislature to contest unpopular legislation. The letter continues:

> At the same time, basic articles of the current Constitution, which institutes Eastern Orthodox Christianity as the formal religion of the nation, and which condemns abortion as a disgusting crime, are being violated.
>
> As a result, the law carries the obvious signs of unconstitutionality and must be annulled as soon as possible; otherwise all of the Orthodox Christian populace of Greece, in order to protect Greece from extinction [afanismo], will assume all the rights that are legal and which follow from the Constitution, since the Greek nation was destined to live and enact its destined role.

Almost all the letters of *Kathimerini* seem to rely on an enmeshed religio-national discourse to make a case against abortion because, in various ways, they find the Greek nation-state's welfare to be specifically and uniquely linked to the populace's *Greek Orthodox* religion. The preservation of the Greek Orthodox Christian *ethnos* emerges as the primary reason the Greek nation's survival is vital and abortion is bad. However, in the case of this priest's letter, the initially strongly stated position on abortion as sin does not lead as clearly to the same conclusion. Just as the Church's official representative unexpectedly considered abortion a problem because of its impact on a woman's physical and emotional (not spiritual) health, so here too, the priest may be seen as making an unexpected move. Specifically, in this letter the Greek nation is *not* clearly positioned as having a unique or privileged destiny because of its Greek Orthodox religion. As the last sentence of the previous excerpt suggests, and as what follows also indicates, the priest might also be articulating a more generalized concern with the future of Greece as a God-loving nation, not a specifically Greek Orthodox nation that is better than other types of religious nations. Regarding Greece's destiny, he speaks of "the peaceful, and in the love of the Lord, survival of peoples on Earth and the spiritual elevation of the peoples' level."

Finally, the letter ends with an interesting gesture. Keeping in mind the fevered pitch of the conclusions of the letters previously discussed, compare the ending of this letter: "Note that the Catholic Church and the Muslims strictly forbid abortion—an action that constitutes a common position for the three religions" (i.e., for Catholicism, Islam, and Orthodoxy). Most letters on the demografiko subordinate an opposition to Greek abortion to claims in favor of the inherent superiority of Greek Orthodoxy as a religion and, even more, of Greek Orthodox nationhood. Any move of potential solidarity with Islam, even an entirely strategic one, would not be possible in their register. In the priest's letter, arguments against abortion and for the survival of the Greek nation as *generically* God-loving are primary, whereas the particular uniqueness of the Greek Orthodox nation as well as the Greek Orthodox religion might be seen as secondary. Indeed, to underscore the significance of a position against abortion, the priest ends by aligning Greek Orthodoxy with both Catholicism and Islam, a surprising move given the strong anti-Muslim sentiment permeating not only demografiko discourse specifically but popular Greek culture as well. This move may well be provocative. That is, the priest might be suggesting that if even the (*justly*) denigrated Muslims have got it right on the issue of abortion, should we not be able to as well? Nonetheless, the reference to these religions is noteworthy in this context.

With the mild exception of the priest's letter, an image of Greece as inherently superior because of its Greek Orthodox religion prevails in *Kathimerini*'s letters. The priest's letter puts that image in bold relief via its own unexpectedly subdued image of Greece as a generically God-loving rather than a specifically Greek Orthodox or even Christian nation. Yet, even the priest's letter firmly represents Greece as inherently being a nation of God.

To become a modern nation-state, Greece negotiates a contraction: from Greek *Orthodox* nation to Greek nation. The absence of the word "Orthodox" from references to the Greek state, as *Kathimerini*'s letters suggest, cannot be taken to mean that the "imagined community" of the modern Greek nation is a secular one. Indeed, the "Greece" that prevails in the letters to the editor of *Kathimerini*, the bipartisanly respected representative of the conservative portion of Greece's public sphere, appears to be much more stridently and religiously Greek Orthodox than the "Greece" of sectors of the Greek Orthodox Church.

The Centrist Letters to the Editor

In this sector of the press, too, a formal Greek Orthodox conception of the Greek nation again emerges. The demografiko continues to be an important national threat; once again there is a marked concern with the nation's territorial and moral integrity, whereas, in contrast to *Kathimerini*'s letters, its explicitly spiritual welfare is not a concern. Intriguingly, abortion itself does not appear as a problem in the letters, although it enjoys a fair share of attention in the actual news coverage of this sector of the press. What is new here is a positioning of the Greek (Orthodox) nation in an economic matrix. Although there is still no questioning of the organization of biological reproduction into (loosely) nuclear families characterized by particular gendered patterns of power (an organization that, though social, is commonly held as natural), there is a strong recognition of the economic forces that are seen as influencing social formations such as the family and old age.

In a letter to *Ta Nea* that protests what the writer sees as the paper's inadequate coverage of the demografiko, we see reference to the Skopiano, a national problem that has been viewed as competing with the demografiko in importance.[20] Skopiano is shorthand for the perceived national problem created by the international recognition of the Former Yugoslav Republic of Macedonia as an independent nation-state (Macedonia's capital is Skopia). The seriousness with which the centrist press tends to view the demografiko is evident.

> What is projected from the mass media every day is the number 1 national problem—namely, the Skopiano. There is almost no discussion of the number 2 national problem (according to the ICAP March poll), which is the low birth rate. I mention here in the academic year 1993–1994, in Eastern Attica alone, 100 elementary school classrooms went unused because of a scarcity of children. In a few years, the 1.3 children that each family gives birth to on average *will not cover the need to guard our borders. Also, retirees will face a problem since there won't be enough working people to pay the pension funds.* (emphasis added)

It is "our borders" that are brought up first in this letter, a concern amply evident in the *Kathimerini* letters. Yet, the immediate change of topic to the issue of the pension fund, instead of any elaboration on other issues related to the borders that are soon to be unprotected, introduces a new element in the social construction of the demografiko. That is, it suggests that the concerns with the demografiko and Greece's future lie in the realm of the economy in addition to that of the nation's territorial integrity. Here we see a strategic deployment of an image of the nation that seems, at first glance, to lack a Greek Orthodox orientation of any sort. In addition, this image of the nation looks to the economy as an important element for fortifying the nation. Furthermore, the particular manifestation of this concern with the economy—the pension fund instead of the state-run health or educational systems, for example (or, more congruent with the letter's initially stated concern, the military's ability to modernize its technologies)—happens to take a form that runs counter to the Greek Orthodox Church's instruction to trust God's providence for the future, *ehi o theos,* and consequently to avoid procuring God's wrath by acting as though human beings can somehow provide for themselves *alone.*

In this context, it is interesting to note the letter's next few phrases: "*We are committing national suicide [aftoktonoume ethnika].* The politicians are indifferent and think only about tomorrow's elections. Why don't the journalists get sensitized? Or maybe it [the demografiko] is not our number 2 national problem?" (emphasis added). Whereas the tone prevailing in *Kathimerini*'s letters is characterized by a worry over the variously mediated effects of abortion as "embryocide" and on the territorial, biological, and spiritual fortitude of the Greek Orthodox nation, here we see a distinctly different concern. The focus slides away from abortion itself, especially from its implications for the life of the spirit (whether national, individual, or embryonic); instead, attention focuses more narrowly on the low birth rate, whose effect here is specifically defined as "national suicide." Thus, the fetus's salvation and a variously fundamentalist Greek Orthodox nation are replaced, respectively, by the material needs of an aging population and the nation-state's capacity to fulfill the socialist promise of its current government.

However, the Greek Orthodox religious terms of *Kathimerini*'s letters do not disappear in the centrist press. They are displaced in part and then redeployed, at times with surprising vehemence, in the context of a discourse of Greek nationalist nationhood. In fact, it is the Greek Orthodox narrative of nationhood that recovers the upper hand even in this segment of the press. Consider another letter to the editor, this one published in the centrist *Eleftherotypia*:

> We are a people who are elderly, lazy, and opportunistic. The low birth rate is getting worse and has also brought with it the aging of the population. The large majority of our youth are lazy and they try to survive opportunistically, either through gambling or by . . . withdrawing funds from the bank via the method of armed robbery!

The member-states of the European Union, the presidency of which our country has for this six-month period, are clearly on the right track! Can we say the same about Greece? The predictions are foreboding. However, despite this, Greece is destined to live and it will live![21]

Here the low birth rate is attributed to the alleged laziness of young Greeks. The right's implication that the high rate of abortion stands as proof of inadequate modernization shifts to a claim that the low birth rate and the generalized low productivity to which it is here connected are evidence of poor modernization. The implicit argument seems to be that to be a proper member of the European Union as a modern nation-state, Greece needs to work harder, *produce more,* and *reproduce* more. Notwithstanding any of this, however, this letter relies on a religious register to make reference to Greece's "destiny."

That this economy-based construction of the modernizing nationalist Greece is connected to a Greek Orthodox construction even in the centrist parts of the public sphere is clearly demonstrated in another letter published at about the same time in *Eleftherotypia*.[22] Although this newspaper has historically been associated with the center, its tone has become increasingly caustic and its content more left-leaning, especially with regard to many of the fiscal and other policies of PASOK's rendition of socialism. The intertwining of socialist and Greek Orthodox discourse can be seen most clearly perhaps in this letter, published on 15 June 1994, responding to an earlier article entitled "The Elderly Lady of the Balkans" published on 4 June. Strikingly similar to the Supreme Court judge's letter published in the right-of-center *Kathimerini*, this letter shows both explicit and implicit evidence of what it calls a "Greco-Christian"—or pronouncedly Greek Orthodox—conception of the nation. The letter also brings up the long-standing policy issue of state support for families with four or more children (referred to as *politeknoi* or "many-childrened").

> This serious statement [the demografiko] and prognosis for the future of *Hellenism and Greco-Christian traditions*—in a similar European climate of angina and social decay, *with Islam's dangerously escalating increase in population* taking on the shape of a dangerous "giant"—creates a very large national obligation *for the Church and the polity* to assume their responsibilities in the face of this national danger.
>
> The Church has an obligation not only to limit itself to its worshipping mission, but to take on and give priority to its primary humanitarian mission. The Church needs to . . . support and create families with many children. And the polity needs to preserve its strength and *also its identity: to wake up from its*

slumber and indifference, and *with positive financial and legal measures* to encourage the creation of families with many children (by taxation of the unmarried, of those without children, of the wealthier classes, and by creating labor units in areas close to the border, taking the initiative *to develop rural Greece financially*). (emphasis added)

Thus, the trope of very large families, which is one of the signs popularly used to indicate Greece's past romantically as much more rosy, is implicitly being repositioned here as a sign of the "awakened" (modern) state. The significance of economic measures for preserving Hellenism in the present and the future in the context of the social problem of the demografiko is unquestionable. The concern with the future is especially clear in the claim that the economic development of the Greek areas close to the border may help to alleviate the low birth rate. The letters to the editor of the centrist daily press suggest that the demografiko's definition as a problem depends on a view of it as a social phenomenon that is both relevant to Greece's economy and a result of that economy.[23] Whereas the previous letter examined in this section worried about the effect of the demografiko on the pension fund, this one goes a step further and actually looks for the demografiko's cause in the economy.

At the same time, however, the continued understanding of the demografiko as a threat is also clear. Moreover, it is a threat, after all, not only because of its economic consequences (e.g., on the pension fund) but also because of its territorial effects. And the way the territorial effects are understood is religious, rather than formally political, for example, or economic in their own right. Specifically, the demografiko is a threat owing to its negative impact on the resistance that Greece offers a burgeoning Islam at its borders. Also under consideration, then, is the demografiko's effect on "Hellenism and Greco-Christian traditions," which, as the letter's syntax implies, together constitute "Greek identity." What is not initially clear as a result of this conjunction of themes is the specific image of the Greek nation that is being assumed here. Is the writer *critically* redeploying a thematics of Greek Orthodox nationalism—the image of Greece as David fighting the noble fight against the Goliath of Islam—within a larger framework of Greek socialism, or does the basic form of this thematics, that is, of an almost fundamentalist Greek Orthodox position, actually signal an unexamined alliance with that position's basic terms?

The writer summons both Church and state to take action, although in different ways and for different reasons, to avert the national disaster he sees the demografiko leading to. The Church is urged to use some of its material wealth to support concretely what is postulated as the solution to the impending disaster, that is, the proliferation of families with many children. The state is encouraged to come out of its sleep and indifference to respond adequately to the major national threat posed by a low birth rate. In both cases, the letter's tone is chastising. If the polity is at all interested in preserving itself, the writer claims, it needs to wake up to the reality of an escalating demographic crisis. If the Church is going to be so preoccupied with the demografiko, there are some practical things it can do to put its money where its mouth is.

All this suggests that a charged Greek Orthodox image of Greece is operative here. That this image is dominant even in letters published by the centrist press is demonstrated in the recurring effort to motivate the state to respond to the demografiko by suggesting that this problem concretely undermines not only Greece's strength but its very identity. The textual context of this reference, as analyzed above, implies that the prevailing matrix of Greek nationhood defines Greek Orthodoxy as its domain even in the (theoretically at least by now) mostly secular sphere of the polity.

Negotiating Modernity with Fundamentalism

In a condensation of the Western European politics of modernity, what emerges alongside the Greek debate on modernization is a particularly charged fundamentalist Greek Orthodox nationalist discourse. The heightened concern with the nation's birth rate, expressed most pointedly in the press's coverage of the demografiko, is a complex fundamentalist response to modernity. Both rightist and centrist coverage of the demografiko evidence the tense encounter between a liberal humanist discourse preoccupied with the modernizing project of the secular nation-state and a Greek Orthodox essentializing discourse of the ethnos. This encounter sometimes yields paradoxical, even schizophrenic social formations. For example, Greek women are often admonished both to use modern contraceptives *and* to have many babies (implicitly, male Greek Orthodox Christian babies) so as to do their part to protect the country from Muslim invasion.[24] Also symptomatic of the tensions between modernity and tradition at the level of Greek public discourse is the strong, albeit implicit, assertion that the Greek modernizing nation is at the same time a fundamentally religious state.

Attached to all this is the presupposition of a religious Greek Orthodox citizen.[25] While the media in general pay close attention to what the reasons for the low birth rate might be and how best to solve this national problem, public discourse simultaneously shows escalating concern with the influx of Albanian, Serbian, Kurdish, and Polish immigrants arriving in an Athens already "overflowing" with Albanian, Filipino, Egyptian, and Ethiopian immigrants, in addition to the more familiar "gypsies." In this larger context, the particular danger presented by the demografiko is repeatedly understood, via a conflation of religious difference and race, in terms of a threat facing Greece from its "Muslim neighbors." The recently internationally acknowledged independent statehood of the Former Yugoslav Republic of Macedonia has exacerbated long-standing Greek ethnic anxieties so that what before was the specter of the invading Turk is increasingly being broadened to include the "growing Islam" to which the demografiko letters refer.

Thus, through the linguistic ellipsis "Greek [Orthodox] nation," which is at best only partially reflected in the national imaginary, the religious component of bipartisan conceptions of Greek nationhood is rendered invisible. Further, it is made largely unavailable for reworking despite an explicit debate focused precisely on reconstructing a national agenda and "redefining Greece." However, the notion of Greece as a form of a Greek Orthodox religious state, were it to be openly acknowledged, might be critically examined for its limitations as well as important strengths, and strategically redeployed.

For instance, instead of repeatedly and unimaginatively focusing on Greek national welfare as a function of the *quantity* of Greek Orthodox *citizens,* there might be a shift of attention to the *quality* of Greek social *institutions,* be they economic, educational, or even military. These institutions are precisely what many Greeks identify as serious national problems, as shown in the last chapter of this book. For example, a woman to whom I spoke at the Family Planning Center, where she had come for an abortion, commented that the state would do better to improve education and health systems rather than worrying about how many children she would or would not have. In any case, she added with a wry smile, "I am not going to be persuaded against having the abortion with the argument that I should keep this child now in order for it eventually to be sent out to get killed in a war with the Turks!" Instead of being preoccupied with the number of babies Greek women (and men, I would add) are having or not having, attention might be better directed at the quality of social institutions and the possibility of transforming the "spirit" of government.

✥

PART THREE

Sexing the Nation

As the Costas Ferris film *To Rebetiko* (1983) begins, we see a group of *bouzoukzides*, a traditional rebetiko orchestra of Greek folk musicians, sitting on wooden taverna chairs on a stage, as is customary for this type of music, performing a song. A caption appears: "Smyrna 1917." The scene unfolds as they sing.

We see an image of a bead curtain in front of a doorway, the beads swaying as though someone just walked through.

> One day history will write how he kicked the beasts out of Athens,
> he got rid of kings and senators, the liars and the fakes. (twice)
> *vasileis kai vouleftades, tous pseftarades kai tous maskarades*
> Over there, at the Defense, all the officers
> he's fighting with them too, Venizelos, who'll bring things to an end
> and every patriot will bring us Equality.

The camera cuts away from the musicians on the stage to a woman giving birth in a dark room and the midwife assisting her. Then back to the stage.

> The Virgin [Mary] stands by our side
> showing the way to our new general
> the hero of National Defense [*tis Ethnikis Aminis*]

The camera cuts again to the woman giving birth. We are looking at her from a point of view above the head of the bed she is lying on. Her head is rolled back and appears upside down to us. She yells loudly. Her left breast is exposed. The song continues:

> who fights and drives our enemies away

As the woman yells again and the midwife pushes down on her belly, the singer repeats:

> The hero of the National Defense
> who fights and drives our enemies away.

And the song goes on:

> The lads of the Defense have got rid of the king
> and they sent him away
> [*kai tou dosan ta pania tou—*]

The camera shows us the midwife stirring cloths for the birth over a huge pot of boiling water.

> so he can go on his way
> [*yia na paei sti doulia tou*]
> so he can devour all he can together with his foreign clan
> [*ton peridromo na trei me to xeno tou to soi*]

The last two verses are repeated and the camera remains fixed on the singer. The camera angle widens and then returns to focus on the singer. He calls out:

> Here's to you, Lefteraki!

Then we hear an infant's scream and see the new mother looking down toward her feet.

> Come see the swords and the scimitars [*yatagania*]
> the flames reach up to the sky
> high, high up there, at our borders
> the blood of the enemy is flowing like a river.
> The lads of the Defense got rid of the king
> the hat [of the Defense] brought us Venizelo
> *tis Aminis to kapelo efere to Venizelo*
> a little cap of the Defense [a soldier] brought little Lefteri
> *tis Aminis to skoufaki efere to Lefteraki*

At this, the midwife comes through the beaded doorway and enters the big empty room with just the musicians playing on the stage. She says, "Congratulations, Panagi. It's a girl." Panagi's face looks shocked and turns. The film cuts to a black-and-white image and the words "Smyrna 1922, The Great Disaster" appear in a frame. Then we see a young brown-haired girl peering out a window on a rainy night. Her hair is in ponytails, her hands crossed under her chin. A small tree in a pot on the windowsill to the right of her face glistens through the rain as we look on.

Chapter 7

NAVIGATING THE NIGHT

❖

Abortion, as already noted, like many surgical operations in Greece, is popularly called an "intervention" (*epemvasi*). Yet, the persistently high national rate of abortion suggests that there is more going on here; at the very least, any "interventionary" aspects of abortion are not being perceived of in an altogether uncomfortable way. In fact, the narratives of sex, love, and contraception that some of the women shared with me reveal an emergent conception of abortion as *natural*.[1] How is it that this happens? In what sense does abortion come to be seen as natural and through which processes does it acquire this meaning? Through which conflicts, what negotiations and resignifications—especially in the context of the charged demografiko discourses penalizing it at the level of the nation, and given a matrix of Greek nationhood imbued with variants of a religious discourse, wherein abortion is formally defined as an act of murder?

I suggest that the understanding of abortion as natural is linked to other beliefs formed by the intimate connection of discourses about religion and the divine, of the nation and Greekness, and of gender and sexuality.[2] All of these come together, and sometimes clash, in ways that render the main trope of modernity, the liberal, clearly bounded, autonomous, and rational *individual*, alien, to varying degrees, to the lived reality of Greece at the present, wherein agon, struggle, and rapid tactical repositionings are a key element.[3] To the extent that the accessibility of other available forms of birth control, which are firmly embedded in local expert renditions of liberal humanist discourse, relies on the subject's formation as an individual, accessibility is impeded, or even prevented, in this discursive context.

That the Virgin Mary, referred to in the excerpt from *To Rebetiko,* and religious discourse in general is intertwined with Greek narratives about national prowess was shown in the previous chapter. That the Virgin Mary is intrinsically connected to certain popular understandings of Greek nationhood is perhaps best exemplified by the National Holiday of 25 March, which simultaneously commemorates both the fight for independence from the Ottoman Empire and the foundation of the Greek nation-state, and the religious holiday of the day that the Virgin Mary allegedly sniffed the *krino*, the lily, the act seen as leaving her pregnant with Christ. But how can it make sense, as the film excerpt presented above demonstrates, to parallel a contemporary pregnant woman to the Virgin Mary, and what exactly is at stake with such a parallel? Moreover, how is it that, at the same moment, the clearly biosocial act of giving birth can be aligned with kicking out the nation's enemies? Through what underground passageways do meanings travel, which collisions are resolved and which left dangling, and what is the pivotal role of gender in this process, so that it can also make sense to parallel the mother in labor as a national hero and, in the very next instant, the newborn Greek fetus/infant itself, a girl in this case, to the nation's enemy?

If the body of the woman in labor is being equated to the nation struggling to get rid of its enemies, *i mana [kai i] patrida,* and hence the act of giving birth with the violence of war, how are we to make sense of Panagi's pronounced dismay when he is informed that the new baby is a girl? Most important, what are the implications of this scene for the version of Greece held dear in the national imaginary? And what is the particular configuration of gendered citizenship that accompanies this version of Greece? It is possible that the masculinized matrix of nationhood, which is here reading birth as an act that is primarily situated in the domain of war, indeed itself an act of war, also renders the birth of a girl, at some level, a metaphorical sign of the loss of the war. To the degree that this is so, this scene from the movie may permit us to witness a charged moment in the construction of femininity in this national context. In effect, this semantic formation may be the site of an injury, of trauma, that marks the production of female Greek subjectivity in collective memory, a miasmatic implantation of sorts that is carried forward culturally and that fortifies the subsequent operation of particular national narratives concerning gender, sexuality, and relationship. In this sense, the discursive production "Greek woman" is culturally branded and, perhaps, scripted to perpetually seek to "overcome" the constructed as endogenous and essential boundary position of "traitor" that *she* phantasmatically may occupy in the Greek national imaginary. And this may occur, moreover, even as her transformation into mother is represented as *miraculously* transporting her into the realm of the national hero and thus providing the only legitimized escape from a citizenship marked by treasonous connotations to appropriate citizenship.

It is quite clear that unexpected reversal, ambivalent signifiers, and constantly receding signifieds animate the national imaginary of modern Greece.[4] In the semiotics of dreams in Greece, seeing a wedding or a pregnant woman is often interpreted as a sign of death. In addressing the question of how abortion, locally defined in some spheres as an act that is almost treasonous, is also seen as *natural,* a gateway is opened on the fraught fields of power in which action and experience are viscerally shaped by national and religious discourses and practices. In effect, as this part of the book shows from another perspective, abortion in Greece is a vortex where stories of what it means to be Greek, what it means to be a *good* Greek man or woman, what it means to be a subject of modernity, and what it means to love, all come together and are refracted in often unexpected ways.

From most U.S. points of view, as well as from many Greek perspectives, a belief in abortion as natural would figure as a sure sign of mental pathology. In fact, it is not that abortion is smoothly and seamlessly seen as natural, nor that abortion is automatically seen as natural, in Greece. Rather, this layer of the meaning of abortion *emerges* at the junction where distinct local understandings of the body and of other forms of birth control render the latter unavailable or simply not properly usable. In this chapter, I attempt to show how an ostensibly inconceivable construction of abortion as somehow natural is in fact a logical product of the interplay between sexual discursive practices and the very discourses of nation and gender that, in the context of the demografiko, yield abortion as a problem of national import. In effect, the prevailing stories about Greece that render abortion legible as an act of treason in that context also work to create notions about the body, *erota* (love-passion), and sexuality that in turn make other forms of birth control practically inaccessible at the site of many gendered Greek subjects. It is in this sense that the body politic and the body are intrinsically linked. The configuration of physical and emotional boundaries yielded by the nationalist and religious discourses circulating in Greece at the present is such that, as this chapter shows, the resulting gendered subject has a sense of the body, the self, and the other that severely problematizes access to the available legitimized means of birth control while also rendering abortion legible to many women primarily as a natural act.

Theory and Praxis

I make two suggestions. The first relates to theory and the politics of identity in the national contexts of modernity in Europe. This chapter's analysis attempts to offer a clear and concise demonstration of the extent to which the nation is not elsewhere or "out there" but effectively "within"—indeed, within people's beds and, so to speak, inside their bodies (Calhoun 1997; Warner 1993, 2000). At the same time, I use empirical material to explore and flesh out the postmodern theoretical contention that discourse produces matter, which Judith Butler has perhaps most powerfully argued for in *Gender Trouble* (1990) and *Bodies That Matter* (1993). Indeed it does and, I think, just how much so cannot be properly understood without carefully attending precisely to that matter and its utterances. Foucault (1977, 1980a, 1980b) rooted his theorizing of discourse as the means of power in belabored analyses of historical materials. I look to the present experience of the body and of relationship, using Greece as a case study, to map the operation of power in the capillaries of the body politic through the episodic circulation of particular discourses, especially those relating to the nation. My argument is that pregnancies, indeed life itself, are the result of culturally specific stories of nationhood and of gender that are involved in the discursive production of bodies and sexualities.

The case of abortion in Greece is a rich site and yields strong contemporary evidence that what is natural comes to be seen as such via political discourses.[5] By thus denaturalizing what is natural for some in Greece, it becomes possible to see better how more of what is seen as nature or given in some way is similarly the product of variously charged discourses, similarly political. At the same time, because abortion is so easily deemed *unnatural* by other constituencies or publics in Greece and elsewhere, this analysis may destabilize comfortable constructions of a self-evident reality. Nothing "just is," as the authors of the T-shirt design inspired by the 1992 L.A. riots knew only too well when they wrote "There Is No Justice, *Just Us*." The meanings of abortion in contemporary Greece help illuminate the radical politics that are indeed *inherent* in making what we call reality visible, in defining what gets counted as natural or good or true, let alone in setting the stakes of the game.

The second contribution of this chapter is to Greece specifically and its current situation (see especially Diamandouros 1997; Mouzelis 1986; Tsoukalas 1991, 1995, 1999). Perhaps unexpectedly, given a local preoccupation with economic indices and macrostructures, which is fueled by the generous European Union monies sponsoring quantitative research, a microsociological approach to the paradox of abortion in Greece reveals the contradictions underlying prevailing stories of Greekness. Abortion puts these in bold relief and permits a deeper understanding of the matrix of nationhood that *vis-*

cerally animates the national imaginary of Greece today. In turn, this leads to a critique of important aspects of the liberal democratic discourse that informs both policy and academic work on the current plight of Greece, as well as other ambivalently modern nation-states. If heard, this may also point to ways out of some of the country's current impasses as it seeks to recraft its identity vis-à-vis the effects of political and economic globalization in late modernity.

God, Greece, and the Nature of Abortion

What is meant by the term "natural" when used to refer to abortion in Greece? It is important to keep in mind that we are speaking of degrees of naturalness and not an all-or-nothing situation. Much as it has become possible to speak and think of degrees of citizenship in the United States and elsewhere, I propose that it is useful to think of abortion as enjoying degrees of naturalization among different constituencies, in Greece and elsewhere (e.g., among certain U.S. groups where abortion occurs at similarly high rates).[6] Although abortion has come to be seen as largely natural for many women in Greece, it is not automatically seen as natural. Rather, abortion *emerges* as natural to a high degree through a trajectory of particular understandings of the gendered and nationalized body and the associated meanings of other available forms of birth control. In this sense, abortion seems more natural because other methods seem less so, all of which appear natural or unnatural to their respective degree because of the larger narratives about gender, sexuality, love, and appropriate citizenship that they are embedded in.

Before proceeding to unpack and investigate the semantic processes through which, in this sense, *Greece* creates the high rate of abortion that is at the same time lamented by the formal public sphere, by medical experts and state discourses as well as many citizens and popular culture, let us get a sighting of just what "natural" might mean in this context. Titika, a friend who participated in the research as both formal and informal informant, brings to the fore what is underlying the ways many of the women I spoke with defined abortion.

At the time of this conversation, Titika was thirty years old. She had been working as a journalist for several years and was paid well to contribute pieces to several important Greek women's magazines. She was single, had no children, and reported having had five abortions. At the time of the interviews, she and I had been friends for about five years, ever since we both worked as interns, and then journalists, at the same Greek weekly newspaper.

Although we had not always stayed in touch very well, as I eventually left the paper and pursued graduate studies in the States, it was as though little had changed when we met during my biannual trips back to Greece.

Her mother, Greek, taught English at a private school in one of the northern Athens suburbs. My mother, who was raised by parents who were both Greek immigrants to the States, is much of a Greek American, and was more so during the early years of our relocation to Greece. In different ways, both our mothers took pride in their version of Anglo-ness and both Titika and her siblings and my sister and I were raised bilingually. As a result, we shared a strong sense of ourselves as partially "outside" Greekness, just as we both sometimes felt more Greek than those Greeks who had never had the experience of feeling external to Greekness.[7] Titika and I met fairly often during the year of my ethnographic work in Greece. In the context of renewing our friendship, we talked at length about issues related to my research. The most explicit statement I received about what it means to think of abortion as natural is an excerpt of one of these conversations.

> *Titika:* I would prefer it if the man took something rather than me. . . . First of all, I would never take the Pill because in general I don't take medicines. And I mean I don't take anything even when I have a headache. I don't take aspirin the day I get my period and I'm in pain. This morning I had a stomach ache . . . I'm not interested in taking something.
>
> *I hurt because there is some natural cause that makes me hurt, it's not that I am not healthy.* And at some point for some reason I will put up with it [*tha to yposto*] and then it will leave me later. And not only because of what I have read . . . *the Pill is a very violent intervention in the hormonal system.* The Pill, I was just reading the other day, we put it in the paper, it is responsible for cancer.

At this point I interrupted her. Choosing to leave aside the issue of just how much we do in fact medicate ourselves in Greece with substances such as caffeine, liquor, and nicotine, as well as by being the country often reported as having the highest rate of antibiotic use, I focused on the notion of intervention that she emphasized. I interjected that abortion could also be viewed as a big intervention in the hormonal system. She looked a little puzzled. I continued, "It could be said that abortion interrupts the hormonal 'balance' of pregnancy, which itself might also be seen as a violent intervention in the hormonal 'balance' of nonpregnancy. In addition," I continued, "the full anesthesia under which all Greek medical abortions are performed could be seen as yet another intervention in the organism's processes. In other words,"

I proposed, "could we not see abortion as at least as much of an intervention as the Pill?" Her response:

> *Titika:* Since abortion is the only acceptable and relatively safe way to . . . to stop that which you don't want to have happen . . . You don't have it . . . you don't have the luxury to think about it, to say, But there is the anesthesia, there is this or that. Therefore you could say, though, Why don't you do something ahead of time? I would never choose to take the Pill because of what you said. I don't agree with the parallel that . . . as much as an intervention on the hormonal system and the turbulence that the Pill provokes, that's like that of beginning and stopping a pregnancy. But it is not the same. Because the Pill, you take it *knowing,* knowing the side effects for life, trying not to cause a natural retrograde course of the hormones for some amount of time, a course that you interrupt [with an abortion], which is not good but . . . it's not the same.

Titika's account fairly blatantly leaves out several other forms of birth control. Absent are the "days," as a version of the rhythm method is referred to, the condom, and the IUD. For a variety of cultural reasons, as I show in what follows, these often do not even enter the picture as options. What is vividly present in the above excerpt is Titika's sense that abortion is not just a stopgap emergency measure. Rather, she insists, it is the *natural* choice. Knowing that the Pill causes side effects "for life" is very different, she argues, than thinking that the pregnancy, should it occur, and the subsequent abortion might potentially disturb the body's hormonal balance for a short time.

This is what everybody I spoke with said in different ways. Even those women who reported agreeing at some level with the formal Greek Orthodox doctrine that abortion is murder still expressed a feeling that, nonetheless, abortion was somehow more natural than other options. Other methods are variously seen as "foreign bodies" or otherwise unacceptable, indeed often violent, interventions. To demonstrate this, we are going to move backward, so to speak, as I trace how the women I spoke with attempt to establish and patrol the boundaries between their body and others—be they human (their lover's) or inanimate (the Pill, the condom, the IUD)—and how nationalist and religious discourses are actually key participants in this project.

It needs to be made clear from the onset that, from what the women I spoke with said about birth control, the country's high rate of abortion in fact indexes something far more complex than what the overwhelming majority of family planning and ob/gyn experts and other voices in various formal Greek public spheres (including the press) repeatedly refer to as "women's inadequate information about birth control methods." This statement relies on tautological reasoning through which the only thing that counts as evidence of having "adequate information of birth control methods" is the decision to *use* these specific methods.

As my fieldwork suggests, the quantity of information women have about certain forms of birth control is a dummy variable in the modern Greek context. Many of the women expounded at great length on the medical disadvantages of various forms of birth control, often referring to specific hormonal substitutes and dosages in remarkable detail. My argument is that the culturally and historically formed fields of power in which Greek women find themselves at the present moment—of which they are, as I show, a corporal congealment—yield the *estrangement* of some technologies of reproduction such as the Pill and the condom, and the *naturalization* of others such as, especially, abortion, and certainly heterosexuality itself. All this happens despite the prevalent representation of abortion in the Greek public sphere as very much an intervention that is hostile to a strongly and almost unanimously desired "pure" national integrity. In many ways, thus, the common vernacular reference to abortion as an "intervention," epemvasi, can best be seen as *ironic*.

More specifically, the narratives of women's subjective experience of sexuality and birth control indicate that the project of having a desirable heterosexual female body actually relies on ways of deploying boundaries that are shaped by and encoded in categories of national welfare. The Greek case offers a vivid illustration of how certain discourses of nationality, a particular "regime of truth" about Greekness and about the nation, effectively, practically, *materially* produce not only notions of citizenship but also the very biological bodies with which they are affiliated. These categories, for many women, render unapproachable the forms of birth control that a modernizing Greece claims to want used at higher rates.

At the same time, the feelings animating "Greek" bodies flow in currents according to a particular *economy of pain*. Here I am borrowing the term *economia* from Greek Orthodox doctrine, where it is used to index a nonlinear hierarchy of sin and grace. A popularized version of this shapes the very cognitive categories within which the body and life itself, including the fetus, is defined and experienced so that in the end it is the Pill and the condom that constitute interventions. The historically produced categories that create the demografiko as a problem also underlie the ways in which sexuality, relationships, and the female body are perceived and delimited. In this way, the narratives of nationhood that yield the low birth rate as a national problem, with all its Greek idiosyncrasies, also produce the high rate of abortion.

As a result, not only do abortion and, in the same move, straight sex come to be seen as natural; they also become vital parts of being Greek. The firmness with which the scripted can be upheld as natural at both the level of the body and the level of the nation is remarkable. As one example, consider what a new friend once authoritatively proclaimed when we were in the midst of a heated discussion about vegetarians. Exasperated, he told me, "Every real Greek [man] eats a souvlaki [pitta] with meat." (Indeed, the version made with pitta bread, tomatoes, tzadziki, and onion, but without meat, is called *touristiko*, or *tourist's* souvlaki!) Several Greek vegetarian and vegan friends certainly did not agree. But the sentiment this person expressed is very popular.

Similarly, judging by informal lore as well as abortion rates, it isn't that much of a stretch to proclaim with authority that every (*real*) Greek woman has had an abortion or two, or more. In fact, two doctors and several of the women I spoke with told me precisely that during my fieldwork. Also, an acquaintance in the United States who worked in Greece for part of the year mentioned that during one of her many visits to Greece she had been told in an almost positive way that every *Athenian* woman has had an abortion. This raises the issue of how abortion can also signal the modernity of which, in another register, *Athinaies* (Athenian women) are considered the privileged embodiment. Obviously, not every Greek woman, or even every Athenian, has had even one abortion, let alone several. But then, neither does every Greek man or woman prefer to eat a souvlaki with meat. The issue is that having an abortion and, for a man, eating meat, may operate symbolically as significant emblems of the production of appropriate gendered nationality.

Part of what is surprising in both these statements is the element of pride that seems to be involved. Being proud about eating meat has to do with the souvlaki and other meat dishes as sites of an intriguing conjunction of, on the one hand, the hidden injuries of class that mark contemporary Greece (it was not so long ago that meat was considered a luxury to be eaten regularly by the few, rarely by the many) and, on the other, Greek narratives of masculinity (what kind of man are you if you can't/won't stomach meat and, by extension, blood; see Adams 1990). On the one hand, just as "real" Greek men must enjoy eating meat, Greek women might be expected to have risky sex, not balking at the possibility of an abortion. On the other, given the confluence of notions of citizenship with the historical construction of masculinity, for Greek women this might mean that at some level they also must enjoy "eating meat," or having sex with the risk of an abortion, and *thus* be "real men" *in order to be real Greeks.*[8]

Key to identifying what is at stake in both these relationships—being Greek and eating meat, and being Greek and having abortions—is the question of what is *natural for a Greek*. To be Greek and not eat a souvlaki with meat seems to be seen by some as unnatural. To a lesser degree, in a way that would never be declared so dramatically or forcefully, to be Greek, or at least Athenian, and not to have had an abortion may also be viewed by a few as unnatural. In both these postulations of what is natural and what is distinctly Greek, the undertones of sexuality are discernible. Certainly the investigation of the social construction of abortion in Greece leads us in this direction. Keeping in mind Titika's words about abortion being somehow natural, sex as an arena of struggle and contestation, as well as pleasure, comes to the fore.

In effect, the issue becomes how narratives about sexuality are deployed in the process of negotiating an "essence" of Greekness and how particular notions of what it means to be Greek are deployed in the process of performing and naturalizing a distinct register of sexuality (Fuss 1989). This requires very careful listening. Before addressing sexuality per se as it is represented in the accounts of the women I spoke with, I situate Greek contraceptive behavior in its larger social context—a key part of which is *agona,* or a historically inflected version of struggle, at all levels of daily life. *Ti kanoume? Edo! Ston agona!* In particular, I draw from scholarly and popular texts to identify and highlight some of the key meanings from which sexuality and notions of the body are constructed in Greece.[9] The next two sections, in different ways, continue to tease out some of the culturally specific understandings of Greekness, of the body, sex, and erota, and of the central role that perceptions of the Greek ethnos and of God play in all this. I use two different sets of data: large-scale empirical research on current feelings of nationalism in Greece, and then a critical reading of minute cultural fragments, the words of a few verses of popular Greek songs. The next two sections also further the project of weaving together an interpretive grid, initiated in part 1 and pursued in different ways in part 2, with which to most attentively read the interview material from my ethnographic work.[10] This is necessary to firmly contextualize the narratives of the Athenian women I spoke with, in an attempt to apply Haraway's (1988, 1991, 188) dictum for situated knowledges, and thus illuminate aspects of what they say that are not explicitly stated.[11] Much the way a prism held in a beam of light works to refract the white light and reflect its rainbow components, the elaboration of aspects of the social and semantic context in which Athenian women live helps to reveal the constitutive narratives of their responses and to anchor my reading of them.[12]

The Nation as Child's Play

A pioneering large-scale study was conducted in 1994–95 on "Youth and History."[13] The aim was a comparative assessment of "the historical consciousness and political beliefs of adolescents" in each of twenty-six countries in Europe and elsewhere. I refer to some of the more spectacular findings as a way of gesturing toward the "cultural air" that Greeks are currently breathing. The results of this study vividly demonstrate the primacy of "the nation" as a category shaping identity formation in Greece at the present historical moment.

Notably, Greeks rank second with respect to the degree of ethnocentrism expressed by respondents from all countries. The country that ranked first is Turkey; those with the lowest scores were France, Denmark, and Sweden. Also associated with ethnocentrism, Greek youth ranked first with regard to the degree of interest they expressed for the history of their own geographic region and/or nation. France and Denmark again had the lowest scores on this; Palestinian Arabs and Turks had the next highest scores.

Another interesting finding of the study is that Greek students are second, following Turkish students, with regard to the importance they give to religious beliefs in their lives. As an interesting comparison, consider that Palestinian Muslim youth came third. The suggestion was made by the researchers coordinating this study that Orthodoxy may have something to do with this finding, but it certainly does not tell the whole story, for, with the exception of Greece, the average score for the importance given to religion in other Orthodox countries (Russia, Ukraine, and Bulgaria) is comparatively low.[14]

Greeks also stand out for the negative feelings they reported toward industrialization. They rank second, along with Bulgarians, in their inclination to vote in favor of a reduction in immigration, while Russia ranked first and Italy third. In addition, and somewhat surprisingly given the fairly recent Greek history of student mobilization against authoritarian regimes like the Papadopoulos junta of 1968, as well as the significant anarchist population of Athens, the young Greeks polled in this survey came first in the strength of their desire to grant the police force more rights.

Yet, Greeks also stood out for the intensity of their belief in democracy as the highest value. Interestingly, and perhaps reflecting the "underdog" culture Diamandouros (1993) argues is part of the heritage of modern Greece, Greek youth had the highest average score in endorsing the definition of democracy as "a welfare state and the protection of minorities," whereas the definition prevailing in northern Europe was of democracy as "government *by* the people *for* the people." Finally, Greek youth were the only ones exhibiting a high rate of acceptance of the proposition that democracy is "inherited from Ancient Greece."

Alongside the above, Greek youth also had the highest score with regard to the positive image they have of Europe. Nonetheless, overall, Greek youth emerge as markedly nationalist in contrast to the youth of the European Union and many other countries (with the exception of Turkey and Palestine). Moreover, the particular brand of nationalism most evident has a strong connection with Greek Orthodox religious beliefs.

Another study, this one focusing exclusively on Greece, examined school textbooks and interviewed teachers across the country in an effort to probe just what children think of as "homeland," or *patrida* (Frangoudaki and Dragona 1997). The findings of this study permit more accuracy in identifying some of the constitutive elements of the narratives of Greekness that enjoy currency and that may also shape women's and men's attitudes toward contraception and inform the very meanings ascribed to the body and sexuality.

Here too, Ancient Greece emerges as a powerfully gyrating node in the Greek national imaginary. The finding of "a devalued understanding of (modern) national identity" vis-à-vis other European nations that seems to animate textbooks is marked. In this cognitive context, the researchers argue, antiquity becomes the way for Greece to rescue its pride and establish its presence in modern Europe (Frangoudaki and Dragona 1997, 169–76).

Overall, the researchers comment that the responses of their sample of educators are characterized by "a generalized xenophobia," and they state, "There is a particularly high level of agreement with statements about 'the invasion of foreigners' and 'the masses of Albanians.' " They cite several very charged responses to the open-ended portion of their questionnaire. These are especially useful in plotting the coordinates of nationalism in Greece. I quote from the study's discussion of these responses: "The most aggressively xenophobic responses are revealing of the fear that the presence of aliens worsens the already low position of Greek society . . . with a dramatic description of everyday life, which is called 'a hell' because of 'the foreigners' who 'scavenge our land.' . . . Perhaps most characteristic of all is the response that says that it is because of the 'foreign invasion' of workers that 'Greece has now become an undeveloped country' " (Frangoudaki and Dragona 1997, 191).

This excerpt along with the preceding discussion of the comparative study of nationalist beliefs puts in bold relief notions I have identified as central. Invasion, intervention, (hostile) foreign (bodies), and struggle or agon are important elements in the popular imaginings of Greek nationhood and personhood alike. Reflecting on the cultural concomitants of this system of beliefs, Damanakis (1997, 78) succinctly states, "It is known that especially after the catastrophe of Asia Minor, the population exchange and the consolidation of the Greek diaspora population, the notion of cultural homogeneity was cultivated in Greece so intensely that even today there is no room for cultural deviation. Thus, the bilingual or trilingual person from Pontos, the Vorioipiroti (from southern Albania) and the Greek American run against the existing cultural inflexibility and constitute a dissonant chord, whereas they should be considered normal expressions of a cultural variety that characterizes contemporary Hellenism which, as is known, is not confined to the modern Greek nation-state's boundaries." Similarly, the historian Avdela (1997, 56) comments that the main characteristics of the image of the Greek national self are continuity, preservation, homogeneity, superiority, and resistance: "Thus formed is a cross-temporal collectivity with flexible cultural boundaries which, as a collective subject that is homogeneous and undifferentiated throughout time . . . maintains an unchanging appearance, and, as national characteristics, the love for the homeland, courage, and the love of freedom: in brief, a cultural entity that neither changes nor accepts influences but rather only resists and radiates."

The issue of nationalism is clearly significant in modern Greek culture and the empirical studies discussed above illustrate its manifestation among youth and in the educational system. However, it is important to remember that I am not arguing that nationalism is a unique characteristic of modern Greece or other similarly distant nation-states. This would too easily slip into an Orientalizing discourse, wherein, increasingly, portions of Eastern Europe, especially the Balkans, are represented as being uniquely in the throes of a nationalist fervor while other nations, such as the United States, are represented as not nationalist. Leaving aside the daily pledge of allegiance to the flag that U.S. elementary school classrooms routinely begin their day with, and the commonly heard "I'm proud to be an American," whatever the phrase's significance to each subject speaking it, the United States is a country that goes to war, often with numerous camera crews in tow, with the predominant justifying claim that either "Americans" or, increasingly, "American values" are at stake.[15] Territory, the modern nation-state's old stand-by rationale for war, is increasingly circumvented for the contemporary United

States. All that is necessary to justify a pronounced, though certainly not unanimous, exhibition of nationalist fervor is the indication that "American lives," always strenuously marked as "innocent," have been put at risk. Nationalism is not specific to Greece or other more or less exoticized countries.

It is part of the condition of late modernity that the nation, as a category, and its specificities in each geopolitical context for different populations remains a powerful constitutive element in the formation of identities or their simulacra. This is true for the United States, the Balkans, and elsewhere, and virtual realities, globalization, and European unification notwithstanding, there is little sign that this is changing. If anything, if England's new housing policy, the recent French reformation of social programs, and the implementation of new German labor laws are any indication, there seems to be an exacerbation of state-building projects based on nationalist discourses that are profoundly racist and sexist in their effects. Particular configurations of citizenship are consolidated while others are rendered marginal at best in a body politic in which, as Butler has argued for the U.S. situation, it may be more accurate to refer to degrees of citizenship.[16] What is perhaps most interesting in the empirical data concerning nationalism among youth and in the educational system of Greece is the insight given as to the specific ways in which the nation is popularly being inflected in the Greek national imaginary. To further explore this domain, I turn to popular culture.

Songs of Sex: Desire and Violation

Haris Alexiou is one of Greece's "big" singers. It is hard to think of a U.S. parallel for her music. It is somewhat of a cross between folk and pop, but with an edge. Something like Carly Simon with verses from Simon and Garfunkel plus the fire of Joplin that keeps it all from becoming schmaltzy. Alexiou has been singing for the past twenty years and each of her records is typically a hit.[17] A critical reading of fragments of her work allows us to focus on what is popularly taken to be natural in Greek sexuality and the ways in which the nation seems to animate this domain.[18] This analysis is not aimed at producing broadly generalizable conclusions but at identifying strands of meaning that are part of the production of gendered subjectivity in Greece and, in so doing, illuminating the deeper recesses of the national imaginary in Greece at the present, a key aspect of the context of Athenian women's lives.

One of Alexiou's most popular songs has the following refrain: "Come, come, come enter me, and come enter me, like an army. Pillage me" (Haris

Alexiou, "Pillage Me," from *Leoforo this Agapis*). These words graphically suggest that a desirable performance of Greek female sexuality may hinge on a posture of surrender, on the issuance of a license to violate. Being pillaged—losing a war—is here represented as a good thing. To be willing to lose everything is taken as proof of love in many cultural contexts. To be willing to do so in this particular register of war, of a battle that one knows ahead of time will be lost or, worse, betrayed (as Ephialtes betrayed the Medes and Cavafy's later poetic rendition of it), may be part of the specificity of Greek love.[19] The precognition of betrayal, coupled with the strongly stated desire to nonetheless give all, is the real proof of love. This is what yields the deep sense of tragedy that often accompanies not only songs of love, but also most stories of love that contemporary Greece tells and lives. Indeed, an a priori assumption of a lack of trustworthiness, testing it and trials of it, may be a significant part of the discursive practices animating Greek relationships of all types.

The surrender that Alexiou sings of is not a retreat. Nor even, necessarily, a sign of loss. Having had the wherewithal to declare such a love, and to *deposit* it or one's self, as this often amounts to, the field of power shifts and the one who gives becomes the one who exceeds the self and in so doing gains power. *Afto katatheto ego. Esy, ti katathetis.* In the refrain, sung by Alexiou with a male accompanying voice, it is a woman who is to be pillaged and it is also she who is issuing the command to be pillaged. Thus, in the terms of the song, she effectively orders the invasion of *her* "territory." Although the invasion might seem to signal loss, in the economy of pain that is in place here, invasion (along with its many certain losses) actually is refigured as a victory. *Her* order is obeyed.

Elaborating this theme of incorporation and reversal further, one of the verses of the song, this one sung by a male voice, is "Show me how beautiful you are; like a conspiracy and like a murder." *San sinomosia kai san foniko.* In other words, like something that has great pain in it—betrayal, violence—but also mystery and excitement. The female lover (*Deixe mou pos eisai oraia*) is instructed to reveal this beauty in the same way that a conspiracy or a murder would be revealed. Again, transgression is brought in and disclosed or exposed, and thus appropriated. In an illuminating refraction of what it may mean to be Greek, conspiracy and murder become signs of the lover's beauty. In the constant play of reversals, the desirable female body is paralleled to great acts of violence and betrayal.

What is the crime the female body is harboring? This is never made explicit. Its power, the sheer power of its beauty, its attraction, may be a large part of it. This is connected to destruction. Destruction of the self or of evil, beauty must inevitably be connected to such powers. In a culture where often things have not been what they seemed or what they presented themselves as being, where all schoolchildren are taught the story of the Trojan horse in a version that renders "us" the perennial potential victims to such gestures, and where superstitions abound, appearances of goodness and beauty can be taken as ingenious disguises for evil. Key to the eroticized female body in Athens today is a display of boundaries transgressed. The female body is thus figured as the site of a crime, a foreign territory, presumably a *hostile* territory, which, however, in having offered itself for pillaging, appears to be absolving the aggressor of any responsibility for the violation. Appears to be. In fact, in so doing, in this hall of mirrors, though the victim—qua commander—may emerge as a victor of sorts, she remains the commander of the losing side and merely saves face by having issued a command for what may well have been an inevitable act of pillaging. As in so many instances where one side is essentially requiring something of the other, the other quickly claims to be freely giving it, thus attempting to establish dominance via its simulation. *Ton adeiasa.*

Alexiou's positioning of a beautiful female lover as a crime site and her representation of the female body as a foreign territory that demands its own conquest together work to underline the precariousness of the balance of power. Most of all, sexuality is graphically represented as a war zone. There is an attempt to refigure loss into gain and win back, or create, an aura of superior power. This move to establish primacy by claiming what is already done or is going to be done to one, as one's own and, even more, by claiming this as a *desirable* state of affairs, in many ways captures the crux of what I am calling the economy of pain that shapes gendered Greek subjectivities. In effect, Greek women may aggressively make of the source of their pain a point of pride and, in many cases, of joy. This dynamic is evident in the ways the women I spoke with describe their experiences of unwanted pregnancies and subsequent abortions.

The story does not limit itself to men and women and the interactions between them. Other discourses play roles in this, too. The foreign territory in Alexiou's song, the female body, which offers itself for pillaging, symbolically may accomplish something else as well: it allows the Greek coed national imaginary of modernity to finally, if momentarily, fulfill the dream and strategically reposition Greece itself as victor. Because the nation is of paramount importance and because it is on *her* back that it finally triumphs, as *she* is "pillaged," *she* is undoubtedly a national hero of sorts for her sacrifice. Yet in the strategic elision that this narrative facilitates, so is *he* who is pillaging. The significant difference is that who she is has everything to do with who is being pillaged, and how (i.e., under whose command), and less to do with the genitalia of those concerned. Gender and desirability are achieved through the appropriate deployment of discourses and tactical repositioning within the field of power.

This play of power is associated with a representation of sex as an unregulated space. Indeed, much as many cultures have done, there is even a long academic history of representing sex as a primitive or raw space that is somehow outside order and social processes, just as more recent scholarly work shows that this is not the case.[20] In Greece, the symbolic move to separate sex from the social is often enlisted by a larger narrative of national pride in which Greeks represent themselves as "a Mediterranean people." *Emeis eimaste Mesogeiakos laos*. What this means is, for example, that a figure like Zorba as played by Anthony Quinn is not just a stereotype of Greeks that non-Greeks draw on. Instead, Greeks themselves can redeploy this trope in a process that is quite similar to the ways that (neo)colonial subjects often negotiate with "Orientalist" discourses (see Clifford 1988; Lowe 1991). In fact, many Greeks themselves underwrite certain Zorba-like characteristics. One friend, a professor at the University of Crete, discussing the demise of an important relationship of his, recently told me, "I am an intellectual Zorba!" He had told his girlfriend, apparently, that he would always need to also have sex outside their relationship, a fact that seems to be very common in Athenian relationships. She had initially accepted this as long as she would be the one he always returned to. But, as it turned out, she was not able to sustain the relationship under this condition. Also, as I was told often during fieldwork, the "essential temperament" of Greeks is radically and uniquely spontaneous—*eimaste afthormitoi anthropoi emeis, den pairnei o trahilos tou Ellina zygo*—and this seems to be linked to a persistent resistance against overt efforts to govern. *Tha mou peis esy ti na kano ego, den eimaste kala. Poios eisai sy re!*

In the midst of all this, straight sex is often represented as the site par excellence where the free spirit of Greece, so to speak, is expressed. This is a gendered freedom, of course. With degrees of adamancy that differ for men and women, straight sex becomes a stronghold that resists the compromises Greece as a nation and Greeks as a people may choose to negotiate with modernity in other contexts. In the face of the confrontation of Greece with modernity and as outlined in Alexiou's songs and hinted at in the popular representations of Greeks as a Mediterranean people, straight sex can emerge as a coed attempt to recuperate the nation's prowess.

It is doubtful that the nation is actually consciously on many people's mind at the time of sexual activity (though I discuss below how another Alexiou song and its misinterpretation by the public suggest that the nation may be more of a concern than one would think). Yet, narratives about national specificity have tremendous power to define what is considered natural both as a category per se and as the specific character attributed to Greekness. As the ensuing analysis of interview material argues, the primacy of the nation as a construct, and Greek national identity in particular, may be very much a part of "the cultural air" that lovers strenuously breathe in and out during lovemaking. This interanimation of the nation and the body both reflects and naturalizes the game of power, the testing of trust that is embedded in a simultaneous performance of spontaneity, the idiosyncratic yet constant movement through a hall of mirrors: the agon.

An additional piece of evidence of the powerful link between the nation and sexuality in the Greek national imaginary comes in another song by Haris Alexiou, "O Ellinas" (The Greek), that was picked up and amply quoted in various news media considerations of the demografiko.[21] The titles of several editorial comments and news articles on the low birth rate make specific reference to the line "Come my love, come, let us make another Greek."[22] The quote stops there in the daily press's use of it. The media's way of quoting the song, along with the content of the subsequent articles on the low national birth rate, make it look like the singer is inviting her partner to have sex with her so that they can have a child, *na kanoume enan Ellina akoma,* and in this sense "make another Greek."

Yet the lyrics of the verse in full are "Come my love, come, let us make another Greek . . . sing and so forget, forgive her mistakes as we do, since Greece [feminine] injures us as nobody else." *Ela agapi mou, ela. Na kanoume enan Ellina akomi . . . me to tragoudi na xehnai, ta lathi tis na syhorai opos ki emeis, afou i Ellatha mas pligoni opos kaneis.* The syntax and the rhythm of the song also increase the ambiguity of the meaning. It may be that the singer is indeed suggesting that they have sex to literally create another Greek who will behave, with the passage of some time, one presumes, like all Greeks (as is implied in yet another rendition of the Zorba dance-as-you-cry theme) and sing to forget his or her pain.

However, it may also be that procreation is not being referenced at all, or was not initially intended to be referenced, and Alexiou is simply inviting her eroticized singing partner to help her cheer others up, through *glendi* (loosely, "partying") and through song. Certainly, the music accompanying the song does not reference the lightness and joy of glendi as much as a diffuse sadness, and the tone of voice in which Alexiou says "Come my love, come" is very seductive. But creating art together, including music, like life itself, can be an erotic experience, even if it may also be at times painful. In an interview at a much later time, Alexiou herself did not correct the interpretation made by the media.

But what is most significant is that the segment of the sentence "Come my love, come, let us make another *Greek*" has been separated out and, seemingly automatically, culturally made sense of as a reference to procreative sex. The song does not say "Let's make another child" or "human being," as might have been the case if the intention of the singer who wrote the lyrics was to sing about procreation. Whether or not sex is being linked to procreation, in an echo of the demografiko discourses, indeed whether or not sex is being referred to at all, the popularity of this song and its specific redeployments in the media are strong evidence that in the national imaginary at least, sex may be intrinsically linked to nationalist feelings. Neither does the song, after all, say "Come, let's make another *person*." Greekness emerges as a key concern within the semantic domain of eroticized activity, whether or not it is sex per se. *Na kanoume enan Ellina akoma. Oxi anthropo. Oxi paidaki. Ellina.* At the same time, as the other words of the song show, Greekness is linked to a tenacious resistance over time against what are figured as the negative effects of the onslaught of modernity, and to a solitary but sturdy sensitivity—the strength to feel deeply—despite the pain caused by what emerges as the primary object of love: the nation.[23]

The central role of the nation in Greek heterosexuality is also evident in the story told to me time and time again about how *we Greeks* do not do well with a lot of scheduling and calculating activity, and definitely not in the sacred area of sexuality, because we are a spontaneous people. *Mesogeiakos laos paidi mou, den ginondai afta ta pragmata etsi.* This particular narrative is one I heard both from experts—doctors, midwives, politicians, and policymakers—and from lay men and women alike. I heard it from several feminists in both categories and I also heard it from a few women who self-identified as lesbian or bisexual. A story about sex as a site in which national prowess is demonstrated is linked to a story about the nation as a site of heroic and passionate, if also violent, love. In this context, passion becomes linked to narratives positioning resistance as a national trait.

Sexuality seems to be imagined as a site where some sort of essence of Greekness is expressed. This essence is construed as consisting primarily of "freedom" or "spontaneity," which is juxtaposed to the disciplines of modernity firmly in operation at other sites, and a unique capacity for the appreciation of pleasure. *O Ellinas xerei na glendaei. Kai o pio ftohos ehei poiotita zois. Tha piei to krasaki tou, tha tragoudisi. Tha pane ta farmakia kato.* At the same time, pain is a central category organizing the sense of self in Greece, and it is to be revered, even as it is to be struggled with. *To palevo. Ti na kano, to palevo.* Add to this nexus of sex-Greece the particularity of agon in Greek sexuality, and we have the backdrop of current understandings about contraception. A sexuality thus rooted in stories of national prowess, violation, distrust, and foreign invasion renders a certain register and mode of "control"—especially through modern forms of birth control—a literally "foreign," itself practically treasonous, notion.[24]

Greek foundational fictions result in particular ways of mapping the body. These in turn render modern scientific methods of birth control, such as the condom and the Pill, foreign bodies and interventions of different types and to different degrees. Positioned in the Greek national imaginary as an elusive stronghold of sorts, sex is figured as a privileged site, perhaps one of the last remaining vestiges of resistance against the onslaught of the very forces of modernity that are otherwise, and at other sites, very strongly desired and endorsed.

In this cultural context, abortion may also emerge as a trophy signifying the victory of Greekness, if not of Greece per se. In a trumping move similar to that of Alexiou's order to be pillaged, the abortions that result from the series of hermeneutic and political negotiations engaged in by modern Greek subjects can be repositioned as signs of a superiority. It is here, at sex, perhaps more than anywhere else, that "we" who are not uptight or rigid, *koubomenoi, xenerotoi kai kryokoloi*, like so many of modernity's European and local ambassadors (*emissarioi*), are finally free to show our true colors and, ostensibly unencumbered at last by external demands of any sort, we can let loose the allegedly unbridled free spirit and passion that even the most deconstructionist of Greek intellectuals eventually return to and take great pride in. *Plaka, plaka, re paidi mou, einai alitheia. Emeis den ta pame ta programmata se tetoia pragmata, eimaste alloiws.*

Another popular Greek song, this one by the brothers Katsimiha, is titled "The Knife-wound of Love" ("Tis agapis mahairia"). Certainly, as women's thoughts on the use of birth control reveal, all is not quite so free and joyful—and certainly not equally so for all parties—in both the proximate regions of sex and its varyingly removed areas of the more nebulous aspects of erota, very loosely translated as sex-love. The stealth, the hidden and surprising injury caused by a knife, accompanies popular understandings of love. Thus, the ostensibly free zone of sex-love is marked by the presence of danger. It can be paralleled to a gray zone, like the contested waters of the Aegean that are claimed by Greece and Turkey alike. Yet there is clearly a distinct narrative of freedom firmly connected to representations of Greek sex, and there is an undertone of superiority to this. In what follows, I look more closely at this conjunction of sexuality and nationalism.

Counting the Days, Forgetting the Nights

Between salt water and land
there is a small ceasefire zone.

Sometimes sand sometimes pebbles sometimes rocks
—Topali, 1999, 35; my translation

How does the narrative of a uniquely Greek freedom animate Greek sex? Having explored ways that national identity is a charged and ever-present aspect of everyday life, we can use this symbolic and political context as a lens through which to examine the understandings of contraception and sexuality of women living in Athens. The stories told further illuminate how sex can be positioned as oppositional within a larger narrative about Greece's modernization. At the same time, in following the often intricate and paradoxical negotiation of the meanings of different methods of birth control, we also witness the process through which abortion comes to be naturalized. Greece itself often remains an implicit category in the women's stories. Yet, seen through the lens of Greek political and popular culture, the underlying nationalist elements of the women's narratives about birth control practice and sex come into focus. It is plausible to consider that the interanimation of the nation and the body can at times be very deep, indeed, visceral. Also at this discursive site as well is suggestive evidence indicating that in Greece, stories about the superiority of the Greek nation may be crucial components in the construction of sexuality, perceptions of the body, and notions of love.[25]

One of the clearest illustrations of this occurs when the women talked about their experiences with a method of birth control locally interpreted by experts and lay alike as rudimentarily scientific and not really modern. This is an amalgam of a version of the rhythm method and other methods such as withdrawal, the condom, or other forms of sex (i.e., oral; anal, referred to as Othomaniko or Ottoman; or involving the woman's breasts, referred to as Ispaniko or Spanish in another interesting conjunction of the nation and sexuality). This amalgam method was referred to as "the days" by many of the women I spoke with. Claims are made in the Greek media, especially in women's magazines, regarding the days as a primitive method. Yet, doctors and many small-scale polls reported in the daily press and monthly women's magazines indicate that this is a very popular method used by Greek women. I begin the analysis of women's narratives about birth control with the days, looking more closely at cases where this included use of withdrawal and/or of the condom, because these best reveal the ways in which sex is viewed by many of the women as being external to efforts to control. After the days, I consider notions of conception itself, of the Pill, and of the condom specifically. To situate the ensuing analysis of the representations of sexuality and birth control put forth by the women themselves, I first present and discuss the corresponding representations of local scientific demographic discourse. In so doing, I also problematize formal survey data on sexuality (itself, I suggest, invested in a particular rendition of the modernization of a nation) and argue that there may be a radical disjunction between large-scale survey data such as the UN *Country Family and Fertility* reports and lived sexual practices.

THE STATISTICS

Recall first the data from the United Nations-Greece (2002) large-scale fertility report on Greece that was introduced in part 1. This report indicates, more specifically, that in 1983, 80 percent of 6,534 married women age fifteen to forty-four reported use of contraception (1). Of these women, 62.2 percent reportedly relied on withdrawal and 22.9 percent on the condom (135). In the follow-up survey conducted in 1997 on a subsample of 504 of the original women, and hence on subjects that were fifteen years older, an even higher level of contraceptive use was found: 91.3 percent in total (135). Of the total sample, 30.7 percent reported using withdrawal and 40.8 percent reported using the condom (43). Finally, in the 1999 survey of 1,026 men and 3,048 women age eighteen to forty-nine (1), 55.5 percent of all nonpregnant sexually active women living with a partner reported using contraception (135).[26] Of these women, 45 percent reported using withdrawal and 39.6 percent reported using the condom; the report comments that "the more modern methods follow at a distance (the pill is used by 4% and the IUD by 6.5%)" (135). In addition, the UN report notes that 4.3 percent of the women of the 1999 survey reported using "periodic abstinence."

While these frequencies indicate exceptionally high rates of usage of birth control initially and then a significant decrease—from 80 percent in 1983 to

91.3 percent in 1997 and then to 55.5 percent in 1999—the specificities of the samples used for each of the 1983, 1997, and 1999 surveys render comparison across the years a difficult affair. As the report itself notes, "Nevertheless, these two samples, i.e., the 1983 and the 1997, are not strictly comparable.... Women interviewed in 1983 were 15–49 years old, whereas the sub-sample of women re-interviewed in 1997 were 15 years older. *Therefore the changes in contraception can only be used as an indicator of the real changes over time*" (135; my emphasis).[27] The sample of the 1999 survey, meanwhile, includes 1,026 men and 3,048 women, all of whom were eighteen to forty-nine years old (1). As I suggest in the respective section of chapter 2, despite the UN report's own qualification, the nonetheless firm and scientific presentation of the results from such disparate samples is problematic at best.

Beyond the serious structural constraints presented by the disparate gender, marital status, and especially age composition of the samples in each of the surveys, and beyond the cultural constraints affecting the efficient administration of such surveys concerning fertility in Greece, it is important to consider the sexual context being represented. At first glance, these data suggest that withdrawal and condoms are quite popular methods of birth control in Greece, and that, at least from 1983 through 1999, a minimum of half but *almost all* of the population was systematically practicing birth control methods considered to be variously modern. Yet, my fieldwork and interview material indicates that lived sexuality in Greece is more complex and distinctly more "messy" than the UN Greece survey findings indicate.

Most important, as I go on to argue in greater depth below, withdrawal and the condom should not be seen as isolated and discreet methods of birth control. Rather, as analysis of the responses of the women I spoke with suggests, both may best be seen as components of a broader method, popularly called "the days." In brief, rather than completely abstaining during "the dangerous days," or systematically using either withdrawal or the condom *throughout* the menstrual cycle, women choose to use the condom or withdrawal, or a version thereof, *during a particular time period* and hence are likely to report that the method they use is the condom or withdrawal. Reported rates of condom use and withdrawal may therefore be misleadingly high and obscure the popularity of the days—a method quite different from the survey's "periodic abstinence"—which remains an invisible category in survey data.

Moreover, the days are usually a zone of time calculated by counting from either the first or last day of the woman's previous period, depending on each woman's particular practice, to the middle of her cycle, and then adding on

Navigating the Night 157

either one, two, three, or even four days, again depending on each woman's particular method, in both directions. The days are often termed "the rhythm method" by the media and many small-scale fertility surveys; however, the actual practices referenced by this phrase are quite different from the precise temperature-taking and monitoring of vaginal fluid consistency that the clinical definition of the rhythm method prescribes, so as to achieve the most accurate identification of "the dangerous days" and to abstain during these days.

Another finding reported in the most recent, 1999 survey presented in the UN report on Greece was that, of the women living in couples, a significant percentage, 24.8, although nonpregnant and sexually active, indeed reported not using any contraceptive method at all (UN-Greece 2002 Report, 135). Again, some portion of this population as well may be using a version of the days (either in tandem with withdrawal, condom, other forms of sexuality such as oral or anal sex, or periodic abstention). However, some women do not consider "periodic abstinence" an appropriate designation for their particular combination method; were not offered "the days" as a formal option (indeed, as the interviews I conducted suggest, women who rely on the days are unlikely to consider it a formal method of birth control); and are unlikely to consider the occasional use of oral/anal sex, masturbation, withdrawal, or even the condom as formal methods of birth control. Therefore, the reported rates of nonusage of birth control may also be misleadingly high.

Meanwhile, a mere 4.3 percent of the 1999 women who reported use of contraception report using what the UN-Greece report refers to as "periodic abstinence" (135). This frequency is on a par with that reported for the usage of the least popular method, the Pill, which is cited as 4.0 percent. Yet, again, it may be that a particular cluster of sexual practices, including oral and anal sex and early withdrawal, is not being recognized as abstention from sex, and that the low rates of periodic abstinence are not truly reflective of the number of women using the days. *Apohi!*

In addition, 6.5 percent of the 1999 women reporting use of contraception report use of the IUD. As I found from my fieldwork, doctors do not prescribe IUDs for women who have not had at least two children, due to a fear that its high correlation with infections renders it a threat to the fertility of women. Finally, the diaphragm continues to appear to be unknown (135). Interestingly, the doctors I asked about the diaphragm all commented that it is not a good method for Greek women because "They do not know their body" and "They do not feel comfortable handling their body." The relative popularity of tampons in Greece, however, suggests there may be more going on here. (Two

Table 1. Contraceptive Methods

1. Withdrawal	230 couples	57.5%
2. Condom	94 couples	23.5%
3. Withdrawal and condom	36 couples	9%
4. Nothing	16 couples	4%
5. Vaginal douches	9 couples	2.2%
6. Contraceptive pill	7 couples	1.8%
7. IUD	4 couples	1%
8. Anal intercourse	4 couples	1%

N=400 couples
Source: Tsikoulas et al. 1981

doctors hastened to add that it is also difficult to find the spermicidal gel required for correct diaphragm use in pharmacies.) Altogether, quite serious questions can be raised about the adequacy of the categories being used in large-scale fertility studies such as those of the Fertility and Family Surveys presented in the UN country reports, as they fail to capture the full range of lived experiences of sexuality in different cultures.

A look at a smaller study supports the above reading of the UN-Greece data. In a 1980 study done in Thessaloniki, the second largest city of Greece, with a sample of four hundred couples, withdrawal (57.5 percent) is the most popular method of birth control, with the condom second (23.5 percent; Tsikoulas et al. 1981). Perhaps mirroring the scientific cultural belief that any version of the days is not really a proper birth control method, this study does not measure any version of the rhythm method or periodic abstinence. Interestingly, however, it does include a category labeled "unnatural intercourse," which refers to anal sex (1 percent).[28] Given such a label, significant underreporting of this method is likely. The total findings are reported in Table 1.

The condom and withdrawal, including their use in combination (an important and interesting addition to the list of options), account for almost 90 percent of contraceptive usage. The so-called most modern methods of the Pill and the IUD are used minimally. And yet, the report also states that in the same sample, 30–40 percent of the couples reported having had one or more abortions. This seems to be further evidence that the reported use of birth control methods is (a) not consistent throughout time; and (b) may be occurring in tandem with some version of the days.

Another report of the 1983 and 1997 national fertility studies presented in

Table 2. Main Method of Contraception

Method	1983		After 1983	
Pill	6	(1.2%)	21	(4.2%)
IUD	10	(2.0%)	37	(7.4%)
Diaphragm	1	(0.2%)	—	—
Gel	5	(1.0%)	—	—
Vaginal douche	6	(1.2%)	14	(2.8%)
Condom	139	(27.4%)	205	(40.8%)
Abstention	—	—	8	(1.6%)
Withdrawal	178	(35.1%)	154	(30.7%)
Woman's sterilization	4	(0.8%)	8	(1.6%)
Man's sterilization	—	—	1	(0.2%)
Other	42	(8.3%)	10	(2.0%)
Nothing	116	(22.8%)	44	(8.7%)
Total	507	(100.0%)	502	(100.0%)

Source: H. Symeonidou et al. 2000

the UN-Greece 2002 report focuses specifically on the time period 1983–97.[29] The results in Table 2 are presented analytically.[30] Again we see that the most popular methods by far are withdrawal and condom. There is a notable increase in the reported use of the condom from 1983 to after 1983 (from 27.4 percent[31] to 40.8 percent), perhaps, as the UN-Greece report (2002, 136) notes, reflecting increased awareness of the risk of AIDS. There is also an increase in use of the Pill, from 1.2 percent to 4.2 percent. Altogether, as noted, the 1997 data report 91.3 percent birth control usage.

Yet, crucially, with regard to abortion, the comparative 1983–97 analysis (Symeonidou et al. 2000) also shows that the number of women who report having had three or more abortions has doubled, from 9 percent in 1983 to 18 percent in 1997 (65). In addition, the percentage of women who reported having had one or two abortions has remained unchanged at approximately 16 for one abortion and 12 for two abortions, whereas the percentage of women who report having had three or more abortions has doubled, from 9 in 1983 to 18 in 1997 (65). Meanwhile, the percentage reporting *no* abortions has dropped from 64 in 1983 to 54 in 1997 (65). A study focused on adolescents (age fourteen to nineteen) conducted by the public District General Hospital of Athens, Alexandra's (Periferiako Geniko Nosokomio Athinon

Alexandra's), where much of my fieldwork took place, shows an increase in abortion for this population from 28.8 percent in 1975 to 35 percent in 1989 (Deligiorgou 1992).

Overall, because abortion rates are likely to be underreported (given the stigma attached to abortion and the ways abortion is linked to demographic discourses), it is reasonable to think that the fairly high incidence of reported abortion in these surveys, as well as the upward trend in the reported abortion rates, suggest that the rates of other methods of birth control, reported in the same surveys, are likely to be unreliable.[32] If effective means of birth control are being used at such high rates, it is difficult to account for the high abortion rates.

Whatever else the statistical data on birth control and abortion in Greece may mean, two things seem certain. First, the statistics themselves are political, in the sense that the respondents' reports of using one method or another are the result of an attempt to negotiate the minefield of what method they think they *should* be using, what methods (combinations or variations thereof) they are *actually* using, what methods the various questionnaires sanction as *legitimate methods,* and, importantly, the larger cultural context of particular notions of national identity and their investments in the realm of sexuality. Second, certain trends may be discerned, at least with regard to the popularity of different responses if not necessarily the use of the methods themselves: (1) although reported Pill usage seems to be slightly growing, it remains a very unpopular response; (2) withdrawal and condom are very popular responses; (3) there is a reversal in the distribution of responses reporting withdrawal and condom, such that now the condom seems to be a more popular response than withdrawal; and (4) although reported usage of some form of contraception is fairly high, there appears to be a steady increase in rates of women reporting at least one abortion. As Symeonidou et al. (2000, 64) put it, "Once again, it is confirmed that abortion is a fundamental method of family planning."

The project of this book is not to clinically ascertain the usage of particular birth control methods, or "fertility choices"—including abortion—among Greeks, numerically or otherwise. Indeed, the very choice of sample, 120 women living in Athens who report having had two or more abortions, reflects a quite different objective. Because Greece has a "high" rate of abortion in the context of a pronounced public concern with a "low" birth rate, this sample was drawn as a particularly dense discursive site for an exploration of the narratives, their collisions and collusions, which engender the nation, the subject, and the body in late modernity. That is, as already stated, my primary objective is to track the vexed cultural and political discourses that coconstitute the gendered subject and the nation in the context of Greece, as a case study of how both the nation and the gendered and embodied citizen in late modernity are discursively *created*. This process has serious consequences for democracy: both in theory and in practice. As sexuality in Greece is being used as one point of entry for the retheorization of *this* junction, it also becomes possible to witness some of the ways abortion becomes culturally legible as a fairly popular means of birth control. The ensuing analysis of women's narratives argues that, partly as a side effect of the clash between the social formations of tradition and modernity in Greece, these discourses also yield bodies and sex that contribute to what is locally considered a very high rate of abortion, an act seen as alternatively treasonous, natural, and painful. Thus, sexuality becomes a rich site for exploring the discursive constitution of elements such as "the individual" as well as life itself, to the extent that an embryo is a part of life, which are often thought of as external from the social. It is with this objective in mind that I examine Greek women's narratives of their relationships and sexuality.

"The Days"

The women I spoke with described the notorious method of the days as a vaguely bounded set of sexual practices that involves a cluster of methods or submethods of birth control (such as withdrawal, the condom, or different types of sexual activity) and focuses on a particular time of the month that is perceived as dangerous.

PERSEFONI

Consider the following fragment from an interview I conducted with Persefoni, a forty-four-year-old divorced journalist for a small radio station. Persefoni has three children and reported having had five abortions. She was very articulate and witty. At times she would smile after having said something very serious. She told me her dream was to become a musician and that she had just recently started trying to develop her talent by working with a group she had found. She was very interested in my research. When I first said I was conducting a study on reproductive practices and abortion, as I would tell the women I approached for an interview in the Family Planning Center, she said, smiling, "Ah, yes, abortion; this is a big issue." *Megalo thema i ektrosi.* After the first interview at the clinic, she and I met several more times at her home and in a café. Below is a small yet telling fragment of the second of the three two-hour taped conversations we had together.

> *I:* Did you use any method of birth control at any of those times [of the abortions]?
>
> *She:* No, I didn't, other than the infamous "days." From the "days" is how it happened to us. (pause) Because nobody counts the nights. (laughter)

As she smiled and looked at me with playful eyes, I laughed as well. As indicated by the material from the forty or so interviews I had conducted before her, she had a point. Attempting to make light of what in her subsequent narrative is rendered a troubled experience with conception and contraception, Persefoni implicitly puts in stark relief one of the main mechanisms connected with Greece's perceived high rate of abortion. As she puts it, with some sarcasm, *nobody counts the nights*. In fact, as I found during my fieldwork, the specificities of the actual messy and highly complicated process of heterosexual intimacy in its Greek manifestations seems not to be taken seriously—or "counted"—even by those with a *scientific* interest in contraceptive behavior or fertility rates, including the large number of experts who are only too willing to advise Greek women on "correct" contraceptive behavior and thus to centrally contribute, as the press discussion of the high rate of abortion would have it, to the desired modernization of Greece. Earlier, Titika gave us a glimpse of how abortion emerges as a natural act. Persefoni directs our attention to how the specificities of Greek sex help make this so.

As demonstrated later in more detail, what is configured in the public sphere as a chief prerequisite for the state-building endeavor of modernization is the secure mooring of an appropriately disciplined, or controlled, Greek female sexuality in heterosexual generationally reproducing matrices. "The nights," as Persefoni calls sex, indexes a space that both appears to evade these disciplinary efforts and, as is suggested by the verse from Alexiou's song about surrender, is also a space in which the complex performance of a nationally inflected *commanding* submission to the energy of contestation is highly eroticized. Like a conspiracy, the performance of abandon in sex must be duplicitous, otherwise it is not erotic. This double-edged play with power— the woman's pro-active and aggressive engagement in "submission" and the couple's positionings and repositionings within this agonistic field—is precisely what Persefoni says is not being counted. Being careful about getting pregnant—in any form—can present a serious challenge to this performance.

From the common Greek saying "Whoever loves, torments" (*Opoios aga-*

paei paidevei), it follows that struggle, even (as informal reports of domestic abuse rates suggest) what would locally be defined as abuse, can operate as a powerful sign of love. *Me talaiporei, me vasanizei, ti na kano omos. Me xriazete.* Feminist efforts notwithstanding, to protest is still largely to appear weak, like a "little woman" (*gynaikoula*); certainly, to report wrongdoing is to be betraying your own home. *An den painepseis to spiti sou, tha pesei na se plakosei.* To permit oneself to be tormented (or "pillaged") is both proof of one's deep love and an invitation for the other to pay back such loyalty—at some imagined and always deferred moment—with love in return. *Ego eimai edo, ki andeho, mi se noiazei.* I know that the stronger the attack, the stronger is your love. So, yes, attack. Pillage me, as Haris Alexiou says. *Love me.* In different ways, certainly in gendered ways, both members of the couple, and not just the heterosexual couple, based on anecdotal evidence that came up during fieldwork, assume this posture and make some portion of the offerings it demands.

For Persefoni, as for many of the women I spoke with, the particular disciplinary practice she is discussing—counting the days since her last period to estimate the so-called dangerous days of ovulation and then "be careful"—appears external and irrelevant to the "us" that is embedded in the field of power that is "the night." However, as we see if we look more closely at the black box of "the nights," in fact we find that this activity is firmly "within" and indeed may at times further enhance the excitement and the gaming of erota's agon. Certainly, the attempt to count, in itself, is very often adamantly represented as a move that is extraneous to and limiting of "the Greek personality." *Bakalistika. Ti eimaste, psilikatzidiko na ta metrame ola!* The strength of the resistance straight sex is implicitly seen to offer to modernity and its demands is underlined when, as Persefoni suggests, the very effort to control sex (by "counting the days" and abstaining from sex during the "dangerous days") is itself what is held responsible for the pregnancy it sought to prevent.

On this score, Persefoni's voice can sound almost punishing. Recall, she wryly claims, "From the days is how it happened to us." In other words, if we had not tried to impose "your" order even here in this crevice of the cuticle of capillary power in contemporary Greece, Persefoni (with some Foucault) can be seen as saying to the nation's modernizing project and its various adherents, What "you" do not want might well never have happened and (the wryness in her tone) *we might be better off too*. In this cultural context, abortion can acquire the undertones of a costly but clear victory, a victory over what is seen as modernity's regulating reach. Yet again, in a different domain and in a different register, *we* did not succumb. This may begin to shed light on the element of quiet pride accompanying the various forms of pain that is nonetheless a part of the experience of abortion in Greece, as chapter 8 argues.

This aspect of sexuality should not overshadow its underbelly. The nights are no innocent, happy realm of unity, absolute spontaneity, and unadulterated physical bliss. Part of what is at stake between the couple is the trustworthiness, or faith, of one gendered subject for the other. This was brought to the fore most clearly in women's descriptions of using withdrawal at particular times of the month.[33] The next two excerpts from the interviews focus specifically on withdrawal and illuminate the struggle that seems to shape the nights.

The Days with Withdrawal

It has been argued that withdrawal is a practice associated with the modern habitus.[34] In a concise and intriguing account of "Coitus Interruptus and Family Respectability in Catholic Europe," Schneider and Schneider (1995) present the existence of a deep connection between nationally inflected projects of modernization and one of the most private sexual practices of the body politic. Matters such as the revaluation of the lira and the resulting difficulty in absorbing the Italians repatriating from the United States are linked to Catholic doctrine concerning contraception as well as to concepts of cultural "advancement" in offering an account of the popularity of withdrawal as a birth control method in Sicily at that time. In what follows, I establish the basic parameters of how the historically and culturally specific connection between modernization and birth control is manifested in contemporary Athens, where the stakes of withdrawal are not in fact the degree of *modernity* of its practitioners but rather the degree of *Greekness* of the subjects involved.

CHRYSSA

Trust is a key issue when considering sexuality and birth control in Greece. Consider what Chryssa, a thirty-five-year-old kindergarten teacher, told me about contraception. Embedded within her narrative is a representation of withdrawal that seems to capture what many of the women I spoke with articulated in different ways. Chryssa is the married mother of two children. In the context of our interview, she spoke at length about a miscarriage she had. Although her medical history card (kept on file at the Center) indicated that she had had four abortions at the Family Planning Center, she, like several others, verbally reported to me having had *no* abortions prior to the one she was now coming to the Center for.[35]

I: And so, about contraception?

She: When I think about it, I can't.

I: What can't you?

She: The spiral [IUD], the Pill, all that. I can't. OK, if it was that my husband doesn't take care and I had had a serious problem, OK, I'd put it on. I hear others say eighteen abortions . . . others eight, etc., who have men who don't have a conscience and don't think. Then I would do it.

So, Chryssa says, if she had had many abortions, then she would use contraceptives. Otherwise, no. Her using the high number of eighteen abortions is more evidence supporting my hunch that she was not accurately reporting her abortions.[36] The quick downscale to eight abortions can be seen as a correction once having realized that, for many, seventeen, fifteen, eleven . . . nine or (even) eight abortions may be "too many."

In any case, the implication of Chryssa's statement is that having many abortions is a man's fault. How? He does not "have a conscience," "he doesn't take care," and "he doesn't think." What exactly does this mean? It is not that he does not put on a condom. In fact, for Chryssa, the option of using a condom seems to be entirely external to the range of options available. The problem, as it is clearly portrayed in Chryssa's words, must be that *the men* do not pull out in time. Moreover, it seems clear, there is a very specific version of withdrawal that is at play here. Could it be that she does not push him out in time or that she does not lift *herself* out in time? Neither of these is presented as an option. The female subject's agency seems fully absent in this matter. Thus, if you've got a "good" man, you do not need "any contraception," as Chryssa says. In so doing two things are clearly illuminated: in the lay understanding of withdrawal, it does not fully count as a method of birth control; perhaps more important, the crux of the matter with contraception in Greece is that for a woman to "take measures" to "protect herself" can be a statement against her partner. Withdrawal, perceived as the least intrusive of methods and one that can be performed by the man himself, does not count. That is, withdrawal is safe. The women's accounts of its use reveal a core dynamic: birth control versus the goodness of the partner. *O syndrofos.* Birth control is figured as a powerful sign of not trusting your partner. To choose *not* to contracept, which here clearly includes choosing to use withdrawal, no matter the deviance this may present to the modernizing goals of the nation, wherein use of the Pill or at least the condom is preferred, is in fact to say, in a specifically Greek register, I am loyal to my partner, I trust him. My trust is such that I boldly agree to play a game of chicken, risking an unplanned pregnancy. The resonance of a Greek foundational narrative that valorizes a firm and genuine display of courage before the premonition of betrayal is clear.

TITIKA

Titika, the thirty-year-old journalist reporting five abortions, also talks about contraception in general, having first told me that she never uses the condom. In this context, the advantages and disadvantages of withdrawal that many of the women alluded to are placed in sharp relief.

> *She:* Look, when I was little, with the first boy with whom I did it, it was the first time for him too so he had no previous experience. And I learned normally [*fysiologika*], naturally [*fysika*], naked [*gymna*], you know, the two things (pats the fingers of each hand against those of the other). Then . . . whoever I met, and I don't know, maybe if I had asked "But where is your condom?" and "Where are you going barefoot into the thorns?" maybe he would have felt an obligation. "He," whoever it was each time. As I told you, I always had a permanent one that I had sex with. I didn't have one today and another tomorrow, except for three times, that is, and I'm now almost thirty years old, by a week. It was a permanent escort with whom, well, you trust him sort of . . . And I never asked for it.

Here the pervasive understanding that straight sex is somehow more honest, or should be, than to use means or permit extraneous influences is further illuminated. The nakedness of male and female genitalia is valued and, I suggest, it is also being used to smuggle in a cultural claim that nonnaked forms of intercourse are not honest in a fundamental way. Titika's statement that she did not use a condom because she "trusted" her partners is a clear reference to withdrawal and to the need to withdraw *in time*. It also underscores both that the condom has the capacity to intervene very deeply in the economy of feeling animating sexuality in Greece, despite its apparent superficiality, and that the use of withdrawal operates as a powerful sign of trust. This is a trust, moreover, for which signs seem to be actively sought by both parties and that, again by both, is tested.

In addition, sex itself emerges as a fraught agonistic field wherein a negotiation of responsibility includes the tactic of playing mum. If she had asked for the condom, she says, then "maybe he would have felt an obligation." But obligation seems to have no place in the domain of sexuality being articulated and performed here. With withdrawal, paradoxically, it seems that to *not* ask for some form of birth control is the appropriate move. This may make withdrawal an even better method. The stakes of this game are the possibility of conception on the one hand, and, one presumes, the "arrest" of the other for having failed after all to be trustworthy—though in this intricate field of struggle, they have succeeded in physically referencing and endorsing *Greece* by displaying an uncontainable desire and "spontaneous" excess. The common expectation of many of the women I spoke with that the partner "at least" financially pay for the resulting abortion can be seen as the dues he has to pay for participating in the game, if not openly as a punishment for his having failed at this aspect of the test.

It might be useful at this juncture to consider the specificities of withdrawal, as well as sexuality more generally, in contemporary Athens in contrast to the case of withdrawal for some of the inhabitants of the Sicilian town where Peter and Jane Schneider (1995) did historical and ethnographic fieldwork. Especially for the Sicilian artisans who have had a high rate of literacy since the late nineteenth century, withdrawal was linked to a more advanced or "enlightened" way of contracepting. This group, like artisans elsewhere in Europe, operated as "a vanguard for the transmission of international socialism to the local level" (185). More intellectual than other residents, especially after 1930, the artisans openly discussed what was referred to as "the French method" of birth control. Indeed, one example cited refers to the artisans' notion at that time that the French were more advanced because "those people, it was said, 'can pick up a glass of water, drink half of it, and put it down without finishing it. We Sicilians, however, can't help but gulp down the whole glassful' " (185). Similarly, among the population of the town, the artisans were considered "most advanced" primarily because they could read.

The authors argue that eventually withdrawal was adopted by a large segment of the population of the Sicilian town and played an important role in the historical decline of fertility in northern, central, and southern Europe beginning in the late eighteenth century. When new methods appeared, such as the condom and diaphragm in the 1920s and 1930s and the Pill in the 1960s, these methods encountered both pockets of continued high fertility and what is interestingly referred to as "an older generation of contracepting veterans who 'did it the hard way' by withdrawing before completing coitus" (Schneider and Schneider 1995, 177).

Withdrawal, or "reverse gear," as Sicilian men euphemistically, and apparently proudly, referred to the practice, operated in Sicily in distinctly different ways than in present-day Greece. Withdrawal seems to have figured as a fairly unanimous prized marker of the modernity of those who practiced it, as a sign of the willpower and control of the man, of the willingness to sacrifice on the part of the woman, and of the good communication and cooperation of the couple (Schneider and Schneider 1995, 184–89). There is, however, one striking similarity between Sicily then and Athens today. Many of the women of the Schneider and Schneider study apparently praised their husbands for being *conscientious* (189), a notion used often by the Athenian women I interviewed, though in the negative, as code for a man who does not "take care" and therefore does not practice withdrawal well.

The different histories of the two nations, as well as the different relative positioning of rural Sicily from the 1930s on and of contemporary and fairly cosmopolitan Athens, paralleled as it is to "the cradle of modern democracy," are likely important factors in the quite different inflection withdrawal acquires as a form of birth control.[37] In what follows, I continue to unravel the specificities of sexuality and birth control in modern Greece, with the primary objective being to track the traces of the nationalist narratives of identity that animate and define the body.

The Days and the Condom

In the arena of struggle delimited by the accounts that highlight the uses of withdrawal, one's partner and oneself are together one agent testing the other's trust in the realm of sexuality. Another agent is the woman's body itself. Here we witness how the body (because of birth or, equally, because of its ostensible opposite, abortion) is figured in the women's narratives as an absolute site of resistance against modernity's efforts to control and regulate sexual behavior. This representation of the body occurs even in the presence of the subject's own claimed firm adherence to and compliance with such efforts. In the next two cases, the exploration of the days as an important liminal method that plays a key part in the use of other methods within Greek heterosexuality continues. These women describe their use of the days specifically along with the condom. In Christina's case, she uses the days and then, at a later time, the condom, which is ostensibly chosen in opposition to the practice of counting. In Ersi's case, where a pleasure in counting is discernible, we see how, as in most of the reported cases of use of the condom in my sample, in fact the days are used simultaneously with occasional use of the condom. In both types of cases, the body itself emerges as a site of an ambivalently dangerous alterity. The body is represented as an active agent that itself participates in the tests of trust animating the field of power of heterosexuality.

CHRISTINA

Christina was thirty-seven years old when we met. She was born in the northern city of Kastoria and had been living in Athens for twenty-six years. She left school after the eighth grade and worked as a hairdresser until she had her children. When I asked her if she goes to church, she smiled and said she'll go later, when she's older. "Then I'll need it," she said. Her hair is bleached blond with the roots starting to show and she wears glasses. She's been married fifteen years and has two children. She told me she has had two abortions. Here is what she said about the days.

> *She:* Yes, from the second time that I got pregnant and onwards we used a condom. Although, I knew my cycle, and we would do it without precautions. I knew my cycle and the days we had to not have intercourse. But after the first abortion I lost the cycle [*ehasa ton kyklo mou*], and since then we used a condom.
> *I:* This happened after the first abortion?
> *She:* Yes.
> *I:* In other words, it stopped being so regular then?
> *She:* No, I didn't have the inclination either to count or calculate. I was irregular. To be more sure.

Christina initially presents use of the days along with abstention or a form of sex other than intercourse. This then became the condom, which, contextualized in the rest of her response, is clearly juxtaposed to "counting or calculating" and thus must mean at least relatively regular, systematic use of the condom. This is not always the case. However, the condom does seem to be perceived as further removed from the domain of calculation than are other methods, such as the Pill, and Christina's response underlines this.

Christina's case is especially interesting because, although she initially seems to be saying that the abortion affected her menstrual cycle by altering its regularity, when I asked her to clarify, perhaps mistakenly phrasing my question in terms of a pathological development in her body, she denies this and in so doing gives a mixed signal. She counters that the reason she decided to use the condom is that she simply is not interested in counting and calculating, as she puts it. Yet, she also reiterates that her cycle had become irregular. In addition, before the first abortion she had been counting and calculating at least enough to say with confidence, "I knew my cycle and the days we had to not have intercourse." This is one of several pieces of evidence that shows there is more ambivalence surrounding counting and what it is made to represent in Greece than the oft-repeated narrative "counting is bad"

170   Sexing the Nation

might suggest. However, it also underscores the great cultural weight that a performance of an aversion to counting carries. Moreover, we begin to see more clearly the contours of the female body as resistant to modernity.

While spontaneity and freedom are highly valorized on the one hand, on the other, statistics of all kinds are also highly revered and, at the level of popular culture and politics, conspiracy theories and all the intricate calculations necessary to project fairly complex series of machinations run rampant. As I have noted, it is sometimes said, in a perhaps confessional tone, that, yes, we Greeks are a paranoic people. And paranoia without ample calculation of hidden alliances and broken promises is hard to imagine. *Eimaste paranoikoi, pos na to kanoume.* There are, it seems, certain types of counting, or sites of counting, where/when counting is culturally valorized. Sex and close relationships are not one of those sites. Even for those like Christina who seem to take pride in being responsible for their reproductive potential in a "scientific" way, in the end the defiance toward the *modus vivendi* associated with people who visibly count seems to win. *Aytos ola ta metraei re paidi mou!*

The tone of her voice when she says "counting or calculating" suggests that this is something she had not been enjoying for a long time. Yet, the change of method occurs only after her first abortion. Is it because the experience of the abortion was sufficiently negative that she decides to take what she perceives as fewer risks? No. In fact, the problem presented is that her body responded oppositionally and diminished any possibility for successful counting behavior, such as that involved in any version of the days, because the abortion "ruined the cycle." The experience of the abortion itself does not seem to enter in as a variable in the cost assessment of various means of birth control—except for its perceived impact on the cycle.

Here another aspect of the operative economy of pain governing the Greek subject's sense of self and definition of body is revealed. According to the story exemplified in Christina's narrative, the abortion that results despite modernity's efforts to regulate what "should not" be regulated (by counting the days of a menstrual cycle and trying not to "freely" have sex during some of them) is followed by the body's act of revenge of a sort, by destroying the very preconditions for the regulating behavior of counting the days of one's cycle. Efforts to control are thus represented as maximally disruptive because not only did the attempt to keep track of her fertile days result in a conception and abortion but, ultimately, it results in the loss of the very orderliness of the body itself, which, according to this narrative, has firmly rebelled.

This idea of the cycle's being "ruined," which recurred very often in the women's narratives, nevertheless suggests that there is an orderliness that *is* desirable, and the orderliness of the body is a big part of that. Again, recall Titika's conception of the inner balance of the hormonal system, the method in the madness that is seen as organic rather than imposed, her emphasis is on what is natural, *fysiologika re paidi mou, fysika, pos na to poume*, and hence of the highest value. This is a balance that the Pill would disrupt in a much deeper and dangerous way than that of the occasional unplanned pregnancy and subsequent abortion. Yet, as Christina's account of her initial use of the days indicates, even the ostensibly external order imposed by counting and calculating can itself be something that gives pleasure to the subject. The process of ordering associated with modernity is not only, and not unproblematically, negative. The pull of modernization, *eksyhronismos* as it is called, in any of its variants, is no less strong for its ambivalence; this means that it is also at times very seductive. As is the national project of modernization for much of the public sphere; for many of the women I spoke with, the method and performances of efficiency can also be very enjoyable discursive practices.

ERSI

Ersi's account shows how the seductions of modernity can be pleasurable. She was forty years old when we spoke. Born outside of Athens, in the region of Aitoloaikarnania, she has lived in Athens for most of her life. She doesn't work outside the home, although she went to trade school and was trained to drive work vehicles. She has two children and told me that at the time of our interview she had had three abortions. She seems to take pride in the fact that *she* "was careful." She knew when the fertile days were supposed to be and, as she told me, she "watched out" during those days. When I asked whether that meant they wouldn't have sex then or he would "pull out," as coitus interruptus is called popularly, she explained that if she and her partner did have sex at that time, they would use a condom.

> *She:* We used the condom. But even that isn't that sure sometimes. That's how we got into trouble [*tin patisame*].
>
> *I:* You don't put it on in time sometimes?
>
> *She:* I don't know, I could never understand it. Because I had always learned when the fertile days are and I was careful. I didn't have an irregular cycle. It was every twenty-eight days, so I knew that you catch on the fourteenth day and I would be guarded [*fylagomouna*] from the tenth to the sixteenth. So it was OK. And if it happened in the interim, we used it. Later, maybe with the birth, the cycle was ruined. I don't know how it happened.

Initially, it sounds like Ersi used the condom, yet her subsequent narrative reveals that it was being used only *on certain days* and in conjunction with efforts to abstain from intercourse. Moreover, though I offer Ersi the idea that it can be hard to get the condom on "in time" as a way of easing the conversation into the nitty-gritty of how power and pleasure operate during sex, she keeps the discussion at a more abstract level. Sex is cordoned off as an almost unexplainable site of excess, an insurrectionary space in which "even" the condom, as she implies, does not successfully assert itself. The agency of the subjects involved is obfuscated and sex, like the female body, has a mind of its own that will not be messed with by any of the subjects involved. As in Persefoni's account, it is *the method itself*—in this case, the condom in conjunction with the days and a version of abstention—that is represented as the reason for the pregnancy. To try to control sex, the story repeats itself, is like playing with fire.

Nonetheless, Ersi's account also shows that the counting and calculating of the days can be a pleasurable practice: there is a mastery of method, an obedient performance of reason, an attempt at science that is put on display.[38] When pressed, Ersi says that perhaps another reason she and her partner got into trouble despite all her careful calculations is that the cycle was "ruined," perhaps because of the birth; therefore, the otherwise valid numbers and estimations of "safety" could no longer hold, for reasons ostensibly outside themselves. Again, the body asserts its own presence. Thus, Ersi's narrative implies, even if we do our best and dutifully, even pleasurably engage in an overtly calculating regulation of sexual behavior, sex is not to be subordinated and the forces of the female body exact their revenge. The "ruin" of the cycle is used in both women's narratives as further evidence that counting the days can be a ludicrous activity. As Persefoni showed, the days are no match for sex that, with the crucial help of the female body's autonomous and unpredictable laws, evades overtly disciplinary attempts.

Intriguingly, as Christina's and Ersi's accounts of using the days with the condom illustrate, birth and abortion were often equated as events that disrupt the body's rhythms. Thus, there is evidence that the two are in some way structurally similar; birth emerges as no less disturbing for its naturalness, and abortion, no less natural for its disruptiveness. In an interesting parallel, it seems possible that, be the stated reason abortion, as Christina claimed, or birth, as Ersi sees it, the fact of pregnancy itself is seen as a trigger event "ruining" the cycle. Hence, in this context, pregnancy, often seen as the natural function or "cause" of a woman, is figured as standing in opposition to what is natural.

As Persefoni indicated, the nights emerge as a domain that in multiple ways resists the laws of the days. In the consideration of the days with withdrawal, we have seen that this does not mean that the couple operates as a united front in the nights. The tests of trust that Chryssa and Titika alluded to in their accounts play a part by confounding the neat categories modernity seems to project onto gendered subjects and sexuality. The agonistic field of power animating the couple is complex and powerful. And a large part of what gives sex its capacity to resist modernity seems to be the female body's perceived refusal to be governed. In effect, the struggle in the field of power of the heterosexual couple feeds into the resistance against modernity by Greek heterosexuality in general. Counting the days does not always work because abortion (which is here represented as modernity's natural result rather than the result of a "backwardness" of the women) or birth (which is seen as the body's own action) "ruins" the cycle. Efforts to control are further frustrated by a physical nature that is aggressively uncontainable and founded on excess. Time and time again, I heard the refrain that the body has its own laws and will not put up with the imposition of others. That it is specifically the female body that serves as a repository for this version of the contemporary Greek resistance story was brought into sharper focus when the women talked about conception proper.

"Catching" Conception

In English, we say we "caught" a cold. In Greek, the word *catch* has several different meanings. We say *kollisa*, which also can mean "I glued," or, in slang, "I became fixated." It is used as an alternate to saying, with regard to the flu or a cold, that "I got stuck [as in glue] with something." However, there is another meaning of *catch* that is more active and referenced by a different word. *Piano* emphasizes the subject's participation in the act, whereas *kollao* is an act of catching that exceeds the subject's own agency. Yet, when the women I spoke with talked about their experiences with conception, they would use the more active word to say they "caught" (*epiasa*) either a presumed embryo or, explicitly, "a child." *Epiasa paidi. Piano efkola ego. Den epiana, to ixera.* As the above illustrates, the semiotics of "catching" in Greek common parlance involves some ambiguity, though the weight is on the more active form of "catching" as a positive value. *Piani poulia ston aera. Ta piani.*

This mirrors the feelings surrounding conception. The body's capacity to assert itself and resist—and conception was often deployed as the key sign of this in the women's narratives—is a matter of pride. Yet, in contrast to the scant Greek psychological literature that I found on this topic (Naziri 1988), my fieldwork suggests that although conception itself may have a positive inflection, the experience does not evoke the same type of pleasure for these women. Rather, it is through its function as a sign of resistance, of a good inherent nature saying no to the bad external efforts to control, and perhaps as a sign of the good functioning of the woman's *capacity* to have a child, that conception brings joy, when it does.

This section continues with the study of agon in the nights by pursuing the complex ways in which the female body is positioned as a site of resistance against efforts to govern, such as those of modern science. This resistance seems to be rooted in the female body's potential to conceive, whether this capacity is perceived of as a divine gift, which is rarely explicitly stated among the women of this sample, or, as was often stated, an inextricable part of the (God-given) *nature* of being a woman.[39] This section also permits a closer viewing of the junctions of these two ways of understanding the female body: how they come together and how they sometimes collide. The traffic between the two makes the project of becoming a good contraceptor much more challenging.

MARIKA

An important part of what colors the ambivalent feelings surrounding conception is whether or not it is seen as the result of a failure of effort to control conception. To appreciate the ambivalence, it is important to keep separate the fact of conception from its function as a sign of the failure of birth control. Expressing the undeniable pleasure that was often associated with the reported failure of the days as a method, and illuminating how this is connected to pride in the body's resistance to "science," Marika, a forty-three-year-old mother of three who told me she had had three abortions, explained to me that the reason the days failed had to do with the particular way she conceives. Here again, though we see an initial report of using the condom as birth control, it quickly becomes clear that what is meant is that she actually counted the days along with the occasional use of the condom.

> *I:* Do you remember what form of contraception, if any, you were using when you got pregnant then?
> *She:* Just a condom, nothing else. At both abortions, actually with all three. Until I took the Pill, there wasn't any other contraception.
> *I:* So condom, sometimes.

She: Yes, not always. That is also why there were the three abortions. You count the days, the doctor had said the days, but in the end it was proven that with me the days don't play that much of a role.

I: Why?

She: Well, I get pregnant easily. Because after the period, usually the first day, OK, you're done, clean. The first, second day, you can do it freely. I can't.

I: You've become pregnant that way?

She: Yes, the last.

Marika worked as a salesperson, and had worked in a store since she was fourteen years old. She has been divorced for the past five years. In her narrative, there is at play a version of the story of the female body as an agent that throws a monkey wrench in the system of (birth) control that attempts to control sex itself. Again there seems to be an element of pride associated with the fact of this evasion. She says characteristically, "It was proven with me, the days don't play that much of a role." It is not simply, as we saw in the previous cases, that the method is flawed because of *sex's* reticence toward such efforts to control. Rather, Marika states, it is that she, or her body, eludes the grasp of the days. As she says, she gets pregnant particularly easily.

In this case, it is not that the cycle "shifts" and hence frustrates all the counting. Rather, the body, in its inherent physical nature, is simply "stronger." The excess of sex, in conjunction with the female body's *arresting* ability to conceive, emerge triumphant over all other forces, including even the doctor's own words. *Syllipsi.* At the same time, the value placed on "doing it freely" is made explicit. Conception and sexuality do not follow the laws motivating the mundane (modernist and state-building) project of calculating fertile days, if they follow any laws, as Marika, like many of the women, represents these practices.

MAIRY

The same theme of resistance of the female body and, along with it, sex itself, is elucidated in what Mairy, a thirty-two-year-old phone company employee born in Arta and mother of two, told me about her experience with contraception. In this case, we have an initial report of "no contraception" that later is revealed to have included withdrawal, the IUD, withdrawal again after she gave birth to her children, and even some use of the Pill.

I: What contraception, if any, have you tried?

Mairy: Nothing.

I: What about interrupted, or the dangerous days, as we call them?

Mairy: No, nothing. I hadn't caught before, first time. [*Den iha piasi.*] I hadn't caught before. For a long time I didn't catch and so I relied on it. I don't catch, I'd say.

I: So after this happened [the pregnancy preceding a period of time during which she had recorded no pregnancy on the rough historical chart I put together with all the women interviewed in the clinic], you did some . . . the "pulling out," as it is called.

Mairy: Yes, yes, that's all. But it didn't work, as you can see [gestures toward the chart]. From 1984 to 1986, after the third [abortion], I put on the spiral. After the births, I didn't wear anything, again with "pulling out." I should have used some contraceptive pills, but it would cause hemorrhaging for me and I didn't use them at all anymore. I had a problem with them. As soon as I started [taking them], the third day, blood would begin. The medicine wouldn't "catch," it bothered me.

Mairy's first use of "catch" emphasizes how she would not "catch" a child. This time the female body is represented as almost stubbornly refusing to conceive, though in so doing again rendering itself outside the domain of efforts to control. The tenaciousness of a resistance narrative is evident. In addition, the female body clearly emerges as the site of an agency that exceeds both the subject herself, as is true of most of the female bodies described in the interviews, and the scope of science as well.

The force of Mairy's body to resist is amplified in its reported response to the Pill. Her body, she tells us indirectly, even has the power to frustrate the effects of the Pill, which, in one of the other uses of the word "catch," is represented as being unable to work on her body. Mairy's body, as it is represented in her words, does not tolerate control of any sort. The way she presents it to me, it is as though it has its own volition. Moreover, both the Pill and the pregnancy are represented as similarly external interventions that are not desirable.

Mairy's narrative positions her body as a site that, in a reverberation of the theme of the free Greek spirit, is offering powerful resistance to modernity. Also, both Marika's proclivity in "catching" and Mairy's difficulty at it are reported in tones of voice that seem almost gleeful; each one's perceived predisposition is redeployed and reported as evidence that the female body frustrates or even cancels out external efforts to control. In fact, Mairy does not seem overly disappointed that she appears unable to get pregnant. To the contrary, she says she "relied" on this, clearly representing her apparent infertility as a good thing. In so doing, the child that she might have "caught" is clearly represented as undesirable, as it was also in Marika's narrative, although for her the *capacity* to get pregnant was a very good thing.

Following from the implicit understanding of contraception as useless, when Mairy later decides she is after all at a higher risk for pregnancy, which now she clearly does not want, she is still not sorry that the Pill, this time, wouldn't "catch." To the contrary, the way she talks about it implies that she takes it as evidence of what she suspected all along: her body follows its own rules, it is mysterious, and it does not put up with being tampered with. She says, for example, that though she "should have" taken the Pill, she did not because "it would cause hemorrhaging." Both her rhetoric and tone suggest that she sees her body as having correctly resisted the Pill; there is almost pride in the fact that this resistance was so strong that even a supposedly objective tool of science was unable to "catch," or work as it should. She may be somewhat ambivalent over her initial period of infertility, yet even there, we see evidence of a congratulatory tone: she "relied" on her infertility. All together, Mairy's words show an implicit assumption that both the Pill and the pregnancy are entities that her body refuses to engage and treats as foreign.

As is hinted at in Marika's words and made clearer in Mairy's, the capacity to "catch" may be good, but it does not mean that what is caught—the resulting pregnancy or fetus—is also good. Marika's proud comment earlier that she "catches" easily can be seen as a product of her having easy access to a child should she want one. What is good, in her narrative, is her body and its capacity to give her many chances for a child, should she decide to have one, *not the child itself*.

Mairy's body's reticence toward external influences is configured as being so strong that not only would it not allow the medicine to do what it was supposed to do, but her body itself would not do what *it* was supposed to do: conceive. In the type of narrative Mairy's exemplifies, both the Pill and the very product of conception emerge as similarly foreign bodies that are not desirable, are interventions, and, hence, are seen by the subject as being understandably blocked by the female body.

Thus we have another paradox. On the one hand, the female body is seen as gifted with the ability to conceive, and doing so easily means doing so well. On the other hand, much as sex itself is proudly seen as frustrating efforts to control, the female body specifically is positioned in women's narratives as resisting external incursions such as that of the Pill and, if the body works very well, even of pregnancy. The female body emerges, almost like Aphrodite, from the narratives of the women I spoke with as a fully formed, unbeatable site of resistance to modernity by the *beauty* of its "inherent nature." This nature, moreover, is represented as one of superior resistance to external interferences because it is *so* natural, perhaps also because it is of the divine, and, much less so, because it is allegedly inherently reproductive. Surprisingly, what is left in the fray of the intersection of these semantic formations is a construction of the pregnancy/fetus as a foreign body, implicitly itself an invasion of sorts.

Taking the Pill, "Catching" Modernity

Mairy's comments also show that forms of birth control other than the days, including the heralded modern and more scientific methods, activate their own paradoxes when inserted in modern Greek heterosexual contexts, themselves the complex products of the ways of imagining and delineating bodies that accompany the nationally invested discourse of sexuality. Counting remains very much an issue; the Pill shares the drawback of involving both counting behavior and premeditation in the immediate vicinity of erota. *Poios ta metraei tora . . . ti ekana ego kai ti esy. Oloi, vevaia, alla afto einai allo thema.* Structurally, family planning experts view Greek women as a group as not quite up to the job of remembering to take a pill every morning at a certain time. As we saw glimpses of in the women's discussions of their bodies as frustrating the days as a method, there is also in discussions of the Pill ample evidence of an understanding of the female body as belonging to a different, higher order than that of other aspects of social reality. The Pill is seen as a source of alterity that goes against this understanding of the body in its own ways. To present the range of these understandings of the Pill, I turn to the comments made by five women.

With regard to counting, the Pill seems to present a significant threat to the currently necessary national founding fiction of the triumph of the "essentially" indomitable and free (hence *spontaneous*) Greek spirit. It is seen as a fairly heavily calculated means of protection and references a woman's attempt to count *herself* in the sense of systematically taking account of her own desires. As a technology of birth control that involves repeated actions, counting, and overt means of regulation, the Pill disturbs the national fiction in that it is presumed to require fairly complex calculation, and therefore premeditation, on the part of the woman, at the core of the stronghold of sexuality. Indeed, the degree to which the Pill represents inordinate calculation is inconsistent with the remarkably effective management of tight time and money budgets that are a necessary part of daily life for many in Athens. An important difference is that with the Pill the site of control is sexuality.

The alleged complexity of the calculations the Pill requires figures importantly in the professional and medical discourses that juvenilize Greek women and configure them as unable to handle their own bodies and keep track of their functions. It is true that increasingly, ob/gyns recommend the Pill, especially to younger women. Not the least of their incentives may be the very attractive financial packages offered to them by pharmaceutical companies producing different versions of the Pill. In the course of my fieldwork I was told of several instances when ob/gyns were sent on attractive summer vacations, with their families in tow, with a particular pharmaceutical company footing the bill. However, gynecologists' support for the Pill as a method for Greek women does not seem to run deep. Many of the doctors I spoke with said the women just don't want it. Some said they would talk to women about it if they only had more time, but with their waiting room full, it was not possible. Almost all said it was only young women *kopeles* who would use it. They typically ask for it themselves. And though women's relationship with their gynecologist can be ambivalent, overall it is a very strong and central one. Certain aspects of science, such as the Pill itself, can be very firmly resisted; the practitioners, however, rarely are. The authority of the doctor himself (there are few female ob/gyns in Athens) was rarely challenged in the stories women told me. The special force of this particular relationship is joined by the larger cultural discourse that disallows calculations in the realm of love; this yields even more strength to the Pill's perceived drawback as requiring extraordinary counting behavior. These cultural formations come together as a formidable obstacle impeding access to the Pill, an obstacle that (despite the media's repeatedly citing a lack of information as the issue) has nothing to do with the degree of information women have on what the Pill is as a medical technology and how it works.

The nexus of the cultural forces concerning counting and the Pill is revealed in the juxtaposition between how two different women, Giannoula and Stella, talked to me about their feelings toward the Pill. Giannoula, a woman who used the services of the Family Planning Clinic, was not given the choice of using the Pill by the medical practitioner she saw there. On the other hand, Stella, referred to me from one of the doctors who helped with this research, had been on the Pill for several years and was planning on going back onto it now that she had given birth to what she hoped would, in the long term, be the first of two, or perhaps three, children. Giannoula expressed disdain for the Pill. Yet, she also made evident the pleasures involved in the technologies of the self associated with counting. Stella seemed almost to be promoting the

Pill in the way she talked about it, though it becomes evident in her narrative that the counting the Pill requires is in fact not as seamlessly unproblematic as she overtly suggests.

GIANNOULA

Giannoula is thirty-four years old, the mother of two children, and has been married for eleven years. She works as an assistant librarian and is also taking classes to become accredited as a librarian. Giannoula is one of the first women I interviewed from the clinic and we connected especially well. She was very interested in my research and worked hard to put me in touch with a few of her friends for interviews. In addition, she and I met many times and, talking very fast as she did, she would tell me a lot, almost too much for me to absorb at times, about not only her life, but her mother's and her grandmother's as well. She was born in Mesologgi and, as she explained to me, that meant certain things.

It is a fairly widespread stereotype, as far as Greek regional stereotypes go, that women from Mesologgi are considered strong fighters. Giannoula, however, gave different depths to the meaning of this. Meanwhile, her mother-in-law is from Sparti (Sparta). Entirely different ball game. Again, very strong women. But cold, with a hard heart. Giannoula was adamant about that. After all, women in Ancient Sparta had told their sons to return as victors in the war with Athens, or to return dead, carried on their shield. *I tan i epi tas.* Win, or die fighting. This was mentioned several times and offered as clinching evidence of the validity of the regional stereotype for women today. (In fact, one of my own grandmothers, my mother's mother, happens to be from Sparti. Though herself a strong woman, she is in some ways the exact opposite of the type of woman Giannoula described. I never shared this with Giannoula.)

Born and raised, as Giannoula put it, in a household of left-wing fighters, she now lives in Kaisariani, one of the neighborhoods of Athens where many of the people of the left who had fought in the Greek civil war eventually settled. For several of our meetings, we agreed to meet at a picnic table in one of the central parks of the neighborhood. It was clear that she was very proud of her neighborhood; throughout our talks, her sense of being part of a lineage of fighters, and of herself as a fighter, was evident. In the passage below I think this comes out especially in the way she responds to a faux pas I made. During this particular interaction we were in the little office at the Family Planning Center; shortly after, she had a visit with one of the medical interns. *Me ton giatro.* This was the first time we talked together.

She: Now this problem with anemia has showed up. This spiral [IUD], it "bled" me out entirely. It emptied me . . . I was feeling that my veins are emptying, that's how much blood I was losing!

I: Is the Pill not a good idea?

She: They told me that it's better to put in the spiral and I've been using the spiral until now. Both for my age and for I don't know what else, it is better to wear a spiral. I've never taken the Pill.

I: And you are, what, thirty years old now?

She: I'm thirty-four years old.

I: Yes, well, I think anyway they don't recommend the Pill here from thirty-five years and up.

She: What, the Pill, I don't want it, I don't even know why I have such a prejudice! With the spiral I was carefree. I didn't have to bother. You know every morning take a pill, such and such a day, such and such a time. Count this, count that . . . I'd be pregnant every day. There's no way. But with the spiral, if I didn't have this hemorrhaging, I wouldn't remove it. Now I removed it, to rest a little. My red blood cell count is down to 28. I take three iron pills a day, food, livers, things like that, to raise the red blood cell count a little and control the anemia, to control the spiral.

My comment referring to the fact that the Center won't prescribe the Pill for women thirty-five and older was meant to offer an explanation for something for which she seemed not to have an explanation that she wanted to share, as she stalled and talked about the IUD. Picking up her reference to her age as a factor in the decision to use an IUD, and momentarily forgetting that age is a charged issue for many women in Greece as elsewhere, I offered it back as an explanation for why not to use the Pill. As her quick response suggests, this was not the right thing to say. By implying that there was something she could *not* have because of her age, I was both rearticulating a discourse of prohibition and, very simply, taken to be saying that she was too old. Her instantly telling me that she did not want it anyway was a way for Giannoula to show that she will not be slighted by medical discourse—or any of its perceived representatives—at any site. She simply does not need or want the Pill. In the dynamic that surfaces time and time again, in all sorts of contexts of Greek women's life, what is to be taken away becomes voluntarily denied and indeed commanded to be taken. And what will not be given is proclaimed to be undesirable.

In Giannoula's case, it is clear that this is not one instance in a united front of resistance offered to medicine or science as a whole but, in another example of the at times opportunistic dynamics of agon in Greek daily life, this is resistance specifically targeting the perceived affront that *denial* of the Pill represents. In fact, Giannoula defers to scientific knowledge and seems to take quite a bit of pleasure in counting, as a detailed recitation of her various blood counts demonstrated. She also seems quite comfortable with the multiple pill-taking that controlling her anemia seems to require. Indeed, in the larger cultural context, being able to use the Pill—more, being *told* to—may also be refigured as a trophy of sorts. It says: *You* are modern. *Sihroni ellinida*.

When Giannoula says she doesn't want the Pill but quickly adds that she doesn't know why she has such a prejudice, she's doing two things: she's acknowledging that she knows it is not considered good form in the current modernizing social context to not want the Pill, and she's acknowledging that she knows that appearing to have a prejudice is undesirable. It is only the undeveloped or the uneducated that do so, as this narrative of modern nationhood goes. With both moves, homage is given to science, to the supposed prejudice-free capacity for reason, and the autonomous liberal individual is reinscribed. Meanwhile, Giannoula also represents herself as a modern woman, even as she denies its main trope. In effect, she is saying, Not to worry, it isn't that I really see the Pill as an intervention in a backward unmodernly fashion. Similarly, when she says that she wouldn't remove the IUD if she didn't have the hemorrhaging, she is saying that she is a good docile subject of modernity. It is not that she views the IUD potentially as a foreign body; it is not that she is being superstitious; it is just that *her body* is acting up. In another variation of the theme that the female body resists modernity, Giannoula disavows the idea that she is intentionally using her body to resist, while at the same time claiming—implicitly but firmly—that it does resist on its own. Thus, in one move, she both resists and yet is not to be held accountable for what could be read as a merely disobedient posture toward the call of modernity. What we see here again are the ambivalent feelings—the desire and the repulsion—that modernity so often seems to generate. Giannoula's account of her blood work and of the treatment of her condition reveal that she is in fact more than happy to count. It may be that the Pill's perceived site of intervention, the "heart" of the female body, the reproductive system, and its direct link to the domain of sexuality are part of what render the counting associated with *it* undesirable.

STELLA

Moving from enjoying "counting," except when in the context of the Pill, the position Giannoula's account exemplifies, to also taking pride and pleasure in taking the Pill, a much rarer subject position, Stella, a thirty-year-old administrative assistant in a private company, who lives in Ambelokipi, talks to me about what looks very much like her pleasure in taking the Pill. At the time of our meeting, she had just given birth to a little girl, who slept in her bassinet on the dining table of their house throughout our two-hour conversation. Stella had gotten married shortly before the birth of the baby and she told me she had had three abortions before getting pregnant with her baby. When I asked her about contraception in general, she replied by talking about the Pill at length.

> *She:* Contraception. Pills. I have not tried anything else, let me tell you. In other words, I have not worn a spiral, or anything. And actually now after my birth [*tin genna mou*] I talked about it with my doctor, what is going to happen, and he said watch out during this time, *because you can catch just like that,* and you don't have a regular cycle and then what will we do. He says, "Listen, the pills" and I say why not spiral? And he answered that he doesn't recommend it to women who haven't finished their family. In other words, he says, "If this minute you told me that you had this one child and you don't want another ever"—ever in quotes of course—"I would say OK, I'll put in a spiral for you and if, *may it never,* something doesn't go well, you don't care. But here you are thirty years old. You have had a child, the most reasonable thing is that you will have a second," and true enough, I will have a second.
>
> I won't insert a spiral because it has various side effects. First of all, it isn't 100 percent sure, it can wiggle around, get crooked coming out, *it can hit you* crookedly, etc. It has various infections which can end up in blocking your tubes, etc. etc. And he says "We'll wait for your first period, when your cycle becomes stable." I'll do a Pap test and I'll take pills again. All this time I had been taking the so-called second-generation pills. They worked for me. That is what I was used to, that is what I took. I didn't have any side effects.
>
> Only, the first time when I had first taken them I had acquired beautiful breasts, quite large. Because I don't have . . . It's my complaint; I would have liked my bust a little larger. When I was nursing I had developed a nice taut, taut, I said how beautiful, I wish it would stay with me, but it didn't and unfortunately we have returned to our originals . . . That's all, not even what they say that you become famished and go to the refrigerator and empty it, never, nothing at all. And now I'll take the third-generation pills. I'll try them. *I don't think they'll . . . I don't expect to have any problem.*
>
> And what they say about "Oh, I forget it and I don't do it" . . . Never

forgot it! And the times that I did forget it, with the second-generation ones you have a margin of twelve hours to take them which with the third-generation ones is six hours I think. So I always take them late at night, around 12:00 to 1:00, so if I forgot it I was surely awake the next morning, 8:00 or 9:00. I was always awake, so I would take it at that time, if I forgot it at night. And I never had a problem.

Pills are a very good way and I tell you I always got into trouble stupidly. In other words, and I haven't gotten into trouble only once either. Fine, the first time we can put it aside, it was pure stupidity, ignorance, the way I was counting the days . . . The other two times, I got into trouble . . . because I decided to stop the pills for a rest and it seems that I'm fruitful too, yes, who knows?

The overriding theme of Stella's account, like Giannoula's, is to demonstrate that she is a good consumer of modern science, a mature sexual agent, a docile gendered subject of modernity. Yet even a woman who openly embraces counting, as Stella does, despite some slight confusion with the hour limit to taking a forgotten pill and the apparent frequency with which this seems to have occurred, also decides she needs to take a "rest" from the Pill and with evident pride thinks of herself as being particularly fertile, or *fruitful*, as she puts it. Moreover, the way she corrects her initial comment that she doesn't think the third-generation pills will work to a more authoritative "I don't expect to have any problem" and the doctor's cautionary "may it [the IUD] never [cause any complications]," display the pervasive cultural reflex to guard against hubris and other forces of evil at all times (by never proclaiming a good thing without qualifying it and never stating a bad thing without somehow exorcising it at the same time). *Mi poume megali kouvenda.* There is a quick attempt to correct that "superstition" (or Giannoula's "prejudice") and superimpose on it the language of reason and of the individual's autonomous agency. Yet, all in all, even at this level of engagement with modernity's Word, the endorsement of science that Stella so generously demonstrates is not enough to cancel out a different understanding of the person as a subject vulnerably located in a field fraught with invisible potentially hostile forces, perhaps even belonging to the dominion of God, as the gold cross around her neck testifies. Resilient, even in this more scientific discursive context, is the sense of a woman's body as following a different (higher) set of rules.

That God or a god is a central part of the subtext in all this is put in bold relief when Stella tells me what it felt like to have her baby. She talks a little about her doctor again, how good he was. She refers to the fact that her parents were anxiously waiting outside her room, along with the son-in-law they weren't sure they'd have until the last minute (her husband had initially been very ambivalent about their keeping the baby and getting married). And then she pauses and looks at me very steadily. "I don't know if you have a child," she says and pauses. I gesture no. "Let me tell you," she continues, "I don't know if I can describe the experience. I don't know what words to use." I smile slightly at her and wait. "Yes, when I bent down and saw that being coming out of me, I felt . . . I felt like a God." *Aisthanthika Theos! Theos!*

The Pill's particular power as intervention, evidence of which can be seen even in this case of a high level of support for the Pill, comes from a notion of the natural that is intimately linked to conceptions of the supernatural—and the human boundary deployments this understanding both prescribes and prevents. Here is an uncanny similarity to the idea enlisted by nationalist discourse in the public sphere: that it is a Greek woman's duty as a (Greek Orthodox) citizen of the modernizing yet children-lacking Greek nation-state to both properly contracept and to appropriately reproduce. Recall Mairy. Although Mairy's lack of desire for a child led her to see her period of infertility as something good, she nonetheless would have liked to have the potential to have a child. A woman's nature is locally configured as God's divine gift, and because in Greece reproduction has been historically constructed as the core of woman's nature, it is her duty as a good *Greek (Orthodox Christian)* not to purposefully interfere with her nature in fundamental ways. *Gia na oloklirothei mia gynaika, prepei na kanei paidi.* Those women who cannot get pregnant, as my subsequent research in one of the main Athenian infertility centers indicates, are often very defensive precisely because there is the implication that they were not worthy of this divine gift, or that they lost the right to it by interfering with it via, for example, an abortion. Meanwhile, women who simply do not want to have children are an invisible, and practically unimaginable, part of modern Greece (Halkias 2003, 224).

ELENA

The placement of a very high value on the inferred natural, almost supernatural, abilities of the female body to both conceive and, more important, resist or, in effect, rule, works both to stigmatize the Pill in many contexts and at the same time to naturalize abortion. Key to this construction is the trope of intervention. Elena is a twenty-year-old woman who was visiting the Family Planning Center for the second time in just over a month. Having just accepted a prescription for the Pill by the Center's intern, she sought me out to tell me how her abortion had gone, before which she and I had done her first interview. Lowering her voice, almost as soon as we sat down she told me she had sex shortly after her abortion. She told me what was going on in her mind during this sexual encounter. In this context, her ideas about the Pill came up. First she refers to the condom. I include her comments about the condom here because they provide an important part of the context for her views concerning the Pill and the related notion of intervention.

> *She:* I was obsessing, afraid I'd start bleeding a lot and things like that. But then I said, wait, calm down. But then I told you that it was that I reacted later, I got stubborn the way I usually do. [*Me epiase to anapodo.*] Well, and I did everything.
>
> While I could have said, I don't know, with a condom, I said no. OK? That's the simplest example. In other words, I didn't want things to change radically. I simply wanted to protect myself *a little,* in other words, so I don't have to put my head again right in the wolf's mouth. But I didn't want anything to change.

In Elena's words, the condom is classified as a drastic measure that would change things "radically" rather than "simply" protecting her "a little." Remembering that she had just previously accepted the prescription for the Pill—indeed, that she had ostensibly returned to the Center a month after the abortion precisely to get a prescription for the Pill—we next had the following exchange:

> *I:* And now with the Pill, you'll be covered, so you won't feel stress.
>
> *She:* Look, all I'm afraid of is that—I'm not sure, maybe it was a bad time when I took the Pill in the past, but it had created a strange psychological state. And generally I'm afraid when I feel something *intervening in my organism.* In other words, if it was possible for someone to have some other method of contraception that doesn't intervene at all, *at all,* that's what I would use. But there isn't any method like that. That's how I feel about it. Now the pills. I feel that they *intervene in my cycle,* that they block *me,* but anyway. I used to get depressed I remember in the past. We'll see.

Elena is not happy to be taking the Pill after all. Her words sum up the quandary many of the women felt they faced with regard to the means of birth control valorized as more modern. On the one hand, the condom would "change things radically"; on the other hand, the Pill "intervenes" in the organism itself, as well as raising the fraught counting issues shown in both

Giannoula's and Stella's accounts. The intervention the Pill constitutes upsets not only the perceived physical matter of the body but the psychological state of the subject as well.

Elena's words also bring into sharper focus the pervasiveness of struggle in the ostensibly free and easy contexts of Greek straight sex. There is the same insistent demarcation of straight sex as a field that will not tolerate restrictions, except perhaps "a little." Furthermore, the disciplinary practices of birth control technologies, including the quite unmodern method of abstention on the day of Elena's abortion, operate both from within the female subject, at the level of her desires and fears, and from without, as do the resistances to these practices. Elena both fights against her *own* impulse to "take care" after her abortion, and eventually resolves what she clearly sees as the troublesome impulse to control herself and limit her sexual activity: by refusing its hold—heroically, we might say—by being "stubborn" and doing "everything," as she put it.

What is here enlisted by this tenacious assertion of a *heroic* I who will not be fully subdued by modernity's pull (even when that pull is experienced as the subject's own desire, as we see in Stella's words) is respect for "nature" as the highest good, being, implicitly, a gift from God. Elena would not, at least until the end of my fieldwork, find a way acceptable to her of "keeping her head out of the wolf's mouth" (what many North Americans call "safe sex"). With this phrase she underlines that the stakes in straight sex in Greece, even if it is "protected," are markedly high: sex remains "a wolf" even if she does manage to keep her head out of its mouth. Elena does not endorse the use of a condom. She will not abstain from sex, even right after the abortion, because she feels that would be an almost cowardly frustration of her desire to combat a fear of consequences. She also does not like the idea of taking the Pill because she sees it as somehow fundamentally tampering with (her) nature. The double bind Elena describes surfaced in the words of many of the women I spoke with. It seems to hinge on an understanding of an essential sanctity of female physiology. Recall Elena's emphasis that the pills "intervene in [her] cycle" and block *her*.

TERPSI

Further evidence of the violation that the Pill constitutes can be seen in the way it is represented as a type of Trojan horse of modernity that brings an assortment of other problems in its wake. While the female body is seen as engaging in various forms of resistance against the Pill, the Pill itself is viewed as arriving with an entourage of physical problems. Both the female body and the Pill are allotted a significant degree of agency. Consider the following dialogue with Terpsi, a thirty-eight-year-old psychologist who is married and has one child.

> *She:* I took contraceptives. I began when I was around seventeen years old, first of all as a way of controlling menstruation since it wasn't regular. But that brought me problems. It brought obesity, in other words, it favored obesity and seriously favored . . . I had serious consequences with body-hair growth. Even though I had done all the tests. In other words, I had done a very good examination. And so I stopped them.
> *I:* I see. How many years were you taking contraceptives?
> *She:* I took them for three years, from age seventeen to twenty, when I stopped. I did a detoxification for about three to six months so that I could get pregnant.
> *I:* And did you become pregnant at that time?
> *She:* Yes I did. In other words, I stopped in the month of May and I got pregnant in December.

Again, contrary to the constructions advanced in demografiko discourses, this woman's higher level of formal education does not prevent her from subscribing to a sense of the Pill as an alien substance smuggling in other problems. Moreover, it is the body's natural, if strange, response to an unnatural stimulus. The strangeness of the response references the degree of alterity of the stimulus. This narrative exemplifies the way the Pill is often seen as transforming the female body, despite the performed docility of the subject, to the point of making it "abject"—that is, horrific because it is familiar but out of place or in excess. It needs to be emphasized that this occurs, despite a pronounced display of docility by the subject, who, very often, has "done," as Terpsi emphasized, "very good examinations" or medical tests. *Ekana poli kales exetasis.* Evident here is another variation of the claim that modernity and its scientific instruments, though seductive and revered, are ultimately impotent when faced with the ferocious forces contained in the female body.

KATERINA

This sense of the Pill as a foreign body instigating trouble at a deep corporal level appears in the narratives of women across the spectrum of lower to upper middle class of my sample and of disparate educational backgrounds.[40] I close this section with the simple phrase of another woman, Katerina, who completed elementary school and worked as a server and cook at a pizza restaurant when we met. She was forty years old at the time of the interview, the mother of two children, and reported having had three abortions. When she mentioned that a friend of hers had suggested she try the Pill, she told me, "I didn't want to take pills, because they say they can bring cancerous growths [*karkinomata*]." This basic understanding of the Pill as a foreign agent that, in altering the body, also brings all sorts of evil, including the much-feared cancer, came up very often in the interviews.

Whatever the specific symptoms cited, my fieldwork overwhelmingly indicates that the socially constructed Greek female body has established itself as an active, indeed formidably so, almost holy, site of *nature* in which the Pill intervenes as a foreign body that messes with the heart (not only literally) of the female body by "blocking," among other things, what is implicitly seen as its God-given capacity to reproduce and thus opening the way for other trespassers. The Greek female body is experienced in such ways that the Pill enters into its domain primarily as a potent, indeed toxic, source of alterity. At the same time, we see that even when it is embraced, the construction of personhood that prevails is a far cry from that of the autonomous rational individual presumed to be the cornerstone of modernity.

Greece versus the Condom

The Greek formation of the gendered subject and the effect of nationalist narratives is further clarified here. Moving from their understandings of the body and the influence of a notion of counting in the realm of the nights, we go to the emotional ground of this terrain. The condom also seems to operate as an invasion of disproportionate magnitude to its physical size. This time, however, the invasive aspect of the method resides almost entirely in its perceived capacity to intervene in the already vexed field of power that are the feelings of love and/or that of sex-love or erota. In contrast to the Pill, the condom is not seen as an intervention in the female body, although a few people did also bring up their aversion to its feel or its smell. *Plastiko, vre paidi mou.* Nor is the condom markedly embedded in the type of counting and calculating that the Pill is, though for a woman to have or to request use of the condom does seem to belong to the same discursive domain, if at a further remove. Nor is the condom seen as interfering in sex proper. Indeed, it was often described to me as something that makes the more valued and sensuous process of erota more like what is often juxtaposed to it as quick and dirty sex. Rather, the related capacity of the condom to intervene in the economy of feeling within the couple, in a way that is intrinsically linked to particular notions of Greekness, seems to be the crux of the matter. At the same time, *not* using the condom sometimes has the extra benefit of articulating a display of courage on the part of women, which also is connected to notions of what it means to be Greek.

While usage of the condom was almost always embedded in the method of the days for the women I interviewed, and only a few single women mentioned using it more systematically in the beginning of a new relationship, comments concerning the condom specifically clarify the depth of the penetration of notions of national identity in the domain of sexuality. The excerpts that follow address the ways in which the condom is also understood to be a foreign body, though differently than the Pill. Thus, we move deeper into some uncharted regions of the domain of subjectivity in Greece.

ELENA

Elena, the young woman who told me she felt that the Pill "blocked" her, later explained her ideas about condoms in more detail. By closely examining her word choice, it becomes possible yet again to trace how Greece figures prominently in the sphere of physical and emotional intimacy—sexuality—that is typically regarded as external to the affairs of the nation. Certainly, the very narrative that holds sex to be a spontaneous expression of a desire fueled by the specifically Greek indomitable free spirit is the same narrative that positions sex and love as being in some important way outside the operation of power, at least in power's state-building guise. The women's narratives amply demonstrate the intertwining of the two. Consider what Elena says, and what she does not say, in the following excerpt of one of our interviews.

> *I:* The condom, the male condom, is that something you don't want as a couple?
> *She:* No, I don't like it. Again I feel that it intervenes somewhere else. I don't know. I don't like it.
> *I:* In other words, it intervenes where? How?
> *She:* I feel that it divides me from the other person and I feel that it's just happening for relief and it seems sort of vulgar somehow. What I'm saying isn't right, I know.

The condom is invasive in that it operates as a wedge splitting the couple apart, both physically and emotionally. *Mas horizi*. It is a barrier between the two bodies that simultaneously influences the flow of feelings between the two lovers. In Elena's words, it is *this* "division from the other person" that defines the condom as an intervention. Of course, this also implies that straight sex *without* condoms, or heterosexual union, is somehow natural, uninvasive, and inherently unproblematic.

But what exactly does the "division" Elena associates the condom with consist of in Greece? Evidence of the Greek specificities of this division is found in the way Elena refers to her partner. Why does she not refer to him as her boyfriend, her lover, or perhaps just tell me the name of her partner? Why does she call him the impersonal "other person"? Part of this no doubt has to do with Elena's attempt to deploy the abstraction of scientific language to appropriately play what she sees as her role in the research I am conducting.

But "the other person," or *o allos,* is a phrase commonly used in modern Greek. It can function as a subtly adversarial reminder to a third party that there is another perspective—beyond that of the speaker—that also asks to be heard. If you and I are talking about something that has an impact on your partner but you do not want to put him or her on the spot and say he or she would be an obstacle, you might say, Well, OK, but there is "the other" too. *Endaxei, pes, na synehiso ego na doulevo, na kano ki afto kai to allo. O allos omos. (Ki aftos ehei apopsi.)* As Herzfeld's (1991b) idea of a poetics of Greek womanhood suggests, the historically produced categories of modern Greek culture make one of women's primary obligations (as *citizens,* I add, for Herzfeld's emphasis is more on women's role as *kin* in that context) to present a show of unconditional loyalty to their male partner and children before the eyes of "foreigners." To do otherwise, for instance as a deployment of many feminist discourses is seen to entail, is an action that can have treasonous reverberations.

Yet, as Herzfeld has argued, Greek women may employ a double voice and thus manage to at once both put on a convincing display of allegiance to male kin for the benefit of the eyes of a Greek or foreign outsider and at the same time advance a critique of their male kin's practices that is legible only to "insiders."[41] Silence often plays an important role in this. In fact, Christiana Lambrinidou, a playwright who has done impressive work helping both Athenian women and members of the Muslim minority of the northern Greek area of Thrace to develop "their own voice" through drama and writing, advised me to use this double voice in writing my book. At the beginning of my research, I told her I was concerned I would not be able to do justice to very difficult material without breaking out of a scholarly voice.

Seen from this perspective, Elena's explanation that the condom is an intervention because it separates her from "the other person" can be interpreted as a coded way of informing me—ostensibly very loyally—that "the other person" also has a point of view, and, in this case, is opposed to the condom. As was often the case, the silenced referent here may well be pleasure. Whether what is at stake is exclusively his pleasure, as the coded reference to "the other" suggests, or hers as well, it is likely that a significant part of the issue with the condom is that it also can constitute a fairly radical intervention in the smooth functioning of the couple, as Elena implies, in yet another way: by directly challenging a tacit agreement concerning the primacy of *his* pleasure.

ELLY

The same strategy of protecting the male partner from the possibility of external criticism is evident in the next excerpt. Calm efficiency, positioned as one of modernity's desired and yet mostly unattainable telltale signs in Greece, translates here again into the woman's use of an abstract scientific language. The national investment of excess in the domain of straight sex, which Persefoni and Elena vividly gestured toward, is revealed in a different manner. I quote from an interview with Elly, a forty-two-year-old public servant who has been married nineteen years. She has two children and reported having had five abortions and one miscarriage at the time of our interview.

> *I:* Do you remember if you had been using condoms before one of these pregnancies?
> *She:* Yes, I was using it but it proved to be ineffective. In other words, conception would happen before ejaculation. That's why it isn't a safe method.

Elena spoke of "the division with the other person" as the reason the condom intervenes and, in so doing, she indexed straight sex as a relatively boundary-free space of excess that is marked by what I argue is a nationally invested loyalty. Elly seems to take a different position. She claims to be against the condom ostensibly because it simply isn't an "effective" method. The reason, she says dryly, is that "conception would happen before ejaculation." This, I suggest, is a particularly flaccid way of saying that either "we," the straight couple, or "he" could not or would not put the condom on in time. This again supports the representation of Greek straight sex as a site of radical spontaneity in which the postulated essence of a uniquely unbounded Greek spirit finds its full expression. Within this space, even the condom figures as an intrusion, despite its apparent mechanical externality. Elly is very discreetly suggesting that this is a domain of such proliferating excitement that conception (*typically*, as her diction implies) happens before what is being defined as ejaculation. The condom's insertion here, especially if introduced at the woman's insistence, in the midst of such profusion of what here emerge clearly as masculine forces of pleasure, would be no less an invasion for its scientific claim to mechanical externality.

The treasonous component that this breech would have for Elly is referenced in her choice of words to describe "the problem" with the condom. She is careful to depersonalize and takes great pains to avoid implying that her partner is at fault. If anything, her claim that "conception happens before ejaculation" suggests the now familiar theme of "but I catch easily" and places responsibility on her. The quiet adamancy with which placing responsibility, or *naming* her partner, is avoided fits into the same culturally and historically specific narrative illustrated in Elena's comments.

The words articulated by Elena concerning sex as "the wolf's mouth" and her simultaneous care not to mention her partner, as well as Elly's words regarding the timing of ejaculation and conception, graphically illustrate how sex and love as discursive practices or stories we tell ourselves about certain activities and feelings are intimately intertwined with stories we tell ourselves about characteristics of our national identity. Moreover, the domain of sexuality emerges as a battle zone rigged with mines. The theoretically most private moments of the couple's life are in fact sites of great power in which, among other things, what is in many ways the *dream* of the nation can finally, if momentarily, be realized. Particular nationalist-inflected simulations of freedom, spontaneity, and resistance are physically performed in contexts of varying forms of emotional intimacy. Recall the accounts of Chryssa and Titika of the days with withdrawal as a method that also contained vivid evidence of the "disadvantages," as family planning experts call them, of using the condom by revealing just how deeply "into" the couple the condom has the potential to intervene. In visibly and tangibly suggesting that trust is not unconditional between the partners, the condom also goes against Greek notions of "a good man"—whether he is a partner of many years, the tried and tested loyal husband of Chryssa, or the "permanent escort" of a short period, of whom Titika nonetheless made clear that it is a point of pride that "you trust him, sort of."

Indeed, if we return to the parallel considered at the beginning of this chapter, with few exceptions, to ask for a condom may be something like proposing that a woman's partner eat a souvlaki without meat! In addition to seeming dispassionate and un-Greek-like, one might be suggesting that one's lover is not a good Greek man. After all, one of the subtler implications of not eating meat is not just that one is not a proper Greek, but that one is not a real Greek *man*, thus activating connotations of being gay or *a poustis*, as the

Greek homophobic colloquialism would have it. In effect, for a man, the implication of sex with a condom can be that he is not quite the hot-tempered and spontaneous and unequivocally "straight" and "honest" *Greek man* he is trying to be, even if he is somewhat convincingly being "a man" by having sexual intercourse with a woman. Moreover, not only is this a veiled attack on the male subject's Greekness and "real" masculinity (being reliable, trustworthy, *me besa*), but it also is a drastic diminishment of the couple's pleasure. For the women, to suggest use of the condom seems in many cases to be nothing less than breaking ranks.

Conclusion

In the context of the cultural politics of Greece today, the reference to abortion as an intervention is most usefully seen as ironic; most of the other modern methods of birth control are viewed as interventionary. The Pill violates the (divine) *nature* of the female body while also being seen as involving a fairly high level of counting and calculating and thus functions as an intervention in the freedom that is seen as inherently characterizing both Greekness and sexuality. The condom may not be a "huge change" in straight sex, as Elena put it, but it does violate an implicit code of trust, it does intervene aggressively in the economy of feeling that animates the tenuous achievement of "the couple," and it does visibly intervene in the construction of sexuality as a "free" site of excess and of abundant, if gendered, pleasure. The IUD, meanwhile, is never prescribed to women below the age of thirty-five unless they have already had at least two children, because Greek ob/gyns feel that the risk of infection, with its attendant danger of infertility, is too high for a woman who has not yet "made her family." The diaphragm is rarely presented as an option by gynecologists. In sum, most preabortion birth control measures culturally coded as modern are not easily legible as feasible options.

The days-with-withdrawal, a less interventionary method, has the advantage of offering fertile ground for playing out a nationally invested game of trust and a sound stage for putting up a performance of appropriate Greek femininity (she trusts and is also strong enough to risk) and masculinity (he is trustworthy). At the same time, both subjects also have the opportunity to reinscribe appropriate Greekness by protecting spontaneity and doing a minimum of counting behavior at the site of sexuality, while also flirting with a significant element of risk. Yet, recalling Persefoni's words, even the cluster of methods called "the days," whether in conjunction with withdrawal, the condom, other forms of sexuality, or abstention, is not always effectively inserted within the fields of power of which the straight Greek couple are a manifestation. Meanwhile, abortion, in the midst of all this, indeed emerges as a simple interruption, *diakopi,* much more than an intervention, *epemvasi.*

To the extent that abortion *is* an intervention, whatever it intervenes in is clearly less valued than either female nature, male pleasure, or the sense of Greekness that shapes and in many ways produces both of these. Meanwhile, the strategic uses to which an unplanned pregnancy and the subsequent abortion can be put further enhance the value of abortion as a choice. Certainly, the persistently high rates of abortion, as well as the frequency of repeat abortions, are important evidence suggesting that, to a significant degree, abortion's advantages compared to other methods continue to be locally interpreted as strong. In this chapter, I have tried to show what is at stake with other forms of birth control. In effect, Greek female subjects run up against nothing less than *Greece* itself.

The high frequency of abortion in Greece can be accounted for in part as the product of friction between disparate Greek configurations of personhood, on the one hand, and, on the other, birth control technologies that are presented in ways that presuppose a very different unit of consumption: specifically, the autonomous, fairly rigidly bounded, and largely nationally divested or, better, *extra national* "mind over body" liberal subject. That is, in this context we cannot accurately speak of "the body" as an objective entity external to the subject's notions of the divine and of what it means to be Greek. Indeed, it manifests symptoms in response to these ideas. On the other hand, it is not the counting and calculating behavior per se of such a subject that is foreign to Greek men and women, a culturally and historically specific amalgam of "bodies" and "psyches," but the visible or discernible exercise of counting (in some way taking seriously one's own interests/desires) in the specific domain of erota or love. After all, Greeks from all walks of life easily and proudly converted their national currency to the Euro in early 2002, with all the intricate counting and calculating that this required. To put in bold relief the disjunction between the liberal individual postulated in local family planning, state, and related expert and policy discourses, and the contemporary Greek gendered subject, I juxtapose the text from a taped and transcribed lesson on birth control that was given by a midwife at the Athenian public Family Planning Center, considered a prototype center.

Overall, the women I spoke with do not in fact see themselves as easily and simply distinct units or *atoma,* though there is an ongoing project, in tandem with the state's modernization, to create the more independent-seeming subjects called *sihrones Ellinides* (modern Greek women). This disjunction between the presupposed "contraceptor" and the lived experience of the self is not a result of Greeks "being bad at setting boundaries," as an AA-inflected pop psychology U.S. discourse about "the other" might suggest, even in the domain of foreign policy. Rather, I am talking about a distinct mode of being that involves a more diffuse way of organizing the self, the ongoing presence of conflict and struggle, and different boundaries altogether.[42]

For example, partners might not think about each other's finances, or not show that they do, but would, as a mixed symbol of both pride and the couple's "community," express disdain at counting or keeping track of what each owes the other. This push would be so strong as to prevent a recognition, verbalized at least, of the fact that the subject who has the financial problems is now owed a significant amount of money. While protecting their pride and performing *love* as a domain that is above such practices (*mizeries*), their finances might be steadily driven to the ground. For the injured party to bring this up within the given configuration of personhood is often to break ranks or even "act like an American." *Amerikanies*. Love means never *visibly* separating yourself out, or counting your own interests, and the politics of what is visible are their own little hornets' nest. One who has mastered the fine art of doing this "under the table" is not guilty of being divisive. The same holds, more or less, in domains other than finance. It entails a particular way of negotiating boundaries and protecting the (different) self.

But, if the expectation that modern Greek women modernly contracept is to be fulfilled, all the complicated and culturally and historically specific stuff of love and definitions and experiences of the body operative in Greece today also need to enter into the equation. In Greek public and more privately articulated discourses at this historical moment, there is a very sharp delineation between "us" and what or who is configured as foreign, or "outside of nature." As in most social systems, what is postulated as natural or a particular rendition of nature itself is a valuable trump card that silences dissent or contains practices deemed deviant and operates as a powerful mechanism of social control. This discourse permeates the nights.

Yet, a concomitant of the particular construction of the Greek gendered subject as person is that, especially in physically intimate interactions, women's efforts to establish boundaries such as those involved in "taking precautions" are themselves dangerous acts. They become such by virtue of their location in the larger cultural context in which Greek Orthodoxy and its communitarian ethics as well as Greek nationalisms currently enjoy wide circulation. For various reasons, having to do with the nation, the couple, and the perceived innate nature of the female body's capacity to reproduce as a divine gift, for a woman to "watch out" during sex is itself a highly dangerous act. She is, at some level, at once challenging the integrity of her partner and indicating that she herself is not entirely trustworthy, as she will not "give her all" unconditionally. Moreover, in an important sense, she is launching an attack against the discursive core of Greece, a Greece that is nonetheless increasingly embracing more modernized modes of behavior in other domains.

Simply put, to risk pregnancy is to prove loyalty, as well as demonstrate a Greek freeness of spirit and, not least, the allegedly irresistible allure of the partner. There may also be some pleasure in establishing whether or not one "catches," as some medical experts suggested when asked why Greece has such a high rate of abortion. But the other reasons impelling the choice to risk pregnancy are clear. As seen from the optic of the ongoing, always contested, and nationally invested Greek configuration of personhood, the so-called modern contraceptive devices that might—in a framework of abstract liberal individualism—appear to be unobtrusive get variously coded in ways that make their use prohibitively invasive in some Greek contexts. The condom "divides" but does not conquer (though it invades), and it raises all sorts of painful questions about trust and betrayal in the process. The Pill "hits" the body, brings all sorts of ills, and is attached to a high degree of counting. The so-called modern forms of birth control are intervening foreign bodies.

Like the Greek female body's intimate affiliation with another foreign body, the penis, the culturally specific understandings of Greek straight sex and technologies of reproduction work to render abortion a natural act. Though the naturalization achieved for both these technologies is of different degrees, in both cases this process is highly political. In this chapter we witness how, in Greece, "natural" bodies are imagined, literally *put together* in certain ways under the aegis of an imagined nationality. These ways, quite political, work to construct as natural some forms of sexuality and some parts of material bodies, animate and inanimate, and not others. In the next chapter, the focus is on how the emotions that animate these bodies in intimate relationship with one another also shape "the couple" as a social formation embedded in an economy of pain that is itself in turn shaped by larger narratives about national identity. *Ena zevgari. Ohi papoutsia.* In this context, beyond being more natural, abortion acquires actively positive connotations. After that, I turn to the nonetheless significant negative dimension that abortion also has, its meaning as a loss of sorts, and the stigma that remains attached to it in present-day Athens.

Chorus: Midwives on Contraception

The Family Planning Center where I met most of the women whose stories are presented here included a weekly, or sometimes biweekly, lesson (*mathima*) on contraception, as the midwives called it. This lesson was taught by one of the midwives to a group of two to six women who were required to attend one such lesson before being given a prescription for the Pill or the IUD. The following is a transcription of the lesson that was given one day by the newest midwife rotated into the Family Planning Center in 1994, Mrs. D. She had asked to use my tape-recorder because she wanted her children to hear her. She had often talked to me about her son and her daughter. I asked if she'd let me keep a copy of the tape for my research and she agreed.

This lesson was one of the few that took place in the office, the room I would conduct interviews in unless the director of the Center was working there, instead of sitting in the other room with the rest of the midwives. Most of the other lessons I observed included slides and took place in the room where the Sterility Department did its microscope work. This was one of the few lessons that did not use slides. Perhaps because of the lack of visual aids, perhaps because Mrs. D was performing this for her children, the actual lecture was more verbally detailed than any of the others I had sat in on. Keeping in mind the body and agency as they are mapped in the narratives of the interviewed women, let us listen now to the main *body* of the lesson they are offered at the Center.

> Mrs. D: . . . We said that these symptoms have almost vanished now [*pane na eklipsoun tora*] because of the lower dosage of hormones that the pills contain. If, despite this, symptoms appear in a woman, we tell her to be patient for about two to three months, during which time the organism gets to know this additional medicine and the symptoms vanish. If, despite all this, the symptoms do not eclipse, which I told you the percentage of them appearing now in recent years are minute, if however, they do not eclipse, the symptoms, then we change the particular type of pill [*skevasma*] for the woman. We give some other type.
>
> Because, as you know, very many circulate on the market from various companies. Another thing which the pill may present to us is that in the middle of the cycle the woman may see on her underwear some drops of blood. This doesn't trouble us. We pass it by without making mention of it [*to pername aparatirito*]. Nor does it create for us any problem. Also, the chances that a woman will develop vaginal infections increase by taking the

little pills [*hapakia*]. Every woman has chances of having a vaginal infection [*na kani mia kolpitida*]. But by taking the pill this symptom may appear more often, and this is due to [the fact] that the ph of the vagina [*kolpos*] drops and it is easier for the germs [*ta microvia*] to develop. And that is why we tell women that they should come in to the office at least once a year for us to see them [*na tis vlepoume*] in order to prevent these symptoms.

If now a woman who uses the Pill as contraception forgets to take the little pill one day, what should she do? First of all, you should know that she is covered, as far as an unwanted pregnancy is concerned, in other words, she is covered for seven hours. If she would take the little pill at 12 at night and she forgets and from 12 at night up to 7 in the morning she has sexual contact, she isn't in danger of getting pregnant. As long as, however, in the morning when she remembers that she forgot to take the little pill, she takes the forgotten pill and that night she takes the pill of the day, normally. Now, if she forgets to take more than one pill, first of all she is in danger of getting pregnant, and secondly, a period will come to her [*tha tis erthi periodos*]. That's why, at that point, we tell women to leave the used box to the side and start a new box with the entire series of pills inside.

Now, if the woman who takes the Pill wants to schedule [*na programmatisi*] a pregnancy, it is good for her to stop the pill for two to three months and then get pregnant. And the reason for this is so that the hormones that the pill contains can be eliminated. Because sometimes the effect of the hormones, if a pregnancy should happen [*prokipsi*] early, or if the woman falls on the slight percentage of failure [of the Pill] that we said, the effect of the hormones could create problems in the baby's formation of organs [*iorganogenisi*], in other words, the child may have some problems. Now, if the woman falls on this slight percentage of failure that we said and she gets pregnant, the pregnancy will have to, as you understand, be interrupted. But this follows since a woman who is taking contraception doesn't want to get pregnant. That's what I had to tell you about the Pill. I don't know, you, miss, since you are more interested, if you'd like to ask some questions?

First Woman: I've heard a lot about the problems of the Pill. I don't know . . .

Mrs. D: Yes, we will talk about that too. Talking here with women, they present various excuses to me with regard to taking the Pill. That doesn't hold, that the Pill can create some problems. Simply the women, or the world, if you like, aren't well informed [*kala enimeromenes*]. The main obstacles that the ladies who come here present [*provalloun*], and we discuss, are that I'm afraid to take the Pill because I'll develop cancer, because I'll grow hairs, because I'll gain kilos.

Now, as far as cancer is concerned, I have to tell you this: In fact, one woman who will take contraception for one year at least covers her organism for many years to not develop cancer of the uterus, the ovaries, and the breast. Also, various gynecological problems, irregularity in the period, and many other problems can be treated by taking a contraceptive pill.

Now, as far as hair growth is concerned, this doesn't hold either. If a woman who doesn't take contraception has some excessive hair growth and she goes to the specialist, the dermatologist in order to cure her problem, the first cure [*therapia*] which will be given from the doctor are the contraceptive pills. Therefore, this excuse doesn't hold either.

Now, as far as weight is concerned, the only kilos that the woman may gain from the receipt of the Pill are two to three and this is due to [the fact] that there is some retention of fluids in the organism, not to the deposition of fat. If the woman happens to gain more kilos this will be due, possibly, to something else. Perhaps to the woman's voracity for food, or to the poor metabolism of her organism, which will not be due, obviously, to the receipt of the Pill. Also, I should tell you that the action of the Pill is influenced by the receipt of other medicines. In other words, if a woman has a cold, a problem with her health, and her doctor tells her, for example, to take antibiotics for three to four days and simultaneously she is taking the Pill, the woman should during this time of seven days, of five, that she will be taking the antibiotics, to use another form of contraception as well. To use the condom, only for the days that she's taking another medicine. Anything else as far as the Pill is concerned?

Second Woman: Do you have to take the Pill all the time even if you know that, say, for a month or for two months your husband may be away on a trip?

Mrs. D: The Pill is taken continuously. Now, if a lady whose husband is, I don't know, a seaman [*naftikos*], and will be away—no, she will take the Pill everyday. Nor do I need to interrupt [*na diakopso*], to say, oh, I'll interrupt for five months so that my organism gets a rest and things like that, which women say. She can take it continuously. As long as, however, she is regular in her visits, she comes to the doctor to monitor her [*na tin parakolouthi*], she has the exams that are necessary. You, miss, something else?

Third Woman: With regard to the Pill, there is something that deters you from taking it. They say that it creates many symptoms. From strokes, they'd tell us, to . . . In other words, everything.

Mrs. D: Listen. When each woman does the tests we said, she meets the prerequisite conditions that we talked about (she doesn't have a health problem, she doesn't have a heart condition, she doesn't have a problem

Navigating the Night 201

with her liver, generally the woman is healthy). She does the tests we said, she comes for the annual visits, then there is no problem. If a woman starts taking the little pill alone, without laboratory exams, without being followed at some special center [*idiko kendro*], then she may have some complications. These hesitations around the receipt of the Pill should not exist. In other words, the excuses that women present don't hold. And I told you from the beginning that this is due to poor information [*kaki enimerosi*] and that the women try to learn one from the other, from the neighbor [female], from the sister-in-law. They don't go to an organized center to be informed and the little that they will hear there will hold and be guaranteed. And now to say some things about the IUD.

What prerequisites are needed here too for a woman to put on/in an IUD [*na vali to spirama*]? Above all, the woman has to have children. To have at least one child. We never put an IUD into childless women [*atokes gynaikes*], to women who haven't given birth. Now, as far as the laboratory examination goes, here too the woman will have to have a good gynecological exam, a Pap test, and a culture of vaginal fluid. If, and only if, these are good, then the woman can put on an IUD. We said that until the woman is thirty-five years old, the woman can take the Pill. From there on we recommend that she wear the IUD. We put an IUD [*forame to spiral*] on childless women only for individuals [*atoma*] with a low intellectual level [*hamilo pneumatiko epipedo*], in other words, a woman who has mental difficulties [*dianoitika provlimata*] and will not remember to take her little pill every day, then, rather than have the woman go have an abortion every month, it is preferable for her to put on an IUD.

The percentage of failure of the IUD is about 1.5 percent to 2 percent, a little higher than that of the Pill. When does it go in? The IUD goes in on the last day of the period. And why do we choose that day? During the duration of the period the uterus has some contractions in order to expel [*na apovali*] the blood. With these contractions, the cervical opening opens and so it is easier for the IUD to pass through into the uterus. Whereas the removal of the IUD, when, in other words, the woman wants to change the IUD and put in a new one, happens outside of the period. We don't want the woman to have a period. In other words, the removal is even easier. Now, as far as the placement [*topothetisi*] is concerned. The placement is painless, I could say. The woman doesn't need to take any anesthetic [*narkosi*], or stay in bed, nothing. She comes from her house, from her work, they put in the IUD, and she leaves. It is a small annoyance [*mia mikri enohlisi*].

Now, if a woman encounters the small percentage of failure that we said the IUD has and she gets pregnant, here too the pregnancy will have to be interrupted, if it is kept, because what is most likely is that a miscarriage will happen. If, however, a miscarriage doesn't happen, it would be good to have an interruption of the pregnancy [*na gini diakopi tis egymosinis*]. The IUDs that are in circulation now in the market cover us for three years. Certainly a woman who will put in the IUD now will have to come in once a year for us to see her, but in three years the old IUD will have to be removed, the exams we said will have to be repeated, and a new IUD will go in. It is being discussed that certain IUDs will circulate, how soon I don't know, that will cover us for five years. At the moment, however, we use the IUDs whose duration is three years.

What, now, can the IUD cause us in terms of complications? The IUD extends the cycle. In other words, if for a woman the duration of the period is three days, four, with the IUD they will become six and likely the quantity of blood will be a little more. This of course doesn't worry us. Also, every woman who doesn't use some contraception, doesn't use an IUD, has a percentage of about 5 percent for an extrauterine pregnancy. The women who wear the IUD have this percentage a little higher. Not, of course, so much so as to consider it a contraindication against using the IUD. That's why we say that we don't ever put in an IUD for childless women. The reason is that, because, yes, on the one hand, the woman doesn't wear an IUD [*den forai spirama*], however she always has chances of having an extrauterine pregnancy. Wearing the IUD, this 5 percent increases, it becomes 6 percent, it becomes 6.5 percent, therefore we don't want to risk this woman having an extrauterine pregnancy, because with the extrauterine pregnancy, as you all know, the tube is removed and the ovary. Therefore, the fertility of the woman is diminished by half. That is the reason we say we don't put an IUD into childless women.

Also, both here and in the Pill, there is an increase in the chances of a woman having a cervical infection, a vaginal infection. But we try to prevent all of this with the annual exam that we impose on women [*epivalloume stis gynaikes na kanoun*]. It is a mistake, a tremendous mistake, for a woman to put in an IUD without having had a Pap test, without having had a culture of vaginal fluid, and a good gynecological exam. Now, as far as the culture of the vaginal fluid is concerned, why do we want it? We want it so that we are certain that in the area of the vagina there are no germs. Why? With the placement of the IUD there are certain maneuvers which happen and certain germs may be dragged along and may enter the cavity of the uterus and create in us some inflammation.

Now, how does the IUD provide to us its contraceptive ability? What does it do, how does it work? The IUD, the element [*to stelehos*] of the IUD is wrapped around with a plating [*elasma*] which is made of bronze. So, entering the cavity of the uterus, the bronze creates a sterile inflammation [*asipti flegmoni*] and the fertilized egg doesn't find appropriate ground to stick to and grow and have the pregnancy develop. That is the one means of action. The other means of action is that the bronze bars the sperm from coming up into the flute of the tube and meeting the egg to have the fertilization happen. Whereas, to the contrary, the contraceptive activity of the Pill is different. In other words, we don't even have fertilization because with the receipt of the Pill the production [*ekkrisi*] of certain hormones which are needed to have ovulation and to have an egg is inhibited, and so the sperm doesn't at all meet the egg to have conception happen. Whereas with the IUD, on the one hand conception happens most of the times but the fertilized egg doesn't find appropriate ground within the cavity of the uterus to stick to and grow, and so it degenerates. Do you want to ask something about the IUD?

Second Woman: Does the IUD bring headaches?

Mrs. D: The IUD, no, it doesn't bring headaches. No, that is chance. It doesn't bring them. If you told me about the little pill, I'd say possibly. No, the IUD, no. The IUD can create, we said, organic problems. A little more blood during the period. After the placement of the IUD we tell all the ladies once the next period comes and finishes to come in, for us to simply do an exam to check that the IUD is in the right place. That first exam is obligatory. From there on, the women can even check by themselves if the IUD is in its place. How can they check it? Putting the index finger of their hand deep inside the vagina and doing a rotating movement so that they meet the little laces that hang from the cervical opening, in which case the IUD is in its place. Of course, if a woman has some doubt and is afraid of doing this maneuver, she can come to the office at any time and say I have a doubt about whether the IUD is in its place, please check it.

What you need to be careful of is during the period, when you change the little pad, to check it always just in case the IUD has been expelled. And why is there a danger that it be expelled? Of course in very small percentages, but I am obliged to mention it to you. We said that the uterus does certain contractions during the period. Those little pains that we feel are contractions of the uterus. And it may sometimes happen with these contractions that the uterus does expel the IUD. I'm telling you, the percentage is slight. It may leave, yes. And that's why we tell women during the days of the period, when they change the little pad, to check it, just in case the IUD has been expelled.

You should know always that the basic prerequisite for you to go to your gynecologist, whether here or outside [privately], regardless if they don't tell you this, is that you be for three days without your period and sexual contact. These are basic prerequisites. Three days without your period and three days without sexual contact. It is a basic prerequisite because the results of the exams are more precise, more guaranteed.

Chapter 8

THE IMPOSSIBLE DREAM:

THE COUPLE AS MOTHER

✥

LOVE (sic)

One day, in a museum, they showed her a painting:

A vivid landscape, nonetheless it exuded a religious calm.
It had something of the fires.
Barren landscape, the place of the skull.
The sky, uncertain. Neither day nor night.

"What is this, our little girl" they asked.

(Once upon a time it was
a small little girl, blond, looked like a cartoon—
with a little red dress
and a childish, little girl's, pocket book. The sun, black.)

"This"
she said, and smiled sweetly with blood dripping from her lips,
"is love."
—Topali, 1999, 31; my translation

The cultural specificities of a preoccupation with *alterity*—what counts as foreign, what constitutes an intervention—that characterizes all members of a collectivity to some degree, including citizens of nation-states, and the specificities of the idiosyncratic and charged forms of agon involved in demarcating what or who is "ours" (*dikos mas*) or *with* us (*eisai mazi mas i ohi*) underlie the high rate of abortion in Greece. Religious and nationalist discourses issuing from and shaping particular sites of Greek collective memory—for example, the representation of the "fall" of Constantinople as a crucial loss for

Greek Orthodox Christianity, the catastrophe suffered by Greek forces in Asia Minor, the Albanian war and the German Occupation, U.S. involvement from the Marshall Plan through the Papadopoulos junta—form a complex web of meanings within which Greek personhood is formed.

One result of this is the very formulation of the demografiko discourses and their configuration of abortion as a national threat and of Greek (Orthodox) births as a panacea for Greek national welfare. The deep-seated anxiety about what is foreign, or a dangerous intervention, and the high value placed on struggle itself are reinscribed here. In this larger context, *testing* the strength and loyalty of the partner, as well as the strength and faith of the self, figure as a privileged site of social intercourse. The struggle or ordeal, *dokimasia* as it is called, is seen as a *trial,* and at times quite specifically in religious terms. Trust and betrayal of trust become key and very volatile issues.

A high use value is implicitly placed on the struggle involved in the process of repeatedly getting pregnant and the subsequent negotiation of a decision to abort. Having shown how abortion in Greece emerges as a natural act, I now examine how, once *naturalized* in Greek culture, abortion goes on to be represented and used in particular ways at the level of the Greek couple. The material presented here demonstrates that abortion is deployed as a potent strategy in the fraught field of power of the Greek heterosexual couple. The specifics of these deployments are varied; however, the narratives of all the interviewed women contained evidence of this use of abortion. For example, in some instances, abortion is used to further secure a relationship that successfully passed through the *dokimasia,* or trial. In others, the abortion experience becomes a catalyst for the termination of a relationship that was not satisfactory. In either way, in most cases abortion is used *to see.*

Thus, not only does there seem to be a cultural and cognitive grid in place that renders abortion easily legible as the most natural birth control method, but abortion emerges as a potent form of political action, no less strategic for the apparent intimacy of its location within the couple. In this context, abortion is in many instances the very glue holding together key elements in the mosaic of the modern Greek nation: the ambivalently individualized self and the Greek couple. In probing this dimension of abortion's meanings and its function as a charged site of contestation *within* the Greek couple, the larger arena of struggle of the nexus of the Greek nation and its substantive affiliate, Greek heterosexuality, is illuminated.

There are few explicit references to the nation and God in the ways the women themselves talk about their relationships. Yet, in the scripts of these relationships, there is evidence of the larger cultural narratives of the Greek ethnos and popular constructions of the divine. In important ways, the Greek straight couple itself is a product of these discourses. I continue here to pursue the argument that the Greek straight couple is one of the primary embodiments and articulations of narratives about national identity and, simultaneously, targeted specifically by nationalist thematics. That abortion emerges as a political strategy within the couple at all, and the particular ways that it does, is a function of the larger historical narratives of Greekness that shape popular configurations of the gendered subject and of love and attraction. Though unmarked, Greece is present here at least as much as is in policy rhetoric and other more clearly distinguishable public spheres—indeed, perhaps more powerfully present in love because it more easily escapes from notice here.

In this chapter I follow the relationship of four Greek straight couples as they unfold in the women's narratives of the experience of pregnancies. Each woman tells a characteristic story about how one or more of her several abortions was positioned in her relationship at the time and what was its perceived impact. As we follow the specific stories of these women, it is again important to keep in mind the larger narratives of national identity and femininity that were traced earlier.

To introduce this consideration of how abortion operates as a strategy aimed at the accomplishment of often disparate ends in the domain of the straight couple, let us quickly survey the fraught field of power that it constitutes. Identifying important landmarks in this difficult terrain is Evangelia, a feminist and psychologist I interviewed for her views on abortion as a Greek feminist. She refers to her personal experience and reveals a vital dimension of the uses of abortion, thus demonstrating just how charged is the agonistic field formed by and through the Greek straight couple.

After she and I finished talking about the Greek feminist movement, her own participation in it, and her estimation of its limitations, we stopped briefly so she could pick up the phone. Her apartment in the coastal Athenian neighborhood of Faliro was fairly large and comfortable; the living room was simple and spacious. I settled into the armchair I was sitting in. I could hear the murmur of Evangelia's voice on the phone in the hallway behind me. I thought of how she had invested so much of her energy and time in helping women throughout the past two decades of her life. At the time of our conversation, she had important differences with the movement, as she and most long-standing feminists referred to it. *To kinima*. But she also continued to feel a strong commitment and she had honored it with a great deal of hard work, at the same time working at establishing her private practice as a psychologist, her marriage, the subsequent divorce, and the mostly single-handed raising of her daughter. At that moment, I overheard the end of her phone conversation. I got the impression she was talking to the man she had told me she has been involved with for the past few years. They were working out dinner plans and it sounded like he would be late coming home that evening.

After she came back to the living room where I was sitting, we picked up our conversation again. She seemed brisker and clearer somehow. "Now, as a psychologist, I believe other things too, which, of course, aren't the political opinion but are tied up with the political. In other words, I believe that it is not by chance that many women who are informed of contraception get pregnant, many women who *know,* as I did in the second abortion. Without essentially wanting to get pregnant, at least at a conscious level, they *do* want it, I believe. It isn't luck or an accident. At bottom, there is something they want to see!" *Kata vathos, kati theloun na doune!*

Evangelia bravely makes the suggestion that at some level women actually want to get pregnant even when they do not want a child. The women are using the resulting abortion(s) along with the pregnancy to learn something about their relationship, their partner, and, I add, themselves. This aspect of the meaning of abortion becomes clear only once we relinquish a view of women who get pregnant and abort as either stupid or uninformed; to my knowledge, it is an aspect that has not been acknowledged or studied for any nationality of repeat aborters.[1] To use abortion in order to see may be an idea that is not imaginable or is sufficiently shocking as to prevent serious consideration.

In putting up for display the next four excerpts from interviews, I hope to nuance the map being charted of national identity, the body, and agency by exploring abortion's meanings at a different site and establishing how, at the site of the Greek couple, abortion is indeed being used as an optic device or a *visual technology,* in the sense that Evangelia suggests above. That it is used thus indicates that "seeing" in the same way, and the same sorts of things, is not otherwise available in the vexed ground of the couple. This also is a telling sign of the economy of feeling of this domain and the cultural patterns governing expression within it.

Each of the women shows us one facet of this realm and abortion's positionings within it. Eleni talks about one of her abortions as a sign of the failure of the relationship she was in. Ismini shows us how abortion can be used first to probe the future of a relationship and then to *avoid* forcing a marriage, contrary to lore and folk opinion. Niki describes how one of her abortions, which seemed not to have changed anything in her relationship with her partner, turned out to have an important effect by clarifying and reinforcing the limits each of them had already established in the relationship. Finally, though initially claiming that none of her abortions had any effect on her relationships, Titika's story illustrates how abortions are seen as revealing "the truth" about a partner. Abortion is positioned in the narratives in quite disparate ways as an instrument that helps the subject, ostensibly passively, to see more clearly. Yet, in many ways, abortion is in fact also being actively used, or deployed, by both subjects in order to *act* on the field of power that the couple occupies and, at times aggressively, compel a retrenchment or realignment of positions.

All four women are highly educated, with a bachelor's degree or higher, and all four were single at the time of our conversations. Almost all media reports and many scholarly accounts of abortion tend to presuppose the *married* couple in their analyses. Yet, the situation of single women offers a condensation of the salient aspects of abortion within the heterosexual couple. The high level of education of these women, meanwhile, may be a factor in the articulateness with which they discuss this aspect of abortion. The dynamics described, however, are representative of those in the narratives of the other women I interviewed. The narratives are excerpts from the actual taped and transcribed conversations with these women; I have done minimal editing to facilitate readability. Each excerpt is prefaced by a description of the socioeconomic position of the woman speaking and followed by a brief analysis of key aspects of the narrative.

Eleni

Eleni is thirty-four years old and single. She works for a private shipping company at the level of middle management and has earned a Master of Arts degree in business from a well-known university in England. She reports having had four abortions and talks at length about her most recent one. This meeting took place in the living room of her apartment in the densely populated downtown area of Kipseli, across from a park. Her apartment was decorated with heavy, solid dark furniture; it looked like the kind of furniture that had belonged to a grandmother and been "carried over," with some solemnity. Juxtaposed to this, the moderate untidiness of Eleni's papers and other belongings scattered on several surfaces of the room gave the space a comfortable feeling. This was her home.

The segment below powerfully illuminates the cognitive terrain within which abortion acquires meaning as an emblem of the perceived failure or shortcomings of a relationship. This was an important element in the majority of the stories I heard, whatever the social class and educational level of the woman involved. Part of what Eleni teaches is that if we are to speak of *a loss* when considering abortion in Greece, it is primarily as the loss of *a dream* about the future of a relationship. Meanwhile, this narrative illustrates some of the ways abortion helps the gendered Greek subject see the limitations of her relationship and, at the same time, helps to build the realization that other hopes held dear may not come to fruition.

> *I:* Do you remember the day you went for the abortion? I want to remind you that whatever you would rather not answer you should feel free to ignore and we'll move on to something else. So, did you go for the abortion alone? Do you remember how you felt when you woke up?
>
> *She:* When I woke up I was fine. When I was going down [to the abortion rooms] I was not well. I was ready to cry when I went down. And I woke up crying. I woke up from my crying. In other words, I felt that I had sobs inside my sleep. And then of course I put on my lovely shield. . . . Because after fifteen days or twenty days have gone by, you forget a little. But at some point it surfaces [*ekdilonetai*] and it comes out [*sou vgeni*] and you don't know how it may come out. It may come out in that you want to go dancing at the *bouzoukia* [a somewhat derogatory word used to reference any of several types of Greek music clubs where people tend to drink a lot, sing, and sometimes dance on the tables]. You may shut yourself inside your home. It may come out in any way. As long as you realize that that is what is coming out for you.
>
> *I:* Did you realize it?
>
> *She:* Well, yes, I know that when I pressure myself where my feelings are concerned, at some moment later it will come out [*tha mou vgi*]. Because I'm not a person who holds things in. I may have patience in many things, but I can't hold my feelings in easily, and the bitterness that I will feel, or something else that I will feel, I know that eventually it will come out. My life has made me see this. We meet and we are together and as long as it goes . . . In other words, I don't see a common course any longer. I may change later.
>
> What else can I tell you? I was shaken, perhaps, by the fact, one afternoon . . . When he was here, before he left—because he works at night, he's a reporter and he works at night—he said, "You know, I belong there out-

side." [Eleni gestured to the window.] "I belong there. Normally, I should be there now." He was referring to the fact that he had just got a divorce, etc.—he hadn't yet got the divorce, they had separated for a year but he hadn't received it—and normally for that reason too he would have to be out and seeing other people, etc. "I have to be there," he said.

But he wanted to think and so he stayed in his house for three days, and all those three days, of course, inside of me the process was going on. I said, "What if the same incident had happened when I was five months [pregnant], when there would be no way to go back, then what?" And he put a damper on it. Maybe I would have been more positive, I would have tried to talk myself into it, tell stories to myself [*na paramythiaso ton eafto mou*].... If I had a warmer family situation of my own or whatever which might draw him into it, which he might like, it might have been different. But I also had a hesitation ... then I, too, because of my professional life and all those things that made me hasten my decision to be more negative, because of that.

But ... Now I don't know.... In other words, things aren't bad between us, but I've reached a point, because I've always had relationships with men who are about forty years old, that I have begun to be unbearably bored because they always come with a whole mess of problems. They suffer the whole problem of being forty-two, forty-five years old, they're separated, some are separated with children. So you find yourself saying, Please, I want a "new generation." I want someone now who is in his thirties, even if that may make him younger than me theoretically, but I don't want the problem of the forty-something-year-old men. And I've started saying that. I say it for fun now, but I think that somewhere inside of me I believe it. In other words, it can't be that I'm just saying it. If it was, OK, I'd say it once or twice. Now I've started realizing that this isn't for me. At last, the forty-something-year-old men have to go home!

I: Their charm is ...

She: All my life I've had relations with that age group. What we say and laugh at is that as I grow older I don't go up in the age group I date. I haven't reached the sixty-year-olds; I've remained at forty! Meanwhile, when you are younger, these things can have a negative influence on you because you think that *you* are wrong. Because they're older and they know and whatever they get across to you, they get it across in such a way that can make you have hang ups. *Na se kanoun koblexiki.* So, when you grow up and you know how to distinguish whether what the other person is saying is really his idiosyncrasy, or weirdness, or insanity (whereas in the past it may have been that you don't realize it and you may even doubt what you think), then you feel happy. They're problematic, best without them.

Because in Greece . . . if you finish school and start college [*na spoudazis*] and you work at the same time, and plus as a woman your brain grows much faster than that of boys. Then they'll have to go to the army [for the obligatory military training Greece upholds] for another two years and the process of work will have to wait. . . . It all adds up to them being about five years behind you. There is a tremendous gap, at least in my generation. But at that time we hung out, my female classmates and I, with men who were twenty-five years old and twenty-six years old. And we'd go up from there. It was normal. When you are twenty-two years old and you work in a company, you're studying, you run around, you're doing things . . . to go out with a thirty-five-year-old man is normal. Such emotional wear and tear. *Tetoia psyhiki fthora.*

She talked more about her boyfriends and the dating patterns of her generation, as she saw them. Then I asked if we could focus in on contraception.

I: Do you remember [using] any means of contraception since August?
She: With condoms and with the days.
I: How do you feel? Do you want it? Do you not want it?
She: I don't want it. But, as we say, "In the face of need, even gods are convinced." *Anagka kai theoi pithondai.* It is horrible, exactly where [*akrivos ekei pou*] . . . the whole process is horrible. And it isn't natural. It isn't. And so we do it with the days. But some day we forgot and it happened.
I: Were you counting together or—
She: No, together. He was too. He knows it all better than me. He understood why I'm a certain way even a week before the period. I get greedy for food, so much so I could eat my toes. *Me piani i tasi gia fai kai troo kai ta podia mou.* He knew the days well. When I'm ovulating, I'm in pain. I can tell when I'm ovulating. But can you tell the two to three days that are before? It happened after . . . I didn't expect it.
I: In this particular case, do you remember the specific night, which you think afterward, was when you got pregnant? Some women say they think they can sense when they got pregnant.
She: I think I knew it, in other words, I had a day in my mind. *Iha mia mera sto nou mas.* In the end it was the next day. . . . But I couldn't say that I could tell . . . that I felt something. I may have had it and it was . . . [motions that it may have been repressed]. Not at all unlikely.

I: Why might it have been repressed?

She: Because I wasn't very familiar with the idea. I was convinced I couldn't get pregnant then. These things are relative to emotions. When you bury them, at some moment they come out.

I: But you didn't say . . . what were your feelings?

She: At the time that I was going I was sad for what I was doing.

I: In other words, what exactly?

She: Because both as a woman I feel that my margins are getting narrower. *Ta perithoria stenevoun.* In what sense? Well, that I don't have the energy [*to kouragio*] to play with my niece, who is now nine years old. Imagine if I have a child and I have to go to the park, and buy it chocolate, etc., etc., and no, I don't want this, I want the other thing. That's why the popular proverb says, "Either get married very young or while young become a monk [or nun]." *I mikros-mikros pandrepsou, i mikros kalogerepsou.* That is, have children while you're young and you have the energy to because afterward you go on the shelf, you are for the shelf, you're not up to such things. . . . A mother of twenty years isn't the same as one of thirty-five. In other words, by your thirty-five years, if you have the ease and you can, OK, but inevitably you have more things against you. . . . You're struggling. *Palevis.* Your defenses are much fewer than those you have when you are twenty years old.

I: . . . Then you were sad because you felt this . . .

She: I was sad also for something that I had imagined that I might do with him and in the end it turns out that it can't happen. That it happened at some moment while it could have happened in September, or one year later, or even now, well, I had mixed feelings about that. An operation that has its own risks . . . The feelings were mixed. And I was: I wanted it, I didn't want it. I went through that. I wasn't unyielding from the beginning, to say no. Nor was I saying from the beginning, Yes, I want it. I was undecided until . . . *Because as long as there is my mother, my father,* oi dikoi mou, *there would be help and you can have peace of mind.* In other words, I have my sisters, I could always . . . you know how it is in the Greek family, and the friends that exist . . . For better or for worse, in the Mediterranean region, people are closer to one another. You don't have a problem. If you want something, somebody will help you. It isn't like England here. My sister was telling me, "Come on, we are here, I'll help you," etc., etc. . . . So, the feelings were mixed.

Eleni shows that going dancing or "shutting yourself inside" can both equally be ways of expressing a sadness that, it is important to note, she sees as having nothing to do with a fetus or a crime of any sort but everything to do with the loss of *a dream* about a relationship. Becoming a mother, as I show in greater detail in the next chapter, is seen as something done *with someone else* and hence operates most powerfully here as a marker of a particular type of relationship (with another adult). It is not so much motherhood per se that Eleni says good-bye to, though it is that as well. But what seems to cause her more sorrow is saying good-bye to a particular type of relationship with this man—one in which Eleni's motherhood *with him,* in effect, would be a possibility. She is also negotiating her own identity as a modern woman. The abortion helped her to see and to establish the limits of her relationship, as well as providing an opportunity for her to test and clarify her own intention and perceived ability to become a mother.

Ismini

Ismini, a psychologist who works for the Secretariat for the Equality of the Sexes as an independent researcher and also at the Center for Research on Women of the Mediterranean, was a new friend. We had met for coffee several times. I enjoyed her company a lot and she also seemed to like our meetings. After we had known each other for a while and I had talked to her quite a bit about the research, I asked her if she would agree to be interviewed. The following is an excerpt from that discussion. She talked to me at length about her relationships in the context of all her abortions. I have selected two excerpts here, first, of her account of her last abortion and then, doubling back, her story of the one preceding it. Both passages offer a vivid illustration of how an unwanted pregnancy is not used in contemporary Athens to force a more serious commitment out of the male partner, as it was in the past. At the same time, both of the following narratives trace an economy of emotions in which love and pain are joined at times in particular and unexpected ways.

As in Eleni's narrative, the specter of Kazantzakis's "down-to-earth" hero Zorba who dances furiously in the sand of the beach as he cries seems to be very present. *Andrikia.* For a Greek woman to be Greek, it seems at times, she must act in a way that is locally defined as "the way of a man." This ostensibly means she should take her blows standing up, without "sniveling"; in practice, when applied to a woman this comes to mean without *any* tears or display of pain at all. To register being *hurt,* not angry or frustrated or disappointed, is to be "like a woman" and hence, in some contexts, not to be properly Greek. *San gynaikoula kani.* This idea of how to be correct as a Greek woman, *sosti,* is tied in with otherwise middle-class notions of what is dignified behavior and what is not (*katinies*), though there is an ambiguous line beyond which too much dignified behavior, especially a lack of a performance of spontaneity, can also become evidence of inappropriate Greekness.

For an example of a woman successfully being manly in a Greek way, consider the following anecdote. When Demetra Papandreou, the second wife of the late prime minister of Greece, Andreas Papandreou, released her book of memoirs from her "life with Andreas" in September 1997, among other events planned to promote the book she appeared at a central bookstore to sign books. Surprisingly, some said, a very long line of people showed up. As a former airline hostess with a reportedly colorful past who had been viewed as the reason for the breakup of Andrea's marriage with the well-respected Greek American Margaret, many were saying her book would be "trashy" and unworthy of Andreas's memory. Yet, there was a long line of people buying it and there was Demetra dutifully signing the books. Unexpectedly, one of the women in line walked up to her, book in hand, and slapped her—apparently once on each cheek. The bodyguard present quickly stepped in and removed the woman from the premises. The press loved the incident. Interviews with anyone present were sought. Throughout all this, Demetra Papandreou made no statement at all. Moreover, when she was asked later if she would press charges, she declined. This is the epitome of "acting like a man" rather than a *gynaikoula*. With this one incident "Mimi," as she is often called, probably earned many more points than her book would get her. *M'arhidia, ohi malakies*. Mimi was willing to take personal insult rather than mar Andreas's memory with a catfight. This counted for many of the Greeks who had considered Andreas their leader.

Ismini's narrative shows that in the context of a relationship, the result is a female subject who subjects herself or manages herself at what is clearly great cost at certain moments, in what is consciously an effort to support the male subject's autonomy. The irony is clear: in forging of herself an individual, the proper Greek female subject takes on burdens, responsibilities, and blame that can make the male production of the individual a much simpler project. Yet, in successfully playing the part, the woman also finds pleasure: the pleasure of being modern or *sosti* or, in a more class-inflected register, a *kyria* (a lady). In ultimately deciding to have an abortion, Ismini is making of herself "a woman" as she understands its normative and markedly nationalized definition. The unplanned pregnancy helped her to see something about her relationship, such that the subsequent abortion figures as a formative moment. In effect, she is performing the self as a person who assumes full responsibility when, if not "careful," she gets pregnant. In this version of the heroic narrative, cluttered as it is with great ambivalence and an attempt to order the profusion of feelings, we nonetheless discern the figure of the woman narrator "composing" herself as we are shown images of the woman who stands tall and single-handedly takes on what are configured as the consequences of *her* actions.

Having just explained to me her doctor's theory of how you know the sex of the fetus (something to do with feelings of heat and other such factors) and her conclusion that the child would have been a girl, Ismini continued with the following.

> *She:* First of all, then, it really touched me. At the time it was a sensitive point for me that I wanted a girl. Second, I believed that my relations with Thodoro at that time—yes, on the one hand, I was separating but I believed that this was the relationship of my life. Really, I had him, I loved him, not anymore at that time, but during the relationship, I had loved him very much, madly, so as to take all that and suffer all that and still not to separate. It isn't only, let's say, that it had entered into my unconscious that it isn't right for me to separate in a moral sense. *I loved him. In other words, I suffered.* And I believed that I'm not going to have another relationship like that. OK, I'll have a relationship but not so much. [*Tha kano shesi alla ohi toso poli.*] And so the idea had come to me that I would want a child from Thodoro, even if I separated.
>
> I discussed it with the doctor. I had the doctor then too who was quite a bit more absolute by then. "Since you have a relationship . . ." he'd say. I asked him, "But how much?" In other words, my father would count the months later, he'll understand that I am . . . The doctor told me not to consider that, parents always think that way—I can't remember what he was telling me—and then they accept it. After the marriage they accept it. They don't try to find out what you did before. They accept it. And he insisted a lot, it was clear, that you have to keep it because you have a relationship, you can get married and have this child. You both work so if you get married you'll have your parents' support too. *Keep it,* he said, *you've already had two abortions, we're not going to go for a third.* And he was very absolute. I was too—he saw me obviously, he realized that I was vulnerable, that I was thinking about it, and he insisted a lot, as much as he could [*oso ton epairne*], and he put me into . . . I told him, OK, I'll think about it. I'll talk about it too with Thodoro. He hadn't come with me, Thodoro, none of the times. I'd go to the doctor alone. I told the doctor, "I'll discuss it and I'll call you tomorrow morning." And he said, "Call me for sure so that I know. If it is, we

shouldn't delay." In other words, if you're going to have the abortion we shouldn't delay, have it right away, or, if you keep it normally, I'll tell you what tests you're going to do, etc.

And I had talked about it a lot with Thodoro. I told him that I didn't care about getting married, that's how I was seeing it. *To iha di etsi.* In other words, I felt that I had the guts to keep it alone and to impose it on my father. But if it is necessary and my father doesn't accept it and he kicks me out of the house, then some financial help. Nothing else from you, in other words. Or also minimally, to play the role of the father. *Stihiodos.* In other words, for the child to know who his father is, and some financial help, nothing else. I'll raise it alone. Let's say a woman who will hold it in the morning when I work, for us to pay her half and half, I can't also pay the rent, and a woman, and everything. And he had said that that was an impossibility, Thodoro. He didn't want a child at all. *Den ithele paidi me tipota.* Generally he was, and he continues to have these same opinions because I bump into him by chance sometimes. I've seen him again from time to time. He continues to be unmarried, to be against marriage, against children. He didn't want a child. I don't know if he ever understood why, but in any case he didn't want a child.

I: Would he give you an argument for why?

She: Social, that social programming, that the world that exists doesn't suit him and he doesn't like it and he doesn't want to bring a child into such a world. That it will suffer, and only if he had tremendous [economic] means to guarantee it for all its life; that with these conditions for him to have it [*na to vgali*] and for it to struggle the way he struggles and everybody struggles, he didn't want to bring a child into the world. And he was absolute on this.

I wanted it, I wanted to keep it, and I remember that it bothered me very much, and I still think about it. In other words, there have been moments even now during some periods of my life when I have said that if I had kept it then, I don't know, it would be ten years old now, it will be now, I don't know, fourteen years old, the girl. I considered it a given that it was a girl. In the end, I concluded that I can't, I can't do it both in opposition to my father and in opposition to Thodoro. Alone I didn't have the qualifications [*den iha ta prosonda*] to keep it, by a long shot [*me tipota*], and I decided to drop it, but that time it bothered me a lot. *Na to rixo.*

And I went and had the abortion at Ygia, with Thodoro together, this time, and we came back. We had even rented an office together. We had opened an office together, which in the one room we had put a bed, and we came back and I slept there after the hospital. *I remember that it bothered me very much and possibly this played a role too in that I separated from Thodoro a month later.* In other words, I considered him responsible. In other words, that if he had wanted I would have kept it because I decided to keep it. If I had the support of my father, or if Thodoro had said OK . . . I don't care about marriage and without a marriage I would have kept it, even if I had a fight with my father, because I believed that he would accept it—my father— but I wasn't sure that he would support me.

In other words, now that I think about it, knowing my father, I believe that he wouldn't have kicked me out. He would have supported me. Yes, on the one hand he would have had a shock, poor him, he would have been ashamed before people because I'd be single. He might possibly have changed houses. He would have had to change a house. In other words, I don't think he could have taken it in the same neighborhood, for people to know that his daughter has a child. We're talking about ten years ago, it was very bad, society has changed tremendously in ten years. Ten years ago . . . In other words, if my father was alive now, and two years ago when he was alive, and I got pregnant and I kept it even without a marriage [*exogamo*], he would have accepted it much better. Not because I would be by then thirty-four years old, but it wouldn't have received such an outcry from society. But ten years ago, there wasn't any way, there weren't out-of-wedlock children, and those women who had out-of-wedlock children were considered whores.

I remember then that they had made it a big issue on TV. The actress Elena Nathanail had kept an out-of-wedlock child.[2] And she was considered the first to keep an out-of-wedlock child. Television presented it in a positive light, not with an accusation. It seemed to be saying that a woman can and has the guts to keep it alone. It was positive. It presented it positively, but it had become an issue. In other words, for months the magazines and the television dealt with Nathanail. Can you imagine that happening now? So the outcry would have been tremendous and yes, on the one hand, I was of the opinion that I don't care what the world says [*den ypologizo ton kosmo*], but my father would not have been able to accept it, to take it, no matter how much he might emotionally want to help me. I believe, then, that very possibly he would change houses or maybe he would rent a house for me far away and pay the rent for me. I don't know what he would have done, but I don't believe that he'd kick me out. I don't believe it, the way I know him now.

Then, though, I remember that I didn't dare to tell him, like that. If I kept it with Thodoro, I would have announced it to him and left. That way it enters in differently too, if you like. We would have appeared later and my father could tell people, "She's married." It is different when there is a man too. My friend did that. Then I didn't dare say it, like that, and I felt Thodoro to be very responsible, because then I wanted to keep it. It bothered me very much and—OK, I say it bothered me, actually I didn't think about it more than two days at the time. But I tell you that repeatedly I think about it still, even now. Of course, I think that my life would have changed completely. I wouldn't have gone abroad to study, and at that time I was working as a secretary and a salesperson because the political science degree is useless. But OK . . . emotionally it bothered me even now. . . .

The problem has nothing to do with the fetus and everything to do with Ismini's dream of becoming a mother. This time as well, however, "becoming a mother" is situated in a particular relationship. Though it is of special importance to her that the child would have been a girl, she says in the beginning that she'd like to have kept it because it was Thodoro's, with whom, despite their impending separation, she felt a very deep connection. It is almost as though his not agreeing with her desire to keep the child was denying her a sign of their love—the end of their relationship notwithstanding. In this context, her decision to abort, represented as inevitable due to financial reasons, can be understood as a sign of her greater love for him. She will not do what she so wants because he does not want it. Her swan song, so to speak, is to honor his wishes, despite the cost to her. *Palikarisia*.

Certainly, needing money to pay for a woman to keep the child during the day is a real need, but it is odd that she places so much significance on it, especially given the work she herself has been involved with at the Secretariat to provide clean, good, state-sponsored day care. Money is being made to figure as the main issue by Ismini, and Thodoro also seems to use money to withhold support of her dream, a dream that would keep them connected. Yet, most important, the pregnancy illuminates the limits of Thodoro's love. Ismini quietly and sadly admits this to herself. He cannot overcome his desire not to have a child just to make her happy, and this says something about the depth of their relationship.

Ismini's narrative also shows how abortion can be used to demonstrate the unfailing depth of her love in good Greek ("ancient") tragic fashion, on the one hand, and her maturity and responsibility as a modern (Greek) woman, on the other. Through this abortion, Ismini, like so many of the women I spoke with, effectively becomes a deeply loving, almost tragically passionate, and yet also properly matured Greek "individual" woman. This construction of her self, and the key role abortion is made to play as a building block in such a project, emerges even more clearly in the way she talked about her *previous* abortion, the "next-to-last," as she referred to it.

> *I:* So your last abortion was when you were twenty-six years old . . .
>
> *She:* Twenty-six years old, yes, ten years ago . . . I had turned twenty-six years old in September. I was twenty-six and a half . . .
>
> *I:* Can I ask you a little . . . so we can close this chapter . . . about the relationship with Thodoro. The last two abortions were with Thodoro?
>
> *She:* The next-to-last possibly was with the other guy, possibly with Thodoro. The last one was definitely with Thodoro.
>
> *I:* Can you tell me a little more about how you felt him to be the day of the operation? Not just the days around the abortion. Did you feel him to be as you wanted him to be, and how did you want him to be?
>
> *She:* Let me tell you. Imagine that in the next-to-last abortion I don't remember at all because I didn't know, I wasn't sure which of the two [men's] it was. I had made sure to take my responsibility myself [*tin efthini mou ego*]. In other words, I didn't let myself really live it in either of the two cases, because with whomever of the two if I had [kept the baby], I felt that I would be fooling him [*ton koroidevo*]. There was a 50 percent chance of deceit. In other words, there was a 50 percent possibility that I'd be deceiving him and I hadn't taken either of the two with me. I had experienced it alone with my friend Rea. . . . Let me tell you, let me remember . . .
>
> *I:* And your friend . . .
>
> *She:* I think that at the abortion, at the hospital, Thodoro had come because . . . No, he had behaved well. In other words, I did not want him to come. I preferred to go with a friend of mine exactly for the reason I'm telling you. I considered it immoral [*anithiko*], according to my personal morality, but he insisted tremendously. In other words, it was incomprehensible to him, he was sure it was his, it would not cross his mind that it wasn't, and he considered it incomprehensible for me to go alone to have an abortion. He was by my side. *Dipla mou.* I don't remember him, though, because I wouldn't let him work on me emotionally [*na litourgisi pano mou synaisthimatika*]. I was paying for it alone. *To plirona moni mou.* I remember that it was with him that I went to the house of my friends to sleep, and in the afternoon the other one [man] came, but he presented himself as a friend.
>
> *I:* To visit.
>
> *She:* Right! The other guy knew about my relationship with Thodoro but knew that we were separating at that time. I had just told him not to discuss it

because I didn't want Thodoro to be put in a difficult position. So the other one came and didn't say a word and the other friend to see me, George, but I think yes, that he was next to me. I just don't remember him, I didn't want him. In the second case, in other words, in the second abortion with him, he was there emotionally. In other words, our relationship was generally such that he was emotionally next to me the way I would want him, I imagine.

Even now if I got pregnant... Can I tell you something? I think that both then and now I felt and feel abortion to be my personal affair. I don't feel that the other person has a part in it. Whereas in my relationships in general I want an emotional relationship, I want an emotional bond, tenderness. I like displays of affection. *Kai hadia.* Abortion, I have the impression, I don't want... I don't think I push the other one away, but it just isn't the same to me. I experience it as a very personal affair. In other words, I don't remember then wanting him to be tender, Thodoro with me, next to me, to support me. I felt that given the situation he could not support me, that it was my affair. *Ek ton pragmaton.*

Now I remember that, because then it was conscious, that I felt it is my personal affair and the other one has no say. OK for him to be there, but even if he isn't, that's fine. In other words, I prefer a [female] friend. Not as an affair of women, not in that sense. It could have. In other words, it could have been a male friend, that's not the issue. I want a person next to me so that they are there when I go and when I come out. If I knew that I was going to sleep for two or three hours at the hospital, I wouldn't want anybody. It is because I come out a bit disoriented and I want someone to hold me. Nobody, I don't think, can stand by me really [*na mou stathi pragmatika*]. *So I prefer to go with a [female] friend rather than with that person. Under no condition do I consider him responsible for the pregnancy. I consider that too my own, that it is my responsibility.*

Generally as a person that's how I am.... I have the propensity to take on responsibilities. Usually I take on more responsibilities than my share [*ap'oses mou analogoun*], but mainly I consider abortion a very personal affair. I didn't watch out and I got pregnant. I make the decision and I am having the abortion. I have it *on my body,* therefore it is my affair. And I believe what I'm telling you and I remember with the question you asked me "How were things then" and I think that even now that's how I'd operate. I wouldn't be interested in having my boyfriend next to me or not. I could go alone, even not with a [female] friend. Ideologically, too, I believe that abortion is a personal affair of the woman and concerns her body.... So, with that reasoning, yes, Thodoro was there simply in the last abortion.

I: In other words, you didn't feel a problem with him?

She: . . . No. I wasn't interested. Simply in the last abortion I resented him because I had the abortion. *Ton kakiona.* Because I wanted to keep it and because of his rejection. Though I recognized that right, the right for him not to want a child, and that's why I had the abortion. I could not force a child on him. *Na tou epivallo ena paidi.* Just, if he had said yes, or if I had had the financial ease to keep it alone, I would have kept it. So I resented his no, regardless if I recognized his right to it.

Thus, again, Ismini reveals that a key component of motherhood, as it is imagined at least, is its capacity to be done with somebody else, somebody one loves. In this, motherhood becomes the sign of an important relationship, even if that relationship, or its form as an active intimate relationship, is gone. Also, Ismini again shows that abortion can be an important occasion for reaffirming a woman's autonomy from her partner; indeed, she emphasizes that it is after all *her* body that undergoes the operation, as much as the abortion may also be a saddening sign of the limits of a particular relationship. Abortion has helped her to see, to echo the words of Evangelia in the beginning.

Niki

Niki, a thirty-seven-year-old single university professor, initially told me that her second abortion had no impact on her relationship. Again, this is a case where the woman reports that her partner was very clear that he did not want children. This presents Niki with the opportunity to examine what exactly it meant to her. When we returned to the issue of her relationship, she said the following in a brief, but telling and surprising, elaboration.

I: Do you remember more about your relationship at the time?

She: Yes, let me tell you, we were doing well. And this was a relationship with a person who had thought things through and had very clear ideas about some things—like not having children. Of course, the fact that I formed a relationship with someone who didn't want children, well, that may say something. I remember that at that time I thought *if* I had insisted . . . and I think that I said *no,* I don't want to, etc., etc. Various such theories. But after the fact of the pregnancy I think that I really did not want it either because I didn't lay a claim on it. I mean one of all those things was the problem, but somewhere too I was pushing this issue onto the future, saying, Well, let's not confront it now, we'll see later. And the constant postponements have probably proved that it was in fact an indefinite transfer to the future, perhaps a cancellation.

After the fact, I thought that despite the fact that a person who didn't want children quite definitively—and who also has never since had children (maybe it was one of the few things in his life on which he was definitive and said no)—despite all this I remember that then he had told me, "OK, if you want the child, let's talk about it." And I had shown somehow no, etc., etc. The child should be wanted by both and such—ridiculous things, in other words. In reality, I think I did not want it either. *Because if I wanted it, I would have fought for it, because there was room for me to do that. Neither the relationship would have collapsed nor anything.* In other words, I did not exhaust the margins. Despite the fact that it has been proven now that he didn't want it ever, in the future either. But I believe that I too had been covered behind all this. In reality I did not want it either. And I did not lay a claim on it. I considered it practically a given that that would happen.

The pregnancy emerges as a test of her partner's desires for their common child bearing, much as Ismini had wanted to mother a child *from Thodoro* and not just to become "a mother." Niki also uses the abortion as a strategy to test and demonstrate her own autonomy or lack of a *need* for children. In this, she seems to think, she underscores her strength. In addition, now the abortion figures in the narrative she shares with me as a sign of the high ground she took: she could have "worked on him," but she chose not to. *Gynaikoulistika pragmata. Katinies.* It is not that there was no possibility of an offer from him. Rather, it was that she *nobly* refused to negotiate for what she seems to feel would have better been openly given. In this way, the unwanted pregnancy brings about a rearticulation and an entrenchment of the established boundaries of their relationship.

In many of the women's narratives, after the process of deciding to have an abortion is put to its disparate uses within the couple, the abortion is often again used within that time frame as a reason for her to have her partner take care of her for a short while. In fact, this surfaces in almost all women's narratives as a fairly important part of the experience of abortion. Just what constitutes "taking care" varies, from buying strawberries to simply sitting reading next to the woman as she sleeps off the effects of the anesthesia. Almost all the women's narratives had instances of such private time, wherein the woman is in some way nurtured and receives the exclusive focused attention of her partner. Niki described her partner's efforts to be nice to her after the abortion.

She: Out of sympathy for me, he took it as an ordeal. No reaction, though. Anyway, he was very clear that he didn't want a child. Neither one of us had any feeling about it as a child, except, "Oh, what happened to you, poor thing, you're the one who has to go through everything, etc." We went to my house afterward; he cooked for me, things like that, to take care of me, etc. Toward *me* though—there was no sadness, etc.

No sadness, she seems to be saying, with a little sadness of her own.

Titika

The effect of abortion as a tool in the solicitation of a particular and practical kind of care for the woman is an important dimension of the use of abortion in Greece. This is put in bold relief again in the words of Titika. She too had initially said that, of her five abortions, none had any effect on her relationships. Yet, as time went on and she quite explicitly, even graphically, explored each relationship with me, she seemed to arrive at quite a different conclusion. Throughout the following excerpt, her descriptions also give more insight into how the pregnancies actually occur and further support the theory of abortion as a visual technology.

She: No, I don't think abortion had an effect on any of my relationships. I would say that in all the cases, with the slight exception of the case of the body builder, because it was not a very real relationship. It was probably during the time of the peak of my interest in him [*tous pollous erotes mou*] that I got pregnant. . . . Not in the beginning, but there, when it starts and flames up and you show tremendous interest in the other, you are very in love. . . .

The first time it was . . . when . . . I was making love with Ianni and . . . It was the usual: I pull out or I don't pull out, I don't know, and he looked at me and he understood "no" and I was dumbstruck [*kai emina*] and I was looking at him like that and he said, "I thought you said 'no' and I said 'yes' " and all of that. Then we were, "It [the pregnancy] will come, it won't come," and it came, of course, sure enough.

The second, which was one of the biggest stupidities of my life, was that since I had the operation and the doctor gave me a very light contraceptive pill to reestablish the cycle [*na epanelthi o kiklos*], as though it won't return of its own, whatever. Which I took. So then later, I stupidly get my period and then I count as though my cycle were normal [*fisiologikos*]. In other words, I count again that here is the middle. But it wasn't my normal cycle. I should have waited for it to even out again [*na strosi pali*].... And we make love and I say today isn't the dangerous day and that, and I get pregnant again right away, in other words.

I: Right after—

She: Yes, I got my period once as a lie [*pseftika*], in other words, and once after that maybe. In other words, very close... I don't know, maybe they had two months difference?

I: Two months difference.

She: That's why and the doctor was very bad... and we were very close.

I: The second. And the third abortion?

She: The first and the second... and... That wasn't, it didn't influence our relationship at all. In other words... oh, with Ianni there was of course always the usual "Now you're going to keep it...." I, from no man, except the German guy, the last one... who... We just didn't have a relationship. There was no relationship [for him to stand on] from which he could tell me. The only thing that very quietly he said once—I imagine that this is also in the... the realization of men of how much they lack in this particular respect because they cannot produce children [*na teknopoiisoun*] that somewhere they want to show that "I was a part of it too," and he said to me... Once that we were saying something about this before the abortion, he said to me, "I can't believe it." He said to me, "Now," like that, when we were talking, "a little Dick," that was his name, "is growing inside you now." I said, "Virgin Mary." Because every single one, especially Ianni and my ex, who the two were the two relationships that were more mature [*mestes*] and like with dreams and I don't know what... They'd be overcome by this thing, this "You should keep it." In other words, as though we're going to make a gesture, suddenly to throw it out there, and it's over, we won't be concerned with her again. And the two first with Ianni, I told you, didn't influence....

With the body builder I would say that... if it were a relationship which I hadn't taken as simply being a sexual thing... the abortion could have influenced it. Because that day I felt very bad and very nervous. Also, with the fact that the other person, no matter how irresponsible he is ordinarily, under the weight of a responsibility that "I should do something," he became even worse. But because I hadn't ever taken him seriously and he was simply, you know, we train together, we fuck each other [*pidiomaste*], and, if we have time, we go and have a drink together... It didn't influence me. It didn't change our relationship in any meaningful way.

And yet, Titika seems to be suggesting that the abortion could have terminated the relationship because it showed him more clearly to be the irresponsible person she suspected him of being. Moreover, she experienced her fourth abortion as having a significant effect on the relationship she was in at that time.

> *She:* With the fourth one, with my ex-boyfriend, it was at the very beginning of our relationship. In other words, we had started going out in January, we first made love in March . . . and in May I got pregnant . . . and it was like that. I can say that it was, it operated, because we did not know each other very well, like with Ianni, *it operated as a thing that brought us even closer.* You know, like, he'd bring me, you know I'd say, "Oh, I'd like to eat strawberries." Without meaning anything, in other words, two months pregnant . . . He'd go and bring me strawberries, and he'd write me funny little poems. I don't know, things like that. . . .
>
> And the last time there was no emotional foundation. I saw it entirely . . . Because the relationship did not exist. It was dead over, when I realized that there wasn't, it was a two-week-old thing [*dio evdomadon pragma*]. It was where I said, "Oh boy [*aman*], I like him. Maybe I can do something with him to help get me over the old one." We had sex twice [*pidikhtika dio fores*], I didn't like it anyway, and in other words, there wasn't anything, any foundation between us.
>
> He was one of the few who . . . I suppose because I am so much older than him too, and he's inexperienced and all that, he didn't try to tell me at all, "Oh, it won't be, don't worry" . . . All of them, every single one of them, when I had the feeling inside me, in my body, that maybe that's the day, all of them would have this attitude, "No, no way, come on, don't worry." All of them, I mean.
>
> *I:* Yes.
>
> *She:* And that's why, it is something that bothers me. It is a very paradoxical dynamic [*oxymoro shima*] that is created that, whereas all of them are at that "come on, no, no way" and all of that, so somewhere inside you say that he doesn't want it either, as much as I don't want it, he doesn't want it, he doesn't want it either. . . . In the end, when it was positive, the pregnancy test was positive, anytime that happened . . . *it would make me livid [m'exorgize].* . . . Suddenly they changed to "Let's keep the baby." What baby? All this time, a little earlier, we were "No way" and then "Let's keep the baby." . . . Where did all this emotion [*olos aftos o sinaisthimatismos*] come from suddenly?

Here Titika shows her anger again at what she sees as the incomprehensible attempt of the partner to "keep it." In so doing, however, she shows also that in that moment when she thinks she might be getting pregnant and he says, "Oh no, no way," she is very interested in seeing his reaction. She is testing him and he is very clearly failing the test. The subsequent "gesture," as she puts it, does little to counterbalance their initial failure to show any interest in a pregnancy and the effort to refute her sense that the possibility exists. *What baby?*

Titika goes on to tell me more about her relationship with the German Greek "boy." In so doing, we again see how abortion "helps women see." Here she says the pregnancy helped her to see how she had been pushing at the relationship, basically creating it, when it shouldn't be because "it wasn't of its own." Her description puts in relief a particular performance of feeling. This man's apparent inability to understand that she was using him to forget somebody else made her have little respect for him. She loses even more respect for him when she realizes he has "no feeling of his own" to bring to the relationship.

> *She:* It was stupid that . . . I was looking inside because I didn't go out, because I was at work for many hours . . . in there. I had to find something in the environment of my life to put my sights on [*sto stohastro*]. So that I wasn't . . . of the previous . . . of my ex.
>
> *I:* Was the previous one at the office?
>
> *She:* No, no, no. I had left. He was at my old job. And essentially, it was something that I started. He's a young kid and it was very easy to. He is polite, sweet, he has an attractive face, he's very tall and very everything, but anyway, and very, like that. A movement like that [she moves her arms as if she is a soldier marching in a parade], not at all at ease. . . . Polite, sweet, and relatively smart kid . . . but certainly not a person I would pick under normal conditions. Simply in my [work] environment I said, yeah, he looks cute. There was no reason for me to make love with this person, in other words, to say that it was purely sexual, then yes, OK. For once in my life I did, or twice, something with a person who . . . That's what was incredibly strange and the thing which made me understand even faster how much of a mistake of mine this was. *In other words, that I was trying to do something that it wasn't of its own.*
>
> Dick . . . because he is very, very shy, and because especially with me he was even more shy. Anytime we were alone together, he was . . . He'd treat me as he treats me at work, and as he treats his pals at work. In other words,

The Couple as Mother   229

never when I told him "I'm going home" he didn't say as I left at least a "bye." He'd sit looking straight ahead. We'd talk about work, OK, "Bye, I'm going," like friends, and even worse yet. So, I started to think either he doesn't like me, which you know was for my ego a little downer . . . In other words, he doesn't like me sexually, or I have to, how to say, *to help* to see what will happen . . . I suppose I was a little bit, I don't know, about it because having been hurt from the previous story, I just wanted to . . . confirm that, OK, I can still manage well. . . . And the first time we kissed, I kissed him. It was not nice, it was nothing, and like, what am I doing here?

I: Why, was it . . .

She: No, he didn't kiss well . . . and . . . and he had this very much that . . . as though there wasn't . . . one feeling that was his own. In other words, *I'd* bring the feeling—which if he was quick he could have understood that it was the desperate effort of a person to get out of trouble with the past, let's say. . . . He would not understand it. Anyone would understand it, but say that it was that . . . He didn't bring some feeling of his own that was at least . . . Shit, man, you know that everyone [*ah, re pousti, xeris pou oloi as poume*], let's say, "they look at Titika at work." "I'm making it with her" . . . nothing. There was not any feeling there . . . not even that "Oh, I'm shy." There wasn't any feeling.

Titika's initial insistence that abortions don't affect her relationships may itself be an important part in the performativity of her identity. She is tough. She stands up to what is being configured as "fate." Yet, the luck of the draw in a gamble with pregnancy is not quite so random but, as I have argued, very much "set up" by the sponsoring discourses of nationhood and their deployments of the divine. However, at the site of pregnancy, the brave gendered Greek subject refuses to concede that anything of value was lost in the struggle. Recall the words of Giannoula from the previous chapter, when she responded to my comment about her age being a reason the doctors wouldn't give her the Pill by telling me she didn't want the Pill anyway. In Titika's case, it is the relationship she did not really want that she says may have been negatively affected by the abortion. Nothing that she wanted, she seems to be saying, in a statement of pride and a clear expression of the familiar reversals of pain, was taken away from her because of the abortion.

Yet, just how much struggle is involved in this situation is put in bold relief by her anger at what she sees as the men's simulation of an interest or "play" with the notion of keeping the pregnancy. She does not like this at all, primarily because of their original refusal to entertain the possibility that conception has occurred on a "dangerous" day even when Titika herself feels quite sure that it is at least a possibility. Certainly, the men's original denial might also be read as an attempt to "think positive," or to not tempt fate, and may well be saturated with the pervasive, if rarely acknowledged, cultural belief that "words do things." *Best not to say what we don't want to have happen.*

However, Titika reads their denial as a clear signal that indeed the pregnancy *is not wanted*. Thus, this particular test is failed and, even if they later express interest in the pregnancy, she is not willing to overlook the initial response, though clearly there is also more yet to be tested. All this further reveals the depth of the struggle and the height of the stakes involved in the process of having sex, getting pregnant, and negotiating an abortion. Moreover, even for the relationships she claims were unaffected by the pregnancy and abortion, the narrative shows both that significant changes occurred in the subject's position and that abortion was indeed used as a visual technology of sorts. Titika's willingness to go into detail with me permits a more nuanced view of the battlefield at the heart of intimate relationships.

Concluding Remarks

In these four narratives, Eleni, Ismini, Niki, and Titika have, in their own voices, carried us through the very vexed, often sad process of negotiating a relationship in the context of an unplanned pregnancy and the decision to abort it. Eleni's narrative illustrates how, at the core of the sadness around abortion, there is often a sense of the loss of a dream of a particular type of relationship with another adult rather than the loss of a fetus or child. This indicates that we may need to rethink current conceptions of motherhood in Greece to include a stronger relational component. As Ismini's narrative also demonstrates, it seems that motherhood is at some level actually more about the relationship between the two adults—even if the formal organization of that relationship collapses, as in Ismini's case—than about the relationship between mother and child, at least when it is still exclusively an imaginary state. Ismini further illuminates the specificities of motherhood as it is imagined in Greece and, in so doing, reveals that abortion can be deployed as a powerful, if last, act of love. In many ways, to decide to abort is to choose to sacrifice one's own desire and offer up the dream of a particular relationship within which motherhood would have been a possibility.

All this resonates with distinct heroism. Titika's account clearly demonstrates this, but nowhere is this dimension of abortion made as clear, if paradoxically, as in Niki's pithy account. She was not interested in "exhausting the margins" and fighting for the pregnancy. As she put it, in the now familiar dynamic, this was probably because she did not want the pregnancy herself anyway. Nonetheless, she chose to abort rather than to "push" the man she was involved with. And, in making this apparently more peaceful choice, as her comments about the rational discussions they had suggest, she also seems to have waged a battle with herself. She says, after all, that she thought to herself, "No, I don't want etc., etc."; she means, I think, both that she didn't want to "insist" and that she didn't want to have a child. Yet, right after telling me this, she sardonically comments, "Various such theorizing." In Niki's account, in other words, we see how the agonistic field of the straight couple cannot neatly be broken down into the woman versus the man or some such notion of the two biological entities involved. In fact, the decision to abort can in some circumstances signal a victory of the woman over herself.

Both Ismini's and Niki's accounts also demonstrate abortion's multifarious uses as a *modernizing* technology. In particular, Ismini's story of her next-to-last abortion shows just how individualizing abortion can be when she tells of how she used it to separate herself from a situation in which she did not know whose sperm had helped create the fetus she carried. Here the heroism of a woman who fights "her own" battles and the stoicism of a Greek Orthodox who "carries her cross" merge together with a narrative about the autonomous liberal subject of modernity. Niki's expression of this includes the very difficult, radically oppositional (in Greece) statement that she simply may not want children. But, in its context, this too is positioned as a sign of her nobility and the willingness to be a good warrior, a Mando Mavroyenous, a Greek Joan of Arc who does not reproduce—not to resist the patriarchy but to better serve her version of who "the good guys" are.

There are few explicit references to Greece and to God in the excerpts presented above. Recall, for example, Eleni's comment about Greek families being closer. Or Titika's retort, "Virgin Mary," when her binational lover started visualizing the fetus as "a little Dick." My argument, however, is that Greece, as a set of stories about what it means to be a human in the world that is moreover attached to a particular geopolitical national context, in fact is *ever present,* shaping the very ways these subjects organize and understand their experience and themselves.

The uses of an unplanned pregnancy, and of the resulting abortion, range from an exploration of the meaning of mothering and testing the partner and the relationship itself to the making of the self into a properly *modern* Greek woman and, at the same time, a properly Greek, if modern, woman. Yet, underlying all this is also an attempt to feel loved and cared for. Whether it means having your partner go out and buy strawberries for you or having him cook you a meal, the unplanned pregnancy and abortion—themselves the product of nationalist narratives—seem to be most useful as a tool in a culturally specific search for love. *With blood dripping from her lips.*

This is not to repostulate the very humanism this book is engaged in interrogating. To the contrary, this emphasizes how pervasive and "within" are those things we have come to think of as being fundamentally external to the inner self, the psyche, and our very desires. In an immediate and material sense, the narratives presented in this chapter show that the nation is at the core of love of various sorts. And love, in turn, is the fuel carrying forward the nation.

Chapter 9

ABORTION, PAIN, AND

AGENCY

✥

About those who really held out
And did not speak.
—Jenny Mastoraki, "Tales from the Deep IV"

In this chapter, we move yet deeper into the zones of contact among nation, women, and sexuality in Greece, always approaching these as vexed products of historically and culturally specific discursive practices and narratives. The focus here is on women's understanding of the role of *others*, primarily that of their partner, and then of society, in the abortions they experience. As I've been arguing, abortion in Athens emerges as both a natural form of birth control and as effective politics in a variety of arenas. This does not mean that there is no pain, or *ponos*, associated with abortion. Indeed, the body is made to bespeak some of the pain of contemporary Greek life that is disallowed at other sites. This is part of what transforms it into a Greek body, and abortion is an important moment in that conversation, both for the subject and, seen from a distance, at the level of society as a whole. I continue to work at spelling out the Greek subject at the site of the couple, always in relationship to a grammar of the nation and of God, by focusing explicitly here on the negative aspects of abortion.

This chapter continues to explore the minefield of the couple and charts the specifically Greek configurations of personhood and agency that underlie the women's stories about their relationships. The narratives of the four women in the previous chapter permit a glimpse of the rough terrain of inter- and intrasubjective politics in Greece and provide a clearer picture of how abortion is embedded in charged fields of power and deployed within these as a strategy. In chapter 7, the consideration of nationalism and its permeation of sexuality revealed the ways in which abortion emerges as natural and other forms of birth control as, to different degrees and in different ways, alien. In the present chapter, we return to sex itself and find that it constitutes a contested zone in the heart of this territory.[1] The focus is narrowed and the question guiding this investigation is: Which designations of agency animate the subject and the intimate life of the couple in the nationally invested domain of erota, or sex-love?

The origins of action, however focused they may sometimes seem, do not reside within one person, nor does social action distinctly issue forth from one person or the other. Postmodern social theory has convincingly argued for the limits of such postulations. The material discussed here contains a wealth of evidence of a class of subjectivity that is distinctly different from that presupposed by Western liberal democratic state-building projects. The women speaking do express an I that is at times hurt, at times angry, at times resigned, but this is not an easily isolatable I, though it is one who, as we see, feels profoundly alone. Yet the configuration of the subject that emerges is diffuse.

To examine this domain, I turn to what the women say about the different forms of pain associated with their experience of abortion. What is their understanding of their partner's role in the abortion and the couple's negotiations of the perceived distance and proximity between the two of them? What exactly is the cost of abortion? That is, why is abortion "bad"? In this context, I examine (1) the ways abortion is seen as a threat to the female subject's health and the underlying conception of the mind-body nexus; (2) the ways abortion in Greece is sometimes seen as taking a life and the contours of the particular, also nationally inflected, moral domain within which these definitions arise; and (3) the refractions of society's position on abortion, thus probing the varied annexations of abortion by disparate nationalist articulations of power, including some forms of feminist mobilization.

As the excerpts below demonstrate, responsibility, one of the cornerstones of the autonomous liberal subject, cannot be treated as a fixed transnational construct. Even in the so-called West, subtle yet important differences are at work. Indeed, these differences may be more important within this geopolitical domain precisely because there is a widespread assumption that social and political policy firmly rooted in liberal discourse can and should be applied in democratic state-building projects across the board. A pivotal particularity of agency in Greece can be found in the gap between the location of *fault* for a given outcome (*poios ftaiei*, originating from the word *ptaio*), and that of *responsibility* for it (*poios ehi tin efthini*, from the word *efthnia*). Here, we witness a critical moment of consciousness and are shown another way that subjectivity is not as clearly bounded, and agency not centralized, within the single human being. The individual, in Greece as elsewhere, is a tentative, contradictory, and ambivalent accomplishment, to the extent that it is accomplished at all. Throughout this process, moreover, the beat of the nation is audible.

Who Is to Blame?

The tensions and friction animating Greek heterosexuality, revealed in the narratives of Eleni, Ismini, Niki, and Titika, are brought into sharper focus when the women talk specifically about what they see as their partner's role in the unplanned pregnancy and during the time of their abortions. The women state that they had more or less adequate support from their partners at the time of making a decision about the pregnancy. Listening more carefully, however, listening to their silences as well as their words, it becomes evident that things are more complex.

Consider what I was told by one forty-two-year-old woman who said she saw abortion "not only as a sin" but as a wrongful interruption of a life. She lives in the mostly middle-class Athens neighborhood of Marousi and, born in the town of Kavala, has lived in Athens for the past twenty-two years. She has a high school diploma and works as a public servant at IKA, one of the major Greek Social Security Agencies. She has two children and reports five abortions and one miscarriage.

I: How was your partner?

She: He stood by me, but he did not intervene in the decisions. In other words, he considered that they were a decision entirely my own and if I said that I'd keep the other child too, he would accept it. Since, however, I could not, therefore there had to be an abortion.

Typically, it seems, the cost of having your partner stand by you is his interference in your decisions, as the "but" above suggests. Yet even in this case, where the man does not intervene, it is he who defines the decision as one that is "entirely" her own. Although the larger frame securely in place in this narrative is the couple's union, there is evidence of significant power differentials at play. It is he who grants her permission to decide "on her own." Moreover, her decision seems ultimately to be determined by what "could" be done rather than being framed in terms of a free choice.

Next, consider the comment of a woman who said abortion is what each woman makes of it, and that for her it has been a situation of deciding on the lesser evil. *To mi heiron veltiston*. Agency is clearly represented here as mercurial and responsibility finally rests precariously on the ostensibly neutral domain of "what can objectively be done." When I asked her to describe any impact the abortion might have had on her relationship, she first talked about how she sees abortion as a trial, then how she had her partner's support but felt the decision was primarily her responsibility.

> *She:* Look, I can't say the abortion brought us into a confrontation with each other, but it put us into a psychological ordeal because we had recently had my little girl, that was a desired pregnancy, and so it was for both of us heavy, let's say. A psychological ordeal. *Mia dokimasia psychologiki*. It also put us into the ordeal of thinking of keeping it, but if we kept it, of course, we would have a lot of problems that we haven't yet resolved anyway, in other words, even without this pregnancy. So we concluded, but *in common*, there wasn't, in other words, disagreement *or, how can I tell you, there wasn't much room for it, on either side*. That's it. *Den ipirhan perithoria*.

Here it is made clearer how "objective conditions" are deployed in a way that lifts responsibility from any one of the subjects involved. In addition, although the decision to abort is made "in common," there is here also a hint of friction. The apparently mutual decision occurred because "there wasn't much room" for disagreements, not because there *were* no disagreements. It is because neither of the two felt they had the financial wherewithal to support another child that neither pushed to keep the pregnancy. Yet, this exhibition of support is not to be confused with an equitable state of peace and unity within the couple. The woman states clearly that there are "sides" here.

Further along in the interview, after she described how her third abortion was more difficult physically, perhaps as she suggests in a move that occurred in several of the women's narratives, because it was more traumatic psychologically, we had an exchange that shed more light on the notion of agency shaping the agonistic field of the couple. What is at once the fixedness and the evanescence of responsibility in Greece becomes clear.

> *I:* How did you feel after the operation with regard to your partner?
>
> *She:* I didn't feel alone. Only, let's say, at some point before the operation I felt, let's say, that I had more responsibility. That I am pregnant and therefore I am the one doing the act. In other words, I could also *not* do it at some moment, if I made that decision. I felt that the dilemma falls on me more. But I didn't have, in other words, I had support in it. My husband helped me to make the decision that I should. *Na paro tin apofasi pou eprepe*. And he

didn't pressure me, and generally we have a good relationship, so I don't have those kinds of problems. We gave a solution to this in common. Simply, in a way, *he took on a piece of the responsibility* because before the operation I felt, like that, *very burdened with feelings.* And of course, later, OK, we didn't have any problem. All this was before.

First, her sense that it is her body that is primarily involved results in her feeling that she is the one who has responsibility for the decision to abort. Then she says that her husband "helped" her to make the right decision. Last, we are told that he agreed, in some sense, to take on a share of the responsibility that, however, is not seen as properly his. A diffuse organization of subjectivity is confounded by a politics of inequality in which the ostensibly less powerful female subject is "taken care of" ethically by the more decisive male partner. This is a configuration of personhood in which the boundaries are semipermeable and responsibility is a dividable element that circulates between and within human beings and that can be repositioned. She observes that because it is *she* who is pregnant, she could potentially single-handedly decide not to have the abortion. The assumption here is that usually decisions are made at more of a remove, certainly in a cognitive space less proximate to her subjectivity.

Another woman, thirty-two years old, who has two children and reports three abortions, offers a more detailed understanding of Greek subjectivities and agency as it resides *between* human beings. She reports on the ostensible lack of differences between her and her partner, and yet also reveals evidence contradicting this. She was born in Athens, has lived in the mostly middle-class area of Kallithea all her life, and works as a mathematician. She has been married eleven years, has two children, and reports three abortions.

> *I:* In your sexual life with him later, did you see any change? Did you feel more distant?
>
> *She:* No, no. Now, I've gone through situations like that independent from births and the abortions, etc. They are emotional swings [*sinaisthimatikes enallages*]—in my opinion, of course—and they happen in the couple [*ginontai sto zevgari*], depending on the psychological and emotional problems that exist between the two. They may start from something like that, because a child, it is a fact—I imagine that it is an occasion for many women for problems that exist to come out, it's not the fact itself. That's why for me too, in these cases, I didn't have such problems. But, they have appeared precisely the same from other causes, let's say, nonsexual, that don't have to do with the gynecological situation. *Akrivos andistoiha.*

I: In other words, more with your work?

She: With work, with life, how are we going to make it, how are we going to do it ... Where you come into disagreement with the other person, you feel the other person doesn't understand you, so those bring this as a consequence. If, for someone, if the weaknesses in communication of a couple are on this matter, the sexual ... We don't have many differences there, in the larger sexual area [*ston evritero sexoualiko tomea*]. In other words, I mean pregnancies, births, we don't have a lot of problems there. For us, they show up in other areas. Maybe, however, I imagine other couples have a weakness there—to solve some problems from the moment that the individual feels that the other person doesn't understand it. For some reason, one person feels unable to communicate and to explain to the other the problem. That's where the distancing appears, which creates what you asked me, I can't remember how you put it exactly.

I: If you feel alone.

She: Yes, when you feel strongly that the other can't understand you, then automatically you'll have a consequence in your sexual life [*stin erotiki zoe*]. I don't know, in that sense. But I didn't have that this time, in this abortion, or in any of the previous ones. Now, with the birth, because a child entered our life ... it was a little difficult. It was very difficult. Again, I see it as natural, we didn't have, you know, reactions, just within natural limits. I imagine, in other words, that with other couples too it enters and disrupts their life. We're not talking about if it is the first child and *both are waiting for it*, where again, though possibly ...

The birth also definitely falls more on the woman. I say it with my own experience, although it isn't very extensive, but the way I've experienced the situations, that's how it is. Because the man, I believe now, learns to love his children and his family *through the woman*. I believe that he doesn't have that filter, from what my husband says, who has read history, there isn't a "father filter." *Patriko filtro*. It is a creation of recent centuries, let's say. From what he reads, of course, because I didn't read these histories, what can I tell you. That's what he says. But I've experienced it that for as long as the couple is doing well ...

That motherhood, or "the instinct of a mother," which is a common trope in everyday Greek speech and is attributed to all women whether or not they have become mothers, might similarly be a historically specific social construction is not a possibility entertained. What is made increasingly clear is that the couple constitutes an agonistic field within which, even when "doing well" and even if not always manifested in the same "larger area," there is a characteristic dynamic of opposition.

The uneven costs of abortion in particular are foreshadowed in another woman's statement about how she sees her relationship as being "well." This woman—who had previously told me of having woken up from the abortion to find her veins on both arms "broken" from the struggle involved in giving her the anesthetic—openly suggests that the costs of abortion, and of the sex that leads up to it, are shouldered more by women than by men. She does not express anger or resentment over this. She feels that her partner goes through exactly the same psychological difficulty. Yet, evidence of conflict is present.

Born in Fokida, a rural region of Central Greece, and having lived in downtown Athens's busy area of Platia Amerikis for the past twenty years, the next woman is a homemaker who has earned a high school diploma plus some professional training. She has been married fifteen years at the time of the interview and has two children. She reports five abortions.

> *I:* How would your husband experience it?
> *She:* He, because he is a very stressful person and a person who is very much afraid of such things, he would go through a lot [*talaiporito poli*]. But they only go through a lot psychologically. We go through a lot both psychologically and physically. That's a big factor. You suffer big damages. *Pathainis megales zimies.* They don't have damages. But, OK, what can we do? As we said, you can't do anything.

The opposition within the couple is not so easily managed. Nor was it common for the women I spoke with to report that their partners were suffering psychologically along with them during the times of unplanned pregnancies and abortions. Perhaps most important, whatever the perceived allocation of emotional pain in these situations, the woman only rarely maintained the kind of resignation expressed above throughout the interview. The more common type of response moves from simply stating that both women and men suffer from an abortion, though women suffer more, to explicitly and with varying degrees of anger raising the question of how the pregnancy occurs in the first place. Aren't there two of us having sex, many of the women seemed to ask. What happened between then and where we are now?

One woman who has two children and reported having had two abortions puts it subtly. Born in the port city of Piraeus adjacent to Athens, she is forty-one years old and has been living in Philothei, one of the wealthier northern suburbs of Athens, for the past five years. She tells me she designs jewelry, but not as a paid job, and that I should just record that she is a private employee "so that we're OK." She has a high school education, goes to church on major holidays, and has been married eleven years. Here is how she portrays the ambivalent state of feeling support from her partner while also experiencing discontent.

> *I:* Your partner was ...
>
> *She:* I had support [*sibarastasi*]. In other words, we had visited the doctor together and, both before and after, the coverage was perfect. At least when you feel someone else feels for you [*na sibasxi kai kapoios allos mazi sou*], it is good. You find some balance. You differentiate other feelings too, complaint, for example: why the other person *doesn't* support you, doesn't understand you, as though it is the woman alone who ... who ... gives birth and ...

This woman suggests that the abortion elicits an intimacy that then allows her to explore deeper feelings about the relationship. It is not that this compassion, or "the feeling that someone else feels for you," is in itself sufficient. It is good, rather, because it allows her, in effect, to see how difficult things are. Though she pauses and then refers to "giving birth" in an attempt to be discrete, it seems clear that what she means is that "it is not the woman alone who" gets pregnant or has sex. Certainly, her comment also reveals yet another understanding of personhood, closer to the dream of the couple as mother, in which it is not just the woman who gives birth. Overall, the above excerpt demonstrates a dynamic that recurs in many of the women's narratives: the abortion situation seems to expose both the shifting power differential and the aloneness that being part of a couple entails.

To clarify this, consider the words of another woman who says she felt support but also simultaneously expresses a complaint. She is thirty-three years old, born in Australia of Greek parents, and has been living in Athens for the past twenty years. She is a homemaker who has been married for fourteen years and has two children. She goes to church one or two times a month. She initially told me she had had two abortions and then, with an almost imperceptible coy spark to her gaze, added, "I'm not sure, have I had three or two, in any case that is why I put in the IUD. *Na'ho kani tris gia dio.*"

Though she falters at times and is obviously nervous, this woman more openly states what the previous woman attempts to keep veiled. Sex, we are unmistakably told, takes two. She is one of those few I spoke with who felt that although the child hadn't yet "formed," she was still killing a life. Also, in the oral history she constructed for me there was marked evidence of a strongly submissive posture toward her partner. In a quiet manner, she told me about her relationship when we were talking about the two or three abortions she reported having.

> *She:* My partner was with me, of course. He . . . you know, other than that we didn't discuss the matter. Maybe it . . . he wasn't as supportive as he should have been, in other words . . . for example, to discuss it. Because sometimes there are some matters that, well, we let them pass by unnoticed. Sure, I didn't have any complications or anything but . . . emotionally it was . . . Generally, there are also cases when the men don't participate. OK, I may take care for it to be . . . for us to enjoy both of us at that moment, but somewhere they aren't as much as they should . . . I'm not that satisfied from the behavior. Not that he treats me badly either, OK?
>
> What you're doing . . . another life, I don't know. You're killing it but, fine, which you are being given, which you conceive and you dismiss. *Pou diohnis.* Somewhere it is a little . . . it requires a little more, a little gentler treatment. Somehow, because I was young too. He was the first man who . . . with whom I had sexual contact.

Though she "overcame" it, this woman feels that it is not fair that her partner wasn't more actively involved in the abortion; after all, she is the one who "takes care for us to enjoy both of us at that moment." She is doing her best both to give him pleasure and to "take measures" so as not to conceive, though it is not clear just what these consist of. She had earlier told me that she never used any form of contraception. Several women told me they take douches with Coca-Cola after risky intercourse because it kills the sperm. A few told me of a special tea they drink. One said hot lemon juice and a hot bath that same night will prevent conception from taking place. The "real time" effect of this woman's comment, however, is likely referencing some form of pulling or *pushing* out, along with, perhaps, an alternative form of sexual activity. Many of the women reporting using no contraception would in fact describe using some version of the days with withdrawal or the condom. Whatever this woman is doing, she makes an effort so that they both may enjoy sex. The issue, as it is stated here, is that she has too much responsibility and he is not taking enough. Complicating the field of responsibility is her sense that when conception in fact happens, it is actually some other force or God that may have played a significant part.

The same theme of an unequal division of responsibility and underlying conflict is echoed in what another woman, forty years old and married for twenty-one years, told me. She completed elementary school and worked in a small nickel-and-dime store that she and her husband own. Born on the island of Mitilini, she has been living in a seaside suburb of Athens, Glyfada, for the past seventeen years. When she went for her most recent of four abortions she told her three children she was having a benign tumor removed because she did not want them to know. She told me that her partner was supportive despite their different desires concerning the pregnancy. Yet, she also described feeling fear toward her partner afterward and openly stated that the pregnancy was the man's fault.

> *She:* I went with my husband. We went home, I laid down that day because I had a little blood. Then I recovered fully. The same day, in other words, I recovered. It was five in the afternoon, I went home, I cooked, we ate, I went and lay down. The next day I was better. But my husband was next to me, even though he wanted me to keep the child. He didn't react. *Den andedrase.*
>
> It was me who felt differently, in sexual activity. In fact, to be honest, I'm afraid of him. When he comes close to me again, in case the same happens to me. *Kai malista ego gia na imai eilikrinis ton fovamai, otan me xanaplisiasi mipos xanapatho ta idia.* I had grown afraid after all, because so many abortions . . . They feel like many to me. We should have taken greater care. Now, whose fault is it?
>
> *I:* Do you see it as being somebody's fault, or is it something that sometimes just happens?
>
> *She:* I don't know. I think it is my husband's fault. *Pistevo pos ftaiei o andras mou.* I don't know. That's how I see it. And just seeing him like that, especially when it is recent like this, it has happened many times, I say, oh, as though I'm afraid of him even. That much. That's how I feel.
>
> *I:* Because in the past you've gotten pregnant.
>
> *She:* Yes, I've had an abortion four times. That isn't a few. And each abortion leaves something behind. . . . I never had back problems. Now, if I get a little tired, my back hurts, everything hurts. You'll say it's the age, the years are getting on. But everything plays a role.

Here the woman says, "We should have taken greater care," though at the same time asking, "Now, whose fault is it?" and looking me straight in the eye. Even though my response provides her with a neutral way out of blaming her husband, she clearly states that she thinks it *is* her husband's fault, implicitly referencing the struggle that the ostensibly calm and measured method of withdrawal actually seems to consist of. She feels that although "everything plays a role," abortion has taxed her body and the pregnancy that caused it was her husband's fault. When she sees him "like that," it is "as though" she is afraid of him. Though this narrative may be partially the product of ambivalence about her own desire, the antagonism at the heart of the couple is brought closer to the foreground.

A pivotal site for these tensions and the shifting positioning of subjects is sex itself. In the next series of excerpts, Greek straight sex itself comes into sharper focus. The image that emerges is a form of battleground. Consider what one twenty-four-year-old single woman with no children and four abortions says.

> *I:* The person with whom you had gotten pregnant, did you still have relations with him when the operation happened?
>
> *She:* Yes, but he is married. He gave me money to have it done. The money is the last thing. *Ta lefta ine to teleftaio.*
>
> *I:* Did you talk with him afterward?
>
> *She:* And what could he tell me? The whole mistake is mine. That was my mistake. That I got involved with him. From that point on, for him to tell me what? That he was sad? *Oti stenohorithike.* For me to do what with that?
>
> *I:* Your mistake, in other words, was what? That you had relations with him? How do you mean that?
>
> *She:* Because the hour that I need him, that I needed him, I didn't have him.
>
> *I:* He can't be there for you . . .
>
> *She:* I would say that I went like someone who has nobody and nowhere to rest, like a dog in a vineyard [*san to skili sto abeli*] and . . . I don't believe that it is possible that I am worth something like that, but it always happens this way, I don't know.
>
> *I:* Which happens this way?
>
> *She:* That I go alone to . . . that I don't make love alone, but I go through all this alone. I don't know how that happens . . . I was saying to myself, Let's see, sometime, can I get pregnant alone to see! (laughter) But it doesn't happen.
>
> *I:* For sure—
>
> *She:* And I believe that it is unfair and it could be different. The way I believe that there isn't "I can't," there is "I won't." And when a person wants . . . Anyway. Complaints. *Parapona.*

This woman's wry attempt to make light of the situation is very revealing. She does not want to attack or accuse her partner. She seems to be saying that it is all his "fault," but that ultimately it is her responsibility for having gotten into such a situation. Yet, with her simple comment that it does take two, she highlights that at some level she also feels that a portion of the responsibility does rest with him. The joke she tries to make echoes the words of the woman

Abortion, Pain, and Agency   245

who lamented that although she does what she can so they can both enjoy sex, she is nonetheless left alone to face the consequences later.

Another woman, thirty years old and just married, spoke more bluntly of what she saw as men's role in the situation. In the process, she fleshed out a picture of the stakes involved in practicing Greek heterosexuality. She reported having had three abortions.

> *I:* How did you decide to start taking the Pill?
>
> *She:* Yes, maybe I thought of it . . . The first is that I did not want another abortion because three are already enough, right? And the marriage . . . You have a greater frequency of sexual contacts than if you have a relationship. *In other words, the danger is more visible. Diladi inai pio oratos o kindinos as poume.*
>
> *I:* Right.
>
> *She:* Yes, when you have a relationship, you may not be able sometimes . . . When two people do not live together, it is difficult. And because I wanted first of all to feel ready and to decide in the end . . . because there is also the age which will have to . . . (pause)
>
> *I:* How old are you? [Glancing at the questionnaire.] Twenty-nine?
>
> *She:* On to thirty. That's it, I decided, for it to be more conscious, let's say. Let me control it at least until I put things in order. *Na to elexo toulahiston mehri na taktopoiiso ta pragmata.* In other words, I did not want to leave it up to chance anymore. *Na to afino sto tihaio.* And since my husband . . . In the beginning, he was pressuring me and I didn't want . . . That's it.
>
> *I:* Your husband was pressuring you to practice contraception? I'm not sure if I understood correctly.
>
> *She:* No, for us to have a child. But men are more . . . (long pause)
>
> *I:* They see it from further away, we said before.
>
> *She: And maybe more irresponsibly.*

As Herzfeld (1991b) has argued in his sketch of a Greek poetics of womanhood,[2] and as was discussed when examining the various meanings attributed to contraception, there is a very high investment in not appearing to betray one's partner, however deep one's own differences may be with him. This means that women will generally be very careful in how they talk about things they blame their partner for. Given this cultural context, the jokes, the quick, wry comments sometimes left to dangle, and the sudden direct meeting of the eyes are especially suggestive. Thus, when the woman above openly corrects me to say that what she really means is that men may be irresponsible rather than just removed, we can hear that a lot more power and passion is

246 Sexing the Nation

involved than simple *parapono,* or "complaint." Another woman is yet more explicit about what most of the women suggested in subtler ways. She is twenty-six years old, single, has no children, and lives in Peristeri. She is a student at one of the community colleges of Athens. She was visiting the Center for her third abortion. In her account we see another possibility: the unplanned pregnancy and subsequent abortion as both the man's fault and the man's responsibility.

> *I:* Now, psychologically, you told me that you have anxiety about your relationship. In your sexual contact, do you see differences from when you learned that you're pregnant?
> *She:* Not yet, no, but I think they'll come up.
> *I:* What are you expecting?
> *She:* I don't know, last time too . . . I was young. Then I considered it a little, how shall I say, a bad coincidence. Despite that . . . I can't avoid it . . . I consider him the main one responsible. *Aytos kyrios efthinetai.* And last time, for a large period of time, I had a problem, at least for a year.
> *I:* You felt, in other words, what?
> *She: I felt that I'm paying for what happens, a distance, and I had no inclination [diathesi], not only sexual, more generally.* The way I felt alone at that moment.

A large part of what is going on here, as in the many accounts of a period of sexual indifference or aversion following the abortion, may have to do with the women's negotiation of their own desire. Indeed, a significant absence from most of these accounts is reference to *her* pleasure; instead, we see a repeated emphasis on *his* fault or her responsibility. This works to construct the speaking subject in a very particular way, almost disembodied, at the moment of sexual contact. In addition, we see the glimmers of a possibility that another way of configuring this field of power is to position both responsibility and blame with the partner. Moreover, that this particular articulation of responsibility and fault occurs in a domain in which female pleasure is largely silent also works to veil the positive aspects of abortion, both in regard to an understanding of it as more natural than other forms of birth control and as an effective strategy or "visual technology" of sorts, as I have argued.

Yet, this woman does speak of her desire and tells me fairly openly that it was absent for almost a year after one of her abortions. Given the taboo against admitting sexual difficulties, this reference is very significant. Moreover, she sees abortion as her having to shoulder the entire "payment" for their sex. She was willing to notch up one of her previous pregnancies and the abortion as "a bad coincidence," but she does not now hesitate to place both blame and responsibility. She is quite clear that she has not forgiven and forgotten.

In almost all of the cases, however, the women usually said that they felt that although it is their responsibility, it is certainly the man's *fault* that they got pregnant. *Einai dikia mou I efthini alla . . . ftaiei aftos!* This distinction is made clear in the words of a forty-year-old woman who has been married twenty-two years, has two children, and reported having had three abortions. She was born in the town of Kavala and has been living in the Athens district of Nea Smyrni for the past thirty years. After high school, she attended secretarial school. Actively religious, she goes to church "on the big holidays for sure, the Virgin Mary's, Christmas, such things, New Year's, Easter certainly." This is much more than the annual Easter eve church attendance many Athenian Greek Orthodox practice.

Alongside her careful and forceful assumption of full responsibility for the pregnancy, her anger and the conflict, not always latent, in the couple are quite marked. Her comment also further illuminates the fraught context in which withdrawal occurs. She too refers to the significant physical cost of the abortion. Having described a range of feelings, starting with "being freed from a burden" to "a nervous breakdown" surrounding each of her three abortions, she goes on to discuss her partner's role.

> *She:* My partner was always with me. Always. Both with my births and the operations, he was always with me. . . . You know, after the pregnancy, because a fight, let's say, "No, you seduced me," "No, it's your fault." He said these things all three times. Fine, it isn't psychologically but somewhere you feel that . . . because you throw responsibilities on the other one too [*rihnis kai efthines ston allon*] . . . In the end, I saw that it is exclusively my issue to not get pregnant again. Do you understand?
>
> *I:* Why? Yes, but why?
>
> *She:* Look, if I wait for my husband to think of me, for example, it doesn't happen all the time. He'll pull out once, he'll pull out the next, he'll pull out the other. "I don't like the condom," this that, you'll get in trouble again [*tha tin patisis pali*]. And I said clearly that it is exclusively my issue, to come have a look at myself because . . . in the end, what happens to the husband? Whereas the woman is traumatized beyond the psychic, there are physical traumas too. Let's not kid ourselves. And who knows what consequences it will have later, isn't that so?

In citing the future consequences of the abortion, she raises the specter of infertility, common in doctors' and other experts' speeches on the negative consequences of abortion. In those contexts, the effort seems to be to scare Greek women, for whom an inability to conceive is in some cases a major stigma signifying nothing less than God's disapproval. Here, however, the woman herself makes an effort to communicate the seriousness of her *partner's* unacknowledged responsibility in all this. Although she willingly takes on responsibility for the pregnancy, this woman is also quite firm in her sense that she is responsible because he is not to be trusted. Sex emerges as a no-man's-land. As this woman concretely puts it, her partner will at some point put his own pleasure first. He is, she says without dramatics, perfectly able to jeopardize her physical and psychological well-being, as well as the much-coveted "future capacity to conceive."

The anger linked to sex and abortion in Greece is put in bold relief in the next excerpt. Somewhat longer, it provides some clues to the source of this disillusionment. Whereas the previous woman claimed that abortions are almost too much for her body, this woman is interested in emphasizing that abortion is far from "just a physical ordeal." She is thirty-five years old, a lawyer, and has been a widow for three years now. She has one child and reported having had one miscarriage and two abortions. As in almost all of the accounts of the 120 women interviewed, the fetus and its life are superfluous concerns, if present at all. As the narrative progresses, the woman expresses more and more anger at her partner and frustration that this is how things are for "all couples."

> *I:* Now, for the two pregnancies that were terminated, do you remember your feelings, thoughts?
> *She:* Yes. I was very much afraid. I felt very badly and very angry.
> *I:* You also felt very angry. Toward whom and why?
> *She:* Toward my husband mostly, I think, because . . . it bothered me. I considered that it was his fault, regardless if that's how it is or not. In other words, that he didn't pay attention [*den prosexei*], that he didn't pull out in time and that I have to go through an ordeal [*na yposto mia talaiporia*] in which he does not participate.
>
> And so that's how I made the decision to insert an IUD, because it bothered me very much. It was a very, very bad experience. One of the worst in my life for very many reasons, not just the physical ordeal *but . . . also because I realized my inability to have company. Syniditopoiisa tin adynamia mou na eho parea.*
> *I:* Your inability . . . ?
> *She:* To have company in my life. But, I don't know, I felt badly to be going to

have an abortion. I felt that I was being put through an ordeal with no outcome [*horis apotelesma*] and that bothered me. And the second was that I felt anger with the result being that I decided to take on the responsibility and now it bothers me, it is something that bothers me even now. In other words, that the women are suggested more for contraception and not men.

And the condom, I've tried it once or twice. I didn't want it either because I felt it to be something very cold [*to enoiotha oti itane kati poli psihro*]. But nor did my husband want it. But also nor had I insisted either that we use it because . . . (long pause).

I: It is difficult because on the one hand there is an impasse because of the methods that exist but—

She: For the men.

I: Yes.

She: I know that but . . .

I: But still.

She: You know, some things can, with logic . . . I know because I've read things, not just in magazines. But, I don't know . . . It still bothers me very much. Perhaps because of the ordeals that I have gone through or I don't know.

In retrospect, I cringed at this. My comment cut off the flow of her thought. More important, I did not realize that my comment about the limited choice of birth control methods would result in this. When I agreed with her response that it is the methods "for the men" that are limited, it was, I realized later, as though I were making excuses for the men. Sitting there in the Family Planning Center wearing the white robe the director had insisted that I wear to look like personnel, it was as if I were saying that therefore, objectively, women need to be the ones carrying the responsibility, thus invalidating this woman's own astute perception of the politics of heterosexuality. This interview taught me to be more willing to ride out silences and moments of difficulty in expression. Thankfully, this woman was strong enough to continue despite the apparent, if inadvertent, invalidation of her feelings by the researcher. Perhaps also because she is a lawyer, she proceeded to work harder to convince me that she was right.

She: I remember once I had gone for some other reason to a hospital and I saw some man who was escorting his wife who was having an abortion—it was obvious—and while, then, he had been patting her on the back, when she left he opened his newspaper like a good gentleman [*san kalos kyrios*] and sat there reading.

Well, of course, you will tell me, What would he do! But I don't know, I believe that . . . that it has to do with the children . . . that everything . . . *For everything, it is the woman who suffers. . . . The man simply observes.* No matter, it is something I don't like, I don't know how else it could be but . . . From friends of mine as well, I know that most men are indifferent. . . . I know a woman who has had fifteen abortions. It seems to me barbarous.

I can't, of course, believe that women take the main responsibility and that's why I decided to use the spiral even though I was afraid. But . . . *I believe that that shows too what the relations of the couple are. Poies einai oi shesis tou zevgariou.*

I: What do you mean?
She: I believe that . . . some things have been delimited, that they belong to us women and some others to men. I . . . that's the difference, and of course I can't do something to change things but, it is my perception. It bothers me.
I: So in those two abortions you had sadness and anger.
She: Yes.
I: And you felt your partner was more distanced. You didn't feel him—
She: Yes. *I felt him to be a stranger. Ton enoiotha xeno.*

Sex is intimately wrapped up with overt power plays. And aloneness accompanies the experience of abortion despite the otherwise diffuse sense of agency. Based on her own experience and that of her friends, this woman describes men as indifferent. In effect, men are at fault for the pregnancies. Yet, she also notes that it is women's responsibility to guard against getting pregnant. That this is so, however, seems to operate as a telling sign of the failure of the couple. This is not just a problem in one area of the couple's common life. Rather, in an intriguing deployment of essentialism, this is seen as reflecting the almost inherent existential inability of a woman to really feel support "inside" or intimacy from a man. Agency collapses into a black hole, leaving the straw figures of the "all-responsible woman" and the "indifferent man," both barely able to stand up.

The woman suffers. The man observes. If abortion were so clearly only about the woman herself, if it were even possible to distinguish "her" from "him" in this field of power as neatly as some of the preceding narratives attempt to do, why would there be so much attention directed toward the partner? The energy focused on placing blame on the male partner seems to serve two important purposes. One, it is covering up for some *other* thing, some hurt, that the women feel even more deeply that the men are guilty of. This, I suggest, is wrapped up with the loss of the dream of real intimacy or a sense of inner belonging, a dream that the diffusely organized, gendered Greek subject intensely craves and pursues while simultaneously being largely incapable of sustaining at deeper levels within the couple. This difficulty has to do with the different ways Greek women raise their sons and their daughters; with the cultural aversion to "strangers," a fluid category, and the heightened fear of betrayal, aspects of the narration of the Greek nation that play an important part in shaping personalities. It also concerns how the present hectic and often dissimulating reality of life in a modernizing Athens fragments the subject. The second important function of the attribution of blame to the male partner may be an attempt to manage the woman's own sense that in fact she is not only responsible but in the end may be the one at fault as well, because, in most cases, she *knew* that he could not be trusted. This may also be connected to a culturally conditioned feeling of guilt for having pursued, to whatever degree, her own pleasure and desire.

The ways women talked about responsibility and blame reveal another dimension of what I have called the operative *economy of feeling* for many Greek heterosexual couples. It shows how the subject's agency is configured in real time so that in the end, men and women collide and collapse into what is experienced, at least by the women, as a fairly painful void. In this matrix of agency, it becomes increasingly difficult to speak with accuracy of a liberal autonomous subject. The implicit critique of the liberal individual that the case of abortion in Greece puts forward is given more force. These representations of responsibility and blame also yield another question. Despite abortion's being seen as more natural and despite its being strategically useful within the field of power of the couple, because there is quite a bit of anger and blame being expressed there must be an important negative dimension to abortion as well. How, then, is abortion in Greece seen as "bad" by the subjects themselves? Why are women talking about fault or responsibility at all?

For What *Is the Partner to Blame?*

There are several reasons abortion is at times seen as "bad" in Greece. A survey of this terrain and its boundaries further illuminates the specificities of the conception of personhood in Greece and the ways in which the nation is, as I argue, viscerally present *within* the subject. Before proceeding with this, it is important to note two reasons *not* found adequate to justify a negative estimation of abortion on the part of the women. First, the demografiko itself does not ever surface in the women's accounts as a reason they think of their abortions as being bad. Not once in the interviews of 120 women, often including two or three follow-up interviews, was the demografiko reported as a reason for concern about an abortion. Indeed, when asked point blank at the end of the interview, almost all of the women, in one way or another, as discussed in chapter 11, said that they considered the demografiko irrelevant. A second reason that is not found adequate to justify a negative estimation of abortion is its formal religious status as a sin, despite, in this case, many women's overt references to it as such.

IS ABORTION A SIN?

The women often referred to abortion as a sin; several also called it a murder or referred to the fetus as "an innocent life." However, the context of these references, along with the widespread absence of an explicit story of sin from women's accounts of their abortions, suggests that these references are a more complicated form of intertextuality with the formal Greek Orthodox position on abortion that the demografiko discourses in the press often underwrite. In fact, close attention to the women's narratives reveals that it is not this dimension of abortion that renders it problematic to them, at least not to a significant degree. Much as lay clergy have become quite lenient as to the formal status of abortion as a sin, so too the women themselves do not seem to be referring to abortion as a sin in the terms of formal Greek Orthodox doctrine.

As Georges (1996a) has shown for women living on the island of Rhodes who have had one or more abortions, and as Herzfeld (1985b) has shown for Cretan sheep thieves, other idioms can be used to bypass the formal Church designation of sin. An alternative morality, a *morality of praxis,* as Petchesky (1990) has called it in the case of U.S. abortion, is put forward. Herzfeld argues that accountability to other humans first, and only afterward to God, shapes the morality of rural Cretan men. Similarly, Georges shows that Rhodean women reference their worry that the child, if born, would go "hungry." Considering this would be a bigger sin, they decide to abort.

In discussing their decision to abort, several of the women I spoke with also referred to this sense of sin. That is, they would mention not being able to give the child shoes to wear, as Georges also observed in Rhodes, or the babies (*ta mora*) their "Babylino" (the Greek brand-name used to refer generically to diapers). *Tha itan amartia.* Intriguingly, stories of no shoes constitute a prominent part of the modern Greek national imaginary. Shoes are a powerful trope for the generation of Greeks who grew up in poor villages during the occupation of Greece by the Nazis and who, very often, did not have shoes to wear. It is these Greeks who flocked to Athens in the postwar period and it is their children who constituted the bulk of my sample.

When asked how they weigh the two "sins," abortion versus giving birth to a child for whom they might not be able to provide "shoes," quite a few answered that abortion was the lesser of several evils. *To mi heiron veltiston.* One woman explained that if she kept the child, the four people already in her family *plus* the new child would all suffer because the same financial resources would have to be divided among more "heads." If she "dropped" it (a popular Greek expression for aborting), she said the decision would be between her and God. This comment shows yet another level of disregard for formal Church doctrine, for the unborn child is formally considered condemned to eternal purgatory because it was not christened a Greek Orthodox. In several cases, women would look me straight in the eye, tell me they felt they had committed murder or a sin, often many, and then also steadily add that that's what they had to do. The process of negotiation with Greek notions of sin is not without its contradictions. One thing is certain: the weight of the designation of abortion as bad, where it occurred, was not because it is an *amartia* (sin), whether sin proper or waste or *krima* (the alternative meaning of the word).

If, then, neither the demografiko discourses in the public sphere nor the Greek Orthodox definition of abortion as a sin is an operative aspect of the pain associated with abortion, why *is* abortion seen as bad by the women I interviewed? In many of the narratives, as I have suggested, abortion is associated with the sense of the loss of a dream. Be this the woman's dream of the couple together becoming "mother" or the dream of a deep intimacy wherein even the decision to abort is experienced *together*, with both subjects equally emotionally involved, it is a dream that is clearly very precious. The way abortion is experienced in reality, in the vast majority of cases, wrecks the dream. And this makes abortion costly.

There are also more concrete ways in which abortion is consciously seen as bad by the women I spoke with. These can be grouped into three broad categories. First, and this aspect was evident in *all* of the women's narratives, abortion is bad because of what it, and especially the full anesthesia under which it is performed in Greece, is perceived as doing to a woman's body. Second, in a few but powerful instances, abortion is in fact seen as causing the loss of a child. Third, Greek female subjects see abortion as bad because society sees it as such. Wisps of the lost dream drift through the narratives of each of these other aspects of the cost of abortion. In total, these sources of pain contain rich evidence of the larger worldview shaping Greek constructions of gendered personhood. They further illuminate the busy intersection of the nation, women, the body, and love.

Abortion and the Greek Female Body

Niki, the university professor whose account of the decision to abort was considered in the previous chapter, described how she would feel if she had to have an abortion now and how she did feel when she had abortions in the past.

> *She:* First of all, it would be much more difficult [now] to interrupt the pregnancy. But I believe again that this would have to do with needs of mine. In other words, with dilemmas I have—to have a child or not have a child—not with the child itself or that we're killing a person, etc. More with my emotional needs in relationship to the whole story and not so much with the child, which, however, I don't know. In any case, I believe that now, either way it would be a much more important and charged experience for me than it was then.
>
> Then it was also a thing somehow, it was another time, a different climate. We were younger too, and it was a climate in which it was, "Oh, yes, abortion." This was a time where things were being called into question. Abortions were considered even a little like bread and butter, no big deal. *Kai ligo psomotiri.* OK, we don't want to have a child at the present moment, let's interrupt the pregnancy. At least personally, I can't say that I had—I was more worried about the whole story, *about what I'd be going through,* and less about the fact itself. The moral aspects not at all, I would say. But not even in the sense that we're killing a person and whether it lives or it doesn't live, etc. I didn't have such . . . I don't remember such.

This irrelevance of a moral register for understanding abortion can be found in most of the stories of the women I spoke with, though not all. What really matters is the effect of the medical act of abortion on the woman's body. In this concern we hear an echo of the negotiating process with modern contraception, indeed the same negotiations that seem to result in the understanding of abortion as more natural. Once faced with an actual pregnancy, that question is opened up again. For most women, as Niki's account illustrates, "the whole issue" of abortion, once it has been decided on, is equated with *"what I'd be going through."* In what follows, we see what exactly this is seen as being.

FERTILITY

It has been suggested that to the degree that abortion is seen as problematic, this is so because it is perceived as a threat to a woman's future fertility.[3] Let us look at one of the few times a woman I interviewed spontaneously told me she had any concern for the abortion's impact on her fertility. It is important to note that she is the youngest woman I interviewed. The following is an excerpt from the interview I conducted at the Center with Natasa, eighteen years old, and her boyfriend. Neither in her interview nor in her medical chart at the clinic were prior abortions reported; thus, her interview was subsequently excluded from the sample. I include this excerpt here because hers was the only interview that showed a pronounced concern with the impact of abortion on her fertility.

> *I:* Now, if we could talk a little about how you feel now that you've gone through the process and you're getting ready to go for the operation.
> *She:* Stress, a lot of stress.
> *I:* Can you say more about that?
> *She:* I'm worried about what will happen with the abortion and after the abortion. *About later, I mean, as regards the—whether I will be sterile or not.*
> *He:* If there's a mistake, if the doctors will take care of her or not.
> *She:* I'm afraid of the operation.
> *I:* In other words, what exactly?
> *She:* During the operation that they do. I haven't been operated on another time. *Den eho ehiristi xana.* I've only had my tonsils removed.

Intent on procuring the abortion with minimum hassle, the two teenagers were very focused on being "good" during their various encounters with personnel at the Center. They had been scolded by one of the nurses and, as they later told me, she had warned them that one of the biggest problems with abortion is that it can cost the woman her future fertility, a common theme among Family Planning Center employees. I myself heard midwives at the Center say this almost every day to women who came in with unwanted pregnancies.

Certainly, this aspect of the concern with abortion's impact on the woman's body may have to do with a cultural preoccupation with reproductive health that targets adolescents in a heightened way. For example, at the private high school I attended in one of the northern suburbs of Athens, one of my friends would routinely tell the rest of us not to sit on the ledge of the school courtyard, where we sometimes sat during break while the boys played basketball in the court in front of us. She would remind us that we need to be careful because we might get a chill (*psixi*), which, she explained, might cause problems for future fertility. Psixi is its own little specter in contemporary Greece. Along with the ever-present *reumata* or unexpected cross-breezes, psixi is always ready to spring up and catch people unaware. But where back pain or just a cold seem to be the more common results for men, for young girls psixi in particular is often seen as a threat to their ability to become a mother. It is believed that girls are also especially vulnerable to threats to their fertility when they are menstruating. Thus, the summers were speckled with blocks of time when one or the other of us "couldn't swim." All girls had an automatic permitted absence from gym class once a month throughout high school. It is in this larger context, I suggest, and with the midwife's recent warning still ringing in her ears, that the girl I was talking with expressed a concern with fertility.

None of the other women brought up preserving fertility as a primary concern. Like the reference to abortion as a sin, future fertility seems to be a borrowed worry. This is made starkly evident in the following excerpt of dialogue between myself and a younger woman, age twenty-two, born in Crete and living in Pangrati for the past sixteen years. This woman's record indicated that she had had two abortions, although in our discussion her current pregnancy is presented as though it were her first. Her words best demonstrate the most serious cost the women associated with abortion.

> *I:* Can you tell me a little about how you feel with regard to the pregnancy that's happened to you?
> *She:* . . . It is very strange. Psychologically I am a big mess. I am very afraid of the intervention. I can't believe that I got pregnant.
> *I:* About the intervention, what are you afraid of?
> *She:* More I am afraid of afterward. Whether there are consequences.
> *I:* Whether there are consequences for your fertility?
> *She:* That, and *if there are consequences for my body.* Will I be able to get up, how will I be.
> *I:* It depends on the woman, but mostly it seems that very many women are fine about three to four hours later.
> *She:* I know because I have a similar experience, not on me, with a friend of mine. We had gone together and afterward she was fine.

This woman's agreement with me that she is concerned about the abortion's impact on her capacity to conceive seems patently superficial and is likely oriented toward avoiding directly telling me, the researcher, that I had got it wrong. But the way she distinguishes her fertility from her body is the most interesting finding here. According to the grammar of this woman's statement, not only is fertility a secondary concern, it is not even a part of the domain of her primary concern, *her body.*

This woman's comment concisely illustrates how a woman's fertility in Greece has been constructed as something that is not, in the end, *hers*. In some important way, her body exceeds itself and does not include in its boundaries the capacity to reproduce. The uterus, the notorious *mitra*, floats upward and comes to rest in a position somewhere near the middle of the national imaginary of *Greece*. Innumerable umbilical cords stream downward, connecting it to men and women alike. Fragile, and a property to be protected, hence open to public surveillance, in many ways fertility, as the entire demografiko discourse demonstrates, figures more as part of the capital of the struggling modern nation than as an aspect of an individual woman's body. And it is always the fertility associated with the female subject, rather than the male, that is the issue in public. The special care given to a woman's reproductive potential may be a corollary of a cultural belief: *Part of what gives me value in your eyes—state, public, partner, other—is this potential loosely located in that liminal space of "here" and more visibly signaled during menstruation.*

There seems to be a prejudicative comprehension that what has given Greek women the status of persons—not only in the private sphere, where it is assumed that all girls will become women who get married and that a woman who is married will go on to have children, but also in the public sphere—and rendered them a powerful social force affecting politics historically has been their capacity as mother. *H mana*. At certain junctions *she* becomes the signifier of Greece as a whole. The more tortured and difficult her life has been, moreover, the more noble. *Like our country*. Trouble in *this* domain, whether appearing "spontaneously" or triggered by some behavior, is a serious cause for wider concern and may operate as a means for gaining a different, more focused form of attention. In many ways, the high frequency of repeat abortion in Greece can be read as a manifestation of just this dynamic at a macro level. The body is made to bespeak the joy, the pain, and the confusion that are not to be granted intelligibility in other spaces.

The biological realization of the capacity to "raise future Greeks" is what distinguishes a mother from women who do not have children, and it is qua mana, at a cultural level, that a Greek woman becomes a full-fledged citizen of the state. Being a mother remains the sine qua non of being a proper Greek woman. *Gia na oloklirothi mia gynaika, prepei na kani paidi.* Yet, ironically, as the words of the women graphically indicate, to the degree that fertility is understood to be a part of the woman's body, it is mostly as a peripheral part when seen from "the inside." Though protected by the polis, including women, here it is not the main fear.

ON BEING "PUT TO SLEEP"

In the exchange that follows, the centrality of simply being worried for one's own health, and the specificities of what this means in Greece, is best revealed. In the beginning, the woman was somewhat subdued, almost defensive about her body being her primary concern; then there is an interesting turnabout near the end of this excerpt, after a comment I make to her about the abortion. In this excerpt, we also see a reiteration of the charged placement of blame on men.

> *I:* Now, if you remember, let's talk a little about after the abortions. Do you remember how you felt after the operation?
> *She:* Well, afterward I had some pains. Pains, you have a little blood too. Because it puts you to sleep, you don't see well. Well, that. Nothing more.
> *I:* Psychologically?
> *She:* Nothing. I was only sad for me, in other words, that we women have to go through these things. *Pou travame afta ta pragmata emis oi gynaikes.* Because I wanted and I did it. I didn't go by force. Because there were so many things, that we weren't ready yet for a second child.
> *I:* What you said, that you were sad for what we go through.
> *She:* Yes, that's it. Because we women—OK, you have the abortion, but from that point on you have the pains, the various things.
> *I:* And, no matter what, you went through a sedation [*narkosi*].
> *She:* It's that sedation which scares me, in case I don't wake up! It is the fear, not whether I was sad about the abortion. And the same for the second abortion. The same. I am an individual that doesn't change. *Eimai atomo pou den allazi.*

Clearly, the most important drawback to the abortion was fear of the anesthesia. It is culturally understandable that women would be cautious, not easily volunteering the name of their main fear, especially with the outcome pending. Thus, the woman's instant agreement with my comment concerning the sedation is especially suggestive.

Another woman, Olga, also makes it clear that the most worrying aspect of abortion is its impact on her body, though her special concern is put in terms of whether or not she will feel "anything." The excerpt shows the negative aspects of abortion for Olga and, at the same time, reiterates one of the strongest positive dimensions of abortion in Greece: its function as a means to solicit special care and attention. This excerpt also provides insight into the process from the point of view of the woman visiting a clinic for an abortion.

She: What can I tell you about how it was? . . . The doctor was . . . First of all, I had a very good relationship with the doctor. He told me, "Let's be serious," and he arranged for me to go the next day with my brother-in-law because my sister was pregnant and he didn't want to put her through the whole ordeal of coming to the ob/gyn hospital with me and the worry. I said, "Will I feel anything?" "You won't feel anything, I'll be there." *Tha katalavo tipota; den tha katalavis tipota. Tha'mai ego eki.*

They take me, they take me to . . . it was the Maieftirio Mitera, you know, the rooms [*oi thalamoi*]. They took me in. They took off my clothes. They put a robe on me. We went inside to the . . . operating room. . . . He [the doctor] was holding my hand. I wasn't, wasn't . . . Fine, I was calm. . . . Anyway, it was done to me. It passed. That's over . . .

I: That's over.

She: That's, that one was passed, how it passed I don't know, I was laughing later. *Gelousa meta.*

Olga's main concern was pain. Her doctor gave her his personal assurance that she would be fine; as he puts it, "I'll be there." I was shown again how deep a relationship women have with their gynecologists. This man's assurance that he would be there seems to makes perfect sense to Olga as a response to her concern about the operation. There is clearly much more at stake in this relationship than simple health care.

Olga's reference to laughing at the end is also very interesting. The significations of laughter in Greek abortion contexts are ambiguous. Considering the numerous instances of laughter I encountered during the research, laughter in this situation is obviously significant. In Olga's case, the laughter seems to have been an expression of relief. But it might also be a sign of having "gotten away with something," something dangerous as she notes "how it passed, I don't know." Recall also the joke made by the doctor in the operating room who was performing an abortion on the overweight young woman. Here it is clear there is laughter that comes when doing something one considers wrong, laughter that helps to manage awkwardness and perhaps even embarrassment. And in Greece there is a deeper connection between laughter and wrongdoing: after laughing a lot, people say, "May it come out well for us." *Poly gelasame. Se kalo na mas vgei.* There is a sense that laughing a lot can result in something bad. *We might be punished for seeming to be carefree.*

Olga's account of how she was most worried for herself, for her health, also illuminates other aspects of the experience and the precarious positioning of the body within them: taking off her clothes, wearing a robe, being held by the hand by her doctor *almost as though she is a child, perhaps even his daughter.* Olga went on to report her sister's position on her abortions, further highlighting just how risky she finds this experience. Yet, through her sister, she is able to avoid looking fearful or overly concerned with her physical health. Olga's sister told her she was "destroying herself" by having the abortions. In one sense, this exemplifies the dynamic I described earlier, wherein relatives, mothers, and caregivers act as guardians of the cultural mandate of motherhood and warn younger women to watch over their capacity to conceive. Not only is this what makes her a *real* woman in the national imaginary but, more practically, it is what is necessary for a good marriage and a materially fruitful family (a leftover from the time when having children meant having "hands" to work and hence bringing in revenue to the family). Olga's use of this reference, however, mines the ambivalence of the sign and flaunts her own blasé attitude toward any threat to her fertility; at the same time, she reveals that abortion (of which she has had several) is nonetheless a serious concern for a woman's general (vaguely defined) health. Olga uses her sister to underscore just how important a risk she herself actually thinks abortion is to her health, and not to her fertility.

For almost all the women I spoke with, being afraid of the impact of the abortion on their body was their biggest concern. Contrary to medical and family planning experts' concern with abortion's effect on women's reproductive capacity, what I heard was a very pronounced concern, if quietly articulated, almost as though knowing it may be considered "silly," with the effect of the anesthesia. Several women told me they were afraid they might not wake up afterward "because something might happen." Many were just afraid of the actual experience of the anesthesia. Typically, it is referred to as "being put to sleep." Many women said they woke up crying and described a feeling of struggling to come out of a deep sleep and not knowing why they were crying. Very few reported any pain beyond mild cramping.

This disjunction is interesting. The culture worries about women's fertility and the women worry about their lives. Even more interesting is that in both cases—both what I am simplistically calling here the demografiko's claim and the women's concern—there is an elision. In the first case, fertility becomes situated somewhere external to the woman's body, both for her and culture alike. In the second case, the source of her life is located in being able to remain awake, and thus, medically imposed sleep surfaces as the prelude to death. Where the "artificial"[4] evacuation of the womb's contents signals the possibility of a *loss of its power,* the forced imposition of sleep harbors the threat of stealing not only consciousness for a few moments but, possibly, life itself.

The escalation characterizing both these anxieties is symptomatic of the concern with foreign bodies that I traced in the chapter on contraception. Be it a vacuum-like device, such as the tube used to extract the lining of the womb, or, in a likely unrecognized acknowledgment of the ancient use of *pharmakon* to reference poison, be it the medicine of the anesthesia, once permitted entrance to the respective domains of femininity-reproduction and humanity-awakeness, the alien force may then depart with more than it was supposed to, having predictably betrayed the trust initially extended to it. Recall the retired Supreme Court judge's comment in the letter to the editor of *Kathimerini*: "many 'friends' have been worse than enemies." These allies purport to help, but in the end they take much more than they offered.

MAGICORELIGIOUS GROUND FOR FEAR FOR ONE'S HEALTH

Concern for the woman's body emerges out of an intricate nexus of various discourses not only of the nation but of God. Though rarely stated explicitly because much is at stake in displaying a social face of strength, almost of defiant bravado, and of faith, both loss of fertility, to the extent that it is an issue, and loss of life through the anesthesia are in some way feared also as possible divine punishments for wrongdoing, though not, it must be emphasized, for sin as it is formally defined.

Let us probe the zone of contact between women's bodily fear when having an abortion and discourses about the divine. Another woman, thirty-three-year-old Stella, talks about how her feelings around abortion have changed over time. As was the case for the majority of the women interviewed, for Stella, even if abortion is bad for some reason other than its capacity to affect her health, it is certainly not so because of its moral status. Rather, she says, it is by virtue of being "bad luck" of a sort. In fact, in this woman's words we see evidence of the diffusely religious, or magicoreligious, ground that helps produce the specific form of fear for the abortion's impact on the woman's health.

> *She:* Look, if you are not ready to keep the child, you don't give that much significance to the fact. At least I didn't. Not that it doesn't hurt you and it doesn't bother you. But somehow you put it behind you much easier when you aren't ready.
>
> In other words, if I was forced to have an abortion now, I'd be a mess. I

wouldn't be able to overcome it because I am ready to have a child and I was ready to take on the responsibilities of the child and I wanted it now.

So, if for whatever reason I was not supposed to have this child, it would have been tragic for me. But at those times in the past, the logical thing was for me not to keep it and the absurd thing would be for me to keep it. Therefore, you know, based on those givens, you put it behind you very fast, very easily.

I: In the third one you promised yourself that you don't want what happened and—

She: The fear that I won't have children again. I believed that three times is already very much, somewhat like bad luck, like a jinx. Not 100 percent that way, but you know . . . You have it once and it turns out that you have [make] another child. *Apodikniete oti xanakanis paidi.* You have it a second time and it turns out you have another child. The fourth, however, will you have it again? And since it happens also on the fourth and I get pregnant, do you then risk ruining that one too? *Ripsokindinevis na to halasis ki afto?* Will you get pregnant again? *Tha xanameinis?* And given that I always wanted children, I wanted a family, so now that I could and I was ready to have it, I wouldn't even think of it. I wouldn't take the risk of having an abortion and not getting pregnant ever again. I was afraid, and for me it would be a great unhappiness to not be able to have children, because I would feel like half a person, entirely unfulfilled.

This narrative has the earmarks of perfect data for a rational-choice model of analysis. At the same time, it also reveals the radical situatedness of what is seen as rational. As Stella says, at certain junctures, having an abortion was the logical thing to do and keeping the child was the absurd thing to do. In fact, in many ways, a *culturally* Greek Orthodox mode of reasoning is in smooth alignment with the logic of rational-choice thinking. The central Greek Orthodox concept of economia refers to the principle by which the lesser of several evils is identified and action is routed (or rerouted) in a way that honors this finding and thus avoids sin. Whatever the sin status of one's actions may be in their own right, this remains and is attributed to one. What is avoided is the extra layer of sin that would be procured if economia itself was ignored.

Stella feels that she would have sinned by having an abortion if she chose to have one when she was married and emotionally ready to have a child, and especially after having already had three abortions. In this case, her fear is, surprisingly, for her fertility. However, it is not really that she thinks that the abortion itself might be negative for her fertility; rather, it is clear that she thinks a divine force or logic might be. The three abortions themselves do not constitute a sin in the way that really matters because she was not then ready to have a child. Although they are a waste of a sort, as she describes it, more important is her inability to provide what she sees as the necessary physical and emotional environment for raising a child. Certainly, with each subsequent conception, the capacity for "waste" grows larger. Here we see evidence of the divine gift and blessing that conception is at some level seen as being. You return it once, twice, thrice . . . *Who knows if it will be extended to you again after that?* Best of intentions notwithstanding, there are limits to God's patience as a bargaining entity. Thus, Stella's concern is her fertility, but only because of its location within a divine order wherein frequent repeat abortions emerge as a challenge and an affront to a divine force that is seen as generously granting. Latent in Stella's explanation of this, moreover, is a dynamic of gaming that includes a component of testing, that is, testing one's luck against some other force. *Including God.* And *tzogos,* or gambling, whether in the stock market, a casino, the racetrack, the various soccer betting games (*pro-po*), or playing cards, is a prominent characteristic of modern Greek society. Certainly, many Greek women's anxiety over the effect of abortion on their body is partially informed by a larger discourse in which the sin they are committing is not murder but not graciously accepting a divine gift.[5]

The women I spoke with invariably referred to their concern for their physical health, as opposed to their fertility, as the main negative characteristic of abortion. The dominant theme is the fear of anesthesia. This fear, I've suggested, contains elements found in larger Greek social formations, such as the historical preoccupation with invasion or assorted foreign interventions under the guise of aid (*xenos daktilos*), and the Christian Orthodox understanding of conception as a divine gift. *Doro theou. Omos kai fovou tous Danaous.* In this amalgam, it is not that an angry God will kill in exchange for the killing of a child, as some extremist members of the U.S. religious right might claim, but that the women may lose themselves, lose their grasp on life, or *let go of it,* and succumb to the sleep of anesthesia, having turned down what is seen as a very important call.

A Brutal Ethics of Life

Look, I . . . The first two abortions I had, since I was young and I couldn't by any stretch keep a child, I was very calm. Now, of course, that my child has grown and I've given birth again, well, it cost me, but I believe that in essence it is the same thing. I told you, it is how you can make use of this fact emotionally. How you see it depending on the conditions of

your life, with the difficulties you are facing, with all of that [*pos na to axioppiisis afto to gegonos synaisthimatika*]. But it does not cease to be a fact that cannot be expelled from the life of a person. *Den apovalletai.* That's what I believe.
—A thirty-two-year-old mathematician, married for twelve years, with two children, reporting having had three abortions.

The second category of reasons offered by the women for why abortion is a negative experience has to do with what I term the situationally specific ethics of abortion in their lives. Carol Gilligan's (1982) formulation of a relational ethics operative for women in the United States has important resonances for the ethics of abortion as they are articulated by women in Greece. In effect, I found that the women's estimation of a negative charge to abortion was related to their relationship and family status. As Stella's earlier comment prefigured, abortion actually changes meaning according to the relational situation the woman finds herself in.

ABORTING MOTHERS

For a few of the women I spoke with, the decision to abort was particularly difficult. All of the women who expressed this were mothers. Although not all mothers felt this way, the experience of having had children is in some instances an important factor affecting the perceived ethics of having an abortion. Closer attention to this group, where this aspect of abortion is exhibited in a condensed form, helps to further map some of the specificities of the *economy of pain* that informs Greek subjectivity and the particular way abortion in Greece may sometimes be configured as causing loss of a life.

The important link between a negative ethics of abortion and feeling pain, and having already become a mother is portrayed in the following short excerpt. A teacher, the mother of two children, compares her feelings about an abortion before she became a mother to a hypothetical abortion after she became a mother.

> *She:* The miscarriage and the abortions didn't bother me. Psychologically, nothing, not at all. But if I needed to do an abortion on the second, it would have bothered me.
> *I:* Why?
> *She:* Because I did not know the experience of pregnancy, I had not gone through it, whereas after the boy it would have bothered me a lot.

This woman had reported one miscarriage and two abortions and says she has no bad feelings about either. However, she goes on to say that if she had to have an abortion after she gave birth to her son, when she became pregnant with her daughter, *then* she would have had a problem. The reason, she tells me, is because at that point she had had the experience "of pregnancy." Obviously she had had that experience during both of her abortions, which are also pregnancies, as well as her miscarriage. Yet, she seems not to consider any of those three pregnancies a proper pregnancy. Moreover, she feels that having carried a pregnancy to term and given birth in itself would have transformed her experience of abortion into a negative one.

This is made perfectly clear in what a sculptor and mother of two, who lives in the upper-class suburb of Kifisia, says about her second abortion.

> *She:* . . . In 1975, it was between the two children, where I felt such a weakness. It happened, that was a mistake. *Etihe, lathos itan afto.* I had had a cesarean with both children and I felt so weak that I could not take a pregnancy and that is why. In other words, I felt that I would not be able to stand up to [*n'andapexeltho*] a pregnancy. In other words, the first pregnancy was, it brought me down a lot [*me katelave poli*]. It was a cesarean too. It took me two years to recover. Imagine, in other words, to have a child and then to take two years to recover.
>
> *I:* It can happen.
>
> *She:* And I could not decide to take on the responsibilities for a second. But there it was perhaps a little, I can tell you, on the second, it was more painful. *When you have a child and you see it, then you feel very bad. In other words, you are closer to the reality, to what is really happening.* Whereas in the first one, where I was young too. I was twenty-two. I can't remember, I didn't even know what was really happening. I hadn't conceived of the whole matter precisely in its full dimensions [*den iha sillavi to olo thema akrivos me tis diastasis tou*]. In the second [abortion] it was traumatic [*siglonistiko*]. *You have one baby and to know that you're ruining another.*

Having already had a child may change the subject's understanding of the ethics of abortion. At the same time, it may not change the decision to abort nor does it compel a definition of the act as murder. Of those women who expressed a charged concern such as that shown here, married women who had children almost always mentioned their children as the lives they are protecting by having the abortion. Single women, and several of the women who already had children, referred to their own life, however indirectly, and said that they could not afford a child right now, or that it just did not fit into their life at the present. Either way, the impact of abortion on existing persons, not on the fetus, was the predominant concern.

MYRTO

Myrto reported three abortions and talked of feelings that ranged from relief at getting rid of a burden to devastation. She was forty years old when we talked, born in the town of Kalamata. She lives in the lower-middle-class neighborhood of Nea Filadelfia and has done so for the past thirty years. She is a homemaker and has finished high school and secretarial school. She goes to church three or four times a year. She has been married twenty-two years and has two children.

> *She:* Well, the first abortion happened because it happened very soon after my first birth. In other words, my son was then two months and I had gotten pregnant.
>
> *I:* Difficult.
>
> *She:* Eh, I took it as that I am getting rid of an additional problem in the beginning. The second ... even though it happened the same year, naturally I can say that it influenced me more. Somewhere I was wavering, to keep it or not to keep the child. It [the child she already had] was still small. ... I thought about it a lot, in other words. But, in the end, I ruled it out. The third, because I had had my second child too, my daughter. That is where in the end I almost lost it.
>
> *I:* Really? What happened to you?
>
> *She:* Now, if someone hears this they'll say that you didn't have it with the first, with the second ... With the third though? And yet with the third I could not sleep for a month. I took sedatives for this matter. ... Eh, until I overcame it, let us say. But of course at the same time, afterward I also put in the IUD. And, let us say, my mind is at peace. [*Isihasa*]. ... Physically, that it is safe now, from that point of view, do you understand?
>
> *I:* Yes.
>
> *She:* I think it can never be overcome. You know how many times I've thought that, I don't know, they didn't influence me much. *But the third. I said that many times I have thought, "Now I'd have another little child of so many years old," let's say.* Very many times I've thought of it.

Myrtos's feelings move from being just a little troubled at the time of the first abortion (which was two months after the birth of her first child) to somewhat more difficult in the second abortion that occurred later that same year, to, finally, being devastated when she had the third abortion after having had her second child. For her, as for a few other women, an abortion after the birth of children is sufficiently painful to motivate action that would prevent the possibility of subsequent abortions.

VASILIKI

The most extreme expression of abortion as actually constituting a form of killing came from Vasiliki. At the time of our interview, she had been married for twelve years and had two children. She too expressed fear for the impact of the abortion on her health, as so many other women did, yet at the same time she voiced concern that in aborting she was actually killing a child. She is twenty-eight years old, a homemaker, and left school after the eighth grade. She reported two abortions. When I asked her if she goes to church, she said, "What can I say! To be churched [sic], rarely. Now, some holidays . . ." *Na ekklisiasto, spania.* This comment shows Vasiliki's sense of humor, but it also suggests what I found to be true time and time again: a sense of abortion as an act with a pronounced ethical dimension is not necessarily accompanied by formal religiosity. Consider Vasiliki's description of the meaning of abortion.

> *She:* First of all, I did not want it. But as soon as I became pregnant . . . Naturally, you entertain the idea because I believe that . . . But anyway a lot came up. In other words, it is also the financial aspect that was in the middle and so I could not keep it. Of course, my husband was telling me for me to decide. He didn't tell me, "You are going to do this" or do the other. He let me decide. Of course, I told him I don't want to keep it. But on the other hand, inside of me I was saying "yes." I was between yes and no. Until I finally made the decision and I went for the operations each time. But psychologically I have not gotten over it yet. I don't know, I feel I've been stigmatized. Psychologically I cannot get over it and I do not believe that I will get over it. And that is why I wanted not to get pregnant again. I still haven't gotten over it and nor will I get over it, I believe.
>
> *I:* Can you say a little more about your feelings?
>
> *She:* First of all, I was a wreck. Because from the moment that you get pregnant [*me to pou menis*], it is as though *you can see it in front of you*, and although I do not know its form [*par'olo pou den xero tin morfi tou*], I feel like . . . Despite my husband telling me that it isn't a formed child, it is very small and that is how you should see it, etc. But it has shaken me up.
>
> *I:* You feel—

She: Yes, I felt it as a child. In other words, a ready child that is ready for you to give birth to it, to hold it, and then for you to lose it. Like that. It is very, very difficult and I don't know.

It is very difficult too to decide, but also with the whole procedure, where are you going, what they are going to do to you, altogether they add up and then you feel a mess. You can't simply pass by something like this, no matter how close to you and no matter what other people tell you. The issue is that it should not happen.

I: It is difficult.

She: Very difficult, and I wish it does not happen to me again because I couldn't. Maybe in the end I would even keep it, I don't know. Maybe too the next one, if it happens, which of course I don't want it to happen again, maybe I'll keep it in case perhaps I'll have again the child I did not have, how can I say, the child that I ruined. [*To paidi pou halasa.*] It is as though I had it alive and I lost it. Something like that. That is how I feel. It is difficult, and it is a shame. *Einai diskolo kai inai krima.*

It is important to note that even in this type of narrative, anxiety about the impact of abortion on the woman's own health and fear of the whole medical process remains a primary issue. Nonetheless, it is clear that Vasiliki experienced pain over the abortion because of her sense of the pregnancy as containing a child. Though her husband told her it is not a "formed" child, her reference to his words figures as an attempt for her to manage her own sense that this does not really matter all that much. "Formed or not . . ." we can imagine her countering. In this, Vasiliki's representation of the fetus is significantly more extreme than most. Although the fetus is always referred to as "the child" by the women of my sample, it does not usually seem to be thought of as a child proper. For Vasiliki, it is actually a child.

Second, evident in this narrative as well is a cosmology within which there is clearly some higher power at work governing the traffic of souls here on earth. She says she thinks that if she gets pregnant again, she might have the child she did not have because of her previous abortion. A possibility that, she hastens to add, she certainly does not want. In this, there is more evidence that some of these pregnancies are, at some level, desired even if not wanted. Similar hints occur in other women's accounts. An underlying sense of some type of intelligence governing the life of souls here on earth seems to animate the stories told of abortion.

Third, although Vasiliki sees the pregnancy, from its very beginning, through the prism of a *mother*—her concern is that the contents of her uterus are a type of child—not only did she choose to have the two abortions *anyway* but, when her narrative, almost "of its own," brings her to the possibility that she might again become pregnant, she concedes that, hopes and wishes notwithstanding, she would likely once more choose to abort. An almost stubborn and fiercely strong subject emerges from this story. *She* is able both to fully acknowledge the life she helped to create and, at the same time, fully insist on her decision to "interrupt" it without flinching at what she sees as being a form of murder, even as she avoids the word.

I tan I epi tas, comes the affirming response swirling out from the mists of time, when Spartan women sent their sons off to battle. *Either return as a victor, or return dead on your shield.* This historical narrative has been used to build a particular construction of regional identity: Spartans are strong, hard people. It has also been lifted from its regionality and used to fuel the representations of the generically Greek mother. Selfless in her care for her children, the idealized Greek mother is a woman who will sacrifice even her own child to uphold the good of the polis.

In these women's stories, the nation is not an explicit concern. The narrative mutates and, despite the resurgence of pronounced local nationalisms in the public sphere during the 1990s, none of the women I spoke with explicitly considered the nation a variable in their reproductive decision making. Yet, a dynamic of sacrifice, of killing in order to save, and of looking the beast straight in the eyes underlies these narratives, and in a way that resonates with the Greek stories of valor and agon that shape a sense of superior national identity. In effect, the nation is beating the drum at the heart of all this. For the women I spoke with, the operative polis is the site of their family or, for unmarried women, their relationship. Thus, the narratives of Greek national identity are transported and reinscribed at the homestead, the *oikos*.

An important piece in the puzzle of how life is seen in Greece actually runs contrary to the framework of the fetus as life. This has to do with how the pregnancy itself is defined when it is unwanted. Invariably, when I asked women how many times they had been pregnant, whether or not they then expressed negative feelings about abortion, they counted only the pregnancies *they had carried to term*. A few who had children asked me if I meant the abortions too, but the vast majority simply answered with the number of children they had. Most of the women who didn't have children and had had three or four abortions openly told me they had had *no pregnancies*. As I conducted more interviews, it became clear that there is a qualitative difference in the women's minds between a pregnancy that results in a child and a pregnancy that results in an abortion. Indeed, the two are not made of the same stuff. This may be the linchpin explaining why it was among mothers in particular that this negative aspect of abortion occurred.

ZETTA

One moment in my conversation with the very first woman I formally interviewed, Zetta, sums up the ethics of abortion in contemporary Greece in a way that is almost poetic. It happened shortly after we had stopped taping and the visit was winding down. At the time we first met, in January 1994, she had been married for eleven years and had two children. She was thirty-four years old. She lives in Menidi, one of the working-class districts of Athens, and invited me to her home for the interview. Her ob/gyn was an acquaintance of mine and he had been talking about my research to some of his patients, helping me to build a sample of women independently from the work I was doing in the public health care system.

Zetta's apartment is small; the living room we sat in was set up in what the civil engineer had no doubt intended as a small entrance hall. The other two rooms in the house had been made into bedrooms, one for Zetta and her husband, and the other, the original living room no doubt, for her two sons. She brought out orange drinks for us. After some initial friendly conversation, the interview began. It went on for almost two hours.

As I prepared to leave, I asked to use her bathroom. Coming back to where we had been sitting, my head was still reeling from everything I had heard in the last two hours. As I subsequently found out, the interviews would in fact typically be very intense interactions for me as well as for the women. Though they were doing most of the talking, they were discussing important sources of pain in their lives that I was being made a witness to. Meanwhile, I needed to stay vigilant, managing the flow of conversation so that the research goals were met, while at the same time assuring the person sitting across from me that I was doing my best to understand what she was laboring to explain and, last but not least, that *I could be trusted*. Trusted for what, it was never entirely clear. But how trustworthy I was is perhaps the main underlying issue of all these interviews. At times, I felt as though I was giving an exam that had the mysterious capacity to keep regenerating itself.

It could be the look away, to the window I had forgotten to check, at just the moment a woman was telling me about the smart comeback she had for her mother-in-law, or the button at the top of my shirt which, judging from the insistence of her gaze, for one woman should have been unbuttoned so that I wouldn't seem so *koubomeni* ("buttoned up") and hence potentially hiding something. There were infinite subtleties and, as I talked with more and more women, I became both more able to identify my many failures and, thankfully, more able to move past them. After all, in some very important way, the women were absolutely right: I am not trustworthy to them. I am a researcher and I am with them at that moment in that capacity. I am not there as a friend when we are doing the interview, even with those few women with whom I did have a friendship. Because the discussion is taking place for the research, because I will be taking what is said and *using* it, even if that happens to be "building theory" and "contributing to knowledge," I am there at that moment as a researcher. Indeed, I am using any friendship toward that end. The most honest thing anybody can do in such a situation is not pretend to be entirely safe. And so I would remind them that our discussion will be used for my research and, in many cases, I would ask them again to grant permission for me to use the interview, once we had finished talking and the woman knew how much and what she had said to me.

I also had a keen sense of the responsibility I had for initiating these encounters. And, certainly, I was always aware that talk is never just talk and that in telling me these stories something that sometimes seemed deep and important was happening for the women I spoke with, even for those who I could tell had tried to keep me "outside" throughout the interview. Several told me something to this effect at subsequent meetings.

Zetta's interview had also felt very intense to me. She seemed to be interested in using my interest, my questions and comments, to help her find out more about her own truths. She told me, for example, that she hadn't realized just how important her husband is to her until now, when she was bringing to mind all the things they've been through together. She told me in a lowered voice, even as we sat there alone in her apartment, that she never really wanted their first child and that this feeling "lasted . . . it lasted, well, for a long time." Zetta also displayed a stiff upper lip when telling me about the sacrifices they had made for their children. It was with a sense of relief that I put the tape recorder back into my bag. And at that moment, she made the comment whose importance, ironically perhaps, it took me a year of subsequent intensive fieldwork to fully appreciate. In many ways, Zetta gave the whole thing to me right there.

I reconstruct her words based on the notes I took when I left: "You know, whatever we say, whatever we think, it is all life. Everything else is well and good, but that's it. That's the truth: it is all life." At that point I put my bag back down, lifted my head, and looked straight at her. She continued: "*We* are life. The air we breathe is life. *Death* is life." I felt something click. She paused, looking around the carefully decorated small living room. "The houses we live in are life." She looked around and added, "*Furniture* is life." I think I nodded. Then she swirled her head around to the bookshelf against the wall next to where we were sitting. "See this bookshelf?" she went on. "This wood? Wood is life." With that, she made her hand into a fist and loudly banged the side of the shelf with her knuckles. "*This* is life!"

Several of the women I spoke with subsequently referred to the fetus as "a life." Not in the first case and not as the main reason that they were upset about abortion. But, at some point, it would come up. This type of life discourse should not be confused with pro-life discourse, U.S. or Greek Orthodox. Zetta is not reifying life. Indeed, she seems to be saying that death, even when it is imposed, is an important part of life. Many women, like Zetta, would express some remorse about one or several of their abortions, but there was also always still a firm pragmatic sense that it needed to be done. Overall, the use of the word "life" to refer to the fetus is very similar to the way Zetta called the bookshelf life. *Death is life*. The overriding trend is for abortion to be viewed pragmatically. Even where emotional pain connected to a negative estimation of the ethics of abortion is reported, it is embedded within this larger discursive context.

Women's generic status as mothers (whether of one or more children) seems to be an important factor influencing Athenian women's feelings about the ethics of abortion. Of those women who reported pronounced feelings of sadness or remorse around one or more of their abortions, almost all were mothers at the time of the difficult abortion and they explicitly linked the specific negative feeling about the abortion to their experience with children they had given birth to.

Yet, there also emerges, even among those few women who define the abortion as some form of sin or even "killing a life," a sense of having done the right thing. Overall, the ethics of abortion that prevail can indeed be summed up in Zetta's defiant comment. Sure, there is "death." Sure, people may even actually deliberately cause it, the way people cut down trees to make furniture, but sometimes this may be the best way of serving and honoring life. This does not mean there is no pain attached. Quietly yet persistently, the narratives of the women reveal that the body has a crucial role in voicing this pain, whether the pain of loss of a potential child or of the dream of the desired intimacy within the couple. In this we see another aspect of the cultural specificity of the formation of the individual in Greece today. Mind and body both are fundamentally social and relational entities and, as evident in many of the women's accounts, they are linked. In addition, the subject's understanding of both physical and emotional feelings are always mediated through larger narratives about national identity and the divine, about what it means to be Greek.

The lack of easily distinguishable boundaries between subjects and the omnipresence of contestation witnessed in the analysis of Greek women's conceptions of who is to blame and what exactly they are to be blamed for, extend to the understanding of life (as including death) and of the individual's physical and mental selves. Everything is connected. And the connections follow intricate underground routes. In what follows I continue to explore how Greek narratives about struggle and valor sometimes collide with narratives about loyalty to those one loves, on the one hand, and patriotism or loyalty to the very nation that bears the narratives about resistance, on the other. Abortion is a powerful optic device in more ways than one.

The Abortion Taboo

The excerpts already presented foreshadow how abortion in Greece also carries another set of costs. This has to do with how it is viewed by society, or people (*kosmos*), as the women would sometimes tell me. In the familiar paradox of a disjunction between daily practice and formal discourse, or between stories told at different sites and to different constituencies, it becomes clear that although Greece may have a very high rate of abortion, this does not correlate to widespread acceptance. Certainly there is much invested in claiming to be at ease with abortion—in not being "like the Americans," with their preoccupation with abortion. Greek concern with abortion is articulated in different registers. As my fieldwork suggests, however, abortion is also more publicly charged with negative connotations in Greece, and not only in the press. And it is no less charged for the specificities of its manifestations at the site of the Greek subject as they have been presented in the preceding two chapters.

Thus, I turn now to a consideration of how abortion's negative dimension can be perceived by other Greek publics. To do so, I rely on a variety of informants. First, we take a quick look at the institutional framework of abortion at the Family Planning Center and how the disparate understandings of abortion held by other constituencies are brought to bear on the women visiting the Center for abortion services. Then, we see how the present climate concerning abortion is marked as different from that of the recent past with regard to an abortion taboo in Greece. To this end, Dr. Jay, a feminist ob/gyn, shares her experience in the autonomous Greek feminist movement. After that, Mrs. Papadopoulou, the head midwife of the Family Planning

Center, offers her insight on the current social status of abortion and its effect on women's choices. From there, I turn back to the women and examine the social context of abortion as it was portrayed in their interviews. Finally, we return to the clinic, and I present anecdotal evidence from my observations there and an incident I witnessed at the adjacent Sterility Center. This last section helps to further problematize the definition of abortion in Greece and to contextualize women's experiences with it, while at the same time shedding light on the complexity and inherent contradictions of the current state-building project of forging the individual in Greece.

THE CLINIC'S PROCEDURE

The role played by the clinic's procedure in the attribution and reproduction of the negative aspects of abortion is significant. It was actually common practice for the Center to give women abortion dates that were a month or more away from the day the women actually visited the center, usually after having done a home pregnancy test and hoping to get the abortion done as soon as possible. But because the law stipulates that abortions are legal up to the twelfth week and because the doctors and medical students performing the abortions had told the midwives at the center that they preferred the pregnancy to be at least five weeks old, many women were scheduled for an abortion during what the midwives estimated was the eleventh week of the pregnancy. "Eleven and two, eleven and three, OK, eleven and five," I heard midwives mutter as they spun the wheel of a little plastic calendar that a pharmaceutical company had provided them all with.

How the pregnancy's age is calculated is another interesting topic in the medical side of the ethics of abortion in the public sector in Athens. The midwives start counting with the first day of the woman's last period, as she reports it to them, thus agreeing to act as though that was the earliest that a woman could conceivably have become pregnant. I say "they agree to act as though" because I was told several times by the midwives that getting your period didn't necessarily mean you weren't already pregnant; that could well be a "false" period! Stories of such cases abound in the lore of the center. Nothing—not even what is taken as common sense—can be trusted, certainly not the women's own word. Things are rarely what they seem, and look how much more complex and demanding all this makes our work.

Then, "the woman," as patients were called by the midwives in private, "the lady," or kyria, in public, got a blood pregnancy test done on the hospital's premises (no external tests would be permitted) and a manual pelvic exam by the intern who was on duty at the time. She would eventually be given a "ticket" and an appointment for an abortion. Each of these steps had to be completed on separate days. Moreover, if the intern was unable to estimate the pregnancy's age by feeling the position of the woman's uterus and if the midwives were unable to prevail with their own estimation based on the little circular calendar they kept in their pocket, or if the intern was very new and had not yet learned that the ultrasound department did not like getting more than two referrals from the center per week (only very ambiguous "special" cases were to be sent for an ultrasound diagnosis of the pregnancy's duration), then the woman was also sent for an ultrasound, again to be done on the premises because "you never know where they got the other ones" (implying they could be falsified).

Certainly the midwives were themselves caught in some very difficult negotiations with a variety of institutional, professional, and personal pressures. Bureaucracy itself, as a vital part of contemporary Greek political culture, has its own mandate in this context.[6] Yet, it was also clear that the midwives—many of whom had chosen to become trained for facilitating birth rather than what the medicalization and institutionalization of ob/gyn services, and the resulting job market's exigencies, had pushed them into—*knew* that most women who wanted an abortion felt that time was of the essence and, I think, this was their way of doing a couple of things. One, delaying the date for the abortion to the estimated eleventh week was a quiet way of punishing women for a crime, which is what most of the midwives I talked with eventually told me outright that they saw abortion as, and, two, constructing themselves as more powerful than the hierarchy allowed them to seem—here they actually have the power to delay the very thing most "ladies" visiting the center want more than anything else at that particular moment in their life. Abortion is the very thing, moreover, in opposition to what they see as their original calling. Meanwhile, both these functions are smoothly accomplished while appearing to be appropriately serving the needs/desires of their superiors, the medical personnel. *The midwife as docile subject par excellence. With all that hostility flying about.*

THE ABORTION STIGMA, FEMINISM, AND THE LAW

Dr. Jay talked to me at length about one phase in her professional experience early on, when she worked in the lower level of the public health system, and her activism around abortion in the autonomous feminist movement. In Dr. Jay's view, Greece used to have a very strong taboo against abortion, until the feminist movement—especially its autonomous branch—began to mobilize support for legalizing abortion. There were many losses involved in that moment of apparent victory, and Jay identifies them as *big* losses. She thinks the biggest win is a Greece (*mia Ellada*) that no longer has such a taboo against abortion. Jay's words about the past help to establish the historical context of abortion in Greece while they also outline the specificities of the abortion taboo in Greece at the present. It is important to keep in mind that most feminist organizations were affiliated with one of the political parties. Those that refused such an affiliation were considered the autonomous, indeed more radical in important ways, feminist movement, and the politics between these groups were themselves charged. When the progressive Family Law was passed in 1981 and abortion legalized in 1986, each sector of the feminist movement had its own claim on it as their victory.

> Dr. Jay: Because time was passing, but slowly, these things were taking hold [*ebedonontousan afta*]. Those who fought some battles in the beginning, and yelled, may have . . . gotten into trouble. They got out of the way. But the thing is, you know, somewhere a foundation was being laid and the next one had a point . . . to start from. That, then, that's where we concluded in the end, with the group [the particular feminist group of the autonomous women's movement which Dr. Jay had been a part of].
>
> In other words, yes, on the one hand, abortion wasn't legalized the way we wanted and in the framework of "abortion-contraception-sexuality" with the liberation of female sexuality being the core. That had been our goal. But, on the other hand, abortion had nonetheless suddenly become a first-page item in the newspapers. People now say the word "abortion" without blushing, and women especially. . . . In effect, it took this matter out of the little cupboard of taboos and made of it a political discourse [*to kanane politiko logo*]. So that's what I consider a success of the women's movement, the autonomous one, of the decade of the 1980s, let's say. That's what the success was in the end, that it took abortion out of the little cupboard of shame . . . and made it political discourse. That it is a claim, that it is a right, that it is a consciousness, that it is, I don't know, things like that . . . for the woman.
>
> Well, that's what I believe happened. . . . Because suddenly you heard even the most out-of-it [*asxeti*] woman who wouldn't have talked to you about sex, or love, or anything . . . telling you . . . "Abortion, yes, I've had five abortions." Where months before, five years ago, she would not have dared to tell. She would not have told anybody . . . that thing.
>
> I: And she would have felt that she was wrong.
>
> Dr. Jay: And that only she has had, and a close friend of hers, and everybody else doesn't know anything. . . . In the end, it came out that everyone knows

and everybody doesn't know. . . . As we said in one of our pamphlets, "Everybody knows about it and we've been keeping it a proudly kept secret." *O kosmos to'hi toubano, ki emis krifo kamari.* Nobody knows about it and everybody is doing it. What is that now? So, hypocrisy.

Dr. Jay represents the present as a mostly taboo-free context for abortion; however, as both the press and the women alike testify from an array of different perspectives, this really is not the case. But Jay helps mark a point of change, a particular site of cultural struggle in which the prevalent terms for understanding abortion socially were challenged and, to some extent, transformed. In so doing, she also vividly portrays the power of the taboo at the time. Before the legalization of abortion in 1986 and the struggle leading up to it, the taboo was much more powerful.

Considering the effects of the legalization of abortion, Mrs. Papadopoulou, the head midwife of the center, also middle-aged, has a different perspective. As I knew from my everyday contact with her and our many conversations, she was not a feminist and did not hold feminists in high regard. Yet, she, like Dr. Jay, saw the period surrounding legalization as an important time of change and, for her as well, the taboo seems to be gone as a result. But her understanding of the change is not the same. Where Jay postulates a fundamental transformation in values and beliefs, Mrs. Papadopoulou suggests that the change in the culture of shame surrounding abortion is not as deep. Moreover, she does not see this as a positive development. Rather, Papadopoulou argues, the law simply provides women with a way out—a vehicle for pushing aside, or covering up, their feelings of guilt.

> *Mrs. Papadopoulou:* . . . But I think that all this sensitization—the law covers the woman, with the . . . insurance books she can have the tests, she can have the abortion itself, all without paying. And somewhere the law may help— you know these things better than me—it may help with the feelings of guilt. It isn't illegal, therefore since it is legal, the feelings of guilt . . . I think they are fewer, in other words.
>
> Or, we see it with the in-take interviews too. They do not present their real problem. If it was the law (if they really believed it), we would not have these cases. But there is the law and I, based on the law, perform the abortion and you see that the women have feelings of guilt. And that shows from the way they talk and how they look, that they do.
>
> *I:* So, maybe you are saying, the law, in the end . . .
>
> *Mrs. Papadopoulou:* And it is too little time for us to say how the law has operated. Isn't that right? To do a statistic.

Mrs. Papadopoulou is suggesting that women continue to have strong feelings of guilt about having an abortion. The law, she suggests, gives them a way to deal with what you and I both know full well is guilt. The law offers women an alibi. Indeed, she implies with her last comment, the law may actually increase abortions. Papadopoulou felt that the women should feel guilty. Though she is very careful to avoid judging the law, from various comments she made in informal conversations, it was quite clear she felt that guilt is the appropriate feeling for the experience of abortion. *I couldn't help thinking, perhaps some of them look so guilty because the personnel here so often blatantly treat them as though they are guilty. Though it was also true that this treatment was mostly reserved for the many racial, ethnic, or national "others" that used the clinic's services and not the Greek women proper, unless they were quite young.*

Even in this short excerpt, the contours of my relationship with Mrs. Papadopoulou come through. She is careful to say that she is not the expert on "women's feelings" and is willing to yield me that turf—knowing full well that this properly belongs to the psychologist, of which the clinic already has one, or the social workers, of which the clinic already had two. Here too, as in the private clinic, my status as a Ph.D. candidate doing research constituted a puzzle for most of the personnel; typically, it was resolved by placing me in the same camp as other nonmedical specialized personnel, such as psychologists and social workers. The difference between a Ph.D. and a Master's seemed to be entirely illegible. Throughout my stay there, she showed much evidence of a concern that my real interest was in eventually getting a job directing the center. She took pains to underline her authority there, even at times pointedly saying within my hearing that she wouldn't let "them" place "any of the psychologists, sociologists, etc." in the position of head administrator of the center. Regardless of this, I found myself liking her more than I expected, partly because it was always very clear to me that she sincerely cared deeply about the center and it was indeed its well-being, rather than her career, that she had foremost in her mind. It was just that the well-being of the center and the midwives that staff it and that of the clients were not in alignment. Also, given the strong religiosity of most of the midwives—indeed, this was part of their training until very recently—along with their strong sense of duty (*kathikon*), I couldn't help thinking that they were in an almost impossible position.

Certainly, the interviews support Mrs. Papadopoulou's sense that, the law notwithstanding, having an abortion was not that simple an affair for the vast majority of women. This is not to say that it was a source of guilt, in the terms of the family-planning, latently Anglo-Saxon, pro-life discourse, which Mrs. Papadopoulou tacitly underwrites. But there were many women who told me that they simply preferred not to tell anyone other than their partner, often not even a friend. This is a quiet but powerful piece of evidence that some form of taboo continues to be associated with abortion. Of the women who said they had told nobody about their abortions, or just one friend, or a sister, the comment made by one woman, Andonia, forty years old and a salesperson at a bookstore, stands out as a strong testimony to the ongoing hold of the abortion taboo, even among Athenian women who consider themselves strong, independent, and modern.

> *I:* And this interests me too, how much this is something unique that has to do with your sense of yourself as a Greek [woman]. *Ellinida.* In other words, how do you see your experience of abortion through the prism of living in a Greek culture? Do you think you felt it differently? More intense, less intense? You thought about it more, you didn't give it much thought?
>
> *She:* Well, I believe I confronted it in a Greek way. *Elllinika to andimetopisa.* Greek and contemporary, of course, not Greek in the retarded sense, the Eastern *tin anatolitiki,* the one we still carry. I think with a contemporary perspective, modern, let's say, modern. You will see further down too, that my life wasn't a conventional one. Fine, my marriage obligatorily [*anagastika*] . . . I could not not have a marriage, but generally I was a revolutionary. *Epanastatria.* A revolutionary both in beliefs and as a way of dealing with certain issues. Of course, not to the point that my mother has learned that I've had an abortion, let alone more, she still has not found out about it. Because even now if I tell her, as I am married with children, she'd say, "Oh!"
>
> *I:* She'd be shocked?
>
> *She:* Oh, of course. Here when I told her that I smoke, she was shocked.
>
> *I:* And with abortion, where would the shock be focused? That you had a relationship? That . . .
>
> *She:* Everything, I don't know, the most important, they'd have fallen on me to marry me off, things like that, and there was no way I would even dare say something. Even now, I hide many things that go on in my house or I don't know what.

Despite her positioning as a rebel, Andonia could not tell her mother about her abortion. Perhaps more telling, during our third meeting, she told me the following, further gesturing toward the cartography of silences and abortion in Greece.

She: . . . I was married by now and this happened to me and . . . with other people very close to me, one or two people, and I didn't . . . I've shared that I had relations within the marriage [extramarital affairs; *iha shesis mesa sto gamo*]. But that I have had an abortion, with nobody. Why? That's what I say—Were the reasons moral? I don't know. Later, I thought about it again. And when I told *you* the last time we talked, later, I said to myself, "Look at how easily you did that." I said it, though, to a young girl, because I believe that if I give her the whole picture she can form a better opinion both about society and about reality.

Further illuminating the comments made by Jay and Papadopoulou, another woman who also represents herself as having had no reservations about the ethics of abortion nonetheless tells me that she and her partner have kept her abortions a carefully guarded secret. Maria was thirty-four years old at the time of the interview. Born in Athens, she had been living in Politia, a mostly upper-middle-class suburb, for the past fifteen years. Maria told me she probably goes to church once or twice a month, plus the holidays. She is married, has had two children, of which one died, and she reports having had two abortions.

I: Now, do you remember the day of the operation? Your feelings?
She: Bad, but because my husband was good, he protected me. We went together. Only the two of us and nobody else came. And other than the two of us nobody else has even found out about it. We don't discuss it with friends, with mothers, with anyone.

Many other women echoed the words of Andonia and Maria. Related and intriguing evidence of the persistence of silences surrounding abortion comes from another of the midwives at the center. Nana was one of the more down-to-earth midwives working there. She would not boss the personnel (janitorial and nursing) the way other midwives would. Also, she took pride in being very methodical and careful and looked up to Mrs. Papadopoulou. Nana referred to her as "the superior" (*i Proistameni*), ostensibly showing deference, but also perhaps indexing the latter's style.

I liked Nana a lot. She could sometimes be very abrupt; in fact, I was often dismayed at the way she openly challenged women whose in-take interview she took about their decision to abort. But there was something endearing about her forthrightness in a space where it was clear that loyalties and alliances were always shifting. Among other things, the midwives got rotated into a variety of different departments at random intervals; this created an intense climate of tension and fear, as each department had its own quirks and different margins for leaving work early and other things the midwives valued.

After several months of being based in the center, I started going to the Sterility Department next door when things were slow at the center. I gained entry there by asking permission from the doctor in charge of the floor and the doctor in charge of sterility, who wrote me a formal note of permission to be present. The Sterility Department had a higher status than the Family Planning Center housed in the same clinic and so, at some level, my ability to move between the two was seen as a potential marker of disloyalty, and even that Mrs. Papadopoulou's fears that I was privately nursing a vision of being head administrator might be right.

At Sterility, I observed intake interviews and exams and had permission, though no private space, to conduct my own interviews with whomever I chose. One morning when I came back to Family Planning after having spent a couple of hours at Sterility, Nana was sitting in the midwives' room and asked me if "they had anything" (*ihe tipota*), meaning any cases. I said there were plenty of people there but none reported abortions. I said this was interesting because it has been suggested that a portion of the population that has fertility problems have had abortions. Nana responded, "Well, do you think they're telling the truth?" Then she said, "Why should they? I wouldn't. And with their husband in front . . . They would risk a lot."

Part of what is at stake in the above exchange has to do with the fact that my new habit of going to the Sterility Department was a reflection of the lack of work being done at the Center. There was a lull during which very few women were coming. Thus, I am indirectly being told by Nana that, contrary to what I may think, my own work won't be furthered by going there and abandoning "the homestead." Also, I demonstrate a mobility that is not available to the midwives and hence create a disturbance in our relationship. Last, my decision to seek approval for access to the Sterility Department was motivated by the recognition that Family Planning's activities were now such that my research time might be more productively spent elsewhere. I had learned a lot from them, but it was time to move on.

Her passive-aggressive undertone notwithstanding, Nana's comments were accurate and very valuable. They showed me how to listen differently and look more closely while in the Sterility Department. They also demonstrate how serious the abortion taboo can in fact be even at the present in Greece. Additional support for the issue Nana raised came from Fotini, the previous medical intern at Family Planning, currently stationed in the Sterility Department, when she told me two stories that support Nana's point—one directly and one indirectly. First, I mentioned to Fotini that I had noticed that Dr. Patsios in Sterility is very adamant and persistent when he asks women if they've had any past pregnancies. "Any at all?" as he would repeat, or "No abortions, no nothing?" *Oute ektrosis oute tipota?* In response, Fotini told me how he had once found a cervix "like this," and she made the shape of an O with her thumb and index finger, in a woman he was examining who had reported that there were no previous pregnancies. Fotini said that the cervix could only be so wide from abortions.

The second story was about a good friend of hers for whom she did an examination. She could tell there had been a pregnancy. It turned out much later that the friend had indeed had an out-of-marriage child. *Everything shows there,* Fotini said as she ended both stories. *Everything (implying "a woman's history") shows there (the cervix).* The female subject's body, especially its interiority, is positioned as the *vasano,* the site that reveals all truth. Agency is severely circumscribed in this nexus of power. The all-telling cervix discloses the truth the female subject withholds, the *miasmatic* truth, it is implied. Moreover, this truth that the subject is represented as pathologically clinging to is always accessible to the ostensibly omniscient scientific gaze.

The inadvertent politics of Fotini's story, as well as the complexity with which history may be transcribed or, better, encoded onto the body become clarified with another story I heard. A woman was prescribed treatment because her cervix was almost sealed shut, despite the five abortions she had had. Perhaps not everything is told by the cervix after all, certainly not linearly, to the scientific gaze.

Yet another important piece of evidence of abortion's continuing strong negative charge with the patients of the Sterility Department showed up about a week later. I was sitting in the Sterility Department's office in a chair to the immediate right of Dr. Theodorou, a woman who, though technically still a medical student doing her internship, was considered one of the doctors—indeed one of the best. The room was usually very crowded on Tuesdays and Thursdays, when Sterility was receiving new patients. There would be Kyriaki, the head midwife of the Department, who also worked at the microscope checking sperm; another midwife, Lili, a Greek Russian woman I knew from her rotation in Family Planning; and a nurse. In addition, there would be about three or four junior interns, stationed in Sterility for that month, and another intern-doctor, though of lower status than Dr.

Theodorou; at that time this was Dr. Patsios. From time to time, there would also be two young women training to become nurses or midwives.

Occasionally the head of the department would also be there. In addition to all these people, and of course the patient with attending family members and/or spouse, there was now me, dressed in the usual white robe, trying to blend in as some kind of intern/trainee. The size of the room was about 15 feet by 15 feet, with a jagged corner, a tiny rectangle taken up by an examination table that was rarely used. Usually, after the intake interview was taken in this room, the patient would be ushered into the adjacent, slightly smaller room to be examined by one of the interns, and a new patient would be shown into the first room. It was a very busy, very crowded place.

On this particular day, I was sitting next to Dr. Theodorou as she conducted intake interviews and explained treatment plans to patients. I was listening to her interview a couple. Theodorou had begun to ask the routine battery of questions when the wife interrupted, saying, "Let me make this easy, the problem is probably my husband's, he has an elevated testicle [*kripsorhis*]." As I had seen her do before, Theodorou said, "Wait, wait, that isn't necessarily so, he may have a problem, but you might also, we don't know. Let's go through all the questions." The woman pulled back and they proceeded with the questions. Once done, Theodorou asked one of the male interns to examine the husband. After some deliberation about where to do this, it was decided that they go to a room outside the Sterility Department. When the intern and the husband left, the wife leaned in close to Theodorou and said, "Doctor, now that the husband isn't listening, I have to tell you that I have had one abortion." Theodorou seemed disoriented for just a second and then immediately said, "OK, that doesn't necessarily matter." When I heard this, I remembered Nana's comment about women not telling the truth about prior abortions!

After about five minutes, the intern came back with the man. Dr. Theodorou outlined their course of action based on the intern's confirmation of the one elevated testicle and of course now also having the information of the woman's past pregnancy and abortion, and the couple left. When they did, the intern stopped Kyriaki from letting in the next patient. Then he said to Dr. Theodorou, "Let me tell you the situation. He asked me not to say anything while they were here. *Both* testicles are elevated. One has been operated on to bring it partly down. The other one can't be felt at all [*den psilafietai katholou*], not even at the mouth or entrance [*bouka*]." Everyone became flustered. They in turn informed him that the woman had reported having had an abortion while her husband was being examined.

Fotini, the intern who had been at Family Planning the previous month and was now stationed at Sterility, was especially interested in what Dr. Theodorou would write on the card recording aspects of each patient's medical history. First, there was concern over what to write about the issue of the testicles and then over the abortion. Fotini pointed out that next time the couple comes it might not be Theodorou who is there. Theodorou kept commenting that "this is the problem that comes up when we let the women bring their cards from downstairs themselves. What if she sees it next time she comes?" she asked, meaning that the women can very well read what's been recorded on their chart as they carry it up from the records office. Someone else in the room said, "We need to have our own code!" Somebody suggested, "What about English?"

Later, when I was back at Family Planning, I relayed the abortion part of the case, saying how right Nana was about some women being wary of disclosing abortions and how now the people at Sterility were trying to come up with a solution as to how to record abortions on the medical charts. The other midwife, Mrs. D, suggested "t.e.," the abbreviation for induced, or "artificial," miscarriage or abortion, and Nana said, in her usual style, "It doesn't take much to figure out what that means, you don't have to be very smart." To me she said that it is an old problem, usually resolved by writing in English.

How interesting, I thought, as I had when this idea was suggested in Sterility earlier. They solve the problem by writing in English. It felt like one of those "representative anecdotes" current social science "thinks with," though I couldn't quite put my finger on why right then. Is a code needed for writing "the truth" about abortion in Greece? Another language? And why English? Why not French? Moreover, what exactly is accomplished by the strategic assumption of a radical alterity on the part of the investigator—what is lost, what is gained, what is hidden or saved, and what is feigned? What new light is shed on the politics of my project by the metaphorical idea of English as the best code for writing "the truth" about abortion in Greece?

Whatever the answers to these questions may be, for different constituencies in different geopolitical contexts, one thing is clear, as this analysis of the perceived costs of abortion in Greece has shown. Deciphering the meanings of abortion is not a simple endeavor. Much as the cervix does not in fact reveal all truth, the surface of abortion as a social phenomenon may be misleading. Perhaps nonlinear reading is the venue that best approximates the multiple levels of truth. Certainly, the attempt to break the code exposes the intricate interweaving of nationalism with discourses of gender and sexuality, which inspires the spirit and animates the body in a modernizing Greece. Abortion is experienced culturally at a multiplicity of sites and by disparate constituencies. At each site the layers of meanings, connected always to stories about the nation and stories about appropriate femininity, are refracted and articulated in code. Contestation is ever-present, and the individual very often an imaginary construct. This nexus, finally, is rigged. Invisible mines can be triggered in a matter of seconds, with results there that are explosive.

PART FOUR

Instigating Dialogues

The Loved Ones

... As it is written, those you love will appear
to you during avalanches, fenced in by iron,
rowing between loud alarms—a deep vessel
all lit up off-shore, with expert marksmen on board.

—Mastoraki, 1998

Figure 14. *Mother*, by Christina Dara. From "Fear and Rage" exhibition, Zoumboulakis Gallery, October 2002. Courtesy of the artist.

Figure 15. "Kapnizete?" ("Do you smoke?") by Ilias Papanikolaou. Zoumboulakis Gallery, October 2002. Courtesy of the artist.

Figure 16. Two women on porch titled *Oi dyo yenies* (The two generations), 1983, by Takis Katsoulidis. Courtesy of National Gallery of Art of Greece.

Figure 17. *O Evagelismos* (The Annunciation), prior to 1924, by Konstadinos Parthenis. Courtesy of National Gallery of Art of Greece.

Chapter 10

REPROSEXUALITY AND THE
MODERN CITIZEN FACE THE
SPECTER OF TURKEY

❖

Politics is about the constitution of the political community, not something that takes place within it.
—Chantal Mouffe, *The Return of the Political*

The demografiko, and most markedly abortion when mentioned in its context, is unilaterally used in the news coverage and editorial and op-ed columns of the left, center, and right-affiliated segments of the Greek mainstream press, and not only in the largely more emotional letters to the editor examined in chapter 6, as an opportunity to air anxieties of ethnos in a way that is gendered and markedly racialized. Elsewhere I have argued that this coverage works, much as the letters to the editor do, to reproduce a particular configuration of nationhood, Greece as a religious state of sorts, and a given range of conceptions of the optimal organization of statehood, of which the strange conjuncture of "socialist" and "fundamentalist" meanings emerges as most prominent (see Halkias 1997, 55–86).

Yet, it is quite clear that the demografiko coverage is also reproducing *subjects* of a particular political order. Interesting differences, indeed a slippage, emerge between the configurations of agency and the body evinced in the narratives put forward by the women and those identified in different segments of the press coverage of the demografiko. Here, men, women, children, families, and couples are all represented and normatively defined as social units or agents, at times primarily and *above all* oriented toward national welfare. That is, they are portrayed as subjects whose overriding concern is being either for or against national welfare, which, in the demografiko coverage, is overwhelmingly defined as the successful biological reproduction of appropriately Greek subjects.

An array of meanings of abortion are made operative in the public sphere

Figure 18. *Eimaste oloi Ypefthinoi* (We are all responsible), 1972, by Kostas Tsoklis. Courtesy of National Gallery of Art of Greece.

that work to position Greek women as the ones to blame for the increasingly evident bankruptcy of "foundational fictions" of the Greek nation.[1] The mainstream Greek press coverage of the demografiko, and its concern with abortion in particular, offers a unique window onto the distinctive image of Greek femininity and citizenship that is linked to the public sphere's ongoing, increasingly high-stakes negotiation of "modern Greece."[2] In this chapter, I focus specifically on the implicit and explicit understandings of femininity and sexuality that animate demografiko discourses. Throughout this discussion, important and often quite radical disjunctions become evident between this set of meanings and those found in the discourses articulated by the women themselves. Perhaps most interesting is the larger picture that emerges from this analysis. In effect, where the women's narratives blame men for abortion, the public sphere press narratives quite clearly blame women. In addition, where the women I interviewed blamed men primarily for "not caring enough," the press news coverage of the demografiko tends to configure Greek women as pronouncedly selfish and uncaring. However, whereas the men were blamed for not caring enough for their partner, the press coverage of the demografiko and abortion very often blames women for not caring enough about nothing less than the nation itself, or, at times, "the Greek race."

To explore this facet of the meaning of abortion in contemporary Greece, this chapter presents and analyzes a few telling fragments of the press news coverage and opinion columns that illuminate recurring stories or tropes that mark demografiko discourses as a whole. In the first section I focus on the gender-nation nexus within this coverage. In the next section I examine more closely how women specifically are portrayed here and argue that although minimal agency seems to be allotted to them as subjects, they are clearly considered subjects who have acted enough to be both at fault and worthy of blame. The third section establishes both the motivation or cause attributed to women for their reproductive insubordination, and simultaneously traces the link to a racialized construction of Greek nationhood that is most pronounced in the centrist press. The next section explores the contrast evident in the significantly lesser coverage of the demografiko and abortion appearing in the left-wing press. I conclude by summarizing the discursive production of competing femininities found in all the coverage of the sample and identify the logical mechanisms through which the nation and gender become intrinsically linked.

Dangerous Turks and Treasonous Greek Wombs

It is impossible to separate the construction of gender from the construction of both race and national identity. Race becomes part of the stuff of gender, and gender is part of what is being used to organize a diffuse and agonistic social reality into clear-cut races and ethnic collectivities that can then be divided up into presumably given nation-states. The strong reaction to Karakasidou's (1997) nuanced and rigorous historical ethnography of ethnicity in Greek Macedonia and of the effects of Greek nationalism on the people of this region is stark evidence of the vehemence with which nationalism patrols the symbolic borders of a postulated homogeneous Greek ethnos. The strength and type of response that book received is also linked to the fact that the author of this incisive analysis of Greek nationalism and the politics of ethnicity is a woman. As a Greek Macedonian woman, she is culturally charged with the moral responsibility to protect "her people," "her family" from all outsiders, even if that means silencing "internal" injustice. Part of the issue, of course, is that it is not so clear who is in, who is out, and which group exactly is "her people." That part of the reaction allegedly included threats of rape is also telling. Perceived as having violated the imperative to protect her larger kin-ethnic-national group from external threat, she herself receives a threat to what is perceived as the core of the integrity of her femininity. Much as narratives of national identity, along with ethnicity and race, inform the culturally specific social construction of gender, so narratives about gender, normative femininity and masculinity, are key elements animating all nation-building projects. This process is usually not easy to trace; it is, however, put into bold relief in the context of the preoccupation with Greece's birth rate that is articulated in the press and other formalized public spheres of Greek political life.

This nexus was perhaps most starkly illuminated, if inadvertently, in the summer of 1995 on the front page of *Kathimerini,* the well-respected Greek liberal-conservative daily newspaper. On 23 August 1995, *Kathimerini* published an article on its front page with the title "Abortions Are Double the Number of Births: Ignorance of Contraceptive Methods." The story began immediately below the fold in the far right column under the paper's lead story, "The Turkish Regime Murders Prisoners." In effect, the placement and wording of these titles argue that a maximally dangerous enemy, the Turkish regime, faces us and meanwhile, "our own" women are busily undermining our strength from within.

The mandate for compulsory motherhood that is articulated in public considerations of Greece's low national birth rate frames Greek women who do not "adequately" reproduce as enemies of the nation. In so doing, the press attempts a partial domestication of the enemy that the Turks are seen as. This conjunction is illustrated with the appearance of these two articles and their positioning. Implicitly, the claim is made that perversely violent subjects surround us: the Turkish regime to the east and northeast, and Greek women in the heart of our own territory, who are busily having too many abortions. We, that is, all Greek male citizens and those few Greek women who are abundantly reproducing, this argument suggests, are on very precarious ground. Just what the danger consists of is a peculiar conflation of the ostensibly free-floating fascism of neighboring Turkey's military regime, implicitly connected to the more generalized evil and inferiority of the racial and religious other that the Turk is represented as, and the allegedly selfish and perverse violence of "our own" women against the nation via the high rate of abortion.

The story itself sheds more light on the rhetorical device evinced in the layout of these two pieces. The portion of the story on abortion that is printed on the front page reads as follows:

> The inadequate information young Greek women have with regard to contraceptive methods is considered by experts as one of the main reasons for the high number of abortions which, in our country, are almost double the number of births. The stunning fact is that one in four girls aged 16–20 years old who visit the Family Planning Center of the Hospital Alexandra report at least one abortion in their medical history. Also stunning are the conclusions of various other scientific studies.
>
> One of these, conducted by the TEI of Athens, found that 30% of those asked—aged 15–19 years old—did not know that the "Papanikolaou test" is not a contraceptive method. Another 16% did not consider syphilis a sexually transmitted disease while 17% believed that Mediterranean Anemia is transmitted through sexual contact.
>
> Most young people learn about these matters from friends and relatives. Of this sample, 99% asked for the introduction of a relevant course into schools. Finally, worthy of consideration is the fact that about 50% does not know that there are family planning services operating in Greece.

In many ways, this excerpt emblematizes the Greek press's coverage of "the reason" abortions occur in the first place. First, we see the automatic move to position abortion in the context of the nation. Abortion's significance is immediately established via a comparison to the national low birth rate, hence making and *naturalizing* an implicit connection between the two, thus portraying the perceived impact on the nation as the main issue. Second, we see the construction of the "ignorance" of Greek women and *their failure* to be well-informed is represented as the cause of an embarrassing number of abortions.

Kathimerini's phrase "the high number of abortions which, *in our country*" (that is, as opposed to the more developed nations we wish to emulate) "are almost double the number of births" references a perceived failure of the nation-building project of modernization. The implication is that no nation whose rate of abortion is so high could possibly be properly modern, or "European." Meanwhile, at the same time that the country's efforts to fully play its role as a member of the European Union reach a new height, there emerges an idiosyncratic concern with modernization, which, paradoxically, relies on a nexus of religious and racial, markedly *fundamentalist* nationalist discourses. That is, the demographic fact—too many abortions—taken as a sign of the failure or serious undermining of the modernizing project is the result of a particular junction of discourses that also yield the belief that a victorious encounter with modernity hinges on an appropriate number of births of, specifically, an appropriate type of infant.

Genetics play an important part in this. Connected to the demografiko's idea of national welfare is a preoccupation with the survival of Greeks as a people and, at some sites, as *a race*. The excerpt above illuminates this. Situating the findings of a study on sexual behavior within the context of the country's high number of abortions and low number of births, while also specifically referencing *Greek* women instead of women in general, for example, puts in relief that the stake in youths' sexual behavior is the survival of the Greek "species." This is amplified with the references to syphilis and Mediterranean anemia, a widely feared and somewhat stigmatized, genetically transmitted blood disease with a high frequency among Greeks.[3] The article reports that the means of transmission for each are incorrectly understood by youth (though at fairly small percentages) to support the main claim that "the inadequate information held by young Greek women with regard to contraceptive methods is considered by experts as one of the main reasons for the high number of abortions which, in our country, are almost double the number of births." Yet, indirectly, the claim is advanced that the very physical health of Greeks, as a species or race, is what is really at stake by youth's allegedly inadequate sexual education. The article seems to be saying with dismay: Young people think the disease of syphilis is not part of what they are gambling with when having sex, though they think Mediterranean anemia is an STD with repercussions on nobody but themselves, when in fact it endangers "us," that is, the biological foundation of the future of Greece.

In tandem, the article attributes both the high rate of abortion and other behaviors seen as being risky for the health of the Greek "race" specifically to women's inadequate knowledge of modern contraceptive methods. Yet most of the data it goes on to report relate to other types of knowledge and are not based on an exclusively female sample. By limiting the reasons for the high rate of abortion to an issue of "knowledge" that, moreover, a specific category of subjects is seen as lacking, the press names women, and minimally the educational system, as those responsible for the current endangerment of the nation itself.

Accompanying the strong nationalist approach to understanding the consequences of Greece's high rate of abortion is a perhaps somewhat paradoxical reliance on methodological individualism. Only *individuals,* rather than nationally inflected discourses of personhood or larger social formations such as "gender roles" or the couple, are seen as responsible for the social phenomenon of repeat abortion. Moreover, within this framework, a zero-sum economy of responsibility prevails, so that the individual person seen as being most proximal to the abortion,[4] and only she, rather than the inseminator, for example, is in this domain given the blame. It is the woman who aborts who is largely seen as guilty of the "sin" *against the nation* that I have shown abortion to be figured as in demografiko press coverage.

In fact, the mainstream right and center press, and to a lesser extent the mainstream left, single out women as responsible for abortion and, moreover, often define that responsibility specifically as a function of a stubborn or backward refusal to accept modern science or, at times, an almost inate inability to master appropriate modern medical means of birth control, and, hence, protect the nation from the metaphorically or actually contaminating and threatening effect of dangerous outsiders. Meanwhile, as shown, the women's own understanding of abortion and contraception and the politics of the couple reveal a quite different allocation of responsibility.

Whither the Agency of Greek Women?

Having examined agency at the site of the gendered subject in part 3, I turn to how agency is mapped at the site of the formally public discourse of the demografiko. The highest resolution image of agency emerges in the news coverage of two medical conferences in the right and centrist press. The moderate right-wing *Kathimerini* makes very clear who is being held accountable for abortion: "For the Greek woman [*Ellinida*], abortion constitutes a method of 'contraception' [*andisyllipsi*]. Gynecologists claim that 'they brainwash' their clients to apply some contraceptive method and not to consider contraception a secondary matter."[5] Leaving aside just what most of the twenty ob/gyns I interviewed told me they tell their clients about contraception, at least partly because of the time exigencies of their work, the effect of this rhetoric is to firmly position women rather than the couple, or the man, as the responsible party. It is women specifically who need to be "informed." Furthermore, it is women who are represented as bizarrely or stubbornly backward, as the paper's representation of the ob/ gyns' rhetoric implies— almost obstinately or defiantly *preferring* abortions instead of using other forms of fertility control, despite "brainwashing."

The article concludes by saying that "the optimistic message of the Association [of Gynecologists and Ob/Gyns] is that in recent years there is a small upward trend in births for the middle class which creates hopes that it will spread also to all the social strata." Giving birth is thus seen as something that "spreads" (*na exaplothi*) without need of the consent or conscious desire of the woman in whose body the event takes place. Reproduction is figured as exceeding the agency of the subjects within whose bodies it occurs. Closing, the article states, "Today, in any case, the birth rate in Greece (1.4 children per woman) is the lowest in Europe." As the careful explanation in parentheses specifies, women are at fault here, whether or not they are capable of also being responsible. The statistic could be per household or, even, per man, as the resignation of "in any case" suggests, because the ostensible bottom line is simply that we need more births regardless of which constellation of subjects is to be responsible for raising them. In this is the promotion of a pronatalist agenda that concertedly targets women.

Echoing *Kathimerini*'s dismay, but putting Greece in a slightly different position, the centrist *Eleftherotypia* reports on the same "Sex Education and Health" conference held by the Greek Society for Family Planning in November 1994: "There is a small but hopeful increase in births in the middle class of our country while the experts hope that this change in behavior will be mimicked too by the farming [*agrotikos*] population. Despite all this, the low birth rate remains an important problem for Greece, *as it is for all the countries of the European Union* except for Sweden."[6]

Instead of focusing on Greece's rate as "the lowest in Europe," as *Kathimerini* did, *Eleftherotypia* attempts to put things in a different perspective. Greece's low birth rate, it suggests, though a serious problem, is not that extraordinary. Especially important, this article does not, initially at least, follow the same tack of focusing on abortion as the main topic of interest in the conference's proceedings. Still, *Eleftherotypia*'s coverage foregrounds the low birth rate. It does not quite so clearly nullify all women's agency by suggesting that the birth rate might "spread." But it does portray a negative image of farmer women who will "mimic," like children who copy what they see, their urban(e) counterparts and thus have more babies.

In the end, this article practically duplicates *Kathimerini*'s coverage of the conference: "From 1974 to today . . . abortions have doubled among Greek women below 18 years of age. In 1974, abortions in those ages covered 5% of the total. Today this percentage reaches 10%. Unfortunately, as the speakers underlined, Greece remains the first country of the E.U. with regard to the number of abortions, while *only* 3–4% of Greek women of reproductive age use the contraceptive pill. Today, two-thirds of Greeks use some means of birth control, and 46% of them use a condom."

Greece's having the lowest birth rate was not a comparison of interest to *Eleftherotypia*, an important difference from the charged fundamentalist nationalist register in circulation, especially in the centrist *Ta Nea* (see below). However, Greece "remains" the country with the highest number of abortions in the European Union. Moreover, it is Greek women's inadequate use of the Pill, "only" 3 to 4 percent, which is seen as the key factor. Altogether *Eleftherotypia* is articulating the modernizing strand of popular Greek nationalism that was evident in some of *Kathimerini*'s news coverage of the demografiko, as we saw in chapter 6.

Where *Kathimerini* focuses on abortion by pathologizing a woman's decision to abort and by referring to the national rate of birth as a legitimate comparison to the rate of abortion, *Eleftherotypia*'s concern with abortion is a function of Greece's relative position in the European Union. The crime here is not against the Greek Orthodox nation by dint of extinction of the populace, but against the nation by way of repeat abortion's function as a sign of inadequate modernity. Being properly European and being properly modern are usually synonymous propositions in Greek vernacular. Relatedly, *Eleftherotypia* emphasizes that "only" 3 to 4 percent of Greek women use the Pill. Although each paper's underlying notion of the Greek nation is distinct, in both cases it is Greek women who are held responsible for the country's perceived primary problem.[7] Also, they have in common an infantilizing image of Greek women who cannot or will not use a contraceptive as simple as the Pill. At the same time, there is a hint that men are doing much better, since we are told of a rate of usage for the condom, a method whose use is commonly thought of as involving only men.

Later the same month, *Kathimerini* covers a different conference, the sixth Panhellenic Conference of Obstetrics and Gynecologists, which was held on 23 to 26 November 1994. Echoing a conclusion that several ob/gyns told me in interviews, the article was titled "Precautions for AIDS Have Decreased Abortions."[8] That this does not in itself mean that the demografiko is "getting better" is revealed in the subheading, which hastens to add "Births in Greece, however, are estimated to be much less than 100,000 this year." In fact, almost all the coverage implicitly and often explicitly argues that cutting down on abortions will automatically boost the birth rate, thus obliterating the Greek female subject's agency. This fragment internally reveals this as a logical fallacy. There is clearly no necessary connection between abortion rates and birth rates, or abortion and birth, as demografiko discourses overwhelmingly suggest.

This article emphasizes that only a threat to one's life—as AIDS is commonly represented as being—can compel a decrease in unwanted pregnancies, and *not* abortion per se. At the same time, the headline indicates that abortion is locally configured as the measure against which even AIDS, a major international public health risk in its own right, is viewed in Greece.[9] Thus *Kathimerini* states: "Fear of AIDS decreases abortions and increases the sales of condoms. The number of abortions in our country, which remains at very high levels compared to other European countries, has dropped during the last two years by 30% whereas the sales of condoms have increased by 25%."

Here it seems that the nebulous, allegedly inadequate "knowledge of contraception" is no longer the salient variable for explaining abortion rates. In its place, we see condom use. While fear of AIDS is represented as very strong, AIDS itself, intriguingly, is shown as important only because of its effect on the abortion rate. In addition, unexpectedly, men shoulder some blame for abortion, as is implicitly suggested by the exclusive reference to the sales figures for condoms. If condoms are such an effective solution to abortions, and their use is popularly seen as hinging on men, it would be logical to assume that men may also be at fault for the inadequate resolution of the abortion "problem." As it continues, however, the article suggests a different answer: "However, as the professor of Obstetrics and Gynecology of the University of Athens, Mr. D. Aravandinos, noted, this does not mean that the change in behavior in the matter of sexual relationships has become common conscience, whereas Professor Kreatsas underlined that 50% of women continue not to take any contraceptive measures."

"The change" references higher usage of condoms which, however, has not yet become "common conscience." Moreover, the quick follow-up with a statistic concerning *women's* contraceptive behavior works to detract attention from any underlying claim concerning men's role in the high rate of abortion. Lest it seem inappropriate to assume that condom use is being connected to men rather than women, consider how the article continues: "According to facts of the Family Planning Center of the hospital Alexandra, 26% of women who use some form of contraception take the pill and 24% insert an IUD, whereas the condom is used by 29% of men." Although it is not foregrounded, these comments make clear that whereas 50 percent of women *continue not to* properly contracept, 29 percent of men *do* use appropriate contraception. The apparently genderless "change in behavior in the matter of sexual relationships" that Dr. Aravandinos calls for acquires a clearer referent in the secondary clause and its pronouncedly gendered component emerges. There, Professor Kreatsas emphasizes that 50 percent of *women* actually "continue not to take any precautions." Thus, it seems, while men are applauded for the current *alleviation* of "a major national problem" due to their 29 percent usage of condoms, women—of whom we must presume that 50 percent *do* properly contracept, at least based on this version of the statistics—are nonetheless firmly held as the ones to blame for its existence as a problem at all. In all this, moreover, the agency of women as a category is minimized in representations of their "good behavior" with regard to birth control and is maximized in representations of their "bad behavior," wherein they emerge as agents who obstinately "continue not to take any contraceptive measures." Thus, though some agency is allotted, it is constrained and polluted by childish and backward feelings and beliefs.

Modern-day Medeas: Insubordinate or Merely Stupid?

Women are to blame, though paradoxically, minimal agency is typically attributed to them. Moreover, they are difficult and stubborn, even belligerent, in their apparent preference for abortion over other forms of birth control. The front-page *Kathimerini* article "Abortions Are Double the Births" states that "all the facts relating to abortion at a young age continue to be disappointing despite the observations of scientists that Greek women have begun at last to 'mature' and to learn how to avoid an unwanted pregnancy."[10] In other words, the article argues, while adult women have finally begun to understand how to avoid an unwanted pregnancy, adolescents, presumably because of their age, are not yet able to overcome the immaturity that until very recently was perceived as *inherently* characterizing *all* female subjects.

Meanwhile, with yet another variation on "the statistics," the article goes on to comment: "The percentage of Greek women who use contraception (the Pill or the diaphragm[11]) is around 10% whereas the absence of information on the methods of contraception is the main reason for the tragic picture our country presents to Europe: it comes first in abortions, which are double the births."

In place of the centrist press's clamoring Muslim hordes ready to cross over Greek borders, here we have a refined version of a European populace looking down at the dismal contraceptive state of Greece. We look more like "the Balkans" than Europe is the implication. Moreover, again it is women who need "information" and it is this absence of information that is the main reason for the crime, here defined as presenting a bad image of Greece to Europe.

Immature, perhaps irrational, and clearly uninformed women who are also portrayed as having mostly minimal positive agency but maximal blame are "the bad guys" in the story of right and centrist demografiko press coverage. This image is enhanced by the additional connotation that they may actually actively choose abortion over other forms of fertility control. A 1993 article reporting on the ninth annual conference of the European Society of Human Reproduction and Embryology is entitled "Greek Women Prefer . . . Abortion."[12] The article focuses on the figures of contraceptive use released by the conference organizer, a professor of medicine at the University of Thessaloniki, Dr. V. Tarlatzis. The finding treated as most significant, given the space it takes up in the article, is that despite the allegedly many good effects of the Pill on a woman's health, "two out of 100 Greek women of reproductive age use contraceptives, the lowest percentage in all the countries of the European Union." Again, Greece is compared to the European Union; again, the main concern is how the country looks to these outsiders; and again, it is what women *do not do* that makes the country look bad in this context. Forms of birth control that *are* used by women, as well as rates of male condom use, simply are not referenced.

The article continues with an interesting twist: the effects of abortion on the female subject are suddenly placed at the center of attention. "Unfortunately, the most popular method of birth control and family planning remains abortion, which has serious consequences as much on the woman's psychological [*psyhiki*] health as on her physical [*somatiki*] health." This reiterates comments made by the representative of the Greek Orthodox Church (see chapter 6). But here the phrasing suggests that while "we" may have a vested interest in her physical health (and she may not care much about her physical health herself), should she not care about her psychological health? If not, the implication is, there is something wrong with her. That is, if she does not care about her mental health, as it is defined for her here, then she is not being rational or psychologically stable.

That women do not use the Pill despite its many alleged good effects suggests a certain backwardness at best. Like a child, in this coverage the Greek woman does not know what is good for her physically, and, like a deranged person, she does not seem to care about what is good for her psychologically. Underlining this emphasis on "the woman's health" and illuminating the higher stakes of just why it is seen as important, the picture that accompanies the short piece is of a pregnant woman wearing a white sheath. The photo of a woman looking like a Virgin Mary operates as a counterpoint to the image of Greek women portrayed in the article. The implication is that in aborting, Greek women voluntarily violate the goodness, indeed the sacredness, they are seen to have *qua pregnant*.[13] The target of this strategic deployment of a discourse concerning women's best interests in the context of a particular matrix of nationhood is made clear.

Another important junction in the representation of women in demografiko discourses occurred after the 1992 publication of *Reproducing the Population: Theoretical Approaches and Empirical Studies* (in Greek) by Professor Nota Kyriazi. Several articles reviewed or referenced it in the mainstream press during 1993 and 1994. This coverage constitutes a significant site in demografiko discourses in that opposing constructions of the gendered female subject appear side by side and the prevailing definition of Greek women is, to a degree, problematized. Kyriazi's rational-choice framework of analysis concluded that Greece's low birth rate is one of the "side effects" of development: "The social and economic changes that have occurred in Greece during the postwar period have created the preconditions for a transference of preferences for children toward other alternative choices, to a change in the hierarchy of preferences with the invasion of new commodities and services, and simultaneously causing an increase in the relative cost of children for parents, mainly as a result of the increased education and external occupation of women [*exoteriki apasholisi*]."[14]

Here abortion is not an issue. Rather, the birth rate is the central concern and a shift in priorities is the causal factor for its drop. When the female subject was not earning income outside the home, jobs were not a factor in deciding whether to have a child. With economic development, however, came jobs for women; thus, development is to blame for the low birth rate— not any of the other factors usually cited (i.e., inadequate information, women's selfishness or immaturity). More specifically, "Economic development has caused two important changes that concern women's position and that have influenced the birth rate: opportunities for external occupation, which affect the birth rate by increasing the value of women's time, and higher education. Education influences the birth rate also by increasing the value of women's time but, in addition, by creating a shift in preferences." Here Greek women are represented as supremely rational, and development is shown to have made the female subject quite logically "shift her preferences" away from child bearing.

Almost overwhelmed by the degrees of agency and rationality that Kyriazi seems to attribute to Greek women, however, the newspaper hastens to emphasize, "Certainly, however, there is also the cost of children and the expenses which negatively influence the birth rate." External factors, likely called on by right-wing *Kathimerini* to emphasize the implication of the PASOK government in the low birth rate, also work to lift some of the blame from women. In effect, however, this reference to external factors also works at a rhetorical level to minimize the realm of free choice that the primarily liberal paradigm of the book attributes to women. I suggest that the newspaper is here working to contain the significant autonomy and acknowledgment of agency women are being granted within the disparate theoretical frameworks Kyriazi presents. In demografiko coverage, modern Greek citizenship is defined in gendered terms: Greek women must reproduce, and appropriately contracept, to fulfill their moral duty as citizens. Thus, Greek women are consistently represented as inherently, essentially, and almost exclusively reproductive beings. This is in complete contrast to the conceptualization of women characterizing most of the disciplinary approaches to demography discussed in the book.

The dominant Greek representation of women in the context of the demografiko is implicitly challenged in yet another paradox. Another *Kathimerini* article reports that the Pill works by "blocking" and "neutralizing" the "natural" hormone that helps to implant the pregnancy in the uterus.[15] The article pursues this representation of women when it articulates the assumption that abortion is always painful for women not only physically but, presumably, emotionally as well: "This pill [*paraskevasma*] has not for the moment made its appearance in Greece and in the rest of the advanced countries it was only minimally made known, despite the fact that it would free women from the painful—and not only physically—experience of abortion."

The newspaper is not referring to the *contraceptive* pill; rather, at issue here is another abortion method, the RU-486 "abortion" pill. In this case, the woman aborts by taking a pill rather than undergoing D and C or asperation under full anesthesia. Given this, it is hard to understand the paper's claim that the pill would ameliorate the negative and allegedly "not only physical" bad effects of an abortion. In the absence of a reference to full anesthesia as something that causes women emotional pain, this claim makes sense only if the mere appearance or external mechanics of abortion as it is performed at the present is what triggers the emotional pain. In other words, it is the mere appearance of the procedure that causes women pain, not the meanings attributed to the procedure or the pregnancy itself.

The article thus implies that disguising the abortion by making it look like a pill-induced menstrual period would suffice to convince women that there is no reason to be sad. Women emerge as only superficially sentient or, at least, very easily emotionally manipulated. It may also be that advancement in medical technology, in particular a new medicine, operates as a node of power that amplifies modernizing discourses. Thus, the display of pride at science's new conquest overrides traditional concern with the low national birth rate and yields a narrative that is, unexpectedly, respectful of the decision to abort. This clarifies that it is not the act of abortion as an objective reality that is the problem here, but particular meanings that come to be associated with it. Most of all, the definition of Greek women as emotionally immature is further fortified.

The image of Greece as advanced in the context of this representation of women is interesting. This article, like most focused on the new abortion pill, shows a remarkable lack of consternation over the contradiction between the implicit claim of Greek women's shallow emotions and the explicit claim that Greece is an advanced nation—second-class categorization of women notwithstanding. In addition, the article unflinchingly attributes the difficulty in promoting RU-486 to the allegedly excessive religiosity of the French: "The reasons could potentially be found in the 'homeland' of RU-486, France, and *the fanaticism of Catholics* against abortions, despite the fact that every year tens of millions of women all over the world resort to this solution for an unwanted pregnancy."

In light of the tenacious religious fundamentalist strand of nationalism running through demografiko coverage, this statement is like the pot calling the kettle black. Especially shocking is the sudden concern registered in most of the articles covering the RU-486 pill on behalf of the women who abort! That all of these somewhat schizophrenic contradictions are installed and unproblematized is symptomatic of the larger pattern of fragmentation, decontextualization, and selective amnesia that characterizes the production of Greece at the present historical moment.

The theme of women's immaturity is also found in the central press. The daily *Ta Nea* published an article titled "Market and Low Birth Rate."[16] It discusses some of the conclusions of sociologists about the effects of the demise of communism on the birth rate in other countries, especially those around Greece. Making clear what is at stake with the persistent negative mention of Greek women's low use of the Pill, the article reports, "The drop in the birth rate can be translated also as *a modernization* of behaviors. Female contraception has been spread with Western pills."

Yet, even in a context heralding modernization, the local Greek idiom of women as subjects lacking adult agency is evident in the choice of the word "spread." Again, it is as though, were it not for "the spread" of female contraception, there would be more births, even if women and their families did not want them. Not only does use of the Pill "spread," but it is sufficient to counteract women's agency with regard to the number of births *desired*. The article continues, "At the same time, [the numbers of] abortions, which were *of necessity* a means of contraception, have dropped *because of [couples'] financial problems*. The same for marriages."

Once more, this is confusing logic. If abortions were "of necessity" a means of contraception, why are financial problems cited as the reason for the *drop* in abortions? Moreover, if financial problems are responsible for the decrease in the abortion rate, how can "the spread" of the Pill also be responsible? The issue seems to be that women are so perversely fixated on abortion that only a shortage of money could stop them from having abortions (and then, bizarrely, proceed to engage in the much more expensive process of giving birth to a child). Meanwhile, their (positive) use of the Pill can only be understood as a product of the influence of the social force of modernization. Again, it is as though it is unimaginable for female subjects to be exercising their agency and making reproductive choices based on other, cultural and historically specific criteria.

Further illuminating a cultural preoccupation, almost obsession, with abortion and the strong investment of this concern with a nationalist narrative, the article's only reference to abortion is about a *drop* in its rates in the Balkan region. Yet the article is accompanied by a photograph of four women in robes, one wearing a scarf, sitting up on hospital beds with the caption "Bucharest 1990. Women resting after abortion." These are the Orientalized "others" whom a modernizing Greece of high abortion rates foregrounds, even in an article focused on the decrease in abortion rates of these countries. The implicit claim is clear: Greek women who abort are "Balkanized."

Saving, or Destroying, the Race of Hellenes

What is at stake with the press's configuration of women in its news coverage of abortions and births? Greece itself, we are told, time and time again. A particularly charged version of this Greece is surprisingly put forward in the centrist press coverage. In the weekly *To Vema,* a routine column, "Common Sense" by Giannis Marinos, offers the most vivid evidence. The vehemence of this column is echoed in many other articles appearing in the centrist *To Vema, Ta Nea,* and *Eleftherotypia.* In one instance, the column analyzes the new legislation forbidding "the commerce of infants."[17] Taking issue with this piece of legislation, the author details why he sees it as counterproductive in terms of the nation's welfare. In this context, in addition to a stark representation of women who do not want to have children as not only backward but insane, the author proceeds to explain why the law matters. In so doing, the link between social production of gender and of race at the site of demografiko coverage in Greece is put into bold relief.

"Numerous exemplary scientists, and also all the political world, have accepted that the demografiko has emerged as the most important danger threatening to extinguish Hellenism. That is, the low birth rate of Greeks, who *prefer to be without children* instead of taking the responsibility of creating them and *perpetuating the species* [*genos*]. Well, with the prosecution of the so-called baby trade, I discern the institutionalization of the low birth rate and the prosecution of women who still accept to have many children." Here centrist and otherwise fairly liberal *To Vema* reaches a surprising climax. Those Greeks who prefer to be without children instead of doing their noble patriotic duty are represented as criminals against the nation by virtue of their selfishness and short-sightedness. The crime is specifically framed in terms of the Greek genos, that is, species or "race."

That the metaphor of national suicide at the hands of *women* specifically is fully endorsed in parts of the centrist press is made blatantly clear. Consider the following excerpt from another extensive article, also by Marinos, published by *To Vema* under the title "A Demographic Crime":

> When a human being [masculine] wants to commit suicide, nothing can stop him. The same holds, it seems, for a society too. And it is more than certain that the society of Greeks who live in the Greek state (the opposite, fortunately, is true about Hellenism outside the borders [*ektos sinoron Ellinismo*]) has, from a long time ago, decided to commit suicide.
>
> ["The society of Greeks"] has voluntarily cut itself off from history and from its linguistic continuity, and cheapened and mocked the cohering values of a people, like the cultural inheritance, tradition, mores, folk music and poetry. It has made fun of and *practically criminalized the love for our homeland* [*patrida*], respect for the religion [*sic*] and metaphysical transcendence, while deifying the mandates of the from-the-waist-down extremities of the human body. This society has condemned competition, meritocracy, philanthropy, and charity as weapons of the ruling classes. It has elevated the violation of the Constitution, of the laws and social ethics, to "democratic conquests" and recently revealed as maximally trustworthy witnesses the criminal convicts and the proven con men who in fact it seems always to trust.
>
> But next to the social, national and moral suicide, what has been cultivated, or at least left to prevail, is the tolerance of *racial degradation* [*filetikos ekfilismos*].

> Why has all this happened? Very simply: The low birth rate has spread for financial reasons, using as alibi an abundance of arguments for freedom, self-determination of the individual, equality of the two sexes and other values appropriately modified to justify the phenomenon.[18]

What is at stake here is nothing less than the survival of *the race of Hellenes*. Although abortion is not openly referred to and the article uses the universal "he," it is women who are being blamed for the death of the nation. In a centrist instance of a gentlemanly aversion to openly deriding "ladies," this op-ed in *Ta Vema* explicitly focuses on the "society of Greeks living in Greece." That it is women who are targeted, and this in the milieu of the stridently racial fundamentalist nationalist discourse that *To Vema* puts forward, is certain. The last sentence's vaguely veiled reference to "the self-determination of the individual" and to "the equality of the sexes" as part of the "alibi" for a lower birth rate is evidence of this.

More proof of the essentialist definition of Greekness being advanced here, and of women's representation as selfish beings who are to blame for a crime against the race of Greeks, appears as the article continues.

> For a moment, it seemed that the state [*politia*] comprehended the danger that not only *threatens our race with extinction* (the internationalists and cosmopolitans who have always fought and continue to fight nonetheless to make us Slavs or Americans, French, English, or Austrians) but will leave us defenseless to our not few treacherous [*epivouli*] neighbors.... Thus some measures were taken for the many-childrened in order to encourage births. Of course, this is the properly Greek and easy, always futile, solution of subsidies for reasons of electioneering (whereas the logical thing would be generous tax allowances and *methodical projection of the importance and value of motherhood*).

From the threat of "racial degradation" this rhetoric moves directly to racial extinction and foreign invasion of Greece. The state is given some of the blame, for not being appropriately responsive to the crisis, but its accountability remains superficial. On the one hand, the state is guilty merely of being Greek by enforcing policies supporting the clientelistic relations modern nationalist discourses have been negotiating with and arguing against throughout Greece's recent history. On the other hand, even if the state's policy efforts weren't so Greek in the mildly derogatory sense used by the editorial, as long as they failed to explicitly and methodically promote motherhood, they would only be scratching the surface of the problem. In the terms of the article, motherhood is the linchpin. It is an inadequate appreciation of motherhood that is dragging the birth rate down, not of fatherhood or even of parenthood generally. And who is to blame for what is here configured as nothing less than genocide by *women* who, in the face of the state's silence on the matter, fail to properly appreciate the significance of motherhood and fulfill their civic duty?

Shedding more light on the cultural assumptions being smuggled in along with the perhaps innocent-sounding call for recognition of the value of motherhood, the article continues:

> As is known, if one working person [masculine] (e.g., in a bank) gets married, he has the right to a spouse subsidy. However, if the other of the spouses is also working, instead of canceling the spousal subsidy, it is doubled. That is, both of them get one! But the subsidy is given from the lawmaker to support the financial burden of the spouse [feminine] who doesn't work and to encourage her thus to have children too. However, when two subsidies are granted to both the working spouses, then *the woman's work is encouraged and having children is discouraged.*

Leaving aside the issue of whether the female spouse "who doesn't work" outside the home is somehow not working at all, it is clearly she whose reproductive choices need to be managed by the state, in opposition, certainly, to both subjects' inferred greedy desire for personal comfort. Thus, the implicit claim here is that this decision is based on a self-indulgent prioritization of *the woman's comfort* over what is hinted at—via reference to racial degradation—as the welfare of *the Greek race*.

The Specificities of the Leftist Press and the Demografiko

As I noted, the left-wing press devotes much less space to the demografiko as a topic. This in itself is significant; it may reflect the ambivalence of this site with regard to demografiko discourses. Yet, it also reveals the difficulty of putting forward a different story. Most prominent of the characteristics of the existing coverage of the demografiko is a marked diminishment, at times absence, of a nationalist frame and a discernible shift of emphasis away from women as the subjects at fault. In addition, however, we see a general endorsement of the terms of 'the problem" of the low birth rate as these are set in other segments of the mainstream press. Also, the focus on more information as the best solution is not problematized, for example, to the extent of considering the nationalistically inflected social construction of the body and sexuality themselves as salient variables.

An article appearing in the left-wing newspaper *Avgi* reveals the somewhat different way of understanding the Greek demografiko and women in this context. Here the *global* demographic problem is the focus, a factor that gives very different meanings to Greece's birth rate and the causes of the Greek demografiko and allows for other potential solutions. At the same time, however, and despite the important differences, this approach does not manage to escape the framework wherein Greece's low birth rate is seen as a legitimate and major national problem. Also, though the author attempts to broaden the unit of analysis, it is still in the end largely the subject women rather than couples that are blamed.

When the author initially speculates about what actions might have prevented the existence of a demographic problem, it is not overtly women who are the primary issue of concern but the process of "family planning" and "people" in general: "If family planning had been developed and applied everywhere there would not be a 'demographic' problem, in the one or the other form. Because people would more or less have the size family that they wanted. They would bring children into the world not by chance, but when they were psychologically, financially and socially ready, under the best conditions."[19]

One interesting implication here is that currently Greeks are not having exactly as many children as they want. Yet the only agents cited as expressing dissatisfaction with the size of Greek families are experts and representatives of the variously nationalist programs for the nation that are quoted in coverage of the demografiko and the press in general. Thus, the left-wing *Avgi* seems not only to be taking as a given the public sphere's call for more babies but also extending its scope and suggesting that people in general are not having as many children as they want.

Another implication, however, is that better family planning will permit them to do so. The reference to family planning represents a move away from the right's and center's familiar tendency to see women as almost exclusively responsible for the demografiko. The common reference to women's lack of information as the source of the problem of abortion shifts emphasis; here, it is instead a slightly broader process that is deemed necessary. Correspondingly, it is people rather than women and their sexual behavior that seem to be the focus.

The operative assumption remains that the high rate of abortion and the low rate of birth together are clearly and unproblematically bad and that the only thing fueling this phenomenon is inadequate information about *modern* forms—one presumes, given the family planning reference—of birth control.

Were this not the issue, the article suggests, all people would avoid abortion. Openly acknowledging that women tend to be pathologized in dominant discourses of the demografiko, and appearing to separate itself from that discourse, the article continues: "If people are educated accordingly, abortions will diminish and the population will develop with more balance. Harmony will exist between the satisfaction of individual desires and the social belief concerning the development of the population. And maybe woman will not be criminalized anymore as the root of all evil."

With the reference to "the satisfaction of individual desires" we see a watered-down version of the motif of women's selfishness as what is keeping the birth rate down. Also, the "education" being called for resonates audibly with the right and centrist press allegations of women's ignorance. Moreover, it seems that the specific process of education is not, for example, a systematic rethinking of Greek heterosexual intersubjectivity dynamics nor a reworking of notions of appropriate femininity and masculinity. Instead, we have again the ever-present term *enimerosi*, indexing more of a how-to on using modern medical forms of contraception: "The avoidance of undesired, untimely pregnancy, the safe use of contraceptive means, the *enimerosi* of scientific progress in this field, sexual education [*agogi*] for reproductive health."

At the same time, the benefit of all this is determined according to its perceived impact on the family, rather than on the woman. These are all "valuable elements that contribute to the good condition of the family." Thus, although the woman is not to blame, it is also still not her interests that are most salient in this public consideration of abortion. The reified family (presumed to be nuclear despite quite different lived Greek realities), the cornerstone of liberal democratic state-building projects, reigns.

Left-wing *Avgi*'s frame of reference, despite its implicit belief in the primary salience of modern contraceptive skills to the Greek phenomenon of a low birth rate and the uncritical endorsement of the demografiko as a problem, nonetheless proclaims that its own position is sharply distinct from that prevailing in the right-wing press, that of the center, and even that of the political left. Consider the footnote appearing at the bottom of this article: "Really, with what preparation is our country going to Cairo [The Conference on Population and Development, 13–15 September 1994]? Let us hope not with scientific and reactionary gibberish of the famous report by the committee of the Parliament on the demografiko. That one where all the wings of the parliament put on a great show of their ability to use anachronistic conjunctions, popularistic references, antifeminism and dormant nationalism."

The sarcasm directed at *all wings* is clear. Moreover, we see fewer signs of the nationalist sentiment authorizing the particular social construction of the demografiko as a serious problem evident in the other sectors of the press. Though the article is still not feminist, the absence of a juvenilization and demonization of women that characterizes right-wing and center press is evident. Yet, both the direct linkage of abortion with the demografiko and the definition of abortion as an issue that concerns women and perhaps also couples rather than discourses or nationalism prove to be tenacious constructs. In the same edition of *Avgi* (8 September 1994), M. Damanaki, then head of the left-wing party Coalition of the Left, is quoted as saying, apropos the UN conference being held in Cairo: "When applied, family planning drastically reduces the frequency of abortion which, unfortunately, in our country, is used as the main method of birth control. . . . Certainly, the right to abortion, legally enforced since 1986, remains indisputable. It is connected with the right to self-determination *for women,* their sexual freedom, the expansion of their choices. . . . No politics of renewing the population can succeed if it doesn't support the right of choice *of the couple*" (my emphasis).

This politics of "renewing the population" is nowhere in question in the left's coverage of the demografiko. Rather, what remains at issue is precisely how best to fulfill the political program of demographic fortitude. Moreover, Damanaki, who initially seems interested in protecting the rights of women with regard to abortion, quickly tacks to the nation's population. In context, this works to legitimize men's power over women's reproductive choice instead of simply broadening the responsibility for abortion to include the male partner. Women's self-determination emerges in this domain as subordinate to the demografiko, even though it is not framed as selfishness.

The same ambivalent effort to trouble an understanding of women as the primary agents responsible for abortion is illuminated in "On Family Planning," an article that appeared in the leftist *Rizospasti*. Citing the unattributed but not surprising fact that 70 percent of Greek women of reproductive age use repeat abortion as "a means of . . . family planning,"[20] the paper quoted the president of the Federation of Greek Women: "There is no distribution of information [enimerosi] about either the positive or negative aspects of the contraceptive pill. And yet, the contraceptive means that will be used by *each woman, each couple,* need to be personalized according to the case and in cooperation with the doctor."[21] Despite a differently inflected strategic reference to the couple, the focus on the Pill suggests that women are the ones who are being held primarily responsible for birth control. Moreover, again, although there is a significant call to "personalize" information, it is not accompanied by a need to adjust imported discourses about contraception to local agonistic negotiations of femininity, masculinity, sexuality, the body and nature, love, trust, and betrayal. Indeed, the source is quoted in a reiteration of the familiar tripartisan trope of enimerosi, the supreme valorization of the purportedly linear dissemination of information to the individual.

The left-wing demografiko coverage is significantly different from that of the moderate-right and centrist coverage in some respects. Most important, it does not evince a specifically nationalist charge, it lacks any concern with Greeks as a race, and it makes a subtle but meaningful shift away from blaming women. However, the basic definition of the low birth rate as a serious national problem and of abortions as a relevant factor are upheld across the political spectrum.

How the Demografiko Manufactures Citizens

Right, center, and left seem to share a definition of abortion as an issue in the public sphere because of its perceived impact on the nation rather than on the rights of the fetus, as is the case in the United States, or the health of the woman as it could be. Much as there is a common domain to the variations of "Greece" in circulation in the press's consideration of the demografiko, there is also a largely shared understanding of "Greek women"; moreover, the two are intimately intertwined. All dominant skeins of nationalist discourses rely on a configuration of femininity and sexuality that is centrally oriented around *the biological reproduction* of the Greek ethnos—be it the Greek race (*fyly* or *genos*, as it is often defined in the conservative and centrist press) or the Greek people (*laos*, as the left and some of the center sometimes has it). The press construction of the demografiko is usually deployed as a racializing reproductive social technology that works to engender the Greek nation in specific—and charged—sexual and gendered, as well as racial, terms. The meanings of abortion in the public sphere are a function of the enlistment of abortion in the service of this nation-state building project.

Thus, abortion and the demografiko, in the vicinity of which abortion almost always appears in public debate, work to fortify particular gendered conceptions of Greek citizenship. Specifically, by further reinforcing the cultural mandate that Greek women biologically reproduce more Greeks in order to be "good women" and serve their nation, the demografiko works at once to enforce normative heterosexuality and motherhood for Greek women and to racialize Greek citizenship. The proliferating discourses of concern with the Greek population's robustness help to police the boundaries of the ambivalently modern Greek nation via a retrenchment of a particular matrix of Greek citizenship. Proper Greeks, according to this coverage, are those subjects defined as Greek Orthodox men, and Greek Orthodox women who give birth to "enough" children. Greek Orthodox women not having "enough," or any, children, as well as all of the Jewish or Muslim Greeks, and certainly the growing number of long-term immigrants, fail to fit this category. Non–Greek Orthodox Greek Christians occupy a gray zone in this territory.

The discursive move that enables the constellation of meanings of abortion as part of the problem threatening the ethnos, and due primarily to Greek women who are violating the strictures of their citizenship by choosing to abort, is no less compelling for its simplicity: the number of abortions is systematically compared to the number of births! That is, abortion rates and birthrates published in the press are systematically compared to one another with no consideration of the differences in the experience and attribution of meaning to each type of pregnancy. The comparison is postulated as though they are somehow made of the same substance. It relies on the assumption that were it not for the availability of medical abortions, those pregnancies that are today aborted (a) would still occur; and (b) would then be carried to term and result in more children. Clearly, neither of these assumptions is valid. Moreover, as the ethnographic material revealed at the level of the gendered subject, these two types of pregnancies are perceived as drastically different. Recall that the women I interviewed did not count as a pregnancy any of the pregnancies that were aborted, referring instead simply to their "abortion" when we constructed a rough table of their reproductive history together.

Why Greek women are not having more children is an analytically separate question from why they are having "so many" abortions. Yet this difference seems not to be visible anywhere in the formal public sphere. In fact, the typical parallel between birth and abortion involves a gloss, a crucial ellipsis, much as the modern Greek (Orthodox) nation itself does. Abortion is unilaterally defined as a birth denied, rather than as a particular form of relationship being tested or denied, and as a logical result of the interface between the exigencies of a culturally specific, politically specific configuration of the subject (body, sexuality, and identity), nationalism, and expert family planning and contraceptive discourses. It is the conflation of the two quite different types of pregnancies, and the underlying practical obliteration of the female subject's agency, that permits the Greek public sphere's almost unanimous conception of abortion as an act that is centrally about the nation, though only in particular ways.

Another important site of agreement that undergirds the press coverage of the gendered subject at the site of the demografiko is a portrayal of the root of the "problem" of abortion: a lack of information on more appropriate methods of birth control, primarily on the part of women. In general, adolescent and adult women and, to a lesser degree, adolescent male students in school are targeted as those who need to receive this information. In addition, in the bulk of demografiko coverage, Greek women are the alternately backward, stupid, or belligerent subjects who are to be blamed and held responsible for what is constructed as a major threat to Greece's future.

In being portrayed this way, Greek women are put into an impossible position at the crossroads of modernizing and fundamentalist nationalist stories about Greek national identity.[22] In all this coverage there are contradictions at work. On the one hand is the public sphere's insistence that women be "good contraceptors" so that the country's bid for modernity may not be undermined. On the other hand, underlying the demografiko coverage in its entirety, is a reinscription of compulsory motherhood (women should have at least *some* children) as a requirement for Greek female citizenship. That is, there is an implicit and often explicit call for women to be "good breeders," to propagate Greeks, at times the Greek *race,* and thus preserve the Greek ethnos. The alternative registers of Greek nationalism that are articulated at the site of the demografiko are largely not matched by alternative configurations of Greek female citizenship. In all stories, abortion, firmly seen as an act done by women, is "the bad guy."

This collision between modernizing nationalist discourses and fundamentalist nationalist discourses at the site of women's bodies is brought to the fore in the centrist press's unabashed claim that *both* abortion *and* other forms of birth control work specifically against the Greek, or Hellenic, race. In general, in the press coverage of all party affiliations, the common parameters of "the Greek woman" stand as proof of a larger, particularly gendered frame of reference that yields a shared truncated vision of Greece's future. A cultural emphasis on reproductive heterosexuality and motherhood as the civic duty of the Greek Orthodox female citizen is coupled with a feminized construction of Greece itself as a gendered entity that is needy of this support, or lifeblood.

In this larger discursive context, the emphasis on motherhood actually becomes the motor effecting the *masculinization*—specifically, the *citizenship*[23]— of the Greek mother, or more precisely, her reconfiguration as a patriot and good Christian who is willing to gallantly give up her life, actually or symbolically, for her country. The transparty insistence on Greece's need for more Greek humans and the consistent portrayal of Greek women (and couples, as the left attempts to add) as responsible for "making" these Greeks together form an opaque nexus that blocks other configurations of nation and gender just as it facilitates traffic between these two. Greece's welfare comes to be seen as *naturally* contingent on Greek women having more newly born Greeks. What is obfuscated is the possibility of either "making" more naturalized immigrants, to name a contentious example, or even, to leave this register further behind, of forging entirely different organizations of state human and nonhuman resources and setting as a new top priority, not the quantity, but the quality, "spiritual fortitude" if need be, not of biological individuals, but of social institutions.

The demografiko is about reinscribing a regime of truth in which the nation, and a particular version of it, has primacy. Beyond the formal status of citizenship, gendered subjects are granted *degrees* of citizenship according to their fulfillment of its needs; in this case, the essential need being advanced is women's heightened␣reprosexuality, that is, sexuality that is oriented toward reproduction and the political institutions based on it (Warner 1993, vii–xxxi). In this discourse, the undertones of a story about productivity or breeding capacity that a farmer, for example, might use are audible. From this perspective, disciplining Greek women and their sexuality, a sign of whose␣unruliness is the frequency of multiple abortions, and incorporating them as docile subjects of a particular political order, along with delineating the symbolic and cultural borders of the nation emerge as the twin concerns of the Greek news coverage of the demografiko.

A beast of the public sphere almost exclusively, the demografiko␣nonetheless works to patrol not only the geopolitical territory of the modern nation-state but the moral borders of the heterosexual regime of Greek nationhood and personhood as well. With its strident valorization of motherhood and constant trumpeting of particular needs of Greece—be it primarily as race, religion, or ethnic nation—the demografiko may be an attempt to contain the aspects of abandon and spontaneity that in more intimate spaces of the national imaginary are strongly desired. Defining Greek women, their role in the polis as well as their sexuality, is as much the issue here as is the identity and future of the Greek nation. The demografiko is a powerful reproductive technology that serves multiple political objectives. Not least of these is a particular political order populated by historically and culturally specific, importantly *docile*, gendered subjects.

The Net

Every time you start a new road in life, do not wait for midnight to find you.
Keep your eyes open night and day because before you there is always a net.

If sometime you get caught in its snares,
nobody will be able to help you.

Alone, search to find the end of the thread and,
if you're lucky, start again.

This net has heavy names that are written in a book with seven seals. Others say it is the guiles of the underworld, and others say the first love of spring.

If sometime you get caught in its snares,
nobody will be able to help you.
Alone, search to find the end of the thread and,
if you're lucky, start again.
—Gatsos, 1992

Chapter 11

A CRITICAL CARTOGRAPHY OF

THE DEMOGRAFIKO'S GREECE

❖

Deconstruction does not say anything against the usefulness of mobilizing unities. All it says is that because it is useful it ought not to be monumentalized as the way things really are.
—Gayatri Chakravorty Spivak, *The Post-Colonial Critic: Interviews, Strategies, Dialogues*

Greece is not a natural entity. Like all nations, Greece is a historically specific political community whose formation is social, ongoing, and always the result of charged contestation. But, tucked into what remains in important ways "the margins of Europe," as it is also "the crossroads between East and West," Greece offers a clear view of the driving forces behind the establishment, however partial and contested, what we think of as the West. In mapping the agon surrounding abortion in Greece, this book has sought to shed more light on the processes by which two of modernity's biggest creations have been produced and, importantly, coproduced: the nation and gender.[1] For a variety of cultural and historical reasons, abortion names some of the key sites of struggle in these projects.

There is one more such site that I would like to turn to now, to bring this work to a close: the site of explicit opposition to the demografiko. At the end of the interviews, I posed a series of pointed and direct questions to many of the women I was speaking with. One set of these questions was simply, "Have you heard of what is called 'the demografiko'? If so, what do you know about it, and what is your opinion?" The responses to these questions are instrumental to this work's effort to instigate a new venue for dialogue, to create a wedge that may intervene and productively destabilize the established terms of public debate, and, potentially, to help to open up another domain of political discussion in Greece today.

As I have argued throughout, the diverse uses abortion is put to, in discussions about the nation, the daily lives of women and straight couples, and in ob/gyn and family-planning discourses, help to mount a larger critique of liberal democracy and its main cornerstones: the liberal state and the individual. The cultural meanings and understandings of nationhood, race, the divine, gender, and sexuality configure Greece almost naturally as a type of religious state. These work at the site of the Greek gendered subject to naturalize abortion to different degrees while making other forms of birth control, as well as pregnancy itself at times, appear to be foreign bodies or invasions. These meanings also belong to the same regime of truth that simultaneously naturalizes the imaginary and continuously contested entity *Greece* itself, as well as the culturally and historically specific practice of both heterosexuality and reprosexuality (Warner 1993). Moreover, this entire operation occurs in such a way that the nation and sexuality are intimately coupled together.

The matrix of nationhood that currently governs various public conceptions of Greek identity often renders abortion a threat to national welfare. However, as the ethnographic data show, abortion has a quite different meaning in the domain of Greek straight sexuality. I have argued that the same cultural preoccupations actually work to make abortion appear to many Greek women as far more natural than any of the modern methods of birth control, including the condom. Given the contemporary nationally invested configurations of heterosexuality, the pattern of routinely getting pregnant and having an abortion emerges, paradoxically, as an indication of an alignment between some Greek subjects' sexual behavior and Greece's purported national interests, that is, as an implicit endorsement of, rather than a challenge to (as the press sees it), the particular Greek matrix of nationhood and the narratives of sexuality that it is connected to. Similarly, although the women I spoke with are largely opposed to the demografiko, this opposition very often is articulated in surprisingly pronounced nationalist terms.[2] Throughout this book I have undertaken to interrogate the discursive and radically political processes through which "Greece" and "Greek women" are born and joined together at the hip; to unravel their "conditions of intelligibility";[3] to start at "the bottom" or, in this case, within the expelled contents of the uterus, in order to unscramble the discursive practices through which nation and women are made to appear in the geopolitical context of Greece at the present as firmly fixed and natural, as well as distinctly separate (indeed, *at odds*), rather than viscerally linked and potentially negotiable.

We have seen how the stories Greece tells of the nation, women, and sexuality and the stories Greek women tell, and are told, about their lives in fact suggest that these subject positions and the affiliated subjectivities are

320 Instigating Dialogues

highly complex, intricate, and at times contradictory productions. That such historically contingent and vexed "social facts," to borrow from Durkheim, as the nation and women come to appear as natural biological or territorial and political entities is but one sign of the intricacy of this operation. This book began with an eclectic survey of at times very intimate aspects of Greek culture, society, and history; it then moved to a close-up look in the bowels of a clinic, at the medical and cultural site of the anesthetized women undergoing abortions. It analyzed what these women said about their personal lives and considered press and media representation of gender and the nation. I turn now to what these subjects consciously and explicitly say about the nation.

Theorizing Resistances

As analysis of the meanings women ascribe to the experience of abortion reveals, Greek women are not "just" a simple by-product of larger meta-narratives, whether seamless or not. There is nothing simple about such a production—much as the observation that each sentence is a product of the rules of grammar is not taken to be an insult to the sentence, nor to the speaker's agency.[4] As Butler says, "To claim that the subject is constituted is not to claim that it is determined; on the contrary, the constituted character of the subject is the very precondition of its *agency*" (1992, 12; my emphasis).

The always partial ways that discourses are refracted at particular sites of congealment means that resistance and power are themselves interwoven and difficult, if not impossible, to untangle. If Greek women and their sexuality are a product of hegemonic discourses about the nation, they are also, at the same time, points of resistances against these discourses. Foucault (1980c, 98) writes, "Power must be analysed as something which circulates, or rather as something that only functions in the form of a chain. It is never localised here or there, never in anybody's hands, never appropriated as a commodity or piece of wealth. *Power is employed and exercised through a net-like organization*. And not only do individuals circulate between its threads; they are always in the position of simultaneously undergoing and exercising this power. *They are not only its inert or consenting target; they are always also the elements of its articulation*. In other words, individuals are the vehicles of power, not its points of application."

To develop this theoretical postulation, and to further elaborate the specificities of how not only individuals but the individual itself as a category are elements of the articulation of power, "the vehicles of power" as Foucault suggests, while clearly also being a historically and culturally specified social construction, I conclude this book by turning to the fairly incisive critiques of the demografiko that the women I spoke with articulated. Thus, from yet one more perspective, we witness how agon shapes nation and the gendered subject alike in Greece.

I first present excerpts that chart the main moves of one genre of resistance. Then I turn to how these apparently oppositional discursive strands also contain elements of an almost blind acceptance of the very terms of power they explicitly seek to oppose. In this context, I also analyze the one newspaper article printed in 1994 that openly opposed the demografiko. Finally, I examine how, in this cultural double voice, there is a discernible irony that puts forward yet another genre of resistance and may help to provoke a more radical rethinking of the terms of Greek nationhood today. Thus, I concretize the argument put forward in this book that the very vehicles for democratization and modernization almost universally used at the present—the concepts of liberal democracy and of the individual—have serious constraints and mark sites of danger.

That is, I examine first the evidence of an outright disagreement with or even refusal of certain aspects of the demografiko discourses. This opposition may be couched in terms that seek to keep the peace or it may be direct. Either way, it is not in question. However, in most cases this opposition is nonetheless embedded within larger narratives that effectively endorse or actively sponsor the nationalism animating the demografiko's nation-building project. Again I turn to Foucault, this time to an aspect of his argument that is largely absent in the rich vein of work seeking to follow from his cue. As he outlined the methodological considerations he felt all thoroughgoing analyses of power needed to take account of, the third of which concerns the omnipresence and fluidity of power, he then turns to the fourth:

> When I say that power establishes a network through which it freely circulates, this is true *only up to a certain point*. In much the same fashion we could say that therefore we all have fascisms in our heads, or, more profoundly, that we all have a power in our bodies. But I do not believe that one should conclude from this that power is the best distributed thing in the world, although in some sense that is indeed so. *We are not dealing with a sort of democratic or anarchic distribution of power through bodies.* . . . I believe that the manner in which the phenomena, the techniques and the procedures of power enter into play at the most basic levels must be analysed, that the way in which these procedures are displaced, extended and altered must certainly be demonstrated; but, above all, what must be shown is *the manner in which they are invested and*

annexed by more global phenomena and the subtle fashion in which more general powers or economic interests are able to engage with these technologies that are at once both relatively autonomous of power and act as its infinitesimal elements. (1980, 98)

In the second section of this chapter, I examine some of the ways in which Greek women's otherwise "resistant," certainly oppositional responses nonetheless are marked by, and at times logically rely on, certain reactionary and clearly nationalist and racist, if not always openly sexist, elements.

Last, incapable myself of resisting the seductions of resistance, I use a brief critical reading of both of the above elements in women's responses to my questions about the demografiko to summarize my own argument against the demografiko and in favor of the use of great caution in policy's uses of the terms of liberal democracy in Greece as well as elsewhere. My foundation for this argument is made up of the ways in which the interviewed women's responses display implicitly, indeed typically entirely inadvertently and often during a lighter moment in our conversation, the element of absurdity that animates popular nationalist discourses in current circulation. But first, the opposition or resistance presented by the women's opinions on the demografiko at the explicit level.

Not "More" Children!

The main thing the women I spoke with expressed an opposition to was the suggestion that they have *more* children. I want to emphasize here that almost none of the women I spoke with expressed opposition to the mandate of motherhood per se, which the demografiko amplifies and underscores but which has been a prevalent part of Greek culture throughout the history of Greece. Rather, it is the idea that they must have a particular, seemingly high number of children that troubles them. Accompanying their opposition to this proposition, the second expression of defiance that I heard time and time again was the idea that if the nation-state insists on such an interest in heightened motherhood, then it should put its money where its mouth is and pay for what it wants. We have witnessed some of the ways the social construction of the couple and Greek women is intimately affiliated with that of the nation. Now there is the opportunity to get a clearer picture of how the couple (and in this context the family) and women are social formations that are also importantly *at odds* with the nation.

Elena, thirty-seven years old and the married mother of two children, responded to my question about the demografiko with some anger. Just what the target of her anger was is not entirely clear. On the one hand, she seems upset that we live "in a world," as this fairly ethnocentric narrative goes, in which having "merely" three children is considered a special accomplishment worthy of reward from the state. This strand of her narrative is reminiscent of the larger one in circulation in demografiko discourses about Greece's "good old times," when people were less "egocentric" and more oriented toward the family and, by extension, the nation. On the other hand, without missing a beat, she also seems very upset with the idea that, given this world, the state could ever have the expectation that people *would* have more children.

> *I:* Have you heard of what is being called "the demografiko"? If so, what do you know about it and what is your opinion?
>
> *She:* Why the women don't give birth? The state gives [them] the subsidy and then it takes taxes from us for the families with many children [*polyteknous*].[5] Now you know who is considered polyteknoi? Those who have *three* children. With the *third* child the state gives you money. Which is inconceivable. [Slight pause and quick rotation of her head] What a point we've reached! How is this going to happen? With what? You cannot take from those who have nothing. [*Ouk an lavis ek tou mi ehondos.*] If you have two children, you're finished—tutoring, schools, doctors, clothes . . . In a little while they'll be giving [money] to those who have a second child.

The turning point where she switches from one reason to be angry to another is immediately after she says "What a point we've reached!" The words preceding this suggest that what is shocking to her is the notion that we are indeed living in a world where having three children is considered "many." The words immediately following it suggest that she is shocked by the state's arrogance in presuming that a couple that already has two children are going to go ahead and have a third. As she says, putting part of what is at stake in bold relief here, "If you have two children, you're finished." The ambivalence Elena shows about the demografiko—on the one hand, implicitly, Yes, why *aren't* we having more kids and yet on the other, Are you crazy, how *could* we?—rests on her adoption of two distinctly different vantage points in very rapid succession. First, she takes the point of view of a romantically imagined Greece of the past, then she shifts to the vantage point of a contemporary couple struggling to make ends meet. The tension between these two constructs is evident. Meanwhile, though her response reveals a pronounced opposition to "heightened" motherhood, there is also an absence of any obvious resistance to other aspects of the demografiko, such as its particular understandings of the national welfare of Greece as contingent on "the replacement of the generations."

Teti, the thirty-five-year-old widowed mother of a four-year-old, echoes the same double anger, accompanied by, at first glance, a similar indifference or, at best, ambivalence as to the issue of the demografiko in general. On closer examination, however, the possibility emerges that in fact this form of opposition extends beyond the particular demografiko fragment concerning her personal, purported national obligation to have more children and includes an important part of how the nation is defined within demografiko discourses. The responses of most of the women who expressed opposition to the demografiko were similar in this.

> *She:* Yes, about the too-low-birth-rate [*ypogennitikotita*]. My opinion is that at this moment my husband has died and I have to raise a child and that child has to have a house, and food, and all this with some quality, and to the IRS and all that I pay a lot. On the one hand, we have a demographic problem and, on the other, I can't raise a child because the state does not provide me with anything, and when we say nothing, we mean nothing. How is it possible that I would have a second too? Shall I take them out to the traffic lights for them to sell tissue packets?
>
> *I:* So there needs to be action on the part of the state for something to happen.
>
> *She:* Clearly.

The way Teti starts her commentary by saying "My opinion is that at this moment my husband has died" makes it evident that she does not think much of either the demografiko or, for that matter, of my asking for her opinion on it. In other words, she seems to be saying, in yet another variation of the always-recurring theme involving the scarcity of money, there is no room for such a thing as an opinion. There is a hard reality here, she juxtaposes. She makes no bones of her disdain for the idea of having more children and is clearly angered at the idea that the nation would ask her to in the face of the state's inadequacy.

As prefigured in Elena's account, the contest between the nation and the woman and the family is not open-ended. In this particular moment of the agon, the nation clearly loses. This time, however, it seems to be a more significant loss. It is not just that this woman sees no reason to comply with the demand that she have another child or two. Indeed, her last comment, about children selling tissues at street intersections, betrays a thoroughgoing, if prejudicative understanding of the primacy of the role race and nationalism play in the discourses of the demografiko and, at the same time, defiance toward it. To shut up the subject position out of which demografiko discourses issue—that of the paternalist Greek nation-state—she takes one of its own favorite terms and turns it against itself. The image of gypsy and Albanian children selling tissue packets to drivers stopped at intersections in Athens is a common recurring trope that is often used to figure the demise of a Greece proper to the "relentless" influx of immigrants. Teti is playing with this. In effect, she is saying, If I do what you (*the nation*) want me to do, you'll just end up with more of what you so dislike. Despite the ambivalence expressed by the support she implicitly extends to "the demographic problem" by legitimizing it as a problem (whereas I referred to it by its nickname, "the demografiko"), the irony in her last comment opens up the possibility of a more deeply critical distance between her and some of the nationalist narratives in circulation.

In many ways, the magnificence of this genre of resistance resides in the mastery with which the women would, in answering my questions, redeploy the very same discourses that contemporary Greek strains of nationalism rely on. It seems clear that in several instances these redeployments are ironic; the answers involve a parody of specifically the state's forms of power along with the sheer refusal to have more children.

This irony isn't necessarily expressed in pointed sarcasm. Amalia seems much invested in being subtle as she shares her views with me. Born in the port city of Piraeus, living now in an upper-class northern suburb of Athens, married eleven years and the thirty-seven year old mother of two children, she reports having had two abortions.

> *She:* For people to be able to have more children, they will have to have more resources [*parohes*]. In other words, from the state there has to be some provision [*pronoia*], from all sides, from the financial and from the social, and more education to the people about how to raise children, because it is not a simple thing. To have children like that, just in general, so the population grows—then you'll see their future! We don't want to end up like the countries of the Third World where there are masses, on the one hand, but the quality goes down.
>
> First of all, there need to be more day care centers so that one can work, since now both have to work, and leave the child somewhere; to have some social care/welfare [*merimna*]; and to have jobs for both—there is also the problem of unemployment! There are many things that have to be improved so people can have children.

Here again, the state is expected to pay if the nation is going to insist on the demand for more children. But even if it pays to encourage women to give birth, this excerpt suggests, the demand just doesn't make sense. There need to be other things offered—in effect, social change. Well, she notes, underlining one of the fallacious assumptions of demografiko discourses, just having more children, that biological fact in and of itself isn't going to change things for the better. It is not an impersonal nation's welfare that she is most concerned with, moreover, but that of the very children that the nation is asking women to have more of. As she says, "To have children like that, just in general, so the population grows—then you'll see their future!"

To clinch the argument against having more children, initially via the humanist and maternal claim that a numerical increase in the population would not be beneficial *for the children,* Amalia shifts back to the needs of the nation and borrows another element from the demografiko discourses. This is one of the ghosts driving demografiko discourses that also haunts the larger discussion going on about Greece's modernization: the Third World. Amalia, like the majority of the women I interviewed, seems to be talking back to these nationalist discourses, saying, Are you really sure you want what you say you want? *This obsession with more babies just might transform you into the very thing you fear.* Even more, she continues to implicitly ask, again by redeploying modernization tropes, isn't the obsession itself a sign of a certain irrationality? Quantity, she notes, in an almost uncanny repetition of the modernizing nationalist claim for the need for Greece's labor force to become better trained and more efficient, as well as larger, is not in itself sufficient to solve the nation's problems. Merely populating the country with more Greek humans does not provide any guarantee of national welfare—be it modern or traditionalist.

Finally, the parodic element of women's opposition to the demografiko's demand that they have more children very often made its appearance as a simple, incisive observation delivered wryly. Christiana is a forty-two-year-old woman who works as a homemaker raising her four children, has been married for twenty-one years, and lives in Peristeri.

> *She:* Look, very well, the demographic problem exists, but they will have to give some incentives so that it can work, so that people can have children. For me it happened, let's say, that I have some ease because of my husband's job. Otherwise, how would I raise these children? Eh, we shouldn't have children just like that, by chance, and leave them to the mercy of God.

Christiana herself doesn't have to worry about money. Yet, she also expresses the view that the state still needs to pay up if people are to have children. Again we see how the demografiko produces friction between the couple and the family on the one hand, and the nation on the other, despite concerted efforts to further enlist the family in the service of the nation-state.

The specific claim Christiana uses to concretize her argument is significant. Rearticulating the religious discourse making up much of the fundamentalist strand of nationalism enjoying circulation in contemporary Greece, she dryly comments that it would not be right to just have children and then trust in God to take care of them. In her statement is a tacit acknowledgment that God is a central part of the issue. At the same time, she seems to be suggesting that the use of God in demografiko discourses may be a little hypocritical. Defending "better" Christianity, Christiana might be seen as implicitly asking the following: Wouldn't the nation-state *itself be sinning* if, in the very process of claiming that the country needs more Christians to defend it from the non-Christians seen as threatening the borders, it required the birth of children who could not be financially supported?

Parody and the strategic redeployment of tropes notwithstanding, the suggestion that the state pay, which was made by almost all the women I spoke with, implies a strongly pro-natalist policy. The strong-arming state the women seem to be asking for in making this suggestion is an aggressively pro-active state, which (ironically, given, for example, how the contraceptive pill and the condom scored on this matter) does *not* appear to be seen as invasive in the stance expected of it. In effect, there seems to be a call for a modality of statehood or a technology of governance that is very close to a rigorous policing of women's reproductive abilities.

In addition, the very unanimity with which the demografiko's demand for more children is contested by the women indicates that this contestation is, among women in Athens, perhaps more hegemonic than policymakers and experts, as well as Greek feminists, may realize. Though the unanimity itself does not undermine the trouble-producing potential of such a stance within the framework of demografiko discourses, it does suggest that we may need to look more carefully at where it is coming from and what else it may be connected to. In fact, certainly with regard to the women I spoke with (both self-declared feminists and not), the stated opposition to the demografiko is very often intimately linked with discourses that are, as Spivak puts it in the quote opening this chapter, quite clearly monumentalized.[6]

Resisting the Demografiko, or Reacting?

As the Foucauldian postulation of an intertwining of power with resistance indicates, the question about women's opinions on the demografiko yielded narratives that also reveal ample evidence of a reactionary set of discourses. Though the women opposed the demografiko's requirement that women have more children, this opposition focused on the state, and their responses nonetheless often rely on rearticulations of dominant discourses of the nation or gender or the divine that do not seem to be deployed in either an ironic or an oppositional way.

Most pronounced here are women's endorsement of several ideas: (1) the idea of the state as an entity that, notwithstanding the strong call for financial incentives, should not interfere in a substantial way with the "rights" of those seen as individuals; (2) the idea of Greece as a nation superior to all others, typically because of its Greek Orthodoxy rather than other reasons, such as the ancient heritage that segments of the press's version of fundamentalist nationalism often articulate; (3) and, especially pronounced, the idea of Greeks specifically as *a race*.

The potentially oppositional emphasis on the state's need to financially support the mandate for motherhood that is advanced on behalf of the nation by demografiko discourses is problematized here by a simultaneous and pronounced reentrenchment of the individual and the family in a markedly nuclear version. In several instances, the women responded to my questions without hesitating to intermingle elements from the story about the need for a stronger state with elements from the story about the obligation to respect the sovereignty of the individual. At times, fragments from disparate versions of Greece and its subjects are placed side by side in a new mosaic of nationhood.

A vivid example of the way these narratives are sometimes transposed onto each other comes in the response of Lydia, a forty-two-year-old doctor who has been married twenty years. She told me she had one child, two miscarriages, and three abortions.

> *She:* I think that both as a woman and as a human being, within the framework of the freedom of the individual, each man, each woman, should arrange their plight alone. If society, or the state, want to intervene [*na paremvi*] and to give, as they do in France, big incentives but in an indirect way to those with many children [*polyteknous*] . . . [that's fine]. In other words, there should be the freedom of the individual and the welfare state, if it wants to give support, and you can generally choose. Generally, I am always of the opinion of possibilities for choice.

Yes, choice, but what is Lydia's choice? She seems to be saying that, be the demografiko as it may, the state should not intervene in the affairs of citizens, at least not directly. Drawing from liberal humanist discourse, she argues that the individual should reign supreme. At the same time, she suggests that the benevolent welfare state, if it is subtle and *French-like*, might perhaps get involved. Most of all, she says, as her response reaches its crescendo, "choice," that centerpiece of liberal democracy, needs to be protected! Forget that the options that emerge or are offered as possible choices are already politically constructed. Forget too that what the subject may regard as a viable choice is also the product of the operation of larger discourses and practices shaping the subject's very desire. Thus, while there emerges in responses like Lydia's something that might more accurately be called disdain for the demografiko, it is couched in terms that wholeheartedly and fully underwrite the particular production of the same liberal democratic state that the strain of nationalist discourses motivated by a call for modernization also seek to achieve. That this state and those subjects have little to do with the matrix of Greek nationhood actually operative in the Greek national imaginary and in the discursive practices of Greek women does not seem to be a factor that the woman—*both as a woman and as a human being*, as she specifies—sees as salient in her argument for choice *within the framework of the freedom of the individual*, as Lydia emphasized.

Surprisingly, France comes up several times in the responses of the women I spoke with. This may reflect the fact that it has offered middle-class Greeks a fairly approachable and desirable alternative for acquiring a university education, at least as much as it reveals the central position France has for many Greeks as an example of a properly socialist state. The French state was typically used as a yardstick against which the Greek state was measured. The response of Irini, age thirty-four and married with one child, shows this clearly. Again, we see the call for the state to shoulder some of the costs faced by women and couples if they do have more children. Intriguingly here the understanding of the state's responsibility extends beyond the dissemination of financial incentives to more substantive social change. Yet, this understanding is laced with a firm reinscription of the bourgeois family, even as the persistent figuration of grandmothers troubles the presumed autonomy of its nuclear version.

> *She:* Yes, I've heard of the demografiko. But I'm not the one who will solve it! Take that glass away from me! *Apeltheto ap'emou to potirion touto!*
>
> Let me tell you something. In 1978, when I got pregnant with the IUD (and it was a difficult decision), when I went to France soon after, I realized that in the end I could very well have kept the child if it wasn't in danger with the IUD. Because there was also a danger of miscarrying with the IUD, of the

embryo not "sitting" well [in the uterus], of having problems, of it coming out or taking out the IUD and creating a problem. It was, in other words, risky.

But let us say that it was a normal pregnancy. There would not be a problem. Going to France where I was studying, the university . . . There was a state day care center for the children in the morning. There was a subsidy then, 2,500 francs, when I could live with 1,500 francs as a student! There were subsidies. From the moment that I had the card, I had the right to it, since I was going legally, in other words, the visa and all that. I mean you had all the possibility. Also, then you had births with the booklet [you could charge births to your national health insurance], what they're doing here now. Then they [Greece] weren't doing it yet.

Therefore, in other words, the relationship was very good. There were classes, parents' school, that had two parts, before the birth and after. The part before the birth taught you more how to change a baby . . . and the part after the birth, supported you emotionally. And all that from the state. . . .

That much doesn't exist in France anymore. They have unemployment. But, I mean, during the time I went there, it supported the family, you could have even two and three children. Here I was forced to take the child to a private school so that it would come home after I did. It isn't easy. You have to, in other words, you have to get the grandmothers into it. And if you put them in, then they get mixed up in other areas too *anakatevondai kai se allous tomis*. Therefore it is very difficult.

Irini is impressed by the way the French state offered a variety of means of support to people having children. The financial subsidy, almost double what she needed to live on, was definitely a big help. She is also especially appreciative of the particular way *the family* was supported. The classes on "how to change a baby," those that "supported you emotionally" after the child's birth: these were considered of exceptional value. In this context, she says, you could have "even two and three children." Thus, she implicitly endorses the idea that women have more children. Irini's appreciation for the various classes on parenthood and for the state's support for the family graphically illustrates the way opposition to the demografiko on the part of the women is often positioned within a register that nonetheless fully endorses the bourgeois family. In these cases, the very social formation that undergirds the ideology of the modern nation-state ends up offering the grounds for opposing its desire.

The tension between the nation and the couple, and especially women who are mothers, that is inscribed on all the women's narratives is put in bold relief in Anna's words. Moreover, the sharp distinction between the state and the nation that seems to be part of what allows women to express their disagreement with the demografiko is illuminated. Anna, a thirty-eight-year-old woman who was born in Arkadia and has been living in Athens for the past twenty-three years, takes on both the state and the nation in her response. This response illuminates the women's common move ultimately to support the nation while critiquing the state. Anna is a civil servant, is married, has two children, and reports having had two abortions.

First Anna appeared to agree with the demografiko. In this context, she expresses clear and pronounced nationalist sentiment.

> *She:* The problem of Greece?
> *I:* Yes, yes.
> *She:* The Turks are going to come in in a little while and they'll throw us out. *Tha boune oi Tourkoi se ligo mesa kai tha mas petaxoun exo.* I don't know which way it is going to take us, I don't know. Because it is a big problem.
>
> You see, most couples, at least I had two [children], most do not have any or they have one. And you tell them, have kids, because one is like none [*to ena inai san kanena*], as they said in the old days. . . . That's what my grandmother said. The one little child is like none. It is bad for the child and for the parents because they put all their attention on him and the child becomes overly protected and feels insecurity. To have everything hinge on only one child? *Na kremesai mono apo ena paidi?* That's why they used to say that one is like none. That's where it came from. But they say, oh, one, one.
>
> I have a cousin and they want to go out to have fun. For it to shut us in, they say? Look, they're partly right too, because you see sometimes . . . Many times I wonder and I say, What are we doing in here [staying at home instead of going out at night]? It doesn't have any effect.

In the next part of her response, she turns to the state's responsibility. Narrating in some detail her recent experiences with her son and his teacher, she seems almost inadvertently to make an argument *against* the basic premise of the demografiko on the grounds of a need for "quality," as Amalia put it. However, it is clear that Anna is not in fact arguing against the demografiko. The larger frame is one in which she is listing the various failures of the state to support the citizenry and give the individual his or her basic rights.

> *She:* But the state does not help you to have children either. When I had the children so many years ago things were not easy like this. I had to leave my job to raise my children. Because then there were not the day care centers

that there are today. I had to pay. If I paid it would be from one to the other [I would have to give all of my salary to the day care provider]. Nothing would be left. I'd have to give it all. What for? Better that I be in my environment so I know also what's going on [*na xero kai ti mou ginetai*]. And the state does not help. Doesn't help you have children. You leave your work, so then there is a financial problem. When you don't have some ease, some property of your own [*kapoia dikia sou periousia*], to have something, to feel some security, you are forced to leave your work. It is a chain reaction. *Einai alisidota ta pragmata.* Who can have children now? The people who have some problem? Most have some economic problem. They haven't solved their economic problem, so they both have to work. Under these conditions, can every woman have children? No. The children now are demanding, they want clothes, whatever they see, they want [*oti thimoundai herondai*]. They ask for anything that comes into their heads.

Anna has established the significance of "the economic problem." In so doing, she also demonstrates that it is in fact the woman who is (doing most of the work of) having children. Then she goes on to the next failure she ascribes to the state.

She: There's no education. At least, I, my children are in high school now. I'm disappointed. A complete disappointment. They get out of elementary school and they don't even know how to talk. If they want to learn [*na mathoun grammata*], they learn on their own. If they don't, they go in as bricks, they come out as bricks [*douvaria bainoun, douvaria vgainoun*]. Nothing.

Generally though, the way you look at the system, as books, as professors... The child is not just for you to tell it, "Read, my boy." Anyone can do that in their home. You have to open his head, so that it starts searching for things [*na arhisi na psahni*]. That is how it is.

Not when you see a child reading—and we're talking about physics classes, where you search yourself and you search yourself [*psahnesai kai psahnesai*]. You can't sit down and learn the rules of physics. You forget them in one day. My son's teacher, I had bought him some books, a series, which he likes and which he is going to follow. His professor, instead of saying, "My child, since you have this, bring it in for the other children to read too," that children today in their majority don't read... Instead he told him, "Where did you find this, do you want to say you're smarter than us? Eh!" Or when he writes something and the teacher gives him whatever [grade] he wants and answers him with "That's how much I wanted to give you, that's how much I gave you." There they stop you, they put brakes on you [*sou vazoun trohopedi*]. Instead of giving you wind beneath your wings ... A brain that is smart *xipnio*, that is bright [*pou inai fotino*], instead of giving it a push to go upward, you keep pushing it downward?

I talked about it with our principal too, there in the Association [the school's Association of Parents]. There are some children who study and we stop them? People get disappointed, generally.

At this point, I expressed agreement with her. She clearly was very concerned about her son. I asked her how he was doing now. She talked about his educational experience a little longer and became calmer.

I: So it sounds like you have some mixed feelings about the demografiko. Is there anything else you would like to say about it?

She: Look, it really is a problem, and it would be nice if we could have four and five and ten children. Minus, though, the difficulties of life are such that unfortunately everyone gets stuck at two, and those are even many. I, for example, would want a third little child, of course not now anymore. My eldest is a student in college now.

A friend of mine had one now. We are colleagues, at the same office. She had three, her children grew up. By chance she got pregnant [*tyhaia emeine*], she's forty-two years old now and she had a baby. Unfortunately, the difficulties are many, and the stuff about rejuvenation and all that, you know how long the rejuvenation lasts? As long as the woman is carrying [*oso egimoni i gynaika*] and everyone pays attention to her because after so many years she is pregnant again. OK, maybe also the first year, when the baby is looking most sweet. Doesn't the woman get shut indoors? Doesn't she suffer? When she works too? I raised them all alone, I did not have mother-in-laws or mothers. Nothing. What will I do? I wake up at quarter to five. In other words, won't I have to sleep at all to nurse the baby? Of course. And can I tell you something? When the relations of the couple are good, they don't need rejuvenations with children. Isn't that so?

Thus Anna emphatically joins the chorus of voices saying, "How can you expect me to have more children without more support?" Her response underlines the crucial role of mothers and mother-in-laws—the "grandmothers" appearing earlier—who step in for services that the women think the state should be providing. What stands out most, however, is that in sharing these views with me she also sheds light on the underlying idea that having more children is potentially a valid request. However, this is so because, as her opening remarks suggest, Greece is indeed in some ways seen as being a superior nation that is threatened by an impending invasion by Turkey. Even having more children seems to be a feasible and potentially successful solution to the problem this represents.

In sum, the tension between the nation and its gendered subjects, and the move to separate the nation from the state are made vividly clear in Anne's response. Moreover, the embeddedness of these within a register of nationalism that runs through most of the responses is also briefly rearticulated. This is brought to the fore with another woman. Eleftheria elaborates her theory specifically about the reason for the high rate of abortion in Greece. She was born in Arta and has lived in Kipseli for the past twenty-nine years. She is a forty-year-old public servant, married, has two children, and reports having had four abortions. She begins first with her analysis of what she refers to as "the social" reasons for abortion.

> *She:* The reason there are so many abortions is social. That is it. It is social, on the one hand, and, on the other, most women who have abortions are either single [*eleftheres*] or married but they do not want a child.
>
> You might tell me why, since there are so many methods of precaution, why this one? Personally, I tell you that this can happen to you the same from many different roads. It happened to me personally first from ignorance, the first time, the second from indifference, and then from collaboration. The last one was obligatory [*ypohreotiki*]. These are the basic roads from where it happens.
>
> And anyway, when you are single . . . the reason "society" and the reason "no obligations," OK. But a married individual after having had some children very much participates in the one child. Because times are not of the sort that would permit you to have . . . In other words, when they used to have seven or eight children, yes, but they did not care if their children would wear shoes, if ten of the fifteen would die. People were entirely indifferent once. They knew one way of making love, making children, regardless of how many would be born, how many would survive.

Eleftheria deploys a notion of contemporary Greece as modern and superior to its primitive early years. Her account also offers a vivid illustration of how a particular way of having sex is linked to a particular state of nationhood. Highlighting what is perceived as an important qualitative difference between reproductive sex and sex that is decoupled from reproduction, she suggests that modern Greeks are more sophisticated and know "more than one way" of making love. That they do, moreover, becomes the sign of their modernity. Alongside this, contemporary Greeks emerge from her narrative as more caring as well. It is not repeat abortion that reveals callousness, as popular culture and experts alike often imply, but repeat births. Thus, the pattern of repeat abortion in fact comes to signify the superior modernization of the Greek nation. A form of the modernization discourse is rearticulated and Eleftheria suggests that her way of making love, where children are not produced though fetuses may be aborted, is precisely a sign of Greece's progress. It is not, clearly, that there are objections to the way modern Greece specifically is being figured in popular and political discourses such as the demografiko.

To the contrary, in a variant of the larger argument I am putting forward, Eleftheria is trying to show how what is being represented as a problem may actually support a particular version of the greater good.

> *She:* They fed them little, many children, let's say the generation of my mother-in-law, they grew up on what, greens, bread, and flour. Well, those generations, it is questionable whether they had meat two or three times per year. Well, now a young person does not pursue a life like that. In other words, to have children, if you don't have enough to support them [*na ta zisis*], to feed them, to educate them . . .

Young people today care more about the quality of life than did the generation of her mother-in-law. Presumably this is also the generation of her mother. Identifying it as her mother-in-law's, a person many married women in Greece have an adversarial relationship with, as well as a potential source of invaluable services such as child care, no doubt reflects her sense of just how wrong those Greeks of the past were. This is a sentiment she would be unlikely to express about her own mother's generation in such a clear way. The opaque conjunction between the strain of Greek nationalism expressed in demografiko discourses that is preoccupied with efficiently and effectively (hence the recurring issue of "quality") modernizing Greece, and the strain of Greek nationalisms relying on a racialized and fundamentalist notion of the ethnos become transparent in Eleftheria's account as she continues. Having painted a bleak picture of a premodern Greece, she goes on to say the following:

> *She:* And you see, and I say it now, those people are usually the way Greece used to be—those are now Albania—where they give birth endlessly [*gennane soridon*]. Turkey, where the lack of education [*amorfosia*] . . . they don't know how to do anything else. They don't have methods of precaution,

while their dogma . . . does not permit [contraception]. They have to give birth, to produce, to fill the earth with Muslims. And we also have the fact that in these peoples, education is about 10 to 15 percent. [They] don't have a higher level of education than that. It is questionable whether it is 10 to 15 percent. . . .

And there is India. There we have a negative religious factor, because they have an uncultured [*apolitisti*] religion. Uncultured religion, I mean that they have a religion that is outside of civilization. In other words, wherever there was civilization, there was also always culture, and in ancient times and always there were educated people. In other words, they did not happen now. They existed at that time, but with another form of education, right? But there were the educated.

But religion, let us say, is negative, it does not leave them room for choice. If you can imagine that in a celebration of fertility that happens over there with those [female] who also are getting high [*mastura*]—they get high over there—and how many are killed over there. And it is a religious celebration that happens just like that, for fun, like our Halloween [*Apokries*].

Eleftheria is by now talking in an openly racist way. The initial elision of a difference between Greece's past and Albania or Turkey in the present demonstrates part of what is at stake in the pronounced statements of modernization and nationalism in circulation in Greece. It also offers insight into contenporary Greek racism against Albanians and Turks: They reflect an element of "us" that we are laboriously trying to overcome while the ever-so-seductive European Union peers on at our performance.

Certainly, the lack of compunction with which Eleftheria proceeds to essentially attack Albanians and Turks on the basis of their imagined ways of having sex continues to illuminate the vital connection between sexuality and nationhood while also reflecting how the fundamentalist nationalist narratives circulating in demografiko discourses are transposed and reanimated by contemporary Greeks in their attempt to craft their own sense of Greekness. Eleftheria suggests that the high rate of abortion, which seems to oppose demografiko tenets, is good. But it is good because it demonstrates that Greeks are not like those hostile, potentially invading foreign bodies across the border (unthinking, uncaring, religious fanatics) that the demografiko also figures as so fearsome. These characters are so feared at least partially because of the resemblance they bear with images of our own past, especially during those four hundred years of being part of the Ottoman Empire that are typically represented as four hundred years of Turkish control.

Eleftheria's narrative also raises a very important question: What about our own Greek Orthodoxy, so vehemently upheld by some segments of the population that the PASOK government's year 2000 decision to get rid of the entry concerning religion on national ID cards provoked intense debate? Indeed, her next comments speak to this.

> *She:* Of course, OK, and our religion does not permit abortion, because if the soul is not born at least for one second, it won't be resurrected according to our religion.
>
> Our religion forbids abortion for one reason, that is that if the baby is born and lives, comes out into the world even for just one second . . . when the dead rise—as our religion says—they too will rise, they will return to their life. Whereas when a pregnancy is terminated it won't . . . It has not become a human being, it has not become fulfilled as a person, therefore it won't ever be. . . . In other words, it won't come back to life. It is as though you . . . you kill it that moment. That's what it believes: murder essentially.
>
> But I don't see, there isn't, at least from the Orthodox Church and the Catholic, there isn't any restriction—in other words, they say it, but it is in a form, nobody intervenes. Because they say, "Well, you had an abortion, you will do . . . two years"—I don't know what they say—"it will be two years before you can take communion," something like that. Then the wrongful act is written off. Something like that, in other words, it is very flexible.
>
> I, of course, agree that it should not happen. Not, certainly, because of religious or other reasons, but because I consider it stupid [*hazo*] to happen. You want to have a child, have it. You don't, don't. There are so many methods of precaution. *And I believe that all those [abortions] that happen, it is a matter that they happen because you don't use certain things correctly—whether those are called contraception, or they are called logic.*

With this, Eleftheria looked up at me pointedly, nodded her head, and concluded her explanation of Greece's high rate of abortion. There was no explicit mention during this part of our conversation of the four abortions she has had. Her comments on Greek Orthodoxy and its position on abortion are intriguing and revealing. Although she is quick to say that her opposition to abortion is not religious, her understanding of the Church's efforts to negotiate a position on abortion is more than casual. It is likely that she believes in Greek Orthodox doctrine and has incorporated it into her life. Yet this degree of faith is precisely what she had been suggesting was one of the important signs of backward or more primitive people. Thus, her explanation ends with a strong affirmation of a distinction between religious belief and reason: she simply thinks it is "stupid" to have "all those abortions." There are, after all, so many precautions, including "logic."

The subject that emerges from all the narratives is clearly portrayed in Eleftheria's words. Contemporary Greek women are the fraught product of contradictory discourses: a religio-racial superiority and the vexed desire to negotiate a perceived divide between tradition and modernity. Refigurations of faith and reason are key to this process. *Logiki*. The idea of repeat abortion as an irrational process is, of course, the prevalent way of viewing the high rate of abortion in Greece, and among certain populations in the United States as well.[7] Chryssa gives us a closer look at the interface between notions of rationality and notions of modernity in this context. Commenting on that pervasive trope of modernization, "informing the citizenry" (*enimerosi*), she tells me the following:

> *She:* For me it is forbidding, let us say.
> *I:* What is?
> *She:* For me it is stupid for someone to have abortions . . . at least today.
> *I:* Why, what is—
> *She:* In the past . . . when I was twenty years old, there was no informing of people, not even coming from the family. What would you say now to your grandfather or grandmother? Inform me or . . . These were things entirely taboo supposedly, etc., etc., and . . . taboo entirely. And they connected sex with . . . reproduction. . . . So there is this too, it still holds, I've identified it [*to'ho entopisi*]. No, I don't know if it still holds, possibly that it still holds, possibly. So they say to a couple, "You plan children, one, two, three at most . . . Then you are to stop your sexual relations." . . . Well, that is a little . . .
>
> It isn't the typical Greek family the way it was twenty or thirty years ago. . . . But unfortunately I see there is even now—the last abortion I had done I had gone to . . . what is it called . . . to Dina's [another public hospital that has a Family Planning Center]. There they told me this, like that, in cold blood [*en psyhro*], young women at my age, maybe younger even, the midwives, and they told me this. It isn't enough, let's say, that I had my sadness [*iha ton kaymo mou*]. I hear that on top of everything. And I say now . . . I did not expect it, of course, but maybe this still holds . . . And from women who were perhaps even five years younger then me.

The picture of a more primitive Greece of the not too distant past that is characterized by people who necessarily "connected sex with reproduction" is clear. Abortion steps in to take the place occupied by contraception in the demografiko story, which holds that to become properly modern, Greek women must contracept. For many of the women I spoke with, to be modern, Greek women must be able to rationally plan their family size and, thus, *to abort*. In a different deployment of a key claim of the demografiko, Chryssa, who has been married eight years, has two children, and reports having had three abortions, suggests that it is in fact abortion that is making Greece modern. Moreover, she registers shock at the idea that women, even women younger than she (she was twenty-seven at the time of the interview), continue to hold the view that sex should be procreative. In fact, it is the midwives of the state-run clinic, Chryssa seems to be saying, in an eerie rearticulation of the pronounced nationalist dynamic of modernization discourses involved in the demografiko, who are the real enemies of the nation.

The Demografiko as Theater of the Absurd

Like a magical rendition of the toy Russian doll that keeps opening to reveal yet another doll inside, abortion in Greece keeps yielding new paradoxes, charting contradictions, tensions, and at times deep fault lines in Greek society. If the midwives who so staunchly defend the pro-natalism of the state while patrolling the borders of appropriate Greek femininity can also be seen as a force of significant opposition to the welfare of the modern Greek nation, it is apparent that what counts as *Greece,* what counts as good Ellinides (Greek women), and how abortion comes to make sense in the midst of all this are not only complex but volatile questions to be grappling with. At the same time, abortion is positioned as a significant site in the negotiation of identity in Greece today, of nation, of gendered subjectivity, and of citizenship, so that it serves as a unique vantage point for surveying the dynamic of power and resistance that characterizes the social and political terrain of late modernity at large.

On the one hand, it is clear that the demografiko can be viewed as an important node in the reproduction of Gramscian hegemonic ideology. One way this is achieved is by using abortion to reinscribe motherhood as a requirement for Greek female citizenship. In the context of demografiko discourses, having children is not only a part of normative femininity, but a projected requirement for appropriately patriotic Greek gendered citizenry. In addition, the press's coverage of abortion effects a retrenchment of what Warner (1993) has termed reproculture, a modality of social life that involves both the strong valorization of generativity, or the belief that one must somehow live beyond one's own life, and the reinscription of forms of sexuality, family, and government that are organized around reproduction, whether heterosexual, homosexual, or bisexual. Nothing less than the nation and its future survival are positioned, *via the demografiko,* as being at stake. Finally, the Greek mainstream press's coverage of the demografiko underscores another notion that works to safeguard the status quo: the source of the nation's main problem at the present, it argues, is women.

On the other hand, the public representations of the demografiko can also activate or exacerbate resistances, as the women's responses to my direct question illustrate. In Gramscian terms, this is a potential site for the development of counterhegemonic ideology. The demografiko gives rise to the opportunity for the similarly public exploration of alternative ways of thinking about abortion, relationship, national welfare, and Greece. Indeed, my presentation and analysis of the women's responses to the demografiko are not only motivated by a theory-building project but also are an attempt to make more public the resistances that the women articulated in private conversation with me.

Yet, especially this portion of the material provokes the retheorization of a Gramscian in favor of a Foucauldian notion of resistance. That is, the often vehement opposition expressed, though conducive to a deeper critique of the nationalist project, is itself riddled with nationalist and racist presuppositions. Indeed, women's very conceptions of their body, sexuality, and love or erotos bear the marks of the stories that constitute Greece as a distinct, presumed to be natural, superior political entity. Moreover, at the site of the media, resistance was very rare. Throughout 1994, there was but one instance of an article or column published in the mainstream Greek press that was explicitly opposed to the demografiko. It is useful to examine this here.

After commenting caustically on the 1993 formation of a parliamentary committee on the demografiko, M. Kondili, a member of the faculty of the University of Patra, and the author of an op-ed piece in *Eleftherotypia,*[8] refers to "the blind nationalist ideology that lies hidden" in the discourse surrounding "the demographic problem" and argues that there is "an attempt to lay guilt on women who, carried away by strange morals and decrepit practices, do not give birth enough so as to fulfill the national mandate. The nationalist ideology is expressed with the subordination of individual interests to the interests of an unreasoning sense of increase, and also of purity, of the ethnos/people."

The project of this book has not been to find what lies hidden in either women's narratives or the press coverage. Rather, I have sought to trace those social formations whose marks are borne on the surface of these texts, to identify, that is, through their textual remains, the relations of power that animate and shape social reality. In this context, the terms with which this excerpt from the press coverage opposes demografiko discourses is especially illuminating. The trope being used to trump the nation is "the individual." There seems to be no adequate basis to refute ethnic claims regarding the growth, and purity, of Greeks as a race other than the equally risky construct of the individual. In this narrative it is Western liberal democracy and its subject that is inscribed as optimal. What is being fought against are Eastern or "backward" claims of a primordial collectivity. Other alternatives, other ways of strategically imagining the nation and its subjects in the geopolitical context of growing globalization and its resistances, are absent.

Nonetheless, within its parameters, the article is firmly oppositional to the demografiko's nationalist and racist terms. The writer goes on to add, "Within the mess of proposed measures of 'social politics,' what stands out is the recriminalization of the right to legal abortions, which are being singled out as mainly responsible for the low birth rate and extremely dangerous for 'national, religious and demographic reasons.'" Undercutting the strength of this critique and patrolling its destabilizing potential is a box that separates it from the news items presented on the same page. In the box is a photograph of the woman writing, as well as a subheading that states that the text is "the opinion of Marianna Kondili, lecturer at the University of Patras, on the domestic discussion concerning the low birth rate of Greeks." Thus, while the newspaper provides space for a fairly strong critique of demografiko discourses, the critique is muted by its emphatic relegation to the status of personal opinion. Haraway's (1991) concept of situated knowledges and her argument concerning science is certainly not an operative part of the hermeneutic grid in a Greece where the grammatical effacement of an author and the graphic portrayal of numbers often are all that is needed to grant a text the status of scientific truth. All together, this article in *Eleftherotypia* offers an ambivalent or veiled critique of key terms of the demografiko.

This example from the press can be seen as emblematizing the way the women negotiated their efforts to articulate resistance. A similar dynamic characterized the ways the women responded to my question concerning the demografiko. They made jokes, at times tongue-in-cheek comments, or simply dry witticisms. In some sense these were statements that worked both to express very direct resistance and to temper it with sardonic humor. These moments seemed to me to incisively reveal how deeply discourses shape our sense of ourselves as subjects who are gendered and raced in particular ways, at times surprisingly so, and who "belong" in varying degrees to one nation, to more, or to none. Here, I argue, are elaborated both the contentious Foucauldian theoretical postulations that discourse *creates* matter, and that wherever there is power there is resistance.

Even in just the excerpts in this chapter we see the full range of meanings that are strategically deployed to respond ironically to demografiko discourse: religion, race, nationality, and the nexus of the three. For example, Elena said, "You cannot take from those who have nothing" in response to the demografiko's mandate for more children. This statement was made with a switch in codes and the use of Ancient Greek, when Elena quoted from the Old Testament: *Ouk an lavis ek tou mi ehondos!* Thus, she draws from one of the main pools of meaning being used in the fundamentalist nationalist narrative of Greekness that informs the demografiko and uses this as the basis of her claim *against* the demografiko. In so doing, she is inadvertently indicating that there is an important inconsistency at work here. The same dynamic is revealed in Irini's retort that she will not be the one to solve the demografiko: "Take that glass away from me!" Again, there is a code-switch to Ancient Greek and religious discourse is used in a dramatic way to refer to the moment of weakness when even the best Christian, Christ himself, questions the need to suffer so much.

Moving from religion to race, one woman posed the hypothetical question about whether a woman should have more children and send them out in the street to sell tissue packets like Albanian and gypsy children do now in Athens. Again, while this fragment mirrors the demografiko's racist postulation of Albanians and the nationals of other neighboring countries as members of a lesser people, it reveals the speaking subject's position that the logic in the demografiko discourse is fallacious, which in turn implicitly exposes the fallacious assumption that "we" are indeed superior. That is, how can we be superior if we are advocating practices that would compel us to behave like those we think of as being lesser? Clearly, it is not that Albanian mothers or parents are somehow worse than Greek parents, as my informant may well have been implying. Rather, social conditions shape the choices they can make in such a way that a behavior assumed to be a reflection of racial characteristics is, momentarily, exposed as a product of social and economic forces.

Also shown here was the comment that "the Turks are going to come in and throw us out," which is exactly what much of the demografiko discourses have as their refrain, though not always putting it quite so frankly. In the redeployment of this idea we have at once the affirmation of a threat from the Turks and, in the exaggeration registered and the tone of voice, the immediate ironic comment that invasion is unlikely, *siga min boune*. Certainly, this woman's criticism of the exaggeration of the statement may also rely on an essentializing nationalist or racist sense of Greece as superior. Yet, the ironic comment also underlines the absurdity of the idea and frames it as, somehow, *funny*.

Finally, another wonderful example from Christiana, who dryly commented that though she herself has no financial problems, she does not see why those who do should have more children and "leave them to the mercy of God." Here again a key fragment of the nationalist narratives of the demografiko is repositioned, and a narrative that primarily seeks simply to oppose the proposition that women should suffer the labor and hardship of having more children is annexed. Yet, in so doing, Christiana also illuminates how the very notion of a nation that is founded on God's will and mercy is problematic because its institution involves the mundane agency of humans who proceed to advocate for, and at times implement, all sorts of contradictory, potentially *sinful* policies. In sum, the depth of the permeation of subjects by particular nationalist narratives, as well as the unchallenged dominance of a liberal humanist discourse, even at sites of otherwise strong opposition to the demografiko and aspects of its formative discourse, confirm the need for further nuancing of theorizations of power.

EPILOGUE:

THEORY AND POLICY

✥

Bodies are *literally* made—or *not,* as in the case of abortion—from discourses. It is not just a metaphor, a figure of speech, or a phatic postmodern refrain. It is perhaps, in the end, only empirically grounded work that can further theory while also proving this point to its skeptics. This study of abortion and the demografiko in Greece offers rich evidence documenting this thesis. Thus, this study both illuminates the politics of modern Greece and extends this theoretical argument. I have argued that it is culturally-specific nationalist discourses that repeatedly produce fetuses and it is these that yield disparate formations of personhood such that the fetus, although often seen as a child, is then aborted. Discourses make both bodies that matter, as Judith Butler (1993) named her important book, and, I suggest, *nations* that *naturalize*—at this historical moment, globally in new ways that are at times unexpectedly violent. The two moves together seem to be viscerally connected, each one mothering the other, united by an invisible but very strong umbilical cord.

This analysis of the interanimation of discourses of nationhood and gender raises several important practical issues for our understanding of liberal democracies and for attempts to shape public policy that supports what is thought of as democracy. For example, the central, if unacknowledged, assumption underlying the popular as well as formally political imaginings of Greece is that of Greece as a form of a religious state. A major preoccupation of current scholarly and policy work has been that both formally religious states and states that simply have a high degree of religiosity (as this is gauged by a varying set of measures) do not have the capacity to be liberal democratic states. Certainly, one interesting way to contest this thesis would be to present an analysis of political culture in a country typically seen as exemplifying the liberal democratic nation-state, such as the United States today, which would document the deep-rooted religiosity that animates it. "The cradle of democracy," Greece is one of those countries that has been targeted by the claim of an inadequate democratization. For example, it has been suggested that one of the reasons for the support Greece extended to Turkey's bid for membership in the European Union may have been a desire to allay its own marginalization due to charges of excessive religiosity. A consequence of one level of argumentation put forward here may be to fuel such claims about Greece. However, as I have argued at another level throughout, the Greek situation actually serves to throw such criticism back on itself by raising the larger question of the efficacy and appropriateness of key terms of liberal democratic discourses.

I suggest that this analysis of the body and nationalism in Greece is an exceptional site for the retrieval of evidence that powerfully illuminates and initiates a counterargument to Huntington's (1996) thesis. In effect, the modern cradle of democracy is, in important ways, an implicitly religious state that, nonetheless, is in the throes of a heightened modernization project that holds democracy as its unspoken sine qua non. The specificities of this perhaps astonishing and postmodern-sounding political project indicate that analytic categories of political science, indeed social science more generally, and of the public policies it informs might be better designed and deployed if they were informed by careful discourse analysis of the cultural and social forms that preoccupy the geopolitical contexts they seek to classify, organize, and govern.

Another aspect of what abortion in modern Greece teaches about liberal democracy and its limitations, at least as it is currently being formulated and implemented via domestic and foreign policies of the United States and Greece alike, has to do with the subject. Late modernity, as the present is perhaps more accurately called, has produced a subject that is in a constant state of flux. Pitted against a variety of totalizing forces, the seduction of an I that stands firm and fixed is powerful, as powerful as are the social formations yielding dividing lines and the associated fragmentation of identity. Thus, what Deleuze terms a schizophrenic society and Foucault names regimes of truth work together in increasingly vehement, yet often self-contradictory efforts to discipline and rigidly *locate* the body politic. Floating above all this is the warm hearth of modernity and a romantic vision of "a home" that yet remains always somehow elusive.[1]

Analysis of the accounts of women living in Athens who reported having had two or more abortions allows us to witness how the process of negotiating national identity intersects specifically with discourses of femininity at the site of the subject. Analysis of the press gives further insight into the agon involved, focusing on the realms of the national imaginary, popular culture, and a formalized public sphere. The narratives articulated by the female subject in Greece reveal another public sphere and other arenas of struggle. There is, clearly, heavy traffic of discourses circulating among these domains. One of the main implicit claims put forward in this book is that the press and women are not the easily distinguishable entities that we commonly think the press and citizens are. Certainly, in light of the anxieties provoked by a modernizing Greece and a rapidly unifying Europe, what it means to be Greek has become a loaded issue, and both the press and women are actively engaged in its, and *their,* redefinition, as much as in a process of retrenchment.

Both the analysis of women's narratives and that of the press's representations teach the necessity to question the extent to which it makes sense to equate the social formation called women in Greece (or men, for that matter) with the liberal subject. I need to emphasize that I am not arguing for a "cultural adjustment" thesis. It is not that we need to adjust policy so that it takes into consideration the romantically imagined, or not, specificities of local, more or less exoticized, configurations of personhood. Rather, the cartography of Greece that emerges from my research argues strongly in favor of the need to *think differently* about both subject and nation alike. Another modality of social thought is needed so that we might more perceptively approach the complex and paradoxical, often very harsh realities of varyingly liberal democratic political orders at the present—be they in the Balkans, Europe, Africa, Asia, including the United States, or elsewhere. It simply does not make good sense, given a geopolitical context in which ideas about the nation-God junction are pivotal to ideas about both personal identity and formal politics at whatever level—and this is not the case only in the Balkans or Islam, we must be able to acknowledge—to talk about the nation and citizens as two distinctly separate entities requiring two different sorts of policy in order to be best tended. Anything aimed at one, I suggest, without addressing the cognitive, semantic, rhetorical, indeed visceral links in the chain connecting the two may very likely fail; at the very least, the unanticipated consequences might surpass in gravity the problems it was aimed at resolving in the first place. Discourses run through both these sites, and many others as well, forming them just as they vex them. The textuality of nation and subject alike is key.[2]

In this matrix of agency, personhood shifts. The human fetus, other human forms of life, the animal and flora life routinely killed or abused in different cultural habitats, all seem situationally to occupy a boundary zone: neither object nor person. They are alternatively attacked or defended by various constituencies. As Zetta said about abortion, knocking on the wood of her bookshelf, death (too) is life. At the heart of democracy reside distinctions that have high stakes attached. These distinctions are cultural and historical products that are contested. In the social landscape populated by the resulting subjects and political entities, constructs such as rational choice, free will, and individual autonomy emerge as powerful tools for the ultimately costly foreclosure of a more radical assessment of the political field.

The nation fills the void of high modern existential angst. Wombs, it seems, in disparate ways in different national contexts to be sure, are asked to fill the empty stores of the (imagi)nation. Babies—both the right amount and the right kind, of course—are, at critical historical junctures, made to figure hope. In the midst of this, it is perhaps the greatest irony of all that abortion is positioned as a constitutive moment in the ongoing (re)birth of the twin construction of the nation-subject.

> May a magic spell protect you
> from snake bites, evil enemies
> and all the healed wounds. (Mastoraki 1998)

The agon that transpires within the cradle of democracy is concisely portrayed by this poem. This analysis of nationalism, sexuality, abortion, and the politics of identity in Greece has sought to track the vexed discursive production of the subject and the nation in order to render visible the seriousness of its political consequences. To the extent that national wounds are "healed" or forgotten in formal policy discourse and social theory alike, the fundamentally historical and cultural basis of the cornerstone of liberal democratic state-building projects, rational decision-making, is erased and the realm of the political circumscribed to our peril. The analysis put forward throughout this book demonstrates the absence of the presupposed "baby" of democracy and, in so doing, urges a reexamination of the unquestioned presuppositions guiding scientific and political projects across the globe.

NOTES

❖

Unless otherwise noted, all translations from the Greek are mine.
The titles of all Greek newspaper articles are given in English.

Introduction
1. According to the most recent national census of 2002, the population totaled 10,964,020 (National Statistical Service of Greece 2002, 3).
2. Butler comments with regard to the violence involved in becoming a gendered subject, "The forming of a subject requires an identification with the normative phantasm of 'sex,' and this identification takes place through a repudiation which produces a domain of abjection, a repudiation without which the subject cannot emerge" (1993, 3). With regard to the implication of violence with the process of crafting identity in a liberal humanist discursive context, she warns, "If through its own violences, the conceits of liberal humanism have compelled the multiplication of culturally specific identities, then it is all the more important not to repeat that violence without a significant difference, reflexively and prescriptively, within the articulatory struggles of those specific identities forged from and through a state of siege" (118). To be able to do so, *to not repeat the violence without a significant difference,* it seems to me that part of the violence that is committed as a function of the discursive operation of power needs to be made visible. It is one of the vanities of this book that it contributes to such a "translation" project by using one specific case to draw the link between the processes of subjection and aspects of the damage that might be recognized as damage by those who do not, a priori, endorse a similar theoretical apparatus.
3. The difficulties associated with an unproblematized usage of these terms to describe aspects of Greece are foregrounded in Herzfeld (1991a). As he clearly shows, the way these terms might work in Greek contexts is complicated by how different histories—classical, Byzantine, and Ottoman—are employed to make a bid for "tradition." Each associated understanding of the future also competes for a claim on the specifics of "modernization." For consideration of the multiplicity of allusions to history at play in elites' attempts to forge Greek nation-

hood, see Herzfeld (1982) and Faubion (1993). A survey of this historical terrain is offered in Kyriakidou-Nestoros (1986) and Vryonis (1978).

Yet, these terms enjoy currency among elites and nonelites alike. For example, focusing especially on notions of womanhood and domesticity in elite nineteenth-century discourse on the relative merits of women's education, and the overlap of such notions with those of nineteenth-century Greek ethnography, Bakalaki (1994b) shows that the basis of the argument put forward in favor of women's education was that it would help make Greece "European" and, implicitly, more modern. Also, as testimony to the widespread anxiety about modernity in the present, Sutton (1994, 240) considers the issue as it applies to the inhabitants of the island of Kalymnos, writing that "islanders posed the relationship of 'tradition' and 'modernity' as the most significant moral issue facing the island today." In addition, see Constas and Stavrou (1995) for extensive analysis and discussion of the challenges facing Greece in the next century. See Lyritzis (1987) for an account of the changing shape of party clientelism, a key bogeyman of modernization discourses, since the demise of the Papadopoulos junta in 1974. On the historical development of party clientelistic relations, see Demertzis (1990). Also, for an analysis of clientelistic politics in nineteenth-century Greece, see Petropoulos (1968). For a review of key monographs dealing with this issue, see Mouzelis (1979).

4 Rosalind P. Petchesky (1990) argues that, depending on the social context, a high rate of abortion can be an expression of fully hegemonic behavior and beliefs *or* a challenge to hegemonic ideology. In Greece at the present, as I argue, it may best be understood as both.

5 For a historically grounded exposition of the characteristics of contemporary Greek political cultures and an overview of the history of the debate concerning modern Greek national identity, see Diamandouros (1993). In his analysis, two political cultures are dominant: the Balkan-Ottoman–Greek Orthodox or "underdog" culture, and the Enlightenment-liberal–democratic-Westernizing or "reformist" culture. As I show in chapter 6, the visions, or discourses, of the nation that I find evidence of in the press coverage of the demografiko largely correspond to these two cultures.

6 All quotes from Foucault appearing in this section are from Foucault (1980c).

7 Influential analyses in this discussion include Bordo (1988, 87–117); Butler (1992, 3–21); de Lauretis (1987); B. Martin (1992, 93–119); Sawicki (1991); Scott (1992, 22–40); Singer (1992, 464–75); Walby (1992, 31–52).

8 For an overview of the rich vein of work concerned with collective memory, see Zelizer (1995). For a nuanced empirical analysis of how contemporary U.S. collective memory contributes to and is informed by particular understandings of national identity, see Schudson (1992). Studies of non-U.S. contexts and how the present has required the reconstruction of the past in ways that are in alignment with the nation-state's current interests are increasing in number. Relevant examples include analysis of collective memory in Russia (Tumarkin

1987) and China (Hung 1991), as well as one of the earlier examples of this work, a consideration of how the reinstatement of the triumph of Muslim Spain was based on a reconstruction of Spanish Islam as an almost egalitarian regime (Lewis 1975). For work examining the contemporary popular negotiation of national identity in Greece, see Tsaliki (1995). Research on the representation of national identity in the media, and its negotiation therein, in various other European contexts is currently fruitful. As a good example of the strand of this work that focuses especially on the content of media texts, and for an overview of the literature, see Hardt-Mautner (1995). Adopting more of a political economy approach are Meech and Kilborn (1992).

9 Feminist theoretical approaches to the discursive production of nature and the biological body have grown in number. Specifically exploring the social construction of biological knowledge concerning gender and sex is Fausto-Sterling (2000). She notes, "Our bodies, as well as the world we live in, are certainly made of materials, and we often use scientific investigation to understand the nature of those materials. But such scientific investigation involves a process of knowledge construction" (28). Also see Haraway (1988, 1989b, 1991); Hubbard (1990); E. Martin (1990a, 1990b).

10 In *The Last Word* (1991), Nadia Seremetakis shows, with an incisive analysis of the cultural form of lament in Inner Mani, a rural area in southern Greece, that the political, social, and cultural terrain can be very clearly viewed from the perspective of a phenomenon not locally explicitly understood as an overtly political or social event in its own right, though widely practiced.

11 Paula Ebgron and Anna Lowenhaupt Tsing (1995) focus on U.S. nationalism and argue that the current emphasis on "giving voice" to minority cultures or communities actually can work as "programs of containment" by promoting "agendas in which communities would be imagined units of independent difference from a dominant white centre"(125). Toward the end of encouraging dialogue among minorities, the authors look at how different groups silence others by deploying their own "allegories of identity," through which their histories are understood, and make a bid for "composing the narrative space of oppression and struggle." They propose that other strategies of identity, such as "dialogue across margins" (144), be tried.

12 The research constitutes a critical ethnography of *discourses* and, as such, takes discourses as its unit of analysis rather than positioning "the press" or "women" as autonomous and clearly isolated subjects. For the sake of brevity and clarity, however, I try to avoid frequent use of what might be seen in some contexts as jargon; and so, after this, I often refer precisely to "the press" and "Greek women." Yet, I want to underline that to keep the field of inquiry as open as possible and to allow room for the specifically Greek constructions of personhood to emerge, as Judith Butler's work suggests, the notion of "women," for example, that underlies this project is that of partially bounded historical congealments of discursive practices that occupy particular subject positions and

both articulate and are articulated by a complicated nexus of discourses. A reification of "women" in what is marked as "clear language" can actually work to obfuscate the very patterns and workings of power that this book attempts to open up and examine. To take "the press" or "Greek women" as the points of origin of this study would be precisely to conceal the historically and culturally specific discourses that produce each category. As becomes clear throughout, my interest is in analyzing these discourses and looking at how they traverse one another, collapse, and collide at two key sites of the nexus of Greek nationhood and gender at the present historical moment. It is only by tracing these, as Foucault and many others have shown, that a thoroughgoing critique of power may be actualized.

13 One of the first works to explicitly address the enlistments of different understandings of sexuality in the foundation of the modern nation-state is Mosse (1985). For a comprehensive and nuanced consideration of this nexus in a variety of national, primarily literary, contexts, see Parker, Russo, Sommer, and Yaeger (1992). More attentive to a wider set of material and also concerned with the conjunctions of gender, nation, and reproduction are Ginsburg and Rapp (1995). This volume offers an excellent example of how a national perception of the very categories of "reproduction" and "population" operates diversely as a discursive construct in the context of disparate nations. See, for example, Anagnost (1995).

1. Greece, Fantasy, History

1 For an insightful analysis of some of the city's pluralities, architectural, historical, and cultural, see Faubion (1993), especially 64–98.
2 For further demographic figures on present-day Greece, see Yfantopoulos (1999). According to a study reported in *Eleftherotypia* on 20 August 2001 that was conducted for the Organization of Urban Transportation and Attiko Metro, the Athens subway company, by urban planning experts preparing for the 2004 Olympic Games to be held in Athens, it is estimated that on any working day during nine months of the year, an average of 5.82 million people are being transported through Athens (during the three summer months this number drops to 4.72 million, as many leave the city at this time). The study is based on data preceding the operation of the Athenian subway, so the current numbers are likely smaller.
3 As this book goes to print, the trial of those arrested is pending.
4 In several instances, when I ordered a *tourkiko* (Turkish) coffee, I was corrected by the waiter and told that I must mean an *elliniko*.
5 This figure was reported in "Telecommunications Have Grown by 16%," *Oikonomiki Eleftherotypia*, 25 July 2001, 22.
6 All the statistics and figures cited in this review of the history of Athens, except where otherwise noted, are presented and discussed in further detail in

Leondidou (1989, 48). Some supplementary information is also drawn from the Greek encyclopedia *Papyros Larous Britannica* 1981, 3: 385–97.

7 By 1896, there are 173,340 inhabitants of the Athens-Piraeus area (Leondidou 1989, 48).

8 Stasinopoulos (1973, 470). For more on the Goudi events, see the section on the history of Greece.

9 Stasinopoulos (1973, 483) reports that the population of Athens in 1920 was 285,000, rather than the 453,000 noted in Leondidou (1989, 156), thus indicating yet a higher rate of growth. The other figures coincide.

10 Stasinopoulos (1973, 510) reports that in 1961 Athens had a population of 1,852,709, and in 1971 there were 2,530,000 inhabitants, marking a 37 percent increase in this area's population. Meanwhile, Greece as a whole had a population of 8,388,553 in 1961 and, ten years later in 1971, this had only grown by 4 percent to 8,736,367.

11 This figure is based on the 2001 National Census (National Statistical Service of Greece 2001).

12 See *Papyros Larous Britannica* 1981, 3: 394.

13 For an insightful exploration of the culture associated with the rebetiko, see Kotaridis (1996).

14 D. Rigopoulos, "A Farewell to the Athenian 60s," Kathimerini, 29 August 2001.

15 For a theoretical discussion of the development of classes in Greece, see Lytras 1993.

16 See Sarris (1992). For an analysis of how the Asia Minor refugees were portrayed in Greek television series, see especially 172–73, 190–95. More generally, the popular genre of "a Greek movie" (*elliniki tainia*) often centered its romantic plot on dramatization of a significant historical moment such as the Occupation by the Nazis, 1941–45.

17 These figures are according to G. Psillas, cited in Miheli (1987, 30).

18 In 1823 Lord Byron formed the Byron Brigade and joined the Greek insurgents who had risen against the Turks. However, in April 1824, Byron died of marsh fever in Mesologi before seeing military action.

19 For more details, see Miheli (1987). She notes that the idealized version of Teresa Makri yielded its parodies later. A journalist visiting Athens was said to have found the by then aged and widowed, and very well-educated, Teresa Black. She had married an English professor at the age of thirty-two, helped translate a book from Italian with one of her sisters, and belonged to one of the city's philological associations. She had given birth to one daughter who survived and three sons, all of whom are said to have died. The journalist who found the middle-aged Teresa made a sketch of her that led to other parodic representations of "the Maid of Athens." Apparently, as Miheli reports, Teresa was nonetheless vindicated when in 1872 the French composer Gouneau wrote and sung a song called "The Maid of Athens," the proceeds from which he sent to Teresa in Athens, who in later years was living in poverty. She died at the age of seventy-eight in 1875.

20 D. Skoufou, "On-line Sales by 100,000 Customers," *Ta Nea*, 13 August 2001, 46.

2. Greek Women

1 The figures discussed here are based on data from the Ministry of Labor and were published in a special article on the Greek pension system and women's work. Vana Marketaki, "Pensions: Equality Arrived a Little Too Early," *Gynaika* (August 2001).
2 The interview was published in Marketaki, "Pensions."
3 In private conversation, many men support this view. A friend who is a member of the PASOK party said to me, "Well, listen, women want equality, right? Well, this is equality."
4 Marketaki, "Pensions."
5 Panagis Galiatsatos, "Listening to . . . the Sidewalk," *Eleftherotypia*, 13 August 2001.
6 The main body negotiating with the government, the largest union of employees, GSEE, has forty-five members in its leadership, of whom, in 2001, only one was a woman.
7 For a detailed account of the history of the struggle for women's right to vote from the first efforts in 1919 through 1956, see Mosxou-Sakorafou (1990).
8 According to Mosxou-Sakorafou (1990, 224), this appeared in an article in the publication *The Greek Woman*, 3 May 1921.
9 For more on this, see Vervenioti (2000).
10 It is important to note the larger political culture of the public sphere, which often does trivialize women's participation. Consider the special magazine of the daily newspaper *Eleftherotypia* for National Women's Day 2000. In this issue, the cover story on women politicians focuses almost exclusively on prominent women politicians' fashion preferences and consists primarily of photos of the women posing in the vicinity of Parliament, thus implicitly emphasizing that women's appearance—rather than their thought or political acumen—continues to be their overriding characteristic, even when they are members of Parliament.
11 These results were published in the UN-Greece report on Family and Fertility Surveys (2002). Thus all references here correspond to the published report. However, I initially studied the data from a printout of the report given to my by Symeonidou.
12 Loizos and Papataxiarchis (1991, 224) notes that there is evidence that approximately 150,000 abortions per year were taking place even in the late 1960s, according to a study done by Valaoras, Polychronopoulou, and Trichopoulos (1969).
13 Cited in UN-Greece 2002 report, 137.
14 In a conference held in Thessaloniki in the middle of April 2002, Dr. Ioannis Bondis is reported as stating, "Abortion is Greece's most widespread means of

birth control, with about 250,000 carried out every year. As a percentage of the general population, this is the highest figure in the European Union." The article continues, "Bondis said about 40,000 of the annual 250,000 abortions are carried out for teenage girls aged 16 and under, while a third of all abortions are performed on married women who would have avoided them had they been sufficiently well off financially to raise another child" (*Kathimerini*, "Dramatic Decrease of Fertility," English ed., 13–14 April 2002).

15 See especially Dubisch (1995). For other rich ethnographic accounts of popular religion, see also Danforth (1989), who describes the anastenaria of St. Helen's in Serres, and Seremetakis (1991) for the mourning practices in the area of Mani. Varvouni (1995) approaches popular worship in Greece through religious folklore. For a concise and illuminating exposition of the lived aspect of Greek religion, see Stewart (1999).

16 As intriguing indirect evidence of the pervasiveness of such a belief system, and as a powerful example of moments of resistance against it, in this case gendered resistance, consider the following poem by Maria Topali (1999), "Servitsio Tsayou" (Dream on a Light Blue Background):

> . . . to descend the stairs within you
> and to turn off the lights.
>
> (And if you don't turn them off
> you shall still find only darkness.
> And then later, deeper, denser darkness,
> like that in the cave of the dragon.)
>
> I, St. George [in nickname form, "Ai Yiorgis"], shall free the all-beautiful one whom I hold captive in my guts,
> I, the Dragon. (57; my translation)

This poem problematizes the dynamic described above by destabilizing the categories "human" and "saint" and firmly reasserting the agency of the gendered subject herself in a strategic redeployment of the traditional narrative of the victorious battle of St. George with a dragon.

17 One interesting story that demonstrates the sense that the saints protect the ethnos was reported on the evening news of *Alpha* on 10 August 2001. Apparently, each year on this date, Corfu celebrates Saint Spiridon, thanking him for his help when in 1716 the island was surrounded by ships of the Ottoman Empire and the local population, which had barricaded itself in the island's castle, prayed to St. Spiridon to be saved. At that time, the story has it, a great storm occurred and the Ottoman battleships were forced to abandon their attempt to invade the island.

18 Another version of a tama that is more prevalent in rural Greece but that also occurs in Athens is the baking of a pie for a particular saint on the day of his or her celebration. Perhaps most common in the celebration of Saint Fanourios,

these pies are handmade by *noikokires* (homemakers), who ask the saint of lost things, as he is considered, to reveal something to them. One of the modern reinterpolations of this particular practice is to ask him to "reveal" a particular sum of money or a husband for an unmarried daughter.

19 A. Boubouka, "A Dance of Billions with the *Tamata*," *Sunday Eleftherotypia*, 12 August 2001, 48; M. Papoutsaki, "The Panagia of Tinos Checks Its Accounts," *Sunday Eleftherotypia*, 13 August 2001, 49.

20 For an excellent analysis of the Papandreou visit and of how the Panagia can be seen as "a symbol of nationhood" in Greece, see Dubisch (1995, 229–49).

21 This is a widely held belief that seems to have begun at the end of antiquity and was subsequently rejected as a paganistic prejudice by the first Fathers of the Church. After the seventeenth century, the Church seems to have accepted this belief, and it introduced a special prayer against the effects (*vaskania*) of the evil eye.

3. What Is Greece?

1 In an article titled "Greece's Identity Crisis" (19 June 2000), *Time* magazine mentioned that the dictator Ioannis Metaxas (1936–1940) initiated the issuance of ID cards. However, a form of Greek ID card preexisted the dictatorship. It is more accurate to say that Metaxas introduced the system of ID cards being issued by the police, which was then carried over after the war as well.

2 The boy was christened a Greek Orthodox Christian in the summer of 2001 by two public figures, the television reporter Makis Triantafyllopoulos and the publisher Odysseas Hadzopoulos, in a ceremony that was widely publicized on all television news broadcasts.

3 These figures concern the public school system. There is also a thriving private primary and secondary school system that charges high tuitions and, in all likelihood, has few such foreign students.

4 C. Katsikas, "100, 000 Foreign Students Sitting at Greek Desks," *Ta Nea*, 13 August 2001, 12–13.

5 The inhabitants of Mani did not pay taxes, refused to honor the order of the state, and often "reappropriated" the public funds of the region of Messinia. They considered Kapodistria responsible for the poor financial situation. Kapodistria imprisoned some members of the large family of Mavromihalaioi. He subsequently refused to see the imprisoned P. Mavromihali, and a misunderstanding occurred when the family interpreted this refusal as an offense. Two of its members then killed him. See Loukos (1988), 375–91.

6 See Papahelas (1998) for a good chronicle of U.S. involvement in Greece.

7 An indication of the seriousness of U.S. involvement can be found in the speech Bill Clinton gave in Athens on 21 November 1999. As noted by the *Washington Post* of that day, "A day after fiery anti-American demonstrations, President

Clinton tried to smooth out a rocky visit to Greece today by acknowledging that the United States was misguided in backing a rightist military coup here 32 years ago." Babington, C. "Clinton Words Cheer Greeks," *Washington Post*, 21 November 1999.
8 For an excellent analysis of the production of national identity in this region, see Karakasidou (1997). With special attention to the role of mothers, see Karakasidou (1996).
9 For example, Cosmas Etolos (1714–1779), a saint of the Orthodox Church, would tell the people he spoke with, "You are not Hellenes, you are not disrespectful, heretics, atheists, but you are reverent orthodox Christians." See Politis (1992, 3, n.3).
10 See an article in the newspaper *Estia* titled "The Refugees and Greece," reprinted in Mavrogordatos (1982, 96).
11 Quoted in Rigos (1992, 229–30). The excerpt was published in the newspaper *To Vema* on 26 June 1978.
12 From a conversation with Neoklis Sarris, who referred to *Lozan Baris Konferansi* (Peace conference of Lausanne), Tutana Klar Belgeler, Turkish translation by Sena Meray (Ankara: University Political Sciences Faculty Publications, 1970), No. 300, unit 1, vol. 1, book 2, pp. 154–55.
13 To see how the definition of who is Greek has varied in the various constitutions of Greece drafted since it became an independent state, see Dimoulis (2000, 35–89).
14 Sarris, private conversation, 24 August 2001.

4. The Demografiko

1 D. Andoniou, "A Pleasant Surprise from the Immigrants," *Kathimerini*, 8 August 2001.
2 For a sample of the more rigorous scientific work in this vein, see Symeonidou (1990); Symeonidou et al. (1992); and Kyriazi (1992). Examples of polemical work in this vein are Emke-Poulopoulou (1994) and Palli-Petralia (1997). For an important example of work opposed to the dominant demografiko narrative, see Kondili (1994). A more polemical counterargument is put forward in a June 1993 pamphlet, "Demografiko: Mia feministiki prosesgisi" (Demografiko: A feminist approach), by the European Forum of Leftists Feminists, published in *Dini* (July 1994), 250–51.
3 The primary sources for the data presented in this section are, unless otherwise noted, the most recent (to 2002) International Family Planning Perspectives for each nation. Its sources are primarily state agencies. In the case of Russia, the statistics are based on figures from the Ministry of Health, although these do not include abortions conducted under the purview of other Ministries. In the case of China, the statistics are also based on figures from the Ministry of

Health, although these do not include data from all of the country's family planning clinics.
4 "More Abortions than Births in Bulgaria," http://www.euthanasia.com/bulgaria.html (accessed 7 October 2000).
5 John Schmid, "In the Former East Bloc, Abortion Remains Norm," *International Herald Tribune*, 16 February 2001.
6 See also Evert Ketting, "Abortion in Europe: The East-West Divide," *Choices* 28(2); and Amelia Gentleman, "Moscow," *Guardian*, 23 September 1999.
7 John Pomfret, "Some Chinese Defy Harsh Approach to Birth Control," *Washington Post*, 11 May 2001.
8 See also J. Dalhburg, "Where Killing Baby Girls 'Is No Big Sin,'" *Toronto Star*, 28 February 1994.
9 "Sex Selection Abortions in China Cause Population Skew," http://www.euthanasia.com/abort-ch.html (accessed 7 October 2000).
10 "India Has Approximately 7 Million Abortions Annually," http://www.euthanasia.com/india2001.html (accessed 7 October 2000).
11 Ian Fisher, "Albanians' Many Children Unnerve Macedonia's Slavs," *New York Times*, 11 August 2001.

5. In the Operating Room

1 This particular dimension to the potential threat I represented wasn't entirely clear to me at the time. After all, to my knowledge, that abortion was legalized in the 1980s was a feat accomplished thanks to the members of the women's movement (its partisan or autonomous branch, depending on who you spoke to). To the extent that legalization was also a symbolic move, conferring status on the groups involved in abortion, including ob/gyns, one might have expected more of an alliance between the groups. In fact, with the exception of very few, mostly female ob/gyns, most doctors exhibited as much anxiety toward feminism and its adherents as anyone. Later, I learned that in fact in mainstream Greek society, the legalization of abortion was often credited to the Panhellenic Socialist Party, which passed the legislation.
2 I visited his office a few times in the ensuing months in an effort to follow up on the generous offers he made to me the day I visited Artemis about helping me with my research by distributing my questionnaires to some of his patients and having them call me to set up interviews. His office was almost entirely covered in white marble. The waiting room had some antique pieces, and music was piped in. The two receptionists' area included a round marble stand, somewhat like a bar, and a computer terminal. His own office also sported a computer terminal on the desk. Of the thirty ob/gyns' offices I visited in the context of my research in Athens, Theodorou's was similar only with Dr. Polakis's, which also had a lot of marble and art, though no music.

3 *Odyssey: The World of Greece*, February/March 1994. Also, in a survey sponsored by *Tempo* (1997), 84 percent of respondents thought the Greek Internal Revenue Service was corrupt and 81 percent thought the doctors of the national health plan were corrupt.
4 Next to the entry *vodi*, the dictionary actually lists ox //dullard, dolt; *vodino*, that which is of *vodi*, is translated as bovine// (meat) beef (*Efstathiadis Group, English Dictionary: English-Greek, Greek-English*, Athens, 1990, 519). In popular speech, however, to say someone is a vodi is to say that he or she is either thick and insensitive, mentally slow, or fat. The *Dictionary of Common Greek* (Foundation of Manoli Triandafyllidi, Aristotelio University of Thessaloniki, 277) also lists a second meaning: being primitive or insensitive. Indeed, to say that someone has done a *hondrada*, literally translated as "something fat," is to say that he or she has been socially inept and done something crass. The term *vodi* is generic for both the male *tavros*, or bull, and *agelada*, or cow. I believe the woman having the abortion was being desexualized in the doctor's joke. While all the connotations of vodi with regard to insensitivity, stupidity, and social ineptitude were salient in the doctor's implied description of the woman on the operating table, I believe that, as in Tasi's consciously sterilized explanation of the joke to me, the main reference was to the woman's weight. I would like to interpret Tasi's lowered voice as an example of her alignment with me, as more of an outsider to sexism, and hence a distancing move between her and the doctor, or her beliefs and the doctor's. Yet, the lowered voice might just as well have been an effort to protect me from losing face for not having "gotten" the joke and an attempt to protect her own status for having brought a visiting researcher who does not understand the simplest joke, hence raising questions about my scientific ability to perform the research in question.
5 This was the price for an abortion in the clinics of the upper-class northern suburbs of Athens in 1994. In 2000 the price is about 100,000 drachmas or $300 U.S.
6 Later, it struck me that there was an anesthetized woman on an operating table and no anesthesiologist, other than the one who was busy with me.
7 SKY, 20 February 1994. 9:45 P.M.

6. Abortion and Nation in the Press

1 This chapter is a modified version of the article "Give Birth for Greece! Abortion and Nation in Letters to the Editor of the Greek Mainstream Press," published in the *Journal of Modern Greek Studies* 16 (1998): 111–38.
2 I refer specifically to abortion's public deployments in the press; these are sharply distinct from the less publicly articulated understandings of many Greek men and women, as I discovered during the fieldwork.
3 This article is based on the analysis of discourses animating the Greek main-

stream press's coverage of the birth rate and abortion throughout 1994, the year of Greece's second term presiding over the Council of the European Union. This chapter presents a detailed rhetorical analysis focused closely on a subsample of six of the letters that most vividly reflect the themes articulated in the majority of those published during the calendar year 1994 in the more rightist *Kathimerini* and the (formally at least) more centrist *Ta Nea*, *To Vema*, and *Eleftherotypia*.

4 There were no letters addressing the demografiko or abortion published in the left-wing *Avgi* or *Rizospasti* between December 1993 and December 1994. However, as I show in the chapter on actual news coverage of the demografiko, the articles on the demografiko that appeared in these papers also reflect a similar religious matrix of nationhood that I find evidence of in the letters to the editor of the right and centrist papers studied here.

5 This chapter offers a set of empirical evidence of the contemporary manifestation of the historical interpenetration of Greek legal-institutional arrangements and the Greek Orthodox Church that, as Elizabeth Prodromou (1994) has argued, has often worked as an obstacle for the "crafting of democracy" in Greece. However, see Prodromou's essay for a solid argument of how there is no inherent incompatibility between Eastern Orthodoxy and "pluralist" democracy. Indeed, as I suggest in the conclusion, even with regard to the notion of Greece as a religious nation-state that is in circulation in the demografiko discourses, were it openly acknowledged, this semantic domain might in fact be strategically reworked so as to greatly facilitate some (and productively reformulate others) of the current national objectives, including the modernization seen as a prerequisite for both EU full membership and a properly functioning democratic state. For a careful discussion of the current relationship between the Greek Orthodox Church and political culture, see Stavrou (1995). For evidence of a Greek Orthodox configuration of nationhood underlying Greek legislation, see Pollis (1992).

6 It is not surprising, then, that much of the cultural studies work concerned with the politics of representing nation and nationality in various geopolitical contexts has centered on literary texts. For a good collection of North American work on stories of nation that helped initiate this line of inquiry, see Bhabha (1990). In his introduction, Bhabha puts the question guiding the work of this collection: "If the ambivalent figure of the nation is a problem of its transitional history, its conceptual indeterminacy, its wavering between vocabularies, then what effect does this have on narratives and discourses that signify a sense of 'nationness': . . . the comfort of social belonging, the hidden injuries of class; the customs of taste; the powers of political affiliation; the sense of social order, the sensibility of sexuality; the blindness of bureaucracy, the strait insight of institutions; the quality of justice, the common sense of injustice; the langue of the law and the parole of the people" (2). In this chapter, as in the rest of the book, I attempt to tease out "the ambivalent figure of the nation" of Greece as it lies

quietly within one of the more intimate aspects of a public discourse centrally concerned with "the sensibility of sexuality."

One of the first pieces of work to explicitly address the enlistments of different understandings of sexuality in the foundation of the modern nation-state is George L. Mosse's (1985) historical analysis of nationalism and sexuality. For a comprehensive and nuanced consideration of this nexus in a variety of national, primarily literary, contexts, see Parker et al. (1992). Attentive to a broader range of material, and concerned specifically with the intersection of gender, nation, and reproduction, are Ginsburg and Rapp (1995).

7 Indeed, Anderson claims that "the newspaper is merely an 'extreme form' of the book, a book sold on a colossal scale, but of ephemeral popularity" (1991, 34). Moreover, he suggests that "the newspaper reader, observing exact replicas of his own paper being consumed by his subway, barbershop, or residential neighbours, is continually reassured that the imagined world is visibly rooted in everyday life. As with Noli Me Tangere, fiction seeps quietly and continuously into reality, creating that remarkable confidence of community in anonymity which is the hallmark of modern nations" (35–36).

8 For an excellent example of analysis focused on this question using the case of China, see Anagnost (1997).

9 For an account of the historical specificities of the development of a public sphere in Greece, see Tsoukalas (1984). For an incisive analysis of the theoretical nexus of the mass media and ideology specifically in the context of Greek nationalism, see Doxiadis (1993).

10 For an overview of the particular aspects of traditional political culture that are singled out as forces interfering with Greece's current project of modernization, see Charalambis and Demertzis (1993). Also, Pollis (1977) offers a glimpse of the cultural forces of "tradition" at work in contemporary Greek politics.

11 For an excellent analysis of these two types of nationalism, and a thorough overview of the literature relating to both, see Lekkas (2001).

12 Examples that stand out for the care with which "tradition" and "modernity" are used as terms guiding an investigation into Greece's present are Mouzelis (1986) and Papadopoulos (1989). Examples of insightful work on other, less overtly political aspects of Greek culture that use a notion of tradition to study identity and the relationship of the present to a Greek past, in addition to Herzfeld (1991a), are Cowan (1990) and Stewart (1991).

13 Dimitiri Tzoumas, "Appropriate Anxiety," *Kathimerini*, 12 February 1994.

14 In modern Greek, Ellada, the word for Greece, is feminine, as is *hora*, the word for "country." *Kratos* and *ethnos*, the words for "state" and "nation," respectively, are both neuter. The implications of the genderedness of "Greece" as female are important; however, a consistent pointed reference to Greece as female in English translation would overly exaggerate the gender's significance in a modern Greek linguistic context. Thus, precisely in the interests of accuracy of transla-

tion for the discourse analysis performed here, from here on I refer to Greece in the appropriate English form without indicating its genderedness in Greek. Nonetheless, I hope that the Greekless reader will remember that, for Greeks, Greece is at some level a female category.

15 The writer is referring to a flurry of sensationalized incidents that occurred in early 1994 regarding satanic worship and its enlistment of violence against both human and nonhuman beings in several neighborhoods on the outskirts of Athens.

16 The specific referent for this is unclear. The term "invisible centers abroad" has been popular, although more so in the past than in the present, and it is especially used to refer to U.S. or specifically CIA influence on Greek political affairs. Here, however, situated as it is in a distinctly religious discourse, it seems to refer to hotbeds breeding the seeds of decay of Greece's *spiritual* integrity. This testifies to the widespread cultural currency of the historically produced preoccupation with the threat of dangerous and not easily discernible intervention that occurs "under the guise" (as the judge puts it) "of mutual aid and philanthropy."

17 A group of specifically pro-life activists, although of very limited membership, has appeared on occasion when legislative reforms were being planned (circa 1986) and has made use of this type of rhetoric.

18 Takis Karathanasis, "Abortions . . ." *Kathimerini*, 18 March 1994.

19 Father Dionysos, "No to Abortions," *Kathimerini*, 17 September 1994.

20 Nikolaos Tritsarolis, "The Low Birth Rate," *Ta Nea*, 7 June 1994.

21 Nikos Athanasopoulos, "Greece Today," *Eleftherotypia*, 5 June 1994.

22 Aristidis Soumakis, "The Aging Population," *Eleftherotypia*, 15 June 1994.

23 Many of the letters published were concerned primarily with proposing various economic measures to fight the demografiko by supporting both the family in general and the many-childrened family (*politeknoi*) in particular. Consider, for example, Daoulas (1994); the letter asks for state-run day care centers throughout the country that will work from 7 A.M. to 5 P.M., for higher subsidies for mothers with many children, for low-interest loans to young couples trying to buy a first house, and for a strict application of the law of "coservice" for couples working in both the public and the private sectors. Prefacing this excerpt from the letter, the editor writes, "Measures to confront the demographic problem confronting Greece are taken below" (Yannis Daoulas, "The Demografiko," *Eleftherotypia*, 22 December 1994).

24 This paradox is resolved in Greek family planning discourse via the somewhat nebulous strategy of emphasizing that the use of contraceptives is important to prevent abortions and "therefore" to permit each couple to more efficiently "plan," rather than to limit, their child bearing.

25 For evidence of the same assumption of Greek nationhood as religious in Greek law, see Pollis (1992), despite the fact that Greek law does postulate Muslims and Jews as "recognized minorities" (Stavros 1995, 9).

7. Navigating the Night

1 Part 3 and the last chapter of this book are based on my fieldwork as a participant-observer at the prototype for Greece's network of state-run Family Planning Centers at the District General Hospital of Athens, Alexandra's, during 1994. In particular, I draw from in-depth interviews, and ususally extensive follow-up conversations, conducted with ninety women visiting the Center and with thirty women I met privately, either as prior friends, through friends, or through other interviewees or via referrals from the ob/gyns I interviewed.

2 For a thorough overview of work on the nation-gender intersection, specifically with regard to the link between nationalism and sexism and from the perspective of sociology and political science, see Yuval-Davis (1996, 1997); and Yuval-Davis and Anthias (1989). For an eclectic interdisciplinary approach to the zone of contact between women and the nation in the context of transnationalism and globalization, see Kaplan, Alarcon, and Moallem (1999). For a cross-cultural survey and interesting analysis of the specific junction of nationalism, religion, and women's bodies, see Friedland (2002). In this survey of specifically religious nationalism and "its preoccupation with both eroticized women's bodies and monies out of national control," Friedland argues that "religious nationalisms invest the human body, its erotic and generative qualities, with enormous import." In particular, using a macrolevel comparative analysis of religious nationalisms in several countries, he argues, "Remaking the collective territorial body and the individual human body are *not only* parallel discursive orders, *but linked ones*" (396; my emphasis). In effect, this article argues persuasively for the very same type of connection that my book does, though using a top-down macrolevel comparative approach. In many ways, my book contributes to the same project while also seeking to illuminate the depth with which this occurs via a microlevel discursive analysis of the dynamics through which this process transpires at a visceral level, using the case of modern Greece. The Friedland article is exciting both for the breadth of its thesis and for the insight with which particular intimate connections are identified, and argued for, among the nation, religion, and the body (as well as money) at a theoretical level and in the concrete empirical political realities of several countries. In this sense, it also offers very strong support for the thesis of this book.

3 The "individual" is itself a political category that is socially, culturally, and historically constructed. The heart of the project of this book is an analysis of power at the site of identity formation in Europe of late modernity by mapping the ways contemporary Greek subjectivization, like other nations', only partially congeals in this particular form. As Foucault (1980c, 98) states, "The individual is not to be conceived as a sort of elementary nucleus, a primitive atom, a multiple and inert material on which power comes to fasten or against which it happens to strike, and in so doing subdues or crushes individuals. In certain bodies, certain

gestures, certain discourses, certain desires, come to be identified and constituted as individuals. The individual, that is, is not the vis-à-vis of power; it is, I believe, one of its prime effects. The individual is an effect of power, and at the same time, or precisely to the extent to which it is that effect, it is the element of its articulation. The individual which power has constituted is at the same time its vehicle." Throughout this book, I track the multiple and often vexed operation of power in the process of negotiating the gendered self, the other, and the nation in Greece at the present.

4 For a vivid description of this economy of symbols and an intriguing analysis of them, see Seremetakis (1991) and Stewart (1991).

5 For an incisive analysis of the ways nature itself is socially constructed, and a thorough review of the relevant literature, see Macnaghten and Urry (1998). In sketching the parameters of a key part of their project, the authors state, "We turn now to a brief account of the history of the relationship between nature and society, in order to understand better how historically the social and the natural were torn apart and some of the different forms taken by this dichotomisation" (7).

6 A lecture given by Judith Butler, Harvard University, Boston, spring 1998, addressed this concept. Her book *Excitable Speech* (1997a) offers a powerful analysis of how speech and personhood intersect in the United States at the present, often explosively, and in so doing implicitly raises questions about linear and static notions of citizenship. In a related vein, the interanimation of sex and citizenship in the United States at the present is examined via a critical reading of dominant images and narratives of sex and citizenship in the U.S. public sphere in Berlant (1997). For an exploration of the layered construction of citizenship in tandem with national identity in the context of Europe, from a macrosociological perspective, see Soysal (1994).

7 Braidotti's (1994) notion of nomadic subjects resonates deeply for my understanding of my identity as researcher of this project.

8 With regard to the argument I make concerning the investment of the practice of eating meat with nationalist connotations, consider the words of the following song, presented on the fairly oppositional television show of Makis Triandafyllopoulos, on channel Alpha, on 18 March 2002. The singer, Giannis Manoulidis, who is not well-known, prefaced the song, titled "The Greek (Man)," by saying that it is dedicated to all meat-eaters. The words of the main verse are as follows: "If you stop the Greek from eating *kokoretsi* [a type of meat], hearts and spleens, if you stop the Greek from eating the little heads [*ta kefalakia*], then he will become an alien and he will look like a tourist. *Tote tha gini allodapos kai tha moizei me touristas.*" Certainly, this song is an attempt to talk back to the recent European Union edict that formally banned the sale of internal organ meat dishes, quite popular with some Greeks, in an effort to contain the spread of mad cow disease. In this sense, it is oppositionally positioned toward larger structures of power that are linked to the project of moderniza-

tion. Thus, at one level, the figure of "the Greek" is being used in the generically masculine to refer to all Greeks, men and women, and this verse makes clear the permeation of nationalism throughout civil society, including the daily practice of eating. Yet, I suggest that the song also illuminates how nationalist discourse is intertwined with a historically specific narrative about appropriate masculinity in particular, at the perhaps unexpected site of eating organ meat, "real" meat dishes, to yield a racist result. The song may be seen as arguing that a Greek man who does not eat heads, hearts, and spleens and kokoretsi symbolically betrays his nationality and is transformed into the implicitly feminized category of alien, or non-Greek. That is, the song may show both that eating particular meat dishes for men and women *alike* is a marker of appropriate or normative Greek nationality and, implicitly, that masculinity *especially* is linked to this practice as a sign of appropriate Greekness. In daily practice, the consumption of the type of meat described in the song is gendered, much as there is a gender coding of drinks. For more on the latter, see Cowan (1991).

9 In an astute observation that applies to social science in general, Tsing (1993, 119) states, "In assessing local knowledge, anthropologists emphasize the said rather than the unsaid of dominant community discourses. Yet a central challenge for feminist anthropologists is to position the cultural statements of their informants politically. This involves paying attention to competing gender formulations variously situated in relation to local groups and hierarchies." In a similar vein, Warren and Bourque (1985, 261) claim, "Understanding dominance and muting requires a broader analysis of the political, economic and institutional contexts in which reality is negotiated."

10 The issue of absence, absence of specific words or of action, and how to interpret it is very important. In many ways, this entire project, exploring abortion in Greece of late modernity, involves the study of crucial absences and listening carefully to different forms of silence. With regard to the specifically Greek gendered dimension of this, see Herzfeld (1991b). He states, "But doing little can also be a dramatic performance: the criterion is whether people notice it. Thus, the difficulty of articulating a poetics of Greek womanhood reflects, not so much any lack of poeticity in Greek women, but, rather, the assumption that poeticity lies only in the bombastic and the verbal. Absences are harder to interpret than presences. Friedl (1985 [1967], 45–46), for example, notes that in Vasilika ritual transvestism at carnival was almost exclusively male-to-female. The women's poetic may indeed have consisted in the extent to which they did not participate; but, since such a stance would register only as an absence, it could hardly satisfy an androcentric canon of proof that demands presence as its main criterion" (82). Indeed, Herzfeld's work in general helps to direct attention to the significance of what is *not* said in Athenian women's responses and hence avoids reinscribing "Greek androcentrism—and its reproduction as verbocentrism—[that] appear as a complex linguistic symbolism"(82). Herzfeld asks, "How, then, do we avoid searching only for *verbalized* notions of female-

ness and its production . . . and how do we seek meaning in what from a male perspective is 'inarticulate' and 'female'?"(83). The path he proposes, which I follow in the subsequent analysis of Athenian women's narratives, is opened via the notion of "mutedness." Preserving his focus on an exploration of Greek femaleness, where my project is to chart Greek femaleness in conjunction with Greek *nationalness,* Herzfeld continues, "There are also female discourses that shy away from verbality altogether (e.g., Messick 1987). These are, in E. Ardener's (1975) sense, 'muted' ideologies. 'Muted' does not necessarily mean 'verbally silent,' since mutedness may take the form of a masking of alternative ideologies with the external signs of androcentric values (i.e., speech). Muting may be semantic rather than lexical" (83). Herzfeld's solution to the methodological challenge presented by the above is to adopt "a contextual approach" (83), which involves interweaving meanings gleaned from disparate social settings in order to interpret the different forms of silence he observes. The challenge this approach seeks to meet is, in a nutshell, "How does one *interpret* without reducing to mere words, and so transcend the effects of history" (84) that are shared in common not only by anthropologists, as Herzfeld states, but by all social scientists and the people they study?

11 The unstated can have disparate political charges. What is not said may be so because "it goes without saying" or is marked as "natural," much as the habitus of different cultures are, according to Bourdieu (1990, 1995). In this sense, silence can be fully hegemonic and supportive of a particular regime of truth. This is the case with much of what is *not* stated by the women I spoke with about the nation and about aspects of normative femininity. Yet, as is demonstrated in the final chapter presenting their responses to the direct question concerning their opinion of the demografiko, the silencing of the significance of narratives about national identity in the accounts of contraceptive use explored here does not index an unproblematized endorsement of the dominant matrix of nationhood in Greece at the present. Nor, certainly, does it mark its absence as a constitutive category for the formation of subjectivity and identity. That silence can be the site of this resistance, as well as others, especially aimed at normative femininity, is also evident, again often in what is unstated or "mutedly" stated, both in this chapter and in the next, where the positioning of abortion in the field of power of heterosexual Greek love relationship is examined. The question of silence and its political significance is vast. At a theoretical level, this issue is linked to the deeper problem of interpretation and hermeneutics. As E. D. Hirsch argues, "The term 'meaning' refers to the whole verbal meaning of a text, and 'significance' to textual meaning in relation to a larger context, i.e. another mind, another era, a wider subject matter, an alien system of values, and so on. In other words, 'significance' is textual meaning as related to some context, indeed any context, beyond itself" (1976, 2–3). Put another way, "If the letter did perfectly realize the spirit, no problems of interpretation would exist. But the great diversity of interpretations compels us to recognize that the letter

must be an imperfect representation of meaning. The intuitionist must therefore be right to insist upon transcending the letter. And how can you transcend the letter except by spiritual communion at a level beyond the letter?" (21).

Meanwhile, empirical studies ranging from Gaventa's (1980) analysis of acquiescence in the Appalachian Valley and why revolution did not occur there, to Basso's (1979) study of how silence is used as a strategic defense against the powerful by Western Apache men in order to confuse and exclude white outsiders, and Bauman's (1983) exploration of how, for the English Quaker men and women of the seventeenth century, the refusal to speak when others expected them to was a form of political protest, all demonstrate the importance of what is not stated, or, at times, even consciously thought. For an excellent and important analysis of what is not stated at a pivotal site of the United States at the present, and how larger patterns of power are both implicated and reflected in silence, rendering it a topos of primary political significance laden with meaning, and thus "data" that are crucial, if also methodologically challenging, see Fine (1992).

The specifically gendered dimensions of silence are also being vigorously explored across the disciplines of the social sciences and humanities. For a brief overview of the issues raised by this literature, see Gal (2002). In different ways, my book contributes to this investigation of the political inflection, uses, and effects of what is not stated, though it is performed. Turning to the specifically gendered aspects of silence, Fine states, "If women's bodies display the individually embodied and negotiated politics of gender, a look at socially constructed shadows and silences reveals those collective spaces in which women's stories have been buried and repressed, and in which women's resistances have been fermenting" (1992, 97).

My attempt throughout this book is to plot the fractures and deflections of these resistances as well as their tactical alliances with narratives and discursive practices of a regime of truth that, at other sites, is vexed or, occasionally, openly resisted. As Tsing (1993) states concerning her account of an ethnographic incident she witnessed among Meratus Dayaks, a group in the rainforest of Indonesia, involving "an ambiguous neonatal death" and "not an infanticide... [as] infanticide is not a locally relevant category," in many ways, indeed most importantly ways unrelated to abortion per se but related more to understandings of the nation-gender nexus, this book is also "about practices at the edge between silence and speech, the area of inchoate understandings without fully developed, public articulations" (115).

12 In describing his vision of analyses of power that should be prioritized, Foucault (1980c) foregrounds the occasional invisibility of power, as noted, and states that "in thinking of the mechanisms of power, I am thinking rather of its capillary form of existence, the point where power reaches into the very grain of individuals, touches their bodies and inserts itself into their actions and attitudes, their discourses, learning processes and everyday lives"(39). My effort

throughout is to use the case of abortion in Greece to track this very subtle, in many ways invisible, and yet vital operation of power.

For an excellent discussion of how nationalist narratives viscerally shape identity in northern Cyprus, becoming embodied in cultural artifacts and memory, see Killoran (1998). She states, "Nationality is inserted into the 'families' shared blood,' the nation's 'sacred soil,' and a national 'family's' metaphorical genealogy" (164). An important part of her argument concerns the disparate strategic uses of Turkish Cypriot blood similarity to that of Greek Cypriots. That is, a particular medical representation of blood similarity is deployed to construct, on the one hand, ethnic homogeneity by Greek Cypriot officials and, on the other, ethnic, national difference by Turkish Cypriot officials. Killoran writes, "A 'national identity,' be it dominant or oppositional, constructed through the body as memory, works to bind individuals to the imagined community by exploiting their sense of self located in the private realm of the home, the family, and the body. Thus, a present sense of self constituted in the 'past' is linked to the 'eternal' image of the nation. *When the voices of nationalist discourses seep into the naturalized world of the body, the voice of nationalism itself remains unquestioned*" (167; my emphasis). In other words, Killoran suggests both that nationalism is experienced at a very deep level of social identity and that it is rarely invoked explicitly, even as it may infuse virtually every aspect of daily life. My analysis in this book reveals that the same holds true in Greece and thus supports the broader claims that nationalist discourse shapes the body.

13 The Korber Foundation, Germany, conducted the research during 1994–95. The sample consisted of 31,000 schoolchildren, fifteen years old, from twenty-six countries. The interview measure contained 280 questions. The Greek portion of this research project was coordinated by Professors Anna Frangoudaki and Thaleia Dragona of Athens University. The results were reported by Mihas in *Eleftherotypia*, 7 July 1997.

14 The researchers coordinating the project are cited as Angela Kindervater and Bodo Von Borries of the Netherlands; see Mihas (1997, 20).

15 Especially after 9/11 there seems to be a resurgence of nationalist sentiment permeating civil society and formal public discourse alike. For an example of the types of "rituals of patriotism" that have reemerged in the United States at the present, see O'Leary and Platt (2001).

16 Invited lecture, Columbia University, New York, spring 1997.

17 The popularity of Alexiou in Greece is uncontestable. She appeals to a very broad base and her music has involved other very popular musicians for the past three decades. As an indication of her popularity, consider how she is presented on one of the main Web sites for rebetika, a genre of music she started her career with: "Many people feel Haris Alexiou to be the most accomplished female vocalist to date. In fact, she is probably one of the most accomplished singers Greece has ever produced.... Often billed and promoted as 'The Female Voice of Greece,' she is what we might classify in the USA as the

archetypical 'Torch Singer.' . . . Alexiou has a voice that bespeaks a rare and understated feminine elegance, as well as a natural and unadorned type of sophistication, that strikes you like a silent thunderstorm when you first hear it" (www.rebetikorow.com; accessed 14 November 2001).

For external confirmation of both the quality and national appeal of Alexiou, as well as an implicit indication of the enmeshment of a particular religious discourse in her songs, see "Modern Greek Music Finally Breaks into American Market," *Christian Science Monitor,* 24 July 1998. After describing how difficult it is for ethnic musicians to enter the U.S. market, the author says, "Leading the campaign into the American market is Haris Alexiou, Greece's reigning goddess of song, whose velvet-brushed, soul-saturated voice is regarded as *the national carrier of contemporary Greek music.* As the country's most successful bridge between music that is at once ancient and modern, folkloric and experimental, she is being introduced to the United States via the redistribution of the successful 1992 Polygram release entitled 'Di Efhon' (With Blessings)—a sleek, edgy work. Despite the new attention and established success in France and Holland, Ms. Alexiou sees a larger challenge in selling Greek music abroad for reasons other than just obscure language or unusual rhythms. 'Greek music takes itself very seriously,' she said in a recent interview. 'It is the music of memory to us. All of our tragedies, all of our modern political problems run through it like lifeblood. You find this essence as deep in the melody of the music as you do in the language, and that is not easily translatable.' Alexiou is part of that collective memory, having grown up in a musical age of the great Greek composers such as Mikis Theodorakis, Manos Hadjidakis, and Manos Loizos, during the country's politically turbulent '60s and '70s. It was then a Greek singer's ultimate honor to be summoned by one of these titans to perform their works. Alexiou ended up working with all of them, shaping a three-decade career into an encyclopedic showcase of contemporary Greek music—from pure Greek folk to fusions of Western jazz and Middle Eastern influences." This article's conclusion also sheds light on how Alexiou herself views the music she performs: "For Alexiou, Greek music, in spite of its 'difficulties,' is a sure thing for anyone who ventures into it, Greek or non-Greek. 'Once you listen to Greek music, you cannot help but be brought in closer and closer to it,' she says. 'Then you find that you can never leave it. It is always with you.'"

18 For examples of work done in this vein, on themes similar to those pursued in my book, that is, work that involves a close critical reading of often very minute cultural fragments to generate advances in theory, see Grossberg, Nelson, and Treichler (1992); McClintock, Mufti, and Shohat (1997); and Parker et al. (1992). For an interesting Greek collection of essays that analyze elements of specifically literary texts of various cultures to explore the conjunction of nationalism and sexuality, see Kalogeras and Pastourmatzi (1996); for a focus on Greek texts, see especially therein Chryssanthopoulos (55–62); Leontsini (135–46); and

Yates (343–50). The above texts are examples of strong and suggestive work that contributes to the understanding of the junction of narratives about the nation, gender, and identity by closely analyzing minute textual fragments.

19 Cavafy, "Thermopylae," in Keeley and Sherrard (1981, 6).
20 For example, Gagnon and Parker (1995), writing about what they call the "sexological" period (from 1890 to 1980) in sexuality research, note that nearly "all theorists of this period agree . . . that sex was a natural force that existed in opposition to civilization, culture or society" (7). Gagnon and Parker argue that the "sexological paradigm" started to be displaced by the 1960s (8). See also Weeks (1985). Gagnon (1990) applies the theory of sexual scripting as a way of analyzing critically "cultural, interpersonal and mental aspects of sexuality" and demonstrates the social constructionist approach wherein sexuality is no longer based on internal drives but is a specific articulation of historical and social circumstances. For a methodical consideration of the construction of sexuality in a specifically political context, see Evans (1993). See Vance (1991) for a consideration of the historically specific dimensions of the study of sexuality.

It might be argued that the groundbreaking book for the scientific study of the full depth of the fundamentally political "construction" of sexuality was Michel Foucault's rigorously empirical study of the historical articulations of sexuality in *The History of Sexuality*, volumes 1, 2, and 3. He persuasively argued that the persistent representation of sexuality as a sphere that is external to the social and the political is itself a profoundly political strategy. Among other important arguments advanced by this work, even the notion of "the liberation" of sex from a formerly repressive regime, characterizing the 1960s, which several of the authors above argue for as "the turning point" in the study of sexuality, itself operates as a technology of power that simultaneously defines, circumscribes, and patrols forms of behavior deemed appropriate for the domain of sexuality as well as constituting different types of political subjects. Echoing the typical consideration of sexuality and, at once, critiquing it, Foucault states, "Sexuality must not be described as a stubborn drive, by nature alien and of necessity disobedient to a power which exhausts itself trying to subdue it and often fails to control it entirely. It appears rather as an especially dense transfer point for relations of power: between men and women, young people and old people, parents and offspring, teachers and students, priests and laity, *an administration and a population*. Sexuality is not the most intractable element in power relations, but rather one of those endowed with the greatest instrumentality: useful for the greatest number of maneuvers and capable of serving as a point of support, as a linchpin, for the most varied strategies" (1980b, 103; my emphasis).

21 "O Ellinas," lyrics by Haris Alexiou, *Kratai Hronia afti i Kolonia* (This cologne lasts for years), Th. Mikroutsikos, L. Nikolakopoulou, H. Alexiou, March 1990, Minos-Emi.

22 See, for example, *Ta Nea,* 6 February 1995 and *To Vema,* 17 February 1995.
23 The full verse is "Since you continue to love the gray seas, since you can look at burned forests, since you listen to Tsitsani and it shatters you, this means that you continue not to have changed! Since you have not been won by your loneliness, since you are not ashamed to shed a tear in front of me, since you continue to listen to the clarinet and be moved, this means that you continue not to have changed! *Come my love, come. Let us make another Greek . . . with song to forget, her mistakes to be forgiven, since Greece injures us as nobody else.* (refrain)" ("O Ellinas," lyrics by Haris Alexiou, my translation).
24 Many thanks to Chandra Mukerji for her insight on this.
25 For a historical and ethnographic analysis of the connection between lived sexuality and economic, and implicitly political, social forces, see Schneider and Schneider (1996). That so-called macrostructures are intrinsically linked not only to an abstractly defined microlevel of social reality, but even to the very experience of pleasure in sexual behavior is empirically demonstrated in this discussion of the change in fertility rates among four classes of Sicilian inhabitants. Though national identity and narratives of nationhood or nationalism are not examined as factors per se, much of the evidence presented illuminates their impact and, in this sense as well, paves the way for a concerted analysis of the interanimation of the nation and the body such as that which I engage in here. I refer to the Schneiders' work on fertility in more detail in the section on the use of "the days" along with withdrawal.
26 The most recent survey also measured 5.8 percent infertile, 3.9 percent pregnant, 9.5 percent not sexually active (no intercourse during the four weeks prior to the interview). These categories are not noted for the earlier surveys. Thus, H. Symeonidou (UN-Greece, 2002) additionally reports that of the most recent sample, "a rather high percentage (24.8) of women, although non-pregnant and sexually active, were not using any contraceptive method."
27 The age coordinates given here for the 1983 sample are stated as 15–49, as I quote here, whereas on page 1 of the UN-Greece 2002 report the age of the 1983 sample is stated as 15–44 years (as I quoted in the first paragraph of this section on the national statistics).
28 Indeed, anal and oral sex are typically excluded from national surveys of birth control.
29 The data presented here are reported in Symeonidou et al. (2000). It is important to take note of the authors' clarification that the comparison being made is between 1983 and "after 1983," rather than 1997, which was the year of the second survey. The reason given for this in this book presentation of the same two surveys, 1983 and 1997, constituting the bulk of the discussion in the UN Greece report, is that the way the question was posed—"What is the main method of contraception that you used after 1983"—does not permit comparisons with 1997 (Symeonidou et al. 2000, 64). It is also explained here that the

question was purposefully posed in this way because a large number of the women of the 1997 follow-up sample had already reached menopause and therefore did not use any method of contraception.

30 In the UN-Greece 2002 report, the results of the 1983 survey are referred to as a percentage of those respondents reporting use of some form of contraception, whereas the results of the 1997 survey seem to be reported in terms of the percentage *of the total sample*, including those who report no use of contraception. This may explain the lack of correspondence between some of the numbers appearing in this table and those referred to in the report, even though they arise from the same survey.

31 This figure is actually reported as being 22.9 percent in the UN-Greece (2002) report authored by Symeonidou, page 135. As I mention above, the discrepancy is likely due to the fact that the UN-Greece report refers to the results of the 1997 survey in terms of the percentages of those who reported *some* use of contraception. However, it is important to note that the report itself states, "The national fertility survey of 1983 showed a proportion of 80 per cent of women using contraception at the time of the survey. A large segment of these women relied on traditional methods such as withdrawal (62.2 per cent) and condom (22.9) (Symeonidou et al. 1997)" (43). In the discussion of the same survey found in the book by Symeonidou and her colleagues (2000), the table I have reprinted here illustrates the percentage of the entire sample that reported use of one or another method; perhaps this is why it indicates that use of withdrawal for the 1983 survey is 35.1 percent and of condom 27.4 percent.

32 Another issue affecting all these statistics has to do with how changes in mores may affect the rate of reporting different birth control methods and, certainly, abortion. This is similar to the phenomenon wherein efforts to challenge the stigma attached to rape may have resulted in reports of higher frequencies of rape without its being ascertainable whether there were in fact more or, conceivably, fewer rapes occurring in a particular area of the United States.

33 In almost all accounts of the use of withdrawal, there was explicit reference to it as a method used during "the dangerous days," thus as a *co-method* with the days.

34 I would like to acknowledge the anonymous third reviewer of my book for Duke University Press, for alerting me to the significance of this work with regard to a comparative understanding of the politics of withdrawal. In particular, the Schneiders' early 1980s research on fertility and birth control practices in Sicily powerfully illuminates the existence of a deep connection between nationally and internationally inflected projects of modernization and the most private sexual practices of the body politic, though finding that withdrawal in Sicily from the 1930s functioned in importantly different ways than it does in Greece at the present. See Schneider and Schneider (1995, 177–94; 1996).

35 This is indicative of what, as I argue throughout this book, are the multi-

valenced meanings abortion acquires in contemporary Athens. Whereas at one level, for example, abortion can be deployed as a sign of the modernity of the woman who undergoes it, at another, as I argue in this chapter, it also operates as a sign of a "traditionally" Greek hardiness and desire to resist. At yet another level, as I argue in the next chapter, an unplanned pregnancy and the subsequent abortion can be used strategically by the couple to test one another's love and to solicit caring. At the same time, however, at the macro level we see that demografiko discourses clearly configure abortion as a negative act that ranges from being a sign of the immaturity and "backwardness" of Greek women to being out-and-out treasonous. Finally, at the level of local community and that of family-planning midwives and other personnel, as I show in the last chapter of this part of the book, abortion, especially repeat abortion, clearly also continues to carry an aura of shame and a stigma. Thus, for Chryssa, like many of the women I spoke with, the fact that abortion is not formally considered a good act, or even a neutral act, seems to weigh more heavily and so she refrains from disclosing the full number of abortions that she has had.

36 It was actually fairly common among the women I interviewed to refer to "other women" or "a friend" who had had more than ten abortions. In my sample of ninety women with medical records reporting two or more abortions performed at the clinic I was stationed in, in addition to another thirty women external to the clinic, there were only three who actually told me that they themselves had had eight or more abortions.

37 In the interests of meeting this chapter's objective of presenting a nuanced and yet thorough reading of the recurring issues involved in the women's accounts of each of an array of practices that emerge as birth control methods in Greece, this section on the days with withdrawal focuses on two fairly lengthy excerpts from the interviews that most concisely concentrate the recurring issues expressed by all the women who spoke with me about withdrawal. More interview material concerning withdrawal that further fleshes out the claims discussed here is presented in the last chapter of part 3, where the costs associated with abortion are the primary focus.

38 For an excellent analysis of the connection between liberal democracy and culturally specific discursive practices of reason and of counting, see Walkerdine (1988).

39 The thirty women I interviewed in a private sterility clinic during the summer of 1994, a sample whose interviews I do not analyze in this book, *all* stated that they considered conception a divine gift.

40 Interestingly, with regard to the Pill, a recent study presented at the second Panhellenic Conference of Family Planning comments that it is a form of birth control that Greek women "don't trust because they believe it causes health problems." Moreover, the condom is seen as problematic, as it is often "not used correctly"; for every one hundred couples who reported using the condom,

there are apparently ten to fifteen pregnancies. This study reports that only 5 percent of Greek women take the Pill, whereas the respective figure reported for "European women" is 30–35 percent. Overall, this study reportedly concluded that Greek women seem to prefer the so-called traditional methods of birth control—the condom, withdrawal, and "the calculation of the fertile days"—instead of embracing the modern methods like the Pill and IUD. The conference this study was presented at took place in Athens on 18–20 February 2000. The unpublished findings were reported in the newspapers *Kathimerini,* 16 February 2000 and *Ta Nea,* 16 February 2000.

41 Herzfeld comments, "A woman—mirroring a reciprocal ambiguity in male attitudes—may castigate men in general or use the generic follies of men to berate her husband or son; but she will stand strongly beside him in the face of a threat from other men. People may seriously mean what they say about being categorically inferior or deficient when talking to outsiders; but these same utterances may also be directed ironically at the group, in which case they convey virtually the opposite implications to its members" (1991b, 80).

42 The role played by the influence of Greek Orthodoxy on this may be significant in another way as well. For example, it has been argued (Iossifides 1991, 153) that for Greek women who have joined a monastery as nuns, "the dichotomy between the body and the soul, the material and the spiritual, is not clear-cut." To the extent that this is an effect of Greek Orthodox doctrine, and that such doctrine permeates Greek popular culture in different ways, the establishment of boundaries in contemporary, ostensibly secular aspects of life in Greece is further problematized.

43 Taped session on contraception at the Center with four women who had come for the lesson, the midwife Mrs. D, and I.

8. The Couple as Mother

1 Though not seen as "an optic device," as I suggest it should be, there is one significant exception that in fact does approach this aspect of abortion: Kristen Luker's (1975) study of "abortion and the decision not to contracept." In this very insightful examination of the factors involved in repeat abortion for women in the United States, Luker argues that the phenomenon of repeat abortion occurs through a fairly intricate process of rational-choice decision making. While I follow suit in arguing that there is a rationale to repeat abortion in Greece, my analysis also advances a critique of reason and its presupposition by Western science.

2 Nathanail was especially famous for her film role as a woman living her last love affair before finding out she is dying of cancer. The song opening the film became famous and continues to evoke misty eyes today. The refrain is "One evening, my Virgin Mary will come to find me, down at the seashore."

9. Abortion, Pain, and Agency

1 For an analysis of how sexuality and prestige, as components of power, are intertwined in Greek sex, see Zinovieff (1991).
2 In this discussion of his ethnographic work in Crete, Herzfeld argues that Greek women's "self-restraint and frequent displays of submission to male dominance do conform to the model in that women *creatively deform* their submission. They perform their lack of performance, as it were. In so doing, they may also implicitly deflect the appearance of submission to their own ends" (1991b, 81). The question thus becomes, "How then does one begin to elicit the subversive strategies of female silence? How does one interpret without reducing to mere words, and so transcend the effects of history shared by anthropologists and the people anthropologists study?" (84). Herzfeld goes on to comment that "this, ultimately, is the local women's dilemma. Unless and until they are enabled to verbalize their resentment in a public context, whatever subversion they bring to their discourse will, in the public world, have the force of the proverbial tree falling in an uninhabited forest" (95). Throughout the book we see many instances of women silently, and parodically, performing their submission to the traditional hierarchy. In this chapter, we see how the interviews sometimes provided them with an opportunity to begin to make their resistance more explicit.
3 This follows also from the notion that "from the women's point of view what makes sex 'natural,' pleasurable, and desirable is that it leaves the door to conception open." Speculating on the high rate of abortion in Greece, Papataxiarchis states, "Sexuality in itself, sealed off from the prospect of pregnancy by contraceptive devices, is seen as undesirable" (1991, 225).
4 The formal medical term for abortion, carried over from an older, more formal dialect of Greek is "artificial miscarriage," or *tehniti ektrosi*.
5 The zone of contact between the body and specifically religious discourses is made most explicit in a different set of interviews I conducted, focused on women visiting Athens's most prestigious private center for assisted reproduction because they could not get pregnant. Although I do not go into that material in depth here, I do want to make note of a general trend. Most of the women I talked with there (as they rested immediately after having had an embryo transfer performed) brought up God within the first few minutes of our conversation. Typically, they simply said "God willing" any time they referred to the operation and their hopes for it. Alternatively, they would go to what seemed like great lengths to tell me that they went to church, or that they tried to be good people, or even that they saw the new reproductive technologies or the specific doctor who runs the clinic as a gift from God. *Theostaltos*. A few of these women even referred explicitly to the charismatic doctor running the Center as *being* God. Their capacity to conceive was, in almost all forty cases, explicitly and directly linked to the will of God.

6 For a studied analysis of Greek bureaucracy and its cultural function, see Herzfeld (1992). A case study of contemporary Greek bureaucracy is insightfully presented in Sotiropoulos (1996). For a thorough overview of the theoretical discussion concerning bureaucracy in the social sciences, see Serafetinidou (2003).

10. Reprosexuality, Greece, and Turkey

1 One of the most important of these is a seamless continuity between Ancient Greece and contemporary Greece. This continuity is typically postulated in markedly phylogenetic or racial terms in the demografiko discourses, which simultaneously tend to lament a break in this continuity at the cultural level. In her book on the national romances of Latin America, *Foundational Fictions* (1991), Doris Sommer looks at how the desire for love and the longing for belonging come together in romance novels in various Latin American countries. My use of the related phrase "founding fictions" in this context is also meant to index the tight, in many ways erotic hold that Ancient Greece has on the modern Greek national imaginary.
2 As examples of work considering the fraught nexus of narratives of gender and nation in the mass media, consider the following work on U.S. forms of nationalism: Giroux (1993); Calabrese and Burke (1992); Davison Hunter (1991).
3 Mediterranean anemia is common in the larger Mediterranean region and occurs in individuals whose biological parents both had a condition that is literally referred to by doctors and lay people alike as "the stigma." The point the excerpt is making in referring to this is that a condition that has historically been seen as a threat to the Greek people is being mistakenly considered a sexually transmitted disease.
4 In "The Rights of the Fetus," Gallagher (1991) uses the increasingly frequent cases of comatose women having cesareans performed on them to argue against fetal rights discourse in the United States precisely because of what she calls "the geography of pregnancy." She states that the fetus cannot have rights superseding those of the woman in whose body it is located. She reviews various laws regulating the use of one person's body to treat another's and concludes that there is no case in which such an invasive operation, as a cesarean, would be legal without the consent of the person to be operated on.
5 "Abortion, the Cheapest Contraception," *Kathimerini*, 5 November 1994.
6 Sophia Neta, "The Bourgeoisie Goes to the Obstetrics Hospital," *Eleftherotypia*, 1 November 1994.
7 Underscoring the importance given to the *Eleftherotypia* 1 November 1994 story is a graphic also titled "The Bourgeoisie Goes . . . to the Obstetrics Hospital." This is a sketch of a plump toddler wearing only diapers. The toddler, with very little hair and big, wide-open eyes, also has somewhat bulging breasts. The toddler is holding a balancing stick at an angle across its chest and walking on its toes on a tight-rope.

8 "Precautions for AIDS Have Decreased Abortions," *Kathimerini*, 27 November 1994.
9 Certainly, this is also partly attributable to Greek society's approach to AIDS in general. As Tsalikoglou (1995) argues, national myths concerning "the indestructibility of the Greek nation and race" are part of what produce a form of "narcissism that creates the illusion of Greece's immunity to the epidemic" (98).
10 "Abortions Are Double the Births," *Kathimerini*, 23 August 1995.
11 The article actually uses the term *diaphragm*, but this is confusing because all formal sources repeatedly state that "the Greek woman cannot use the diaphragm," and, indeed, it is very difficult to find in Greece. All ob/gyns I spoke with said it is not used, and many told me they would never recommend it to "the Greek woman" because she cannot or does not want to touch her body in this way. This was reiterated by one of the guest gynecologists appearing on one of the most popular afternoon talk shows on Greek television, Anna Drouza's *Boro* (I can!), which was devoted to the topic of sex education on 25 April 2002.
12 "Greek Women Prefer . . . Abortion," *Kathimerini*, 10 June 1993.
13 She is holding her somewhat swollen belly with folded hands and looking down toward her stomach. Her long brown hair is falling to one side of her face. The picture is large, about 5 by 4 inches, and the background is nondescript: a curtain ahead of her, a black frame of some sort on the wall behind her that could visually index the fairly common practice of many Greek households of displaying a religious icon, or more than one, although the frame is never black. She actually occupies only one fourth of the frame and the image is romantically out of focus.
14 Quoted in "Consumerism and Births," review of *Reproducing the Population: Theoretical Approaches and Empirical Studies* by Nota Kyriazi, *Kathimerini*, 4 November 1993.
15 Thalia Ioanidou, "Interruption of Pregnancy with a Pill," *Kathimerini*, 22 February 1994. My emphasis.
16 "Market and Low Birth Rate," *Ta Nea*, 26 July 1994. My emphasis.
17 Giannis Marinos, "Murder Is Permitted, Pity No," *To Vema*, 31 July 1994. My emphasis.
18 Giannis Marinos, "A Demographic Crime," *To Vema*, 28 August 1994. My emphasis.
19 Melina Volioti, "Best To Be Quiet?," *Avgi*, 8 September 1994.
20 Anna Drouza, *Boro* (I can!), 25 April 2002. A poll conducted during airtime found that 85 percent of the viewers who called reported having had abortions.
21 "On Family Planning," *Rizospasti*, 18 September 1994. My emphasis.
22 I am grateful to Chandra Mukerji for help in clarifying how Greek women are caught between fulfilling the state's modernizing need for them to be "good contraceptors" and simultaneously remaining desirable within Greek heterosexual fields of power by upholding a sexuality that shuns "precautions" of the medical sort as "interventions" and "foreign bodies."

23 For an analysis of the ways these two have co-constituted each other, see Brown (1988).

11. The Demografiko's Greece

A small portion of the material analyzed in this chapter has been presented and analyzed in somewhat different form in Halkias (2003).

1 Certainly, biological females have existed throughout the history of humanity. Women, I suggest, are a historically specific phenomenon, just as are nations. "Nationalism was not the whole, but only the most important part of the tacit consensus forged in the late nineteenth century as to what would count as politically appropriate identities. It played a central role in the development of 'essentialist' thinking that was also basic to the way race, gender, sexual orientation and other sorts of collective identities came to be constituted.... 'Essentialism' refers to a reduction of the diversity in a population to some single criterion held to constitute its defining 'essence' and most crucial character. This is often coupled with the claim that the 'essence' is unavoidable or given by nature.... Put another way, it has been the tacit assumption of modern social and cultural thought that people are normally members of one and only one race, one gender, and one sexual orientation, and that each of these memberships describes neatly and concretely some aspect of their being. It has been assumed that people naturally live in one world at a time, that they inhabit one way of life, that they speak one language, and that they themselves, as individuals, are singular, integral beings. All these assumptions came clearly into focus by the late nineteenth century, and all seem problematic" (Calhoun 1997, 18).

2 Another indication of the lack of a gender-based distinction in the permeation of subjects of its territory with nationalism can be seen in a suggestive study of Athenians' representations of crime and criminals. It was found that the image of the criminal held by women, as opposed to that held by men, is marked by a strong national element: the strongest characteristic of this representation was that of "the Albanian." See Zarafonitou and Mandoglou (2000, 108).

3 Judith Butler (1997a) uses this phrase to refer to the contexts that make some utterances and not others appear problematic. In her discussion of censorship in the United States she performs "a case study" that defends the thesis that "the conditions of intelligibility are themselves formulated in and by power, and this normative exercise of power is rarely acknowledged as an operation of power at all" (134).

4 I am grateful to Bennett Berger for the many discussions we had together during 1992–93 on hegemony and culture.

5 *Polyteknoi* is a term used in policy discourse that, at different points in time, has referred to families that have a minimum of anywhere from three to five children.

6 The least visible and most prominent of these being that which suggests that

Greek women are individuals with rights that are in opposition to the incursions of a state that is perceived of as hostile and a society that is at times cumbersome in its demands. For a powerful analysis of how Marx, in "On the Jewish Question," and Foucault in much of his work each interrogate this type of discourse, see Brown (1995, 111–20). She extends the Foucauldian critique by arguing, in effect, that this liberal humanist discourse effectively genders the liberal state and the individual alike.
7 See Luker (1996) for a review of these positions and for a powerful case against them based on the specificities of aspects of U.S. teenage and poverty cultures.
8 Marianna Kondili, Op-ed, *Eleftherotypia*, 10 September 1994.

Epilogue

1 Craig Calhoun (1997, 19) writes, "Home, it has famously been said, is the place where they always have to take you in. In an important sense, it is this sense of having a home that many people derive from ideas of membership in a nation. Even when this sense of having a home is not immediately tied to any specific 'nationalist' political project, it is a powerful facilitator of such projects; it paves the way for mobilizing people in solidarity with the rest of 'their' nation; it encourages an identification with one's nation that makes it attractive to think of it as superior because that implies a certain superiority for oneself."
2 This textuality of subject and nation, which this book has sought to demonstrate and explore, and in so doing firmly argue for, should not be understood as a lightness or effervescence. The textuality of the subject and the nation that is created historically through agon and tactical realignment ultimately, in every given present, carries formidable weight. "Nevertheless the nationalist principle as such, as distinct from each of its specific forms, and from the individually distinctive nonsense which it may preach, has very very deep roots in our shared current condition, is not at all contingent, and will not easily be denied" (Gellner 1983, 56).

REFERENCES

❖

Adams, Carol J. 1990. *The Sexual Politics of Meat*. Oxford: Polity.
Allison, Graham T., and Kalypso Nicolaidis. 1997. *The Greek Paradox*. Cambridge, Mass.: MIT Press.
Althusser, Louis. 1971. "Ideology and Ideological State Apparatuses: Notes toward an Investigation." In *Lenin and Philosophy and the Other Essays*, trans. Ben Brewster, 121–73. London: New Left Books.
Amemiya, Kozy Kazuko. 1993. "The Road to Pro-Choice Ideology in Japan: A Social History of the Contest between the State and Individuals over Abortion." Ph.D. diss., University of California, San Diego.
Anagnost, Ann. 1995. "A Surfeit of Bodies: Population and the Rationality of the State in Post-Mao China." In *Conceiving the New World Order: The Global Politics of Reproduction*, ed. Faye D. Ginsburg and Rayna Rapp, 22–41. Berkeley: University of California Press.
——. 1997. *National Past-Times: Narrative, Representation, and Power in Modern China*. Durham, N.C.: Duke University Press.
Anderson, Benedict. [1983] 1991. *Imagined Communities: Reflections on the Origin and Spread of Nationalism*. London: Verso.
Anzaldúa, Gloria. 1987. *Borderlands/La Frontera*. San Francisco: Spinsters/Aunt Lute.
Ardener, Shirley, ed. 1975. *Perceiving Women*. London: Malaby Press.
Asad, Talal. 1994. *Genealogies of Religion: Discipline and Reasons of Power in Christianity and Islam*. Baltimore: Johns Hopkins University Press.
Avdela, Efi. 1997. "Hronos, istoria kai ethniki taftotita sto elliniko sholeio" (Time, history, and national identity in the Greek school). In *"Ti ein' i Patrida Mas?" Ethnokedrismos stin Ekpaidefsi* ("What Is Our Homeland?" Ethnocentrism in education), ed. Anna Frangoudaki and Thaleia Dragona, 39–71. Athens: Alexandria.
——. 2003. *Yia Logous Timis: Via, Synaisthimata kai Axies stin Metemfyliaki Ellada* (For words of honor: Violence, emotions and values in post–Civil War Greece). Athens: Nefeli.
Avdela, Efi, and Aggelika Psarra, eds. 1997. "Xanagrafodas to parelthon: Synhrones Diadromes tis Istorias ton Gynaikon" (Rewriting the past: Contemporary path-

ways of the history of women). In *Siopires Istories: Oi Gynaikes kai to Fylo stin Istoriki Afiyisi* (Quiet stories: Women and gender in historical narration), 15–120. Athens: Alexandria.

———. 1994. "Gender-Related Discourses and Representations of Cultural Specificity in Nineteenth-Century and Twentieth-Century Greece." *Journal of Modern Greek Studies* 12: 75–112.

Banet-Weiser, Sarah. 1999. *The Most Beautiful Girl in the World: Beauty Pageants and National Identity.* Berkeley: University of California Press.

Barrett, Michele. 1991. *The Politics of Truth.* Stanford: Stanford University Press.

Barrett, Michele, and Anne Phillips, eds. 1992. *Destabilizing Theory: Contemporary Feminist Debates.* Stanford: Stanford University Press.

Basso, Keith. 1979. *Portraits of "The Whiteman": Linguistic Play and Cultural Symbols among the Western Apache.* Cambridge: Cambridge University Press.

Bataille, Georges. 1986. *Eroticism: Death and Sensuality.* Trans. Mary Dalwood. San Francisco: City Lights Books. Originally published as *L'Erotisme,* 1957.

Battaglia, Debbora. 1995. *Rhetorics of Self-Making.* Berkeley: University of California Press.

Baudrillard, Jean. 1988. *Selected Writings.* Ed. M. Poster. Stanford: Stanford University Press.

Bauman, Richard. 1983. *Let Your Words Be Few: Symbolism of Speaking and Silence Among Seventeenth-Century Quakers.* Cambridge: Cambridge University Press.

Benedict, Helen. 1992. *Virgin or Vamp: How the Press Covers Sex Crimes.* New York: Oxford University Press.

Benhabib, Seyla. 1990. "Epistemologies of Postmodernism: A Rejoinder to Jean-François Lyotard." In *Feminism/Postmodernism,* ed. Linda J. Nicholson, 107–30. New York: Routledge.

Berger, Bennett. 1995. *An Essay on Culture: Symbolic Structure and Social Structure.* Berkeley: University of California Press.

Berlant, Lauren. 1997. *The Queen of America Goes to Washington City: Essays on Sex and Citizenship.* Durham, N.C.: Duke University Press.

Bhabha, Homi K., ed. 1990. *Nation and Narration.* London: Routledge.

Bordo, Susan. 1993. *Unbearable Weight: Feminism, Western Culture, and the Body.* Berkeley: University of California Press.

Bourdieu, Pierre. [1977] 1995. *Outline of a Theory of Practice.* New York: Cambridge University Press.

Bourdieu, Pierre, and Jean-Claude Passeron. 1990. *Reproduction in Education, Society, and Culture.* Trans. Richard Nice. Newbury Park, Calif.: Sage.

Braidotti, Rosi. 1989. "Organs without Bodies." *differences: A Journal of Feminist Cultural Studies* 1(1): 147–61.

———. 1994. *Nomadic Subjects: Embodiment and Sexual Difference in Contemporary Feminist Theory.* New York: Columbia University Press.

Brown, Wendy. 1988. *Manhood and Politics: A Feminist Reading in Political Theory.* Totowa, N.J.: Rowman and Littlefield.

———. 1991. "Feminist Hesitations, Postmodern Exposures." *differences: A Journal of Feminist Cultural Studies* 3(1): 63–84.
———. 1995. *States of Injury: Freedom and Power in Late Modernity.* Princeton: Princeton University Press.
———2001. *Politics Out of History.* Princeton: Princeton University Press.
Browner, C. H. 2001. "Situating Women's Reproductive Abilities." *American Anthropologist* 102(4): 773–88.
Browner, C. H., and Carolyn F. Sargent. 1996. "Anthropology and Studies of Human Reproduction." In *Medical Anthropology: Contemporary Theory and Method,* revised ed., ed. Carolyn F. Sargent and Thomas Johnson, 219–34. Westport, Conn.: Greenwood.
Burchell, Graham. 1993. "Liberal Government and Techniques of the Self." *Economy and Society* 22(3): 267–83.
Butler, Judith. 1990. *Gender Trouble: Feminism and the Subversion of Identity.* New York: Routledge.
———. 1992. "Contingent Foundations: Feminism and the Question of 'Postmodernism.'" In *Feminists Theorize the Political,* ed. Judith Butler and Joan W. Scott. New York: Routledge.
———. 1993. *Bodies That Matter: On the Discursive Limits of "Sex."* New York: Routledge.
———. 1997. *Excitable Speech: A Politics of the Performative.* New York: Routledge.
———. 2000. *Antigone's Claim: Kinship between Life and Death.* New York: Columbia University Press.
Butler, Judith, and Joan W. Scott, eds. 1992. *Feminists Theorize the Political.* New York: Routledge.
Butler, Judith, Ernesto Laclau, and Slavoj Žižek, eds. 2000. *Contingency, Hegemony, Universality: Contemporary Dialogues on the Left.* London: Verso.
Byron, George Gordon. 1839. "Made of Athens." *The Poetical Works of Lord Byron.* London: John Murray. Vol. 4. 338-40.
Calabrese, Andrew, and Barbara R. Burke. 1992. "American Identities: Nationalism, the Media, and the Public Sphere." *Journal of Communication Inquiry* 16(2): 52–73.
Calhoun, Craig. 1994. "Introduction: Habermas and the Public Sphere." In *Habermas and the Public Sphere,* 3d ed., ed. C. Calhoun, 1–48. Cambridge, Mass.: MIT Press.
———. 1996. *Democracy and Difference: Contesting the Boundaries of the Political.* Princeton: Princeton University Press.
———. 1997. *Nationalism.* Buckingham, England: Open University Press.
Calotychos, Vangelis, ed. 1997. *Cyprus and Its People: Nation, Identity, and Experience in an Unimaginable Community, 1955–1997.* Boulder, Colo.: Westview.
Carey, James, ed. 1988. *Media, Myths, and Narratives: Television and the Press.* Newbury Park, Calif.: Sage.
Carlson, Elwood, and Megumi Omori. 1998. "Fertility Regulation in a Declining

State Socialist Economy: Bulgaria, 1976–1995." *International Family Planning Perspectives* 24 (December).

Charalambis, Dimitris, and Nicolas Demertzis. 1993. "Politics and Citizenship in Greece: Cultural and Structural Facets." *Journal of Modern Greek Studies* 11: 219–40.

Cheah, Pheng, and Bruce Robbins, eds. 1998. *Cosmopolitics: Thinking and Feeling Beyond the Nation.* Minneapolis: University of Minnesota Press.

Classen, Constance. 1997. "Engendering Perception: Gender Ideologies and Sensory Hierarchies in Western History." *Body and Society* 3: 1–20.

Clifford, James. 1988. "On Orientalism." In *The Predicament of Culture: Twentieth-Century Ethnography, Literature, and Art.* Boston: Harvard University Press.

Clifford, James, and George Marcus, eds. 1986. *Writing Culture: The Poetics and Politics of Ethnography.* Berkeley: University of California Press.

Clogg, Richard. 1992. *A Concise History of Greece.* New York: Cambridge University Press.

Cockburn, Cynthia. 1999. *The Space between Us: Negotiating Gender and National Identities in Conflict.* New York: Zed Books.

Cohen, Anthony P., and Nigel Rapport. 1995. *Questions of Consciousness.* New York: Routledge.

Comninos, A. C. 1988. "Greece." In *International Handbook on Abortion*, ed. P. Sachdev, 210. New York: Greenwood.

Condit, Celeste Michelle. 1990. *Decoding Abortion Rhetoric: Communicating Social Change.* Urbana: University of Illinois Press.

Constas, Dimitri, and Theofanis G. Stavrou, eds. 1995. *Greece Prepares for the Twenty-first Century.* Washington, D.C.: Woodrow Wilson Center Press.

Cowan, Jane K. 1990. *Dance and the Body Politic in Northern Greece.* Princeton: Princeton University Press.

———. 1991. "Going out for Coffee? Contesting the Grounds of Gendered Pleasures in Everyday Sociability." In *Contested Identities: Gender and Kinship in Modern Greece*, ed. Peter Loizos and Evthymios Papataxiarchis, 180–202. Princeton: Princeton University Press.

Cowan, Jane K., Marie-Benedicte Dembour, and Richard A. Wilson. 2001. *Culture and Rights: Anthropological Perspectives.* New York: Cambridge University Press.

Crenshaw, Kimberle. 1991. "Demarginalizing the Intersection of Race and Sex: A Black Feminist Critique of Anti-discrimination Doctrine, Feminist Theory, and Antiracist Politics." In *Feminist Legal Theory: Readings in Law and Gender*, ed. Katherine T. Bartlett and Rosanne Kennedy. Boulder, Colo.: Westview.

Crimp, Douglas, ed. 1988. *AIDS: Cultural Analysis, Cultural Activism.* Cambridge, Mass.: MIT Press.

Dahl, Robert A. 1998. *On Democracy.* New Haven: Yale University Press.

Dakin, Douglas. 1972. *The Unification of Greece, 1770–1923.* London: Ernest Benn.

Damanakis, M. 1997. *I Ekpaidefsi ton Palinnostoudon kai Allodapon Mathiton stin*

Ellada (The education of repatriated and foreign students in Greece). Athens: Gutenberg.

Danezi, Ioannis. 2001. "Natural Methods of Family Planning." *Oikoyeneiakos Programmatismos* (Family planning), news bulletin of the Greek Association for Family Planning, no. 22 (summer).

Danforth, Loring M. 1989. *Firewalking and Religious Healing: The Anastenaria of Greece and the American Firewalking Movement*. Princeton: Princeton University Press.

———. 1995. *The Macedonian Conflict: Ethnic Nationalism in a Transnational World*. Princeton: Princeton University Press.

Da Vanzo, Julie, and David Adamson. 1997. "Russia's Demographic Crisis: How Real Is It?" *Center for Russian and Eurasian Studies, Labor and Population Program* (July).

Davison Hunter, James. 1991. *Culture Wars: The Struggle to Define America*. Scranton, Penn.: HarperCollins.

de Certeau, Michel. 1984. *The Practice of Everyday Life*. Trans. Steven F. Rendall. Berkeley: University of California Press.

De Cillia, R., M. Reisigl, and R. Wodak. 1999. "The Discursive Construction of National Identities." *Discourse and Society* 10(2): 149–73.

de Lauretis, Teresa, ed. 1986. *Feminist Studies/Critical Studies*. Bloomington: Indiana University Press.

———. 1987. *Technologies of Gender*. Bloomington: Indiana University Press.

Deleuze, Gilles, and Félix Guattari. 1983. *Anti-Oedipus: Capitalism and Schizophrenia*. Trans. Robert Hurley, Mark Seem, and Helen R. Lane. Minneapolis: University of Minnesota Press. Originally published as *L'Anti-Oedipe*, 1972.

Deligiorgou, E. 1992. "Pregnancies and Abortions in Adolescence." In *Sexual Behavior and Health*. Athens: Family Planning Association.

Demertzis, Nikolaos. 1990. "I Elliniki Politiki Koultoura sti Dekaetia tou 80" (Greek political culture during the 1980s). In *Ekloyes kai Kommata sti Dekaetia tou 80: Exelixeis kai Prooptikes tou Politikou Systimatos* (Elections and parties during the 80s: Developments and the potential of the political system), 70–96. Athens: Hellenic Political Science Association.

Diamandouros, P. Nikiforos. 1993. "Politics and Culture in Greece, 1974–91: An Interpretation." In *Greece, 1981–1989: The Populist Decade*, ed. Richard Clogg. New York: St. Martin's.

———. 1997. "Greek Politics and Society in the 1990s." In *The Greek Paradox*, ed. Graham T. Allison and Kalypso Nicolaidis. Cambridge, Mass.: MIT Press.

———. 2000. *Politismikos Dyismos kai Politiki Allagi stin Ellada tis metapolitefsis* (Cultural dualism and political change in metapolitefsi Greece). Athens: Alexandria.

Diamond, Irene, and Lee Quinby, eds. 1988. *Feminism and Foucault: Reflections on Resistance*. Boston: Northeastern University Press.

Dimoulis, Dimitris. 2000. "Laos, Ethnos kai Polites stin Elliniki Syntagmatiki

Istoria tou 19ou Aiona" (The people, the nation, and citizens in Greek constitutional history of the nineteenth century). *Thesis* 72: 35–89.

Dini: A Feminist Journal. 1994. Special issue on *Motherhood* (July).

Douglas, Mary. 1966. *Purity and Danger: An Analysis of the Concepts of Pollution and Taboo*. London: Ark Paperback.

Doumanis, Mariella. 1983. *Mothering in Greece: From Collectivism to Individualism*. New York: Academic Press.

Doxiadis, Kyrkos. 1993. *Ethnikismos, Ideologia, Mesa Mazikis, Epikoinonias* (Nationalism, ideology, media of mass communication). Athens: Plethron.

Drettakis, Manolis G. 1996. *Demografikes Exelixeis Sin Ellada, 1961–1990* (Demographic developments in Greece, 1961–1990). Athens: Foundation for the Resolution of the Demographic Problem.

Dubisch, Jill, ed. 1986. *Gender and Power in Rural Greece*. Princeton: Princeton University Press.

———. 1995. *In a Different Place: Pilgrimage, Gender, and Politics at a Greek Island Shrine*. Princeton: Princeton University Press.

Du Bois, Page. 1991. *Torture and Truth*. New York: Routledge.

Du Boulay, Juliet. 1984. "The Blood: Symbolic Relationships between Descent, Marriage, Incest Prohibitions and Spiritual Kinship in Greece." *Man* 19: 533–56.

During, Simon, ed. 1993. *The Cultural Studies Reader*. New York: Routledge.

Eagleton, Terry. 1991. *Ideology: An Introduction*. London: Verso.

Ebgron, Paula, and Anna Lowenhaupt Tsing. 1995. "From Allegories of Identity to Sites of Dialogue." *Diaspora* 4(2): 125–51.

Elshtain, Jean Bethke. 1981. *Public Man, Private Woman: Women in Social and Political Thought*. Princeton: Princeton University Press.

Emke-Poulopoulou, Ira. 1994. *To Demografiko* (The demographic problem). Athens: Hellene.

Engels, Friedrich. [1884] 1972. *The Origin of the Family, Private Property and the State*. London: Penguin.

Epstein, Debbie, and Deborah Lynn Steinberg. 1996. "All Het Up! Rescuing Heterosexuality on the Oprah Winfrey Show." *Feminist Review* 54: 88–115.

Evans, David T. 1993. *Sexual Citizenship: The Material Construction of Sexualities*. New York: Routledge.

Fang, Y. 1994. "'Riots' and Demonstrations in the Chinese Press: A Case Study of Language and Ideology." *Discourse and Society* 5(4): 463–81.

Faubion, James. 1993. *Modern Greek Lessons: A Primer in Historical Constructivism*. Princeton: Princeton University Press.

Fausto-Sterling, Anne. 2000. *Sexing the Body: Gender Politics and the Construction of Sexuality*. New York: Basic Books.

Featherstone, Kevin, and Kostas Ifantis, eds. 1996. *Greece in a Changing Europe: Between European Integration and Balkan Disintegration?* Manchester, England: Manchester University Press.

Fine, Michelle. 1992. "Silencing and Nurturing Voice in an Improbable Context:

Urban Adolescents in Public School." In *Disruptive Voices: The Possibilities of Feminist Research*, 115–38. Ann Arbor: University of Michigan Press.

Fonow, Mary Margaret, and Judith A. Cook, eds. 1991. *Beyond Methodology: Feminist Scholarship as Lived Research*. Bloomington: Indiana University Press.

Foucault, Michel. 1977. *Discipline and Punish: The Birth of the Prison*. Trans. Alan Sheridan. New York: Vintage.

———. 1980a. *Herculine Barbin: Being the Recently Discovered Memoirs of a Nineteenth-Century French Hermaphrodite*. Trans. Richard McDougall. New York: Pantheon. Originally published as *Herculine Barbin, dite Alexina B*, 1978.

———. 1980b. *The History of Sexuality. Vol. I: An Introduction*. Trans. Robert Hurley. New York: Vintage. Originally published as *Histoire de la sexualite. Vol. I: La volante de savoir*, 1976.

———. 1980c. *Power/Knowledge: Selected Interviews and Other Writings, 1972–1977*. Ed. C. Gordon. New York: Pantheon.

———. 1982. "Afterword: The Subject and Power." In *Michel Foucault: Beyond Structuralism and Hermeneutics*. Ed. Herbert Dreyfus and Paul Rabinow. Brighton, England: Harvester.

———. 1988a. *The History of Sexuality. Vol. III: The Care of the Self*. Trans. Robert Hurley. New York: Vintage. Originally published as *Histoire de la sexualite. Vol. III: Le souci de soi*, 1984.

———. 1988b. "Technologies of the Self." In *Technologies of the Self: A Seminar with Michel Foucault*. Ed. L. H. Martin, H. Gutman, and P. H. Hutton. Amherst: University of Massachusetts Press.

Frangoudaki, Anna, and Thaleia Dragona, eds. 1997. *"Ti ein' i Patrida Mas?" Ethnokedrismos stin Ekpaidefsi* ("What Is Our Homeland?" Ethnocentrism in Education). Athens: Alexandria.

Franklin, Sarah, and Helena Ragon. 1998. *Reproducing Reproduction: Kinship, Power, and Technological Innovation*. Philadelphia: University of Pennsylvania Press.

Fraser, Nancy. 1989. *Unruly Practices: Power, Discourse, and Gender in Contemporary Social Theory*. Minneapolis: University of Minnesota Press.

———. 1992. "Rethinking the Public Sphere: A Contribution to the Critique of Actually Existing Democracy." In *The Phantom Public Sphere*, ed. Bruce Robbins, 1–32. Minneapolis: University of Minnesota Press.

Fraser, Nancy, and Linda J. Nicholson. 1990. "Social Criticism without Philosophy: An Encounter between Feminism and Postmodernism." In *Feminism/Postmodernism*, ed. Linda J. Nicholson. New York: Routledge.

Friedl, Ernestine. 1986. "The Position of Women: Appearance and Reality." In *Gender and Power in Rural Greece*, ed. Jill Dubisch, 42–52. Princeton: Princeton University Press.

Friedland, Roger. 2002. "Money, Sex, and God: The Erotic Logic of Religious Nationalism." *Sociological Theory* 20(3): 380–425.

Fuss, Diana. 1989. *Essentially Speaking: Feminism, Nature and Difference*. New York: Routledge.

———. 1991. *Inside/Out: Lesbian Theories, Gay Theories*. New York: Routledge.

Gagnon, John H. 1990. "The Implicit and Explicit Use of the Scripting Perspective in Sex Research." *Annual Review of Sex Research* 1: 1–43.

Gagnon, John H., and Richard G. Parker. 1995. *Conceiving Sexuality: Approaches to Sex Research in a Postmodern World*. New York: Routledge.

Gal, Susan. 2002. "Between Speech and Silence." In *The Anthropology of Politics*, ed. Joan Vincent, 213–21. London: Blackwell.

Gal, Susan, and Gail Kligman, eds. 2000. *Reproducing Gender: Politics, Publics, and Everyday Life after Socialism*. Princeton: Princeton University Press.

Gallop, Jane. 1988. *Thinking through the Body*. New York: Columbia University Press.

Garber, Marjorie. 1989. "Spare Parts: The Surgical Construction of Gender." *differences* 1 (fall): 137–59.

Garber, Marjorie, Paul B. Franklin, and Rebecca L. Walkowitz, eds. 1996. *Field Work: Sites in Literary and Cultural Studies*. New York: Routledge.

Gatsos, Nikos. 1992. "To Dihty" (The Net). In *Fysa Aeraki Fysa Me Mi Hamiloneis Isame* (Blow, breeze, blow, don't lessen until). Athens: Themelio.

Garber, Marjorie, and Rebecca L. Walkowitz, eds. 1999. *One Nation under God? Religion and American Culture*. New York: Routledge.

Gaventa, John. 1980. *Power and Powerlessness: Quiescence and Rebellion in the Appalachian Valley*. Urbana: University of Illinois Press.

Geertz, Clifford. 1973. *The Interpretation of Cultures*. New York: Basic Books.

Gefou-Madianou, Dimitra. 1993. "Mirroring Ourselves through Western texts: The Limits of an Indigenous Anthropology." In *The Politics of Ethnographic Reading and Writing: Confrontation of Western and Indigenous Views*, ed. Henk Driessen. Saarbrucken, Germany: Breitenbach.

Gellner, Ernest. 1983. *Nations and Nationalism*. Ithaca, N.Y.: Cornell University Press.

———. 1988. "Trust, Cohesion and the Social Order." In *Trust: Making and Breaking Cooperative Relations*, ed. D. Gambetta. Oxford: Blackwell.

Georges, Eugenia. 1996a. "Abortion Policy and Practice in Greece." *Social Science and Medicine* 42: 509–19.

———. 1996b. "Fetal Ultrasound Imaging and the Production of Authoritative Knowledge in Greece." *Medical Anthropology Quarterly* 10(2): 1–19.

Giannuli, Dimitra. 1995. "Greeks or 'Strangers at Home': The Experience of Ottoman Greek Refugees during Their Exodus to Greece, 1922–1923." *Journal of Modern Greek Studies* 13: 271–87.

Giddens, Anthony. 1971. *Capitalism and Modern Social Theory: An Analysis of the Writings of Marx, Durkheim, and Max Weber*. Cambridge: Cambridge University Press.

Gilligan, Carol. 1982. *In a Different Voice: Psychological Theory and Women's Development*. Cambridge, Mass.: Harvard University Press.

Ginsburg, Faye. D. 1998. *Contested Lives: The Abortion Debate in an American Community*. Berkeley: University of California Press.

Ginsburg, Faye D., and Anna Lowenhaupt Tsing, eds. 1990. *Uncertain Terms: Negotiating Gender in American Culture.* Boston: Beacon.

Ginsburg, Faye D., and Rayna Rapp, eds. 1995. *Conceiving the New World Order: The Global Politics of Reproduction.* Berkeley: University of California Press.

Ginsburg, Faye D., Lila Abu-Lughod, and Brian Larkin, eds. 2002. *Media Worlds: Anthropology on New Terrain.* Berkeley: University of California Press.

Giroux, Henry A. 1993. "Beyond the Politics of Innocence: Memory and Pedagogy in the 'Wonderful World of Disney.'" *Socialist Review* 23(2): 79–107.

Glenn, Evelyn Nakano, Grace Chang, and Linda Rennie Forcey, eds. 1994. *Mothering: Ideology, Experience, and Agency.* New York: Routledge.

Goffman, Erving. 1959. *The Presentation of Self in Everyday Life.* Garden City, N.Y.: Doubleday.

———. 1974. *Frame Analysis: An Essay on the Organization of Experience.* Boston: Northeastern University Press.

Gourgouris, Stathis. 1992. "Nationalism and Oneirocentrism: Of Modern Hellenes in Europe." *Diaspora* 2: 43–71.

———. 1996. *Dream Nation: Enlightenment, Colonization, and the Institution of Modern Greece.* Stanford: Stanford University Press.

Graham, B. 1998. "The Past in Europe's Present: Diversity, Identity and the Construction of Place." In *Modern Europe: Place, Culture, Identity,* ed. B. Graham, 19–52. London: Arnold.

Green, Donald P., and Ian Shapiro. 1994. *Pathologies of Rational Choice Theory: A Critique of Applications in Political Science.* New Haven: Yale University Press.

Greenhalgh, Susan, ed. 1995. *Situating Fertility: Anthropology and Demographic Inquiry.* Cambridge: Cambridge University Press.

Grossberg, Lawrence, Cary Nelson, and Paula Treichler, eds. 1992. *Cultural Studies.* New York: Routledge.

Gupta, Akhil, and James Ferguson. 1997. *Anthropological Locations: Boundaries and Grounds of a Field Science.* Berkeley: University of California Press.

Gusfield, Joseph. 1966. *Symbolic Crusade.* Urbana: University of Illinois Press.

Habermas, Jürgen. 1989. *The Structural Transformation of the Public Sphere: An Inquiry into a Category of Bourgeois Society.* Trans. Thomas Burger. Cambridge, Mass.: MIT Press.

———. 1991. "The Public Sphere." In *Rethinking Popular Culture: Contemporary Perspectives in Cultural Studies,* ed. Chandre Mukerji and Michael Schudson, 398–404. Berkeley: University of California Press.

Halkias, Alexandra. 1997. "Democracy Revisited: Abortion and Agon in Modern Greece." Ph.D. diss., University of California, San Diego.

———. 1998. "Give Birth for Greece! Abortion and Nation in Letters to the Editor of the Mainstream Greek Press." *Journal of Modern Greek Studies* 16: 111–38.

———. 2003. "Money, God and Race: The Politics of Reproduction and the Nation in Modern Greece." *European Journal of Women's Studies* 10(2): 211–32.

Hall, John A. 1987. *Liberalism: Politics, Ideology and the Market.* Chapel Hill: University of North Carolina Press.

Hall, Jonathan M. 2002. *Hellenicity: Between Ethnicity and Culture.* Chicago: University of Chicago Press.

Hall, Stuart. 1979a. "Culture, Media, and the 'Ideological' Effect." In *Mass Communication and Society,* ed. James Curran, Michael Gurevitch, and Janet Woolacott. Beverly Hills: Sage.

———. 1979b. *Policing the Crisis.* New York: Macmillan.

Hallin, Daniel. 1986. *The Uncensored War: The Media and Vietnam.* Berkeley: University of California Press.

———. 1994. *We Keep Americans on Top of the World: Television Journalism and the Public Sphere.* New York: Routledge.

Halperin, David M., John H. Winkler, and Froma I. Zeitlin, eds. 1989. *Before Sexuality: The Construction of Erotic Experience in the Ancient Greek World.* Princeton: Princeton University Press.

Haraway, Donna J. 1988. "Situated Knowledges: The Science Question in Feminism and the Privilege of Partial Perspective." *Feminist Studies* 14(3): 575–99.

———. 1989a. "The Biopolitics of Postmodern Bodies: Determinations of Self in Immune System Discourse." *differences* 1 (winter): 3–43.

———. 1989b. *Primate Visions: Gender, Race, and Nature in the World of Modern Science.* New York: Routledge.

———. 1991. *Simians, Cyborgs, and Women: The Reinvention of Nature.* New York: Routledge.

Harding, Sandra, ed. 1987. *Feminism and Methodology: Social Science Issues.* Bloomington: Indiana University Press.

Hardt-Mautner, Geraldine. 1995. "'How Does One Become a Good European?' The Press and European Integration." *Discourse and Society* 6(2): 177–205.

Hart, Janet. 1996. *New Voices in the Nation: Women and the Greek Resistance, 1941–1964.* Ithaca, N.Y.: Cornell University Press.

Hart, Laurie Kain. 1992. *Time, Religion, and Social Experience in Rural Greece.* Lanham, Md.: Rowan and Littlefield.

Hartouni, Valerie. 1997. *Cultural Conceptions: On Reproductive Technologies and the Remaking of Life.* Minneapolis: University of Minnesota Press.

Hartsock, Nancy C. M. 1990. "Foucault on Power: A Theory for Women?" In *Feminism/Postmodernism,* ed. Linda J. Nicholson, 157–75. New York: Routledge.

Harvey, David. 1989. *The Condition of Postmodernity.* Oxford: Blackwell.

Henshaw, S. 1990. "Induced Abortion: A World Review." *Family Planning Perspectives* 22(80).

Henshaw, S., S. Singh, and T. Haas. 1999. "The Incidence of Abortion Worldwide." *International Family Planning Perspectives* 25, January suppl.

Herzfeld, Michael. 1982. *Ours Once More: Folklore, Ideology, and the Making of Modern Greece.* Austin: University of Texas Press.

———. 1985a. "'Law' and 'Custom': Ethnography *in* and *of* Greek National Identity." *Journal of Modern Greek Studies* 3: 167–85.

———. 1985b. *The Poetics of Manhood: Contest and Identity in a Cretan Mountain Village.* Princeton: Princeton University Press.

———. 1986. "Within and Without: The Category of 'Female' in the Ethnography of Modern Greece." In *Gender and Power in Rural Greece,* ed. Jill Dubisch, 215–33. Princeton: Princeton University Press.

———. 1987. *Anthropology through the Looking-Glass: Critical Ethnography in the Margins of Europe.* New York: Cambridge University Press.

———. 1991a. *A Place in History: Social and Monumental Time in a Cretan Village.* Princeton: Princeton University Press.

———. 1991b. "Silence, Submission, and Subversion: Toward a Poetics of Womanhood." In *Contested Identities: Gender and Kinship in Modern Greece,* ed. Peter Loizos and Evthymios Papataxiarchis, 79–97. Princeton: Princeton University Press.

———. 1992. *The Social Production of Indifference.* Chicago: University of Chicago Press.

———. 1997. *Cultural Intimacy: Social Poetics in the Nation-State.* New York: Routledge.

Hirsch, E. D., Jr., 1976. *The Aims of Interpretation.* Chicago: University of Chicago Press.

Hirschon, Renee. 1978. "Open Body/Closed Space: The Transformation of Female Sexuality." In *Defining Females,* ed. Shirley Ardene. London: Croom Helm.

———. 1989. *Heirs of the Greek Catastrophe: The Social Life of Asia Minor Refugees in Piraeus.* Oxford: Clarendon.

Hobsbawm, Eric J., and Terence Ranger, eds. 1983. *The Invention of Tradition.* Cambridge, England: Cambridge University Press.

———. 1990. *Nations and Nationalism Since 1780: Programme, Myth, Reality.* Cambridge, England: Cambridge University Press.

Holst-Warhaft, Gail. 1997. "Song, Self-Identity, and the Neohellenic." *Journal of Modern Greek Studies* 15 (fall): 232–38.

———. 2000. *The Cue for Passion: Grief and Its Political Uses.* Cambridge, Mass.: Harvard University Press.

Horkheimer, Max, and Theodor Adorno. 1972. *The Dialectic of Enlightenment.* Trans. John Cummings. New York: Seabury.

Horn, David G. 1994. *Social Bodies: Science, Reproduction, and Italian Modernity.* Princeton: Princeton University Press.

Hubbard, Ruth. 1990. *The Politics of Women's Biology.* New Brunswick, N.J.: Rutgers University Press.

Hung, W. 1991. "Tianaman Square: A Political History of Monuments." *Representations* 35: 84–142.

Huntington, Samuel P. 1996. *The Clash of Civilizations and the Remaking of World Order.* New York: Simon and Schuster.

Iossifides, A. Marina. 1991. "Sisters in Christ: Metaphors of Kinship among Greek

Nuns." In *Contested Identities: Gender and Kinship in Modern Greece,* ed. Peter Loizos and Evthymios Papataxiarchis, 135–55. Princeton: Princeton University Press.

Ives, Edward D. 1974. *The Tape-Recorded Interview: A Manual for Field Workers in Folklore and Oral History.* Knoxville: University of Tennessee Press.

Jacobus, Mary, Evelyn Fox Keller, and Sally Shuttleworth, eds. 1990. *Body/Politics: Women and the Discourses of Science.* New York: Routledge.

Just, Roger. 1989. "Triumph of the Ethnos." In *History and Ethnicity* (ASA Monographs 27), ed. Elizabeth Tonkin, Malcolm Chapman, and Maryon McDonald, 71–88. London: Routledge.

Kahn, Susan Martha. 2000. *Reproducing Jews: A Cultural Account of Assisted Conception in Israel.* Durham: Duke University Press.

Kalogeras, Yiorgos, and Domna Pastourmatzi. 1996. *Nationalism and Sexuality: Crises of Identity.* Thessaloniki, Greece: University of Thessaloniki Publications.

Kaplan, Caren, Norma Alarcon, and Minoo Moallem, eds. 1999. *Between Woman and Nation: Nationalisms, Transnational Feminisms, and the State,* Durham, N.C.: Duke University Press.

Karakasidou, Anastasia. 1996. "Women of the Family, Women of the Nation: National Enculturation among Slavic Speakers in Northwestern Greece." *Women's Studies International Forum* 19(1–2): 99–109.

———. 1997. *Fields of Wheat, Hills of Blood: Passages to Nationhood in Greek Macedonia, 1870–1990.* Chicago: University of Chicago Press.

Karlekar, Malavika. 1995. "The Girl Child in India: Does She Have Any Rights?" *Canadian Women's Studies* (March): 40–58.

Keeley, Edmund, and Philip Sherrard, eds. 1981. *Voices of Modern Greece: Selected Poems by Cavafy, Sikelianos, Seferis, Elytis, Gatsos.* Princeton: Princeton University Press.

Killoran, Moira. 1998. "Nationalism and Embodied Memory in Northern Cyprus." In *Cyprus and Its People: Nation, Identity, and Experience in an Unimaginable Community, 1955–1997,* ed. Vangelis Calotychos, 159–70. Boulder, Colo.: Westview.

Kitromilidis, Paschalis. 1996. *Neoellinikos Diafotismos* (Neo-Hellenic enlightenment). Athens: Publications MIET.

Kligman, Gail. 1990. "Reclaiming the Public: A Reflection on Creating Civil Society in Romania." *East European Politics and Societies* 4: 393–438.

———. 1995. "Political Demography: The Banning of Abortion in Ceausescu's Romania." In *Conceiving the New World Order,* ed. Faye D. Ginsburg and Rayna Rapp. Berkeley: University of California Press.

———. 1998. *The Politics of Duplicity: Controlling Reproduction in Ceausescu's Romania.* Berkeley: University of California Press.

Kodzamanis, Basis, and Lilly Maratou-Alibrandi. 1992. *Oi Demografikes Exelixeis stin Metapolemiki Ellada* (Demographic developments in postwar Greece). Athens: New Borders, Livanis Press.

Kondili, Marianne. 1994. "Sholio yia to Demografiko" (Comment on the Demographic Problem). In *Dini: Feministiko Periodiko* (July): 144–48.
Kondili, Marianne, and Angelika Psarra. 1986. "Gennate Yiati Hanomaste" (Give birth because we are disappearing). In *Dini: Feministiko Periodiko* (December): 34–41.
Kotaridis, Nikos, ed. 1996. *Rebetes kai to Rebetiko Tragoudi* (Rebetes and the Rebetiko Song). Athens: Plethron.
Kyriakidou-Nestoros, Alki. 1986. "Introduction to Modern Greek Ideology and Folklore." *Journal of Modern Hellenism* 3:35–46.
Kyriazi, Nota. 1992. *Anaparagogi tou Plithismou: Theoritikes Prosengiseis kai Empeirikes Erevnes* (Reproducing the population: Theoretical approaches and empirical studies). Athens: Gutenberg.
———. 1998. "Women's Employment and Gender Relations in Greece: Forces of Modernization and Tradition." *European Urban and Regional Studies* 5(1): 65–75.
Laclau, Ernesto. 1990. *New Reflections on the Revolution of Our Time*. London: Verso.
Laina, Maria. 1998. "Hers, #8." In *The Rehearsal of Misunderstanding: Three Collections by Contemporary Greek Women Poets. Bilingual Edition. The Cake by Rhea Galanaki, Tales of the Deep by Jenny Mastoraki, Hers by Maria Laina*, ed. Karen Van Dyck. Hanover, N.H.: Wesleyan University Press.
Laqueur, Thomas. 1990. *Making Sex: Body and Gender from the Greeks to Freud*. Cambridge, Mass.: Harvard University Press.
"Last Chance Sisyphus." 1993. *The Economist*, 22 May, insert.
Lay, Mary M., Laura J. Gurak, Clare Gravon, and Cynthia Myntti, eds. 2000. *Body Talk: Rhetoric, Technology, Reproduction*. Madison: University of Wisconsin Press.
Lekkas, Pandelis. E. 2001. *To Paihnidi me ton Hrono: Ethnikismos kai Neoterikotita* (Playing with time: Nationalism and modernity). Athens: Ellinika Grammata.
Leondidou, Lila. 1989. *Poleis tis Siopis: Ergatikos Epoikismos tis Athinas kai Peiraia 1909–1940* (Cities of silence: The settlement of workers in Athens and Piraeus 1909–1940). Athens: Cultural and Technological Foundation ETBA.
Leontis, Artemis. 1995. *Topographies of Hellenism: Mapping the Homeland*. Ithaca, N.Y.: Cornell University Press.
Lewis, Bernard. 1975. *History: Remembered, Recovered, Invented*. Princeton: Princeton University Press.
Loizos, Peter, and Evthymios Papataxiarchis. 1991. "Gender, Sexuality, and the Person in Greek Culture." In *Contested Identities: Gender and Kinship in Modern Greece*. Princeton: Princeton University Press.
Lorde, Audre. 1984. "The Master's Tools Will Never Dismantle the Master's House." In *Sister Outsider*. New York: Crossing Press.
Loukos, Christos. 1988. *Andipolitefsi Kata tou Kyverniti I. Kapodistria 1828–1831*. (Opposition to Governor Kapodistrin 1828–1831). Athens: Themelio Press.
Lowe, Lisa. 1991. *Critical Terrains: French and British Orientalisms*. Ithaca, N.Y.: Cornell University Press.

———. 1996. *Immigrant Acts: On Asian-American Cultural Politics.* Durham, N.C.: Duke University Press.

Lowe, Lisa, and David Lloyd, eds. 1997. *The Politics of Culture in the Shadow of Capital.* Durham, N.C.: Duke University Press.

Luker, Kristin. 1975. *Taking Chances: Abortion and the Decision Not to Contracept.* Berkeley: University of California Press.

———. 1984. *Abortion and the Politics of Motherhood.* Berkeley: University of California Press.

———. 1996. *Dubious Conceptions: The Politics of Teenage Pregnancy.* Cambridge, Mass.: Harvard University Press.

Lyritzis, Christos. 1987. "The Power of Populism: The Greek Case." *European Journal of Political Research* 15: 667–86.

Lyritzis, Christos, Ilias Nikolakopoulos, and Dimitris Sotiropoulos. 1996. *Koinonia kai Politiki: Opseis tis Tritis Ellinikis Dimokratias, 1974–1994* (Society and politics: Aspects of the third Greek democracy, 1974–1994). Athens: Themelio.

Lytras, Andreas. 1993. *Prolegomena stin Theoria tis Ellinikis Koinonikis Domis* (Prelude to the theory of Greek social stratification). Athens: Nes Synora.

MacCormack, Carol. 1994. "Ethnological Studies of Medical Sciences." *Social Science and Medicine* 39 (fall): 1229–35.

Macnaghten, Phil, and John Urry. 1998. *Contested Natures.* London: Sage.

Malkki, Lisa. 1994. "Citizens of Humanity: Internationalism and the Imagined Community of Nations." *Diaspora* 3(1): 41–68.

Marketaki, Vana. 2001. "Pensions: Equality Arrived a Little Too Early." *Gynaika* (August): 22–27.

Markezinis, Spyros. 1966. *I Politiki Istoria tis Neoteris Ellados: 1824–1964* (The political history of modern Greece: 1824–1964). Vol. 1. Athens: Papyros.

Martin, Emily. 1987. *The Women in the Body: A Cultural Analysis of Reproduction.* Boston: Beacon.

———. 1990a. "The Egg and the Sperm: How Science Has Constructed a Romance Based on Stereotypical Male-Female Roles." *Signs* 16 (spring): 485–501.

———. 1990b. "The Ideology of Reproduction: The Reproduction of Ideology." In *Uncertain Terms: Negotiating Gender in American Culture,* ed. Faye D. Ginsburg and Anna Lowenhaupt Tsing, 300–314. Boston: Beacon.

Marx, Karl. 1978. "The German Ideology." In *The Marx-Engels Reader,* ed. R. C. Tucker. New York: Norton.

Mastoraki, Jenny. 1998. "Tales from the Deep." In *The Rehearsal of Misunderstanding: Three Collections by Contemporary Greek Women Poets. Bilingual Edition. The Cake by Rhea Galanaki, Tales of the Deep by Jenny Mastoraki, Hers by Maria Laina,* ed. Karen Van Dyck. Hanover, N.H.: Wesleyan University Press.

Mavrogordatos, George. 1982. *Meletes kai Keimena gia tin Periodo 1909–1940* (Studies and texts on the period 1909–1940). Athens: Sakkoulas.

———. 1983. *Still-Born Republic: Social Coalitions and Party Strategies in Greece, 1922–1936.* Berkeley: University of California Press.

Mazower, Mark, ed. 2000a. *After the War Was Over: Reconstructing the Family, Nation, and State in Greece, 1943–1960*. Princeton: Princeton University Press.

———. 2000b. *The Balkans*. London: Phoenix.

McClintock, Anne, Aamir Mufti, and Ella Shohat, eds. 1997. *Dangerous Liaisons: Gender, Nation, and Postcolonial Perspectives*. Minneapolis: University of Minnesota Press.

McKinnon, Catherine. 1989. *Toward a Feminist Theory of the State*. Cambridge, Mass.: Harvard University Press.

McNay, Louis. 2000. *Gender and Agency: Reconfiguring the Subject in Feminist and Social Theory*. Cambridge, England: Polity.

Meech, Peter, and Richard Kilborn. 1992. "Media and Identity in a Stateless Nation: The Case of Scotland." *Media, Culture and Society* 14(2): 245–59.

Michaels, Walter Benn. 1992. "Race into Culture: A Critical Genealogy of Cultural Identity." *Critical Inquiry* 18 (summer): 655–85.

Miheli, Lisa. 1987. *Athens in Minor Tones*. Athens: Dromena.

Mill, John Stuart. 1975. *On Liberty*. New York: Norton.

Minh-ha, Trinh T. 1989. *Woman, Native, Other: Writing Postcoloniality and Feminism*. Bloomington: Indiana University Press.

Mintoff Bland, Yana. 1996. *Nobody Can Imagine Our Longing: Refugees and Immigrants in the Mediterranean*. Austin, Tex.: Plain View Press.

Modleski, Tania. 1991. *Feminism without Women: Culture and Criticism in a "Postfeminist" Age*. New York: Routledge.

Mohanty, Chandra. 1991. "Under Western Eyes: Feminist Scholarship and Colonial Discourses." In *Third World Women and the Politics of Feminism*, ed. Chandra Mohanty, Mary Russo, and Lourdes Torres, 51–80. Bloomington: Indiana University Press.

Moraga, Cherríe, and Gloria Anzaldúa, eds. 1981. *This Bridge Called My Back: Writings by Radical Women of Color*. New York: Kitchen Table/Women of Color Press.

Mosse, George L. 1985. *Nationalism and Sexuality: Middle-Class Morality and Sexual Norms in Modern Europe*. Madison: University of Wisconsin Press.

Mosxou-Sakorafou, S. 1990. "The Suffrage of Greek Women." In *Istoria tou Ellinikou Feministikou Kinimatos* (The history of the Greek movement), 213–34. Athens: n.p.

Mouffe, Chantal. 1992. "Feminism, Citizenship, and Radical Democratic Politics." In *Feminists Theorize the Political*, ed. Judith Butler and Joan W. Scott, 369–84. New York: Routledge.

———. 1993. *The Return of the Political*. London: Verso.

Mouzelis, Nicos P. 1978. *Modern Greece: Facets of Underdevelopment*. New York: Holmes and Meier.

———. 1986. "On the Concept of Populism: Populist and Clientelistic Modes of Incorporation in Semiperipheral Politics." *Politics and Society* 14(3): 329–48.

———. 1995. "Greece in the Twenty-first Century: Institutions and Political Culture."

In *Greece Prepares for the Twenty-first Century*, ed. Dimitris Constas and Theofanis G. Stavrou. Washington, D.C.: Woodrow Wilson Center Press.

Mukerji, Chandra. 1989. *A Fragile Power: Scientists and the State*. Princeton: Princeton University Press.

———. 1997. *Territorial Ambitions and the Gardens of Versailles*. Cambridge, England: Cambridge University Press.

Mukerji, Chandra, and Michael Schudson, eds. 1991. *Rethinking Popular Culture: Contemporary Perspectives in Cultural Studies*. Berkeley: University of California Press.

Nandy, Ashis. 1994. *The Illegitimacy of Nationalism: Rabindranath Tagore and the Politics of Self*. Delhi: Oxford University Press.

National Statistical Service of Greece. 2002. *H Ellada me Arithmous, 2002. (Greece in figures, 2002)*. Athens: National Statistical Service of Greece.

National Statistics on Social Security and Health. 1995. Athens: National Statistical Service of Greece.

Naziri, D. 1988. "La Femme Grecque et l'Avortement: Etude Clinique du Recourse Repetitif a l'Avortement." Ph. D. diss., University of Paris.

Nicholson, Linda J., ed. 1990. *Feminism/Postmodernism*. New York: Routledge.

Nietzsche, Friedrich. 1989. *On the Genealogy of Morals and Ecce Homo*. Ed. and trans. Walter Kaufmann. New York: Vintage.

Norris, Pippa, ed. 1997. *Women, Media, and Politics*. New York: Oxford University Press.

Ortner, Sherry, B. 1989. *High Religion: A Cultural and Political History of Sherpa Buddhism*. Princeton: Princeton University Press.

Paige, Karen, and Jeffery M. Paige. 1981. *The Politics of Reproductive Ritual*. Los Angeles: University of California Press.

Palli-Petralia, Fani. 1997. *I Atekni Hora: Demografiki Exelixi-Prooptikes* (The childless country: Demographic evolution and developments). Athens: Sideris.

Pandelidou-Malouta, M. 1992. *Gynaikes kai Politiki* (Women and politics). Athens: Gutenberg.

———. 2002. *To Fylo tis Demokratias: Idiotita tou Politi kai Emfyla Ypokeimena* (The gender of democracy: Citizenship and gendered subjects). Athens: Savvalas.

Panourgia, E. 1995. *Fragments of Death, Fables of Identity: An Athenian Anthropography*. Madison: University of Wisconsin Press.

Papadopoulos, Yannis. 1989. "Parties, the State and Society in Greece: Continuity within Change." *West European Politics* 12(2): 55–71.

Papagaroufali, Eleni. 1990. "Greek Women in Politics: Gender Ideology and Practice in Neighborhood Groups and the Family." Ph.D. diss., Columbia University.

———. 1999. "Donation of Human Organs or Bodies after Death: A Cultural Phenomenology of 'Flesh' in the Greek Context." *Ethos* 27: 283–314.

Papagaroufali, Eleni, and Eugenia Georges. 1993. "Greek Women in the Europe of 1992: Brokers of European Cargoes and the Logic of the West." In *Perilous*

States: Conversations on Culture, Politics, and Nation, ed. George Marcus, 235–54. Chicago: University of Chicago Press.

Papageorgiou, Nike-Rebecca. 1986. "Sto Vytho" (In the Deep). In *Tou Linariou Ta Pathi/O Megas Mirmigofagos.* Athens: Agra.

Papahelas, Alexis. 1998. *O Viasmos tis Ellinikis Demokratias: O Amerikanikos Paragondas (1947–1967),* (The rape of Greek democracy: The American factor). 9th ed. Athens: Estia.

Papataxiarchis, Evthymios. 1991. "Gender, Sexuality and the Person in Greek Culture." In *Contested Identities: Gender and Kinship in Modern Greece,* ed. Peter Loizos and Evthymios Papataxiarchis. Princeton: Princeton University Press.

Papyros Larous Britannica. 1981. Vol. 3. Athens: Papyros.

Parenti, M. 1986. *Inventing Reality: The Politics of the Mass Media.* New York: St. Martin's.

Parker, Andrew, Mary Russo, Doris Sommer, and Patricia Yaeger. 1992. *Nationalisms and Sexualities.* New York: Routledge.

Pateman, Carol. 1988. *The Sexual Contract.* Stanford: Stanford University Press.

———. 1989. "The Patriarchal Welfare State." In *The Disorder of Women.* Cambridge, England: Polity.

Patton, Cindy. 1990. *Inventing AIDS.* New York: Routledge.

Paxson, Heather. 1997. "Demographics and Diaspora, Gender and Genealogy: Anthropological Notes on Greek Population Policy." *South European Society and Politics* 2(2): 34–56.

Petchesky, Rosalind Pollack. 1990. *Abortion and Woman's Choice: The State, Sexuality and Reproductive Freedom.* Boston: Northeastern University Press.

Peterson, Peter. 1999. "The Global Aging Crisis." *Foreign Affairs* (January/February): 42–55.

Petropoulos, John. 1968. *Politics and Statecraft in the Kingdom of Greece, 1833–1844.* Princeton: Princeton University Press.

Politis, Alexis. 1992. *Romandika Hronia, Ideologies kai Nootropies stin Ellada tou 1830–1880* (Romantic years, ideologies and mentalities of Greece in 1830–1880). Athens: Etairia Meletis Neou Ellinismou-Mnimon.

Pollis, Adamantia. 1977. "The Impact of Traditional Culture Patterns on Greek Politics." *Greek Review of Social Research* (English ed.) 29: 2–14.

———. 1987. "The State, the Law, and Human Rights in Modern Greece." *Human Rights Quarterly* 9: 587–614.

———. 1992. "Greek National Identity: Religious Minorities, Rights, and European Norms." *Journal of Modern Greek Studies* 10: 171–95.

Polyzos, Nikos I. 1984. "I Egatastasi ton Prosfigon tou 1922: Mia oriaki periptosi astikopoiisis" (The installation process of the refugees of 1922: A boundary case of urbanization). Ph.D. diss., Ethniko Metsovio Polytexnio, Tmima Arhitektonon, Athens.

Polyzos, Nikos I., George Tziafetas, Dimitris Tzaousis, Ira Emke-Poulopoulou, and Haris Symeonidou. 1988. *Evropaiki Demografiki Koinotita: I Thesi tis Elladas*

(European demographic community: The position of Greece). Athens: Greek Association for Demographic Studies.

Probyn, Espeth. 1993. *Sexing the Self: Gendered Positions in Cultural Studies.* New York: Routledge.

Prodromou, Elizabeth H. 1994. "Toward an Understanding of Eastern Orthodoxy and Democracy Building in the Post–Cold War Balkans." *Mediterranean Quarterly* (spring): 113–38.

"Prometheus Unbound: A Survey of Greece." 2002. *The Economist,* 12 October, insert.

Rabinow, Paul, ed. 1984. *The Foucault Reader.* New York: Pantheon.

Radway, Janice. 1984. *Reading the Romance: Women, Patriarchy, and Popular Literature.* Chapel Hill: University of North Carolina Press.

Rafael, Vicente. 1993. "White Love: Surveillance and Nationalist Resistance in the U.S. Colonization of the Philippines." In *Cultures of U.S. Imperialism,* ed. Amy Kaplan and Donald E. Pease. Durham, N.C.: Duke University Press.

Rajaretnam, T., and R. V. Deshpande. 1994. "The Effect of Sex Preference on Contraceptive Use and Fertility in Rural South India." *International Family Planning Perspectives* 20(3).

Rich, Adrienne. 1979. *On Lies, Secrets, and Silence.* New York: Norton.

Rigos, Alkis. 1992. *I B' Elliniki Demokratia 1924–1935: Koinonikes Diastaseis tis Politikis Skinis* (The second Greek democracy 1924–1935: Social dimensions of the political scene). Athens: Themelio.

Riley, Denise. 1988. *Am I That Name? Feminism and the Category of "Women."* London: Macmillan.

Robbins, Bruce, ed. 1993. *The Phantom Public Sphere.* Minneapolis: University of Minnesota Press.

Rousseau, Jean-Jacques. 1967. *The Social Contract and Discourse on the Origin of Inequality.* Ed. Lester G. Crocker. New York: Penguin.

Russell, Andrew, Elisa J. Sobo, and Mary S. Thompson, eds. 2000. *Contraception across Cultures: Technologies, Choices, Constraints.* Oxford: Berg.

Said, Edward. 1978. *Orientalism.* New York: Basic Books.

Sant Cassia, Paul, and Constantina Bada. 1992. *The Making of the Modern Greek Family: Marriage and Exchange in Nineteenth-Century Athens.* New York: Cambridge University Press.

Sarch, Amy. 1997. "Those Dirty Ads! Birth Control Advertising in the 1920s and 1930s." *Critical Studies in Mass Communication* 14: 31–48.

Sarris, Neoklis. 1982. *Kypros: H Alli Plevra* (Cyprus: The other side). Vol. 2 of *The Diplomatic Chronography of the Dismemberment of Cyprus According to Turkish Sources, Book A, 1955–1963.* Athens: Grammi.

———. 1992. *Elliniki Koinonia kai Tileorasi* (Greek society and television). Vol. 2. Athens: Gordios.

Sawicki, Jana. 1991. *Disciplining Foucault: Feminism, Power, and the Body.* New York: Routledge.

Schneider, Jane, and Peter Schneider. 1995. "Coitus Interruptus and Family Respectability in Catholic Europe." In *Conceiving the New World Order: The Global Politics of Reproduction*, ed. Faye D. Ginsburg and Rayna Rapp, 177–94. Berkeley: University of California Press.

———. 1996. *Festival of the Poor: Fertility Decline and the Ideology of Class in Sicily, 1860–1980*. Tucson: University of Arizona Press.

Schudson, Michael. 1992. *Watergate in American Memory: How We Remember, Forget, and Reconstruct the Past*. New York: Basic Books.

———. 1995. *The Power of News*. Boston: Harvard University Press.

Scott, Joan Wallach. 1988. *Gender and the Politics of History*. New York: Columbia University Press.

———. 1992. "Experience." In *Feminists Theorize the Political*, ed. Judith Butler and Joan W. Scott, 22–40. New York: Routledge.

Sedgwick, Eve Kosofsky. 1990. *Epistemology of the Closet*. Berkeley: University of California Press.

Seferis, George. [1961] 1993. *Delphi*. Trans. C. Capri-Karka. *Charioteer: An Annual Review of Modern Greek Culture* 35(94): 12–24.

Serafetinidou, Melina, 2003. *To Fainomeno tis Grafeiokratias: I. Theoritiki Sizitisi* (The Phenomenon of democracy: The theoretical discussion), vol. 1. Athens: Gutenberg.

Seremetakis, Nadia. 1991. *The Last Word: Women, Death and Divination in Inner Mani*. Chicago: University of Chicago Press.

———, ed. 1993. *Ritual, Power and the Body: Historical Perspectives on the Representation of Greek Women*. New York: Pella.

———, ed. 1994. *The Senses Still: Perception and Memory as Material Culture in Modernity*. Boulder, Colo.: Westview.

Shapiro, Michael J. 1997. *Violent Cartographies: Mapping Cultures of War*. Minneapolis: University of Minnesota Press.

Singer, Linda. 1992. "Feminism and Postmodernism." In *Feminists Theorize the Political*, ed. Judith Butler and Joan W. Scott, 464–75. New York: Routledge.

Smith, Anthony D. 1999. *Myths and Memories of the Nation*. New York: Oxford University Press.

Snitow, Ann, Christine Stansell, and Sharon Thompson, eds. 1983. *Powers of Desire: The Politics of Sexuality*. New York: Monthly Review Press.

Sommer, Doris. 1991. *Foundational Fictions*. Berkeley: University of California Press.

Sotiropoulos, Dimitris A. 1996. *Populism and Bureaucracy: The Case of Greece under PASOK, 1981–1989*. Notre Dame: University of Notre Dame Press.

Soysal, Yasemin Nuhoglu. 1994. *Limits of Citizenship: Migrants and Postnational Membership in Europe*. Chicago: University of Chicago Press.

Spivak, Gayatri Chakravorty. 1990. *The Post-Colonial Critic: Interview, Strategies, Dialogues*. Ed. Sarah Harasym. New York: Routledge.

Stamiris, Eleni. 1986. "The Women's Movement in Greece." *New Left Review* 98–117.

Stasinopoulos, Epaminondas K. 1973. *Istoria ton Athinon: Apo tin Arhaiotita os tin Epohi mas* (History of Athens: From antiquity to our times). Athens: Costas Kouloufakos Press.

Stasinopoulou, Olga. N.d. *Kratos Pronoias* (The welfare state). Athens: Gutenberg.

Stavros, Stephanos. 1995. "The Legal Status of Minorities in Greece Today: The Adequacy of Their Protection in the Light of Current Human Rights Perceptions." *Journal of Modern Greek Studies* 13: 1–32.

Stavrou, Theofanis G. 1995. "The Orthodox Church and Political Culture in Modern Greece." In *Greece Prepares for the Twenty-First Century*, ed. Dimitri Constas and Theofanis G. Stavrou, 35–38. Washington, D.C.: Woodrow Wilson Center Press.

Steinberg, Deborah Lynn, Debbie Epstein, and Richard Johnson, eds. 1997. *Border Patrols: Policing the Borders of Heterosexuality.* London: Casell.

Stewart, Charles. 1989. "Hegemony or Rationality? The Position of the Supernatural in Modern Greece." *Journal of Modern Greek Studies* 7: 77–104.

———. 1991. *Demons and the Devil: Aspects of the Moral Imagination of Modern Greek Culture.* Princeton: Princeton University Press.

———. 1999. Magic and Orthodoxy. *Archeologia* 72, 8–13.

Survey. 1997. *Tempo*, no. 5 (7 July): 14–18.

Sutton, David. 1994. "Tradition and Modernity: Kalymnian Constructions of Identity and Otherness." *Journal of Modern Greek Studies* 12:240.

Svoronos, Nikos. 1999. *Analekta Neoellinikis Istorias kai Istoriografias* (Selections of neo-Hellenic history and historiography). Athens: Themelio.

Symeonidou, Haris. 1990. *Apasholisi kai Gonimotita ton Gynaikon stin Periohi tis Protevousas* (Employment and fertility of women in the area of Athens). Athens: Ethniko Kendro Koinonikon Erevnon.

———, et al. 1992. *Koinoniko-Oikonomikoi Prosdioristikoi Paragondes tis Gonimotitas stin Ellada* (Socioeconomic factors affecting fertility in Greece). Vol. 1. Athens: Ethniko Kendro Koinonikon Erevnon.

———, et al. 1997. *Koinoniko-Oikonomikoi Prosdioristikoi Paragondes tis Gonimotitas stin Ellada* (Socioeconomic factors affecting fertility in Greece). Vol. 2. Athens: National Center for Social Research.

———, et al. 2000. *Epithimito kai Pragmatiko Megethos Oikoyeneias: Gegonota tou Kyklou Zois. Mia Diahroniki Prosengisi: 1983–1997* (Desired and real family size: Life-cycle events 1983–1997). Athens: National Center for Social Research (EKKE).

Tatsis, Nikolaos. 1995. *Koinoniologia: Koinoniki Organosi kai Politismiakes Diergasies* (Sociology, social organization and cultural processes). Athens: Odysseas.

Taussig, Michael. 1997. *The Magic of the State.* New York: Routledge.

Topali, Maria. 1999. *Servitsio Tsayou* (The tea setting). Athens: Nefeli.

Tsakalogiannis, Panos. 2000. *Syhroni Evropaiki Istoria: Apo ti Vastili sto Teihos tou Verolinou, 1789–1989* (Contemporary European history: From Bastille to the Berlin Wall, 1789–1989). Vol. 1. Athens: Estia.

Tsaliki, Liza. 1995. "The Media and the Construction of an 'Imagined Community': The Role of Media Events on Greek Television." *European Journal of Communication* 10(3): 345–70.

Tsalikoglou, Fotini. 1995. "A New Disease in Greek Society: AIDS and the Representation of 'Otherness.'" *Journal of Modern Greek Studies* 13(1): 83–98.

Tsing, Anna Lowenhaupt. 1993. *In the Realm of the Diamond Queen*. Princeton: Princeton University Press.

Tsoukalas, Constantine. 1984. "The Making of the Modern State in Greece." *Mediterranean Peoples* 27–28: 83–101.

———. 1991. "'Enlightened' Concepts in the 'Dark': Power and Freedom, Politics and Society." *Journal of Modern Greek Studies* 9: 1–22.

———. 1995. "Free Riders in Wonderland; Or, Of Greeks in Greece." In *Greece Prepares for the Twenty-first Century*, ed. Dimitri Constas and Theofanis G. Stavrou. Washington, D.C.: Woodrow Wilson Center Press.

———. 1996. "Peri Tromokratias" (Of terrorism). In *Taxidi ston Logo kai stin Istoria: Keimena 1969–1996*, ed. Panayotis Kafetzis, 97–102. Athens: Plethron.

———. 1998. *Eidola Politismou: Eleftheria, Isotita kai Adelfotita sti Syhroni Politeia* (Idols of civilization: Freedom, equality and brotherhood in the contemporary polity). Athens: Themelio.

———. 1999. *Exousia os Laos kai os Ethnos: Peripeteies Simasion* (Power as "the people" and as nation: Adventures of meaning). Athens: Themelio.

Tuchman, Gayle. 1978. *Making News*. New York: Free Press.

Tumarkin, N. 1987. "Myth and Memory in Soviet Society." *Society* 24(6): 69–72.

Turner, Bryan S. 1984. *The Body and Society: Explorations in Social Theory*. New York: Blackwell.

Turner, Victor. 1974. *Dramas, Fields, and Metaphors: Symbolic Action in Human Society*. Ithaca, N.Y.: Cornell University Press.

United Nations-Greece Report. 2002. *Fertility and Family Surveys in Countries of the ECE Region, Standard Country Report, Greece*. United Nations Economic Commission for Europe and United Nations Population Fund. Economic Studies, no. 10, by Haris Symeonidou. New York: United Nations.

Vaiou, Dina. 1995. "Women's Work and Everyday Life in Southern Europe in the Context of European Integration." In *Women of the European Union: The Politics of Work and Daily Life*, ed. M. D. Garcia-Ramon and J. Monk, 61–73. New York: Routledge.

Vance, Carole S., ed. 1989. *Pleasure and Danger: Exploring Female Sexuality*. London: Pandora.

———. 1991. "Anthropology Rediscovers Sexuality: A Theoretical Comment." *Social Science and Medicine* 33(8): 875–84.

van Dijk, T. 1988. *News Analysis: Case Studies of International and National News in the Press*. Hillsdale: N.J.: Erlbaum.

Van Dyck, Karen. 1997. *Kassandra and the Censors: Greek Poetry Since 1967*. Ithaca, N.Y.: Cornell University Press.

——, ed. 1998. *The Rehearsal of Misunderstanding: Three Collections by Contemporary Greek Women Poets. Bilingual Edition. The Cake by Rhea Galanaki, Tales of the Deep by Jenny Mastoraki, Hers by Maria Laina*. Hanover, N.H.: Wesleyan University Press.

Varika, Elena. 1992. "Andimetopes me ton Eksyhronismo ton Thesmon: Enas Dyskolos Feminismos" (Facing the modernization of institutions: A difficult feminism). In *I Ellada ton Gynaikon* (Women's Greece), ed. E. Leontidou and S. R. Ammer, 67–80. Athens: Enallaktikes Ekdoseis/Gaia I.

Varvouni, M. G. 1995. *Paradosiaki Thriskeftiki Symberifora kai Thriskeftiki Leografia* (Traditional religious behavior and religious folklore). Athens: Odysseas.

Verdery, K. 1996. "Whither 'Nation' and 'Nationalism'?" In *Mapping the Nation*, ed. G. Balakrishan, 226–34. London: Verso.

Vervenioti, T. 2000. "The Adventure of Women's Suffrage in Greece." In *When the War Was Over: Women, War, and Peace in Europe, 1940–1956*, ed. Claire Duchen and Irene Bandhauer-Schoffmann. London: Leicester University Press.

Visaria, Leela, Shireen Jejeebhoy, and Tom Merrick. 1999. "From Family Planning to Reproductive Health: Challenges Facing India." *International Family Planning Perspectives* 25 (January).

Vryonis, Spiros, Jr., ed. 1978. *The "Past" in Medieval and Modern Greek Culture*. Malibu, Calif.: Undena.

Walby, Sylvia. 1992. "Post-post-modernism? Theorizing Social Complexity." In *Destabilizing Theory: Contemporary Feminist Debates*, ed. Michele Barrett and Anne Phillips, 31–52. Stanford: Stanford University Press.

Walkerdine, Valerie. 1988. *The Mastery of Reason: Cognitive Development and the Production of Rationality*. New York: Routledge.

Ware, Timothy. 1997. *The Orthodox Church*. New York: Penguin.

Warner, Michael. 2000. *The Trouble with Normal: Sex, Politics and the Ethics of Queer Life*. Boston: Harvard University Press.

——, ed. 1993. Introduction to *Fear of a Queer Planet: Queer Politics and Social Theory*. Minneapolis: University of Minnesota Press.

Warren, K., and Bourque, S. 1985. "Gender, Power, and Communication: Responses to Political Mating in the Andes." In *Women Living Change*, ed. S. Bourque and D. R. Divine. Philadelphia: Temple University Press.

Wedeen, Lisa. 1999. *Ambiguities of Domination: Politics, Rhetoric and Symbols in Contemporary Syria*. Chicago: University of Chicago Press.

Weeks, J. 1985. *Sexuality and Its Discontents: Meaning, Myths, and Modern Sexualities*. London: Routledge and Kegan Paul.

Wharton, Annabel Jane. 2001. *Building the Cold War: Hilton International Hotels and Modern Architecture*. Chicago: University of Chicago Press.

Williams, Patricia J. 1991. *The Alchemy of Race and Rights: Diary of a Law Professor*. Cambridge, Mass.: Harvard University Press.

Williams, Raymond. 1981. *The Sociology of Culture*. New York: Schocken.

Yanagisako, Sylvia, and Delaney, Carol. 1995. "Naturalizing Power." In *Naturalizing*

Power: Essays in Feminist Cultural Analysis, ed. Sylvia Yanagisako and Carol Delaney, 1–22. New York: Routledge.

Yfantopoulos, Y. 1999. "Demographic Trends and Socio-economic Indicators in Greece and the EU." In *About Greece,* 146–59. Ministry of Press and Mass Media, Secretariat General of Information, prepared by the Laboratory of Political Communication. Athens: University of Athens.

Yo, Zeng et al. 1993. "Causes and Implications of the Recent Increase in the Reported Sex Ratio at Birth in China," *Population and Development Review* 19(2): 5–8.

Yuval-Davis, Nira. 1996. "Women and the Biological Reproduction of 'the Nation.'" *Women's Studies International Forum* 19(1–2): 17–24.

———. 1997. *Gender and Nation.* London: Sage.

Yuval-Davis, Nira, and Floya Anthias. 1989. *Woman-Nation-State.* London: Macmillan.

Zarafonitou, Christina, and Anna Mandoglou. 2000. "I Koinoniki Anaparastasi tou Eglimatos kai tou Eglimatia" (The social representation of crime and of the criminal [in Greece]). In *Poinika 59: Antieglimatiki Politiki II. Eikosiepta Akomi Meletes yia ta Oria, tous Orous kai tis Katefthynseis tis* (Criminal policy II. Twenty-seven additional studies on its limits, terms and directions), ed. Nestor Kourakis, 77–121. Athens: Sakkoula.

Zelizer, Barbie. 1995. "Reading the Past against the Grain: The Shape of Memory Studies." *Critical Studies in Mass Communication* (June): 214–39.

Zerubavel, Yael. 1995. *Recovered Roots: Collective Memory and the Making of Israeli National Tradition.* Chicago: University of Chicago Press.

Zinovieff, Sofka. 1991. "Hunters and Hunted: Kamaki and the Ambiguities of Sexual Predation in a Greek Town." In *Contested Identities: Gender and Kinship in Modern Greece,* ed. Peter Loizos and Evthymios Papataxiarchis, 203–20. Princeton: Princeton University Press.

Žižek, Slavoj. 1987. *The Sublime Object of Ideology.* London: Verso.

INDEX

✢

Abortion: and AIDS, 91, 299–300; and anesthesia, 259–64, 304; and the body, impact on, 255–64, 268–69; and couples, impact on, 208–33, 235–52; and doctors, 97–100, 102–12; ethics of, 264–73; and fertility, 248–49, 255–59, 261–64; and laughter, 260; legalization of, 41–42, 91, 276–79; and midwives, 275–76; and modernity, 4–6, 131–32, 295, 299, 336, 339–40; and mothers, 265–71; and nationalism, 120–26, 295–96, 306, 313–16; as natural, culturally, 6, 135–55; vs. other birth control, 155–98; pain of, 14, 236–74; and patriotism, 6; perceptions and attitudes about, 100–101, 121, 254, 265, 274–86; press coverage of, 113–15, 120–26, 295–306, 340; procedure of, 274–76; as resistance, 6, 55, 164; responsibility for, 236–52, 259; secrecy surrounding, 89–90, 280–81; as sin, 252–55, 263–64; statistical data for, 4, 40–45, 80–85, 90–91, 156–60; surgical operation of, 108–11; taboo of, 274–86; and tradition, 4–6, 131–32; uses of, 208–33; as visual technology, 210–31, 247, 274. *See also* Demografiko; Identity, Greek; Religious discourse

Abortion rate: in Bulgaria, 80–81; in China, 83–84; in Greece, 1, 4–6, 78, 160; in India, 84–85; in Macedonia, 85–86; in Romania, 81–82; in the Russian Federation, 82–83
Agency, 2, 14, 166, 185, 210–33, 235–86, 291–93, 297–301, 304, 305, 310, 314, 321, 344; retheorizing, 345–48
Aggelopoulou, Iana, 22
Agon ("struggle"), 11–12, 144, 319, 346; as battleground, 197, 198, 245–52; and the couple, 208; as minefield, 144, 155, 161, 231, 245; and sex, 163, 164, 167, 188, 190, 193, 194, 241
AIDS, and abortion, 91, 299–300
Alarcon, Norma, 363 n.2
Albania, and national gendering, 55–56
Albanians, 343; as immigrants, 127; and No Day incident, 55–56
Alexiou, Haris, 148–54, 164, 368 n.17, 370 n.21, 371 n.23
Anagnost, Ann, 83, 352 n.13, 361 n.8
Ancient Greece, and Greek identity, 50–51, 59–60, 66–68, 116, 146. *See also* Greece
Anderson, Benedict, 10, 115, 361 n.7
Anesthesia, fear of, 259–64, 304
Anthias, Floya, 363 n.2
Ardener, E., 366 n.10

Asia Minor: catastrophe, 61–62, 147, 208, 312; racism against refugees, 68–71
Athens: appearances in, preoccupation with, 31–34; economy of, 25–27; historical background of, 23–25; present day, 21–23. *See also* Ancient Greece, and Greek identity; Identity, Greek
Avdela, Efi, 147

Bakalaki, A. 350 n.3
Balkans, 147, 148, 301, 306, 347; joke about, 72, 74
Basso, Keith, 367 n.11
Bauman, Richard, 367 n.11
Bekou, E., 36–37
Berlant, Lauren, 364 n.6
Bhabha, Homi K., 360 n.6
Birth control. *See* Contraception
Birth rate. *See* Demografiko
Bodies: and modernity, resistance to, 6, 169–71, 174–79, 182–90; and nationalism, 2–3, 45, 135–55; production of, by discourses, 8–10, 138–39, 142, 259–64, 345
Bordo, Susan, 350 n.7
Boundaries, cultural, 5, 92, 98, 104, 112, 272–74; and anesthesia 259–64; and eating meat, 92; and flesh, 22–23, 31–33, 137; and national identity, 66–74, 114, 137, 293, 313, 347; "pop psychology" notions of, 197; in relationships, 225, 252; and religion, 45–50, 186; and the research, 5, 8, 19, 96–98, 100, 104, 107, 109, 272, 281–86
Bourdieu, Pierre, 366 n.11
Bourque, S., 365 n.9
Braidotti, Rosi, 364 n.7
Brown, Wendy, 102, 378 n.23, 379 n.6
Butler, Judith, 138, 148, 321, 345, 349 n.2, 350 n.7, 351 n.12, 364 n.6, 378 n.3
Byron, Lord, 28–31, 353 n.17

Calabrese, Andrew, 376 n.2
Calhoun, Craig, 379 n.9
Cartoons (by K. Mitropoulos) 37, 47
Charalambis, Dimitris, 361 n.10
Chryssanthopoulos, 369 n.18
Chrystodoulos, Archbishop, 53–55
Citizenship, 207, 292; and gender, 136, 148, 162, 186, 313–16; and motherhood, 7, 258, 294, 314–16, 323, 340
Clinic, private, narrative of day at, 89–112; public, Family Planning Center, 91, 274–76, 278–79, 282–85; Sterility center, ethnographic data on, 102–8, 112, 283–85, 358 n.2
Conception, "catching," 174–79, 198
Condoms: frequency of use, 159–60, 298–302; vs. "the days," 169–76; vs. the Pill, 187; women's thoughts on, 190–95, 214
Constas, Dimitri, 350 n.3
Contraception, 298–305; as alien, 141–42, 255; alternative forms of, 243; in Bulgaria, 43–44, 81; in China, 83; and demografiko discourse, 299–304, 312, 315; and Greek women, 141–42, 155–205, 299–302; in India, 84; and invasiveness, perception of, 6, 141, 154, 189–90, 198, 262, 320; midwives on, 199–205; narratives on, 140–41, 162–205, 214; and national identity, 162–99; quantitative data on, 40–45, 80–85, 156–60; in Rumania, 81–82; in the Russian Federation, 82–83; and trust, in relationships, 165–69, 208. *See also specific methods of contraception*
Couples, heterosexual: and national identity, 135–53; impact of abortion on, 208–33, 235–52; narratives of, 209–30, 237–51
Cowan, Jane K., 361 n.12, 365 n.8
Cyprus, and Greek history, 63–64

406 Index

Dakin, Douglas, 59–60
Damanakis, M., 147
Danforth, Loring M., 118, 355 n.15
Dara, Christina, 288
"The days" (birth control method), 156–58, 162–63; and condoms, 169–71, 174; and other forms of sex, 155,158, 159; and the rhythm method, 155, 157–58; and withdrawal, 165–69
De Lauretis, Teresa, 350 n.7
Deleuze, Gilles, 346
Delphi (Seferis), 17
Demertzis, Nicolas, 350 n.3, 361 n.10
Democracy, liberal: foundations of, 2–4, 7,14, 196–98; and Greece, 77–86; limitations of, 162, 345–48; and the United States, 138, 147
Demografiko, 1, 75, 77–86; bills proposed about, 79–80; and contraception, 299–304, 312, 315; and gender, 6; and Greek youths, 128–29; and Macedonia, 78; and modernity, 4–6, 131–32; narratives about, 324–36; and nationalist discourse, 6, 322–37, 341–44; press coverage of, 113–32, 291–316, 341–42; and racism, 337, 342–44; as reproductive technology, 7, 113–34, 291–318; resistance to, 319–35, 341–44; and the retirement system, 36–37, 127–30; and tradition, 4–6, 131–32. *See also* Women, Greek
Diamandouros, P. Nikiforos, 118, 350 n.5
Diaphragm, 158, 195
Dimoulis, Dimitris, 357 n.13
Doctors, 195, 297; and abortion, 97–100, 102–12; Aravandinos, Dr., 300; Asprikadi, Tasi, 89, 92–96, 102–3, 107–10; Jay, Dr., 274, 276–78, 281; Kreatsas, Professor, 300; Polakis, Dr., 98–100, 358 n.2; Theodorou, Dr., 102–8, 112, 283–85, 358 n.2; and women patients, 97–100, 180, 259–60
Dokimasia ("trial"), 208

Dowries, and Greek women, 36
Doxiadis, Kyrkos, 361 n.9
Dragona, Thaleia, 368 n.13
Drouza, Anna, 377 n.11, 377 n.20
Dubisch, Jill, 49–50, 355 n.15, 356 n.20
Durkheim, Emile, 321

Ebgron, Paula, 351 n.11
"Economy of pain," 142, 171, 252, 265
Elytis, Odysseus, 116
Emke-Poulopoulou, Hra, 357 n.2
Enimerosi ("informing the citizenry"), 142, 310, 311, 313, 315, 339
Epemvasi ("intervention"), 12, 41, 96, 135, 142, 196
Ethics, of abortion, 264–73
Etolos, Cosmas, 357 n.9
Evans, David T., 370 n.20

Fallmerayer, Jakob Phillip, 68
Family Law of 1981, 36, 41, 277
Family Planning Center, 91, 274–76, 282–85
Faubion, James, 35, 350 n.3, 352 n.1
Fausto-Sterling, Anne, 351 n.9
Feminism, 102, 192, 209, 276–78, 328
Ferraios, Rigas, 59
Ferris, Costas, 133
Fertility, and abortion, 248–49, 255–59, 261–64
Fine, Michelle, 367 n.11
Foucault, Michel, 138, 346, 350 n.6, 352 n.12, 363 n.3, 367 n.12, 370 n.20, 379 n.6; on power, 8–10, 321–23
Frangoudaki, Anna, 368 n.13
Fraser, Nancy, 116
Friedl, Ernestine, 365 n.10
Friedland, Roger, 363 n.2
From Medea to Sappho: Insubordinate Women in Ancient Greece (art exhibit), 50–51
Fundamentalism, 80, 128, 130–32, 291, 296, 305, 315, 328, 337, 343

Gagnon, John H., 370 n.20
Gal, Susan, 367 n.11
Gaventa, John, 367 n.11
Gender: and abortion, 11, 17; and Albania, 55–56; and Athens, 17–18, 28; and citizenship, 136, 162, 186, 313–16; and demografiko, 6; and Greek Orthodoxy, 41, 45–50, 122; and national identity, 8, 135–37, 289; and nationalism, 55–56, 72, 74, 137, 143, 293–97. *See also* Masculinity, Greek; Men, Greek; Women, Greek
Georges, Eugenia, 253
Gilligan, Carol, 265
Ginsburg, Faye D., 352 n.13, 361 n.6
Giroux, Henry A., 376 n.2
Gourgouris, Stathis, 116
Graikoi, and Greek History, 66–68
Gramsci, A. 340
Greece: attitudes toward abortion in, 100–101, 121; and democracy, 345–48; as Greek Orthodox state, 115–16, 118, 120–32, 207, 252–55, 262–64; historical analysis of, 57–75; and nationalism, 118–32; 293–97, 306–9, 328–40 in the press, 115–18; psychologists in, 97; public sphere in, 116–18; representations of, 2, 19–20, 289. *See also* Athens
Greek identity. *See* Identity, Greek
Greek Orthodoxy, 121–26; and abortion, 141, 253–54, 338; and demografiko, 124–32; and gender, 41, 45–50, 122; and Greece as religious state, 115–16, 118, 120–32, 207, 252–55, 262–64, 289; and ID cards, 53–56; and national identity, 124–32; and women, 45–50; and youths, 145–46. *See also* Religious discourse
Greek press. *See* Press, Greek
Greek youth. *See* Youth, Greek
Grossberg, Lawrence, 369 n.18
Gynecologists. *See* Doctors

Habermas, Jürgen, 116–17
Hadjidakis, Manos, 369 n.17
Hamilou Pneumatikou Epipedou ("not smart or cultivated"), 99–100
Haralambidis, C., 70
Haraway, Donna, 15, 144, 342, 351 n.9
Hardt-Mautner, Geraldine, 351 n.8
Hatdzifotis, I., 121, 124
Hellas, and Greek history, 66–68
Herzfeld, Michael, 2, 66–68, 118, 192, 246, 253, 349 n.3, 350 n.3, 361 n.12, 365–66 n.10; and "a poetics of womanhood," 51–52, 192, 246
Heterosexuality, Greek. *See* Couples, heterosexual; Sexuality
Hirsch, E. D., Jr., 366 n.11
Historical analysis: of Athens, 23–30; of Greece, 57–75; politics of national identity, 50–51, 59–60, 66–68, 116, 146
Hobsbawm, Eric J., 115
Homosexuality: female, and bisexuality, 153; male, 194–95; and nationalism, 164
Hubbard, Ruth, 351 n.9
Huntington, Samuel P., 346

ID cards, changed format of, 53–56
Identity, Greek, 1–2, 10, 66–75; and Athens, 17–18, 28–30; characteristics of, 55, 66; and contraception, 162–99; and demografiko, 1, 7, 10, 113–14, 142–43, 291; and gender, 72, 74, 135–37, 293–94; and Greek couples, 209; and Greek Orthodoxy, 124–32; and the Greek press, 115–18; and Greek youths, 145–46; and ID cards, format of, 53–56; and modernity, 137–39; and No Day, 55–56; politics of, in contemporary and ancient Greece, 50–51, 59–60, 66–68, 116, 146; and religious discourse, 121–26; representations of, 11; and sexuality, 6, 143–98, 335–37

408 Index

I dyo yenies ("The two generations," Katsoulidis), 289
Immigrants: from Albania, 127; anxiety about, 77–79, 146; to Athens, 25. *See also* Asia Minor; Racism
Infanticide, 83–86
I Sholi ton Athinon No. 2 ("The School of Athens No. 2," Vakirtzis), 24
IUD, 158–59, 182, 195, 199–205, 300

Jokes, 34, 342; about Greece and the Balkans, 72, 74; in the operating room, 104; on the radio, 112; about sex, 163, 245

Kalogeras, Yiorgos, 369 n.18, 377 n.8
Kaplan, Caren, 363 n.2
Kapnizete? ("Do you smoke?," Papanikolaou), 288
Karakasidou, Anastasia, 293, 357 n.8
Katsoulidis, Takis, 289
Keeley, Edmund, 370 n.19
Kemal, Mustafa, 61, 71
Kenderis, Kostas, 50
Kilborn, Richard, 351 n.8
Killoran, Moira, 368 n.12
Kinito ("mobile phone"), in Athens, 22–23
Kligman, Gail, 82
Kondili, Marianna, 341–42, 357 n.2, 379 n.8
Korais, Adamandios, 59
Kotaridis, Nikos, 353 n.13
Kyria ("a lady"), 217, 275
Kyriakidou-Nestoros, Alki, 350 n.3
Kyriazi, Nota, 303–4, 357 n.2, 377 n.14

Laina, Maria, 87
Lambrinidou, Christiana, 192
Laughter, and abortion, 260
Law 1609, 41, 91, 124
Lekkas, Pandelis, 361 n.11

Leondidou, Lila, 23, 25–27, 353 n.6
Leontis, Artemis, 116
Listening, 144–45, 155, 237, 316
Loizos, Manos, 369 n.17
Loizos, Peter, 41, 354 n.12
Loukos, Christos, 356 n.5
Love (Topali), 207
The Loved Ones (Mastoraki), 287
Luker, Kristen, 374 n.1, 379 n.7
Lyritzis, 350 n.3
Lytras, Andreas, 353 n.14

Macedonia, 60–61, 66, 68, 75, 78, 80, 127, 132, 293–94; and demografiko, 78; and politics of reproduction, 85–86
Macnaghten, Phil, 364 n.5
"magical" thinking, 262–64, 269. *See also* Women, Greek; Religion
"Maid of Athens ere we part" (Byron), 29–30
Makri, Teresa, 29–32, 353 n.18
Male children, preference for, 83–86
Mandoglou, Anna, 378 n.2
Martin, B., 350 n.7
Martin, Emily, 351 n.9
Marx, Karl, 379 n.6
Masculinity, Greek, 101, 136, 143–44, 150, 194, 195, 216, 221, 311, 315, 364 n.8
Mastoraki, Jenny, 235, 287, 348
Mazower, Mark, 63
McClintock, Anne, 369 n.18
Meech, Peter, 351 n.8
Meidani, Marina, 91
Memory, collective, site of trauma, 28, 62, 66, 136, 207, 248, 348
Men, Greek, 114, 143, 146, 166, 168, 169, 250, 293, 312, 347; and contraceptive use, 40–43, 299, 302. *See also* Women, Greek
Midwife, head, 274, 278–82
Midwives, 340; and abortion, 275–76; on contraception, 199–205

Index 409

Miheli, Lisa, 353 n.16
Mikroutsikos, Th., 370 n.21
Mitropoulos, K. 37, 47
Moallem, Minoo, 363 n.2
Modernity: and abortion, 4–6, 131–32, 295, 299, 336, 339–40; and national identity, 137–39; and nationalism, 115–16, 148; and women's bodies, 6, 169–71, 174–78, 182–90
Money, 103, 105–6, 128, 138, 165, 196, 197; and finances, 303, 306, 330–31, 344
Mosse, George L., 352 n.13, 361 n.6
Mosxou-Sakorafou, S., 38, 354 n.7
Mother (Dara), 288
Motherhood, and Greek women's citizenship, 7, 240, 258, 294, 308–9, 313–16, 323, 340
Mothers, 5, 254, 258; and abortion, 265–71
Mouffe, Chantal, 291
Mouzelis, Nicos P., 118, 350 n.3, 361 n.12
Mufti, Aamir, 369 n.18
Mukerji, Chandra, 371 n.24, 377 n.22
Music: Alexiou, 148–54; The Brothers Katsimiha, 154; Gatsos, Nikos (*The Net* as song), 317; Manoulidis, Giannis, 364 n.8; *To Rebetiko* (film), 133–36; rebetika songs, 27; "Trompe-L'oeil-Realité" (Costas Haralambidis) 70. *See also* Zorba
Muslim Greeks, 314
Muslim Turks, 71–72, 78, 124, 291–17

Nathanail, Elena, 220
National Council of Greek Women, 38
National discourses, and the Greek body, 10, 138, 142, 198, 235, 345
National Holiday of 25 March, 136
National identity. *See* Identity, Greek
Nationalism: and abortion, 120–26; 295–96, 306, 313–16; and the body, 2–3, 6, 10, 135–98, 293–97, 313–17; in the clinic, 104; and demografiko, 5, 6, 322–37, 341–44; and gender, 143; in Greece, 62, 77, 118, 144; and Greek women, 14, 320–35; and Greek youth, 145–48; and invasion, fear of, 146–47; and masculinity, 136; and modernity, 115–16, 148; and No Day incident, 55–56; and personal relationships, 207–33; and the press, 115–18, 128–29, 295–97, 306–16, 341–42; and religious discourse, 121–26; and resistance, 328–44; in the United States, 147–48
Nation-state, 308, 316, 323–28
Nelson, Cary, 369 n.18
The Net (Gatsos), 317
New Democracy (political party) 65
New York Times, and Macedonia article, 85–86
Nietzsche, F. 102
Nikolakopoulou, L., 370 n.21
No Day incident, and Greek identity, 55–56

O Evagelismos ("The Annunciation," Parthenis), 289
Olympic Games, 22

Pandelidou-Malouta, M., 39–40
Panhellenic Socialist Party (PASOK), 21–23, 36, 65
Papadopoulos, Yannis, 361 n.12
Papageorgiou, Nike-Rebecca, 112
Papahelas, Alexis, 356 n.6
Papandreou, Demetra, 49, 216–17
Papanikolaou, Elias, 288
Paparigopoulos, C., 68
Papataxiarchis, Evthymios, 41, 354 n.12, 375 n.4
Parker, Andrew, 352 n.13, 361 n.6
Parker, Richard G., 370 n.20
Parthenis, Konstadinos, 289

PASOK (Panhellenic Socialist Party), 21–23, 36, 65
Pastourmatzi, Domna, 369 n.18
Peripoiimenes ("taking care of one's appearance"), 32
Petchesky, Rosalind P., 253, 350 n.4
Petropoulos, John, 350 n.3
The Pill, 140–42, 159–60, 176–91, 199–205, 298–301, 304, 306
Poetics of womanhood, 51–52, 192, 246
Politicians, men: Kapodistrias, Ioannis, 59; Karamanlis, C., 49, 63–65; Kolettis, Ioannis, 60; Makarios, Archbishop, 63–64; Mitsotakis, K., 39, 65, 79; Papandreou, Andreas, 39, 49, 65, 216–17; Papandreou, George, 55, 62, 64–65; Plastiras, Nikolaos, 63; Simitis, C., 37, 53–55, 65, 78, 117; Trikoupis, Harilaos, 60; Venizelos, Eleftherios, 61, 64, 69, 71
Politicians, women, 39–40; Apostolaki, Milena, 39; Bakogianni, Dora, 39, 65; Damanaki, Maria, 39, 312; Gennimata, Fofi, 39; Merkouri, Melina, 39, 50–51; Palli-Petralia, Fani, 357 n.2; Papandreou, Vaso, 39; Papariga, Aleka, 39
Politis, Alexis, 357 n.9
Pollis, Adamantia, 360 n.5, 361 n.10, 362 n.25
Power, 1, 7, 9, 12, 14, 15, 23, 38, 57, 59, 113, 122, 137–38, 149–55, 162–63, 174, 191, 198, 208, 209, 235–36, 237, 261, 304; Foucault on, 8–10, 321–23. *See also* Resistance
Pregnancies, different types of, 270, 304, 314
Press, Greek: coverage of abortion, 113–15, 120–26, 295–306, 340; coverage of the nation and the demografiko, 113–34, 128–29, 291–316, 341–42; excerpts and analysis of, 113–32, 291–317; and Greek identity, 115–18

Prodromou, Elizabeth, 360 n.5
Public policy, considerations for, 345–48
Public sphere, in Greece, 116–18

Race, 6, 7, 10, 12, 86, 114, 293, 294, 296, 306–9, 313, 315, 316, 320, 325, 339, 342, 343
Racism: and Asia Minor refugees, 68–71; and the demografiko, 337, 342–44; and immigrants, 77–78
Ranger, Terence, 115
Rapp, Rayna, 352 n.13, 361 n.6
Religious discourse: and abortion, 120–26, 207, 252–55, 262–64; and the nation, 115–16, 118, 207, 252–55, 262–64; and national identity, 45–50, 121–26. *See also* Greek Orthodoxy
Reproculture, 340
Resistance: abortion as, 6, 55, 164; and democracy, 345–47; to the demografiko, 10, 115, 132, 319–35, 341–44; female body as, 174–79, 183; to modernity, 183; retheorizing, 321–23, 340–44; to science, 175, 178, 182, 189
Responsibility, for abortion, 217, 236–52, 259, 297
Retirement system, and demografiko, 36–37, 127–30
Rhythm method, 155, 157–58. *See also* "The Days" (birth control method)
Rigos, Alkis, 357 n.11
Romania, George, 35
Romioi, and Greek history, 66–68
RU-486, 83, 304–5
Russo, Mary, 352 n.13

Saints, and daily life, 45–46
Sappho, 50–51
Sarris, Neoklis, 14, 72, 74, 353 n.15, 357 n.12
Sawicki, Jana, 350 n.7

Schneider, Jane and Peter, 168–69, 371 n.25, 372 n.34
Schudson, Michael, 350 n.8
Scott, Joan Wallach, 350 n.7
Seferis, George, 17, 19, 116
Serafetinidou, Melina, 376 n.6
Seremetakis, Nadia, 351 n.10, 355 n.15, 364 n.4
17th of November (terrorist group), 21–22
Sex: as battleground, 197, 198, 245–52; and conflict, 163, 164, 167, 188, 190, 193, 194, 241; and the couple, 208; as minefield, 144, 155, 161, 231, 245
Sexuality: bisexuality, 153; heterosexuality, 6, 7, 11, 14, 142, 151, 163, 169, 198, 208, 311, 313, 315, 320; homosexuality, female, 153; male, 194–95; narratives on, 162–98; and national identity, 6, 143–98, 335–37; and nationalism, 164; other forms of sex, 158. *See also* Couples; Women, Greek
Sherrard, Phillip, 370 n.19
Sicily, withdrawal in, 168–69
Sin, abortion as, 252–55, 263–64
Singer, Linda, 350 n.7
Skopiano. *See* Macedonia
Sommer, Doris, 352 n.13, 376 n.1
Sotiropoulos, Dimitri A., 376 n.6
Souvlaki, 143–44, 194
Soysal, Yasemin Nuhoglu, 364 n.6
Spivak, Gayatri Chakravorty, 319, 328
Stasinopoulos, Epaminondas K., 353 nn.8–10
State, 308, 316, 323–28
Statistics, formal abortion, 4, 40–45, 80–85, 90–91, 156–62, 171, 298
Stavrou, Theofanis G., 350 n.3, 360 n.5
Stewart, Charles, 355 n.15, 361 n.12, 364 n.4
Sutton, David, 350 n.3

Symeonidou, Haris, 40, 160, 357 n.2, 371 n.26, 372 n.31

Tarlatzis, V, 302
Theodorakis, Mikis, 369 n.17
Topali, Maria, 155, 207, 355 n.16
To Rebetiko (film), 133–35
Treichler, Paula, 369 n.18
Triandafyllopoulos, Makis, 364 n.8
Trichopoulos, 354 n.12
"Trompe-L'óeil-Realité" (Haralambidis) 70
Trust: and contraception, 165–69; in relationships, 174, 195, 208
Tsaliki, Liza, 351 n.8
Tsalikoglou, Fotini, 377 n.9
Tsing, Anna Lowenhaupt, 351 n.11, 365 n.9, 367 n.11
Tsoklis, Kostas, 292
Tsoukalas, C., 117, 361 n.9
Turkey, 61, 63–65, 68, 71–72, 113, 343; and article on abortion, 294–95; and demografiko, 78; fear of invasion by, 5, 294, 337, 343
Turks, Muslim. *See* Muslim Turks
Tzoumas, Dimitris, 119, 361 n.13

UN *Country Report of Fertility and Family Surveys* (2002), 40–45, 156–60
United States: attitudes toward abortion in, 100–101, 121; and nationalism, 147–48
Urry, John, 364 n.5

Vakirtzis, Yiorgos, 24
Valaoras, 40–45, 354 n.12
Vance, Carole, 370 n.20
Varvouni, M. G., 355 n.15
Vervenioti, T., 354 n.9
Violence: as conflict, 13, 15, 21, 23, 59–63, 65–72, 140–41, 149, 153, 171, 173, 181, 198, 242, 268, 270, 273, 286, 294, 295, 299, 347; in constitution of

412 Index

the subject, 3, 162, 185, 196, 197, 236, 316; and democracy, 345–48; of doing research, 15. *See also* Racism; Sex
Virgin Mary, 47–49, 133, 135–36, 232, 289, 302
Visual technology, 197; abortion as a, 210–31, 247; research as, 15
Vlahos, G., 69
Voting rights, Greek women and, 38–39
Vryonis, Spiros, 350 n.3

Walby, Sylvia, 350 n.7
Walkerdine, Valerie, 373 n.38
Warner, Michael, 340
Warren, K., 365 n.9
Weber, M. 5
Withdrawal, as contraceptive method, 159–60, 165–69, 176, 195, 243, 248
Women, Greek, 35–52; and agency, 297–306; appearance of, preoccupation with, 31–34; bodies of, 6, 169–71, 174–78, 182–90; and citizenship, 7, 136, 186, 258, 294, 315–16; and contraception, 141–42, 155–205, 299–302; and demografiko, 37, 113, 291–316, 319–36, 341–44; and doctors, relationship with, 97–99, 180, 259–60; and dowries, 36; and family burden, 36–37; and Greek identity, 2, 10, 50–52, 142, 215–17; and Greek Orthodoxy, 45–50; juvenilization of, 180, 312; and nationalism, 320–35; and retirement system, 36–37, 128–29; and voting rights, 38–39; and work, 35–37. *See also* Couples, heterosexual; Men, Greek
Women politicians, Greek, 39–40. *See also* Politicians, women
Work, and Greek women, 35–37

Xenophobia, of Greeks, 97, 146

Yaeger, Patricia, 352 n.13
Yfantopoulos, Y., 352 n.2
Youth, Greek: and demografiko press coverage, 128–29, 296; and nationalism, 145–48; and notions of fertility, 257; at public clinic, 256
Youth and History (large scale study), 145
Yuval-Davis, Nira, 363 n.2

Zarafonitou, Christina, 378 n.2
Zelizer, Barbie, 350 n.8
Zinovieff, S., 375 n.1
Zorba, 70, 151, 216

Alexandra Halkias is a lecturer in sociology at Panteion University, Greece.

✣

Library of Congress Cataloging-in-Publication Data
Halkias, Alexandra.
The empty cradle of democracy : sex, abortion, and nationalism in modern Greece / Alexandra Halkias.
p. cm.
Includes bibliographical references and index.
ISBN 0-8223-3311-2 (cloth : alk. paper)
ISBN 0-8223-3323-6 (pbk. : alk. paper)
1. Abortion—Political aspects—Greece. 2. Abortion—Social aspects—Greece. 3. Fertility, Human—Political aspects—Greece. 4. Fertility, Human—Social aspects—Greece. 5. Sex—Political aspects—Greece. 6. Nationalism—Greece. I. Title.
HQ767.5G8H35 2004
363.46'09495—dc22   2004001306